Ethics, Nationalism, and Just War

Ethics, Nationalism, and Just War

MEDIEVAL AND CONTEMPORARY PERSPECTIVES

Henrik Syse and Gregory M. Reichberg, editors

The Catholic University of America Press
Washington, D.C.

Copyright © 2007
The Catholic University of America Press
All rights reserved

The paper used in this publication meets the minimum requirements of
American National Standards for Information Science—Permanence of
Paper for Printed Library Materials, ANSI Z39.48-1984.
∞

LIBRARY OF CONGRESS CATALOGING-IN-PUBLICATION DATA
Ethics, nationalism, and just war : medieval and contemporary perspectives
/ Henrik Syse and Gregory M. Reichberg, editors.
    p. cm.
  Includes bibliographical references and index.
    ISBN 978-0-8132-1502-0 (pbk. : alk. paper) 1. Just war doctrine—
History. 2. War—Moral and ethical aspects. 3. Military ethics.
4. Nationalism—Moral and ethical aspects. I. Syse, Henrik, 1966–
II. Reichberg, Gregory M. III. Title.
    U21.2.E85 2007
    172'.42—DC22   2007003475

Contents

Acknowledgments — vii

Introduction — ix

PART ONE. The Medieval Roots of Just War

1. Thinking Morally about War in the Middle Ages and Today — 3
   JAMES TURNER JOHNSON

2. Taming Warriors in Classical and Early Medieval Political Theory — 11
   JOHN VON HEYKING

3. Augustine and Just War: Between Virtue and Duties — 36
   HENRIK SYSE

4. Just War, Schism, and Peace in St. Augustine — 51
   PHILLIP W. GRAY

5. Is There a "Presumption against War" in Aquinas's Ethics? — 72
   GREGORY M. REICHBERG

6. Poets and Politics: Just War in Geoffrey Chaucer and Christine de Pizan — 99
   KATE L. FORHAN

7. Reflections on Medieval Just War Theories: A Commentary on Part One — 117
   GERSON MORENO-RIAÑO

PART TWO. Contemporary Problems of War, Nationalism, and Ethics

8. Maintaining the Protection of Noncombatants — 151
   JAMES TURNER JOHNSON

9. Protecting the Natural Environment in Wartime: Ethical Considerations from the Just War Tradition — 190
   GREGORY M. REICHBERG AND HENRIK SYSE

10. U.N.-Authorized Interventions: A Slippery
    Slope of Forcible Interference? 218
    ANNE JULIE SEMB

11. Ethical Uncertainties of Nationalism 246
    DAN SMITH

12. The Sort of Nationalism and Patriotism That
    Europe Needs 267
    ANDREAS FOLLESDAL

13. Defining and Delivering Justice: The Work of the
    Ad Hoc International Criminal Tribunals 290
    JAMES MEERNIK

14. The Legitimacy of Anticipatory Defense and
    Forcible Regime Change 323
    DIETER JANSSEN

15. Genocide: A Case for the Responsibility of the Bystander 352
    ARNE JOHAN VETLESEN

16. The Ethical Core of the Nation-State: A Postscript
    to Part Two 372
    J. PETER BURGESS

    Contributors 385
    Index 389

Acknowledgments

The essays in part one, with the exception of those by Johnson and Gray, were first presented at a panel organized by the "Politica" section of the American Political Science Association in September 2000. Our thanks to Professor Cary Nederman for organizing that panel and encouraging the subsequent publication of its papers. Reichberg's essay on Thomas Aquinas was originally published in the *Thomist* 66, no. 3 (2002); we thank the journal for allowing it to appear here in revised form. The essays by Johnson, Reichberg and Syse, Semb, Follesdal, Smith, and Vetlesen in part two were originally part of a special issue of the *Journal of Peace Research* published in June 2000. Our gratitude to chief editor Nils Petter Gleditsch and the journal's publisher, Sage, for permission to use the essays, and also to the many referees who took part in evaluating the essays then. All of them have been updated for the current volume. Likewise, we thank the *Journal of Military Ethics* for allowing us to reproduce a revised version of Janssens's essay on preventive defense, which appeared in 2004 in vol. 3, issue 2.

Our thanks to Nansenfondet of the Norwegian Academy of Arts and Sciences, the Norwegian Defense Department, the Ethics Program of the University of Oslo, and the Norwegian Research Council for grants that made work on this volume possible.

And finally, our heartfelt thanks—including the thanks of each of the authors—for the diligent and thoughtful comments of two referees who read the entire manuscript for the Catholic University of America Press. Their insights have helped make this an even better volume.

Introduction

The face of armed conflict changes every week and every day, but the underlying moral questions remain, remarkably, much the same. Taking this continuity as our point of departure, we focus in the present volume on some basic issues in ethics and philosophy that are related to the use of armed force as these were developed by thinkers in late antiquity and the Middle Ages. We do not remain in centuries-old history, however. Moving ahead from the historical and philosophical background, we also introduce several pressing issues of our own day.

Assessing war in moral terms means asking *whether* war can ever be rightly fought; if so, *why* or *for what reasons* armed force should be used; and finally, *how* or *with what means* war may be executed. In the European tradition, sustained and systematic reflection on these issues began in the Middle Ages, with precursors in antiquity. With the renewed interest in the idea of "just war" that we have witnessed over the last half century, it is essentially to that medieval reflection we are here returning, albeit adapting and updating it to achieve a better fit with a world different from that of knights and Scholastics.

In this book we have sought to identify a number of core issues associated with the ethics of war. Given the historical genealogy of this reflection, it is only natural that the first half of the volume is devoted to an examination of how the medieval originators of military and war-related ethics conceived of the problems at hand. While these historical essays, spanning thinkers from Ambrose in the fourth century to Christine de Pizan in the fifteenth, will be of considerable historical interest to medievalists in particular and historians in general, they are mainly meant to elucidate the underlying moral problems of war and to help us see how they can be formulated, understood, and tackled even today.

The second part of the book moves us ahead to our own political surroundings. It addresses issues that lie at the heart of current challenges in the international sphere, yet have generally received less attention

x   Introduction

in current debate than problems associated with terrorism and its ramifications. Noncombatant immunity, environmental destruction, U.N.-authorized interventions, nationalism, preemption, war crime tribunals, and the responsibility of bystanders—intellectuals not the least among them—are issues that will remain crucial to the debate about war for decades to come. Addressing them in a calm and balanced way—and reminding ourselves of their importance at a time when they are easily eclipsed—is incumbent upon us.

War and Normative Thought

War is not the sort of activity that can be fully understood from a purely descriptive point of view. It confronts us with provocative moral issues of life and death. The decisions made—and institutions erected—about war, peace, and the relationship between states and peoples have concrete and dramatic ramifications for millions of people, many of them civilians with little stake in, and no responsibility for, the wars waged. Students and scholars therefore need to take seriously the normative dimensions of war and violent conflict so as to participate in the current debate about whether and how armed force should be used. They should do so not primarily as activists but as thoughtful individuals and members of communities who understand both *what* is at stake and *why* certain courses of action should or should not be recommended. The chief aim of the current volume is to make a contribution to this vital task.

Normative analysis of the kind contained herein may not always lead us to firm conclusions or definite stands, but it will help clarify questions of right and wrong, or even good and evil. The basic assumption is the relatively simple one that certain acts and attitudes are damaging to the dignity of human beings, while others promote that dignity. Therefore, human actions, and the ideas and ideologies behind them, must be defined and discussed so that we may see more clearly how human well-being and dignity can be protected. Even if we find ourselves disagreeing about means as well as ends, about what is "right" and what is "good," ethical analysis is required if we are to gain better control of the destructive forces that humankind has too often shown itself capable of unleashing. The alternative is a moral nihilism, which offers no hindrance to human violence and destruction.

PART ONE

The Medieval Roots of Just War

*WHILE THE ESSAYS in this book span a number of theoretical perspectives, many of them are inspired by the just war tradition. The essential idea behind just war thinking can be summed up in two points:
(1) While many wars can and should be stopped, preferably before their inception, war is and remains an inescapable fact in the world. The option of using armed force can never be disregarded once and for all.
(2) While war cannot be totally abolished, it is possible to restrain it. Given the enormous destruction that wars cause, we are morally obliged to find ways of regulating the use of violent force and of educating those who employ that force (or make the decisions to do so). Through vigorous and critical questioning of the motives and means of war, the just war tradition insists that there can be rules even in hell, as Michael Walzer has put it. The challenge is to make these rules as convincing and stringent as possible, so that both politicians and soldiers will feel their force.*

This leads us back to the medieval horizon of moral reflection. One conspicuous element in most of the medieval authors discussed herein is their emphasis on virtue and character as preconditions for justice in war. They had the belief, deemed naïve or at least insufficient by many modern thinkers, that men and women may come to possess a sort of virtue—even if only an incomplete one, due to the omnipresence of sin—that will render them more likely to be compassionate, even in the grave circumstances of war. While we may rightly doubt whether many knights, princes, or ordinary soldiers lived up to that ideal, it has acquired new significance in more recent debates about war. In the twentieth century, carrying on into the twenty-first, unspeakable brutalities have been committed against ordinary men and women: prisoners have been tortured and abused, civilians robbed and raped, and whole classes of people have been sentenced

2 The Medieval Roots of Just War

to die the most horrendous of deaths. Simultaneously, we have seen great acts of bravery as well as significant acts of restraint. In educating politicians, soldiers, and officers in ethics, it is becoming ever clearer that virtue and moral honor are not irrelevant relics from a distant past but rather living ideals of great importance.

"Just war" is not merely a set of theoretical ideas or dry rules—it expresses an ideal of the "just warrior," referring not only to men and women in uniform but to the entire chain of human beings who make decisions and perform fateful actions as the use of armed force is being contemplated or actually takes place. For this reason, understanding the medieval background of just war theorizing is not only of academic interest; it is highly useful as well.

1

Thinking Morally about War in the Middle Ages and Today

JAMES TURNER JOHNSON

Do medieval views of war have any relevance today? There are clearly enormous differences between life in the Middle Ages and life today, differences in social relationships, forms of political order, assumptions about the natural and supernatural world, available technology, and so on, which shaped warfare as they did every other aspect of everyday life. Since historical distance tends to present a somewhat abstracted and idealized picture of medieval warfare, the differences may loom as even more distinctive, with an image of knights in armor colliding on the field of battle contrasted to various models of contemporary warfare: ethnically or religiously motivated civil wars conducted by motley armies of irregulars often no more than bandits with automatic rifles, in which noncombatants are intentionally targeted, escalating to ethnic cleansing or even genocide; warfare by terrorism, where the battlefield may be a shopping mall or an airliner and the enemy hides his combatant status and intention as part of his method of attack; the threat of war by weapons of mass destruction; warfare by precision-guided munitions used by a force effectively invulnerable to the enemy's weapons. Given such enormous and striking differences in the landscape, moralists who have wished to answer the question of relevance with a "Yes" have more often than not focused on the inner world of values, where it is possible to argue for a commonality among individuals, communities, or cultures in which the everyday differences among our lives count for less, or do not count at all. Regarding war, one way of thinking about the relevance of the just war idea is to argue this way, taking the just war principles as having worth and binding power that is essentially the same for all times, so that the issue is how to apply these unchanging principles to different historical contexts.

I think, though, that we can never understand these ideas fully except through their concrete formulation and application in different historical contexts, and thus to attempt to remove them from their history is a mistake. To reflect morally on war is to enter the historical stream of moral reflection on war and seek to learn from it, not seek to escape it to some more abstract level. Accordingly, we must not make too much of the differences in the historical landscapes of our own age and the medieval period (itself made up of many quite different historical landscapes), but we need to recognize and learn from similarities we find there. Relevance, in this view, arises from such reflective encounter with history. I want to carry this argument forward by considering two of the central problems addressed by just war tradition: what authority is necessary for justified resort to armed force and what constitutes right conduct in the use of such force.

In the case of the question of authority for use of force, contemporary usage presents us with two rather different models. First, there is a model that reflects the assumptions of mainline political theory and practice and is found in international law: the authority to use force is to be found in the state or in some "competent" authority deriving from the state, such as the United Nations or alliances of states. While this is fundamentally a moral model expressing central just war conceptions about political order, one of the most prominent examples of this way of thinking about the authority necessary to use force is political realism, where the existence of the state is the primary datum, and the justice of resort to force is translated into the question of national interest. Recent religious and philosophical just war thought, by contrast, typically reduces the question of authority to second place after the question of just cause. The authority required for use of force is, accordingly, that which acts so as to serve the just cause already determined. It may be the authority of a state, but in particular cases, when the state is judged not to be serving the cause of justice but some other actor is doing so, the latter may be judged to have right authority. Both these models effectively remove moral content from the idea of the authority necessary for resort to armed force: the first by absolutizing the state and its interests, the second by locating the judgment as to justice elsewhere (notably, in the judgment of the moralists) and giving the authority a secondary, reactive role. Moreover, they are in fundamental tension with each other, pulling in essentially opposite directions. Taking them on their own terms, one effectively has to choose between them.

Here is a case in which I believe it is informative to reflect on the idea of authority to use armed force as it developed in the medieval context. A convenient point of departure is Thomas Aquinas's statement in his question "On War" in the *Summa theologiae* (II-II, q. 40, a. 1), in which he defines what is necessary for a just war, beginning with the requirement of sovereign authority. There are two ways to reflect on this position, one in terms of Aquinas's thinking in itself, the other in terms of the historical development of this idea on which he drew and which his position encapsulates.

As to Aquinas's position in itself, there are three points to note. First, to require sovereign authority for the use of force is a form of limitation, ruling out this use to others without such authority. Theologically this echoed Augustine's sharp distinction between just war as a public activity and use of force for private purposes as inherently unjust because tinged with sinful self-love. In the medieval context this same distinction was important for another reason: it distinguished *bellum*, war, as an activity on behalf of the common good, from *duellum*, the duel, use of arms by individual knights and nobles without sovereign authority. In the history on which Aquinas immediately drew, making this distinction was a way of seeking to limit recourse to arms in a society in which such recourse was often claimed as a birthright. The second main thing to note about his position in itself is that sovereign authority in his thought referred not simply to the fact of rule but to the moral conception of good rule. A frequently quoted passage in medieval just war thought was Romans 13:4, in which the ruling authority is described as having the right to use the sword as "the minister of God." From Augustine forward in Christian thought this was understood to refer to the ruler's responsibility to ensure order in accord with the will of God. This same conception is found in Aquinas's treatise on princely rule, where it is explained by reference to the natural law. Also in that treatise Aquinas explored at length the ruler's responsibilities to ensure the good of his subjects, within the context of the larger human common good. This is a significantly fuller concept of sovereignty and its responsibilities than found in the realist conception of the state and the national interest, for it seeks conceptually to link the ruler's responsibility to his own political community to broader responsibilities to the public good outside that community and to an overarching conception of the moral order of all things. While the best contemporary way to describe such a broader concept of the role and responsibility of sovereignty may be debated, I suggest that Aquinas's example serves as a reminder of the importance of developing such a concept. It may also be that we can learn from the particulars of his own formulations. Finally, the third main thing to note about his way of describing what is necessary for justified resort to armed force is that the requirement of sovereign authority has the first priority. The logic of his argument places the responsibility to determine whether there is a just cause, to avoid evil intentions, and to achieve the end of peace among the responsibilities of the sovereign to serve the public good, the larger common good, and the natural order. While, in principle, others may advise the sovereign on these matters, he alone bears the final responsibility for deciding and acting on the decision. This contrasts markedly with a recent trend in just war thought to consider just cause as prior to right authority. One wonders whether contemporary moralists wish implicitly to reserve to themselves the right to make the final judgment as to just cause, even though they bear no responsibility for the consequences of their decision. Of course, in contemporary views of the state and of sovereignty, little is said about their having a moral content, and it may be that the moralists' position follows by default. But if true, again this reminds us that the medievals were onto something profoundly important about human communities in exploring the moral dimensions that properly come with authority over the lives of others. Not only on this general point but also on the relation of the responsibility of sovereign authority to the decision to resort to armed force, the perspective we find in Aquinas's prioritization of sovereign authority over just cause and the other *ius ad bellum* requirements offers a significant corrective to recent ways of thinking about the use of force.

It is useful to remember that in the immediate context in which he wrote, the late thirteenth century, Aquinas had not yet moved into the magisterial position he later came to occupy. In his own context, what he said about princely rule and the just resort to force stand as windows on ideas that were developing before him and around him. On the matter of authority to use force this relationship is especially clear. A fundamental problem for medieval society, as suggested above, was widespread violence. On one hand this followed from the knights' arrogation to themselves of the right to use arms on their own authority and to their own purposes. But this was only one aspect of a society that had not yet developed adequately robust institutions of public order. A broader dimension of this problem was widespread banditry and warlordism. If duellum among members of the knightly class kept the higher ranges of feudal life in turmoil, banditry and warlordism afflicted the other orders of society as well, terrorizing peasants on the land, townspeople, merchants, and travelers of all sorts.

It was in response to both the narrower and wider dimensions of this problem of widespread, endemic violence that, beginning in the late tenth century in regions of France where the problem was at its worst, local bishops came together in council and began to issue statements anathematizing the perpetrators of such violence, setting off specific groups of people—those mentioned above and those connected with the Church, plus the property of all those mentioned—as not involved in violence and therefore not to have violence directed against them, and calling on the royal authority to suppress the malefactors. Collectively known as the "peace of God" movement, this effort cast a long shadow. Effectively this movement established the pattern for later concerted development of moral thinking about two important issues in the use of armed force: the restriction of authority to use such force to the highest levels in the political order and the marking off of noncombatants as not to be directly, intentionally made the subjects of attack. This concerted development began with the canonist Gratian in the middle of the twelfth century and continued via his successors over the next hundred years. This was the development that Aquinas's treatment of war directly reflected and on which it depended.

On the question of authority, the canonists' collective work restricted the right to have recourse to arms to those persons with no temporal superior, thus effectively institutionalizing the outlawing of knightly duellum and the phenomena of banditry and warlordism begun in the peace of God movement. This was important both for social cohesion in the temporal sphere and for removing the right of the religious authorities to initiate war on behalf of the Church or Christian religion. Though the final rejection of war for religion in Western culture did not come until after the horrific experience of the post-Reformation religious wars, the rejection of such war in fact may be traced to major canonical writers of the thirteenth century (such as Innocent IV), who defined such severe limits on the right to authorize war as to remove it, except in the case of the need to defend the faith against aggression.[1] When we seek to think about the differences between views of religion and war in Western culture and in Islam, we would do well to examine the consideration the canonists brought to bear and the arguments they made for their conclusion limiting the right to the sword to the sphere of temporal rule.

The peace of God movement and the work of the later canonists are also instructive, I suggest, for how we should think about the problem of limitation in the use of force, the *ius in bello*. In contemporary moral discussion these limits are usually framed in terms of two moral principles, discrimination and proportionality. One never encounters these terms in the medieval writers. Rather, as noted already, they approached noncombatancy by identifying certain classes of people as not taking part in war and therefore not to be attacked in war. Contemporary moral thought on discrimination does not get to these classes of people until the second stage in moral reasoning, and at times it has had to do so over claims that modern societies are so structured that everyone participates in the war effort or that various forms of social links with the warriors make all members of the enemy group equally deserving of attack. By contrast, the medieval approach focuses narrowly on function and sharply distinguishes those who directly participate in bearing and using arms from those who do not. This is an approach that continues to be used in the international law of armed conflicts; it offers a useful alternative or embellishment to reasoning from the principle of discrimination.

The case of the idea of proportionality is similar. Though widely referred to as a guide in contemporary moral thought on war, this is not

---

1. For a brief discussion of this development and a translation of the relevant passages in Innocent IV, see "Innocent IV (c. 1180–1264): The Kinds of Violence and the Limits of Holy War," in Reichberg, Syse, and Begby, 2006: 148–55.

how the problem of limitation of the means of war was approached in medieval thought. There is certainly room for such a moral principle in thinking about conduct in war, a teleological principle to go alongside the deontological principle of discrimination. But the principle of proportionality has proved difficult to apply in practice, and there sometimes seem to be as many interpretations of what it requires as there are interpreters. The different natures of the two principles of discrimination and proportionality suggest part of the difficulty in using them: persons used to deontological moral reasoning are less at home with teleological thinking, and vice versa. But a deeper problem has been disagreement—or lack of understanding—on what proportionality is intended to measure. In any case, as with the idea of noncombatant immunity, medieval thought sought to limit the means of war in a more direct and concrete way, by seeking to ban the use of certain weapons. Though the weapons are of course different today, this is an approach that still is employed to good effect in international law. The benefit in either case is clarity. When making a combat decision, one knows beforehand that certain weapons, or types of weapons, are off limits because of their effects; one does not have to pause to determine how to measure proportionality, then seek to measure it for the case at hand. There may still be a place for a broader moral calculus of proportionality in the conduct of war; yet moralists might learn also from the clarity of the medieval approach.

The question of relevance from one historical period to another is finally one of interpretation. I have argued for an understanding of war and its limitation that requires entering into a stream of reflection, debate, and dialogue as it has developed over history, as opposed to a view that sets up certain ideal principles defining the moral limits to war and then seeks to apply them to the particular problems at hand. There are certainly things to be said for both models. But opting for the latter means that, in principle, no matter how interesting historical cases may be, they are finally irrelevant to the case at hand, for what is necessary is getting the principles and values straight, then applying them rigorously to the contemporary case. My argument has been, though, that these principles and values have themselves come to be known through historical efforts to grapple with specific problems, problems recognizably not unlike our own, and that we learn what those principles and values mean as well as how to use them by understanding the history of their origin and use.

From this perspective the Middle Ages bear a special relevance as the period in which just war thinking first coalesced as a systematic and coherent way of defining the use of armed force in relation to the goods of common life and of limiting the use of force so as to minimize the threat to such life. The question is not so much how can this be relevant for us today as it is how it could ever be judged irrelevant.

REFERENCES

Reichberg, Gregory, Henrik Syse, and Endre Begby, eds. 2006. *The Ethics of War: Classic and Contemporary Readings.* Oxford: Blackwell.

2

Taming Warriors in Classical and Early Medieval Political Theory

JOHN VON HEYKING

> *As a first sign you will observe that [a man of strength] finds all his pleasure and all his delight in being in arms, and in just wars, and in defending all just causes, quarrels, and holy arguments.*
>
> Honoré Bonet, *The Tree of Battles*

Medieval political theory is often accused of being arcane and incapable of speaking to contemporary political problems. This appearance seems especially true when it comes to contemporary thinking on war: what do the likes of Tertullian, Origen, Ambrose, and others have to say about nuclear weapons, apocalyptic terrorists, dictators, and tribal genocide in postcolonial Africa? In fact, medieval political theory has a lot to say about these issues, and its voice is actually being heard in public discourse. For example, one can see the pacifistic tradition of Tertullian and Origen in the stance against war articulated by the American Catholic bishops in their public statements, and the attitude toward "infidels" among members of al-Qaeda is reminiscent of the way some medieval Christians viewed heretics. Pacifism and denying the humanity of one's enemy seem to some to be the only two choices to us, as they seemed to be the only choices to the early medieval thinkers. Neither accounts for the real world of politics, as the former demands an unattainable level of political virtue and the latter demands that we renounce our humanity (as the first choice also does). Fortunately, our moral choices are not restricted to these two options any more than they were for the early medieval writers. This chapter surveys the dynamics of just war thinking in the early Christian period and examines Ambrose's attempt to moderate political and military ambitions, as well as the religious fervor, of his contemporaries, in a way that was sufficiently realistic to understand that the psychological and philosophical complexities behind war made its elimination impossible.

Medieval political thinking on just war often aggravated a tension evident in classical political thought between virtue and actively displaying (and glorifying) that virtue. Theorizing about just war in both traditions had to contend with the reality that a significant portion of the population—the active, political class—thought war was simply fun. As one twelfth-century troubadour sang: "I love the gay Eastertide that brings forth leaves and flowers . . . but it gives me great joy to see, drawn up on the field, knights, and horses in battle array . . . and when battle is joined, let all men of good lineage think of nothing but the breaking of heads and arms. . . . I tell you I find no such savor in food or in wine or in sleep" (Bertrand de Born, quoted in Bloch, 1964: 293).[1] Similarly, the *Song of Roland*, a kind of medieval *Iliad*, idealizes warriors, whose courageous souls go to heaven, as if courage alone were enough for this. However, many commentators point out that medieval just war theories could account for the love of glory only by making it serve God; that is, war was meant to glorify God and just war became holy war, which made war a much more serious enterprise (Russell, 1975: 13).[2]

By having war serve God, medieval just war theory decreased the number of just causes for going to war that were listed by the pagans. For example, Cicero and Aristotle regarded glory—human glory—as a just cause for going to war, but that was considered idolatrous by the early Christians up to Ambrose (the period under consideration in this essay) (Aristotle *Nicomachean Ethics* 1177b14; Cicero, 1983 [*De officiis*; hence-

---

1. I thank Professor E. A. Goerner for this reference.
2. Similarly, the *Song of Roland* is an elegy about the war between Charlemagne's forces and the Muslims at Roncevaux. Conversely, some commentators, such as James Turner Johnson, overlook glory as a cause for just war in the just war tradition (see his summary of the tenets of the tradition in Johnson, 1999: 28).

forth *DO*]: 3.86–87). If medieval just war theories limited the number of purposes for war by removing wars for glory, they seem to have removed some of the *internal* limitations for the means of waging wars with a just cause. For instance, Ambrose sharply distinguishes between the treatment of heretics and nonheretics in warfare (see *On Tobias* 15.51; see also Swift, 1983: 97–99).

Conversely, the classical view limited the *means* by which wars could be fought by attempting to harness the love of glory to the performance of honorable deeds. For instance, Cicero's teaching on just war (whose ultimate purpose is peace) is associated with his stringent account of what constitutes glory and by his understanding of virtue (as appropriateness) and expediency. Thus, while medieval just war theory teaches the classical pagans how to curtail the ends of war, classical pagans teach the medievals how to limit its means. Can the two be reconciled? Can the classical understanding of glory be reconciled with the medieval imperative that apparently reserves glory to God alone?

Perhaps counterintuitively to us moderns, the classical understanding of glory shows how the love of glory can actually serve as a *restraint* in waging war.[3] As we shall see, Ambrose tried to incorporate most of Cicero's understanding of glory into his own transposition of Ciceronian political thought into Christian idiom, in part as a means to moderate what was then the Christian articulation of participation in war by attempting to channel the sense of war making as a mode of play into higher pursuits. His effort advanced Christian thinking beyond the just war thinking of previous Christians, such as the pacifism of Tertullian and Origen, and Eusebius's Constantinianism, but it was not completely successful because fighting heretics for Ambrose was not governed by the same rules of just war as wars against others.

This essay is divided into four parts. The first part examines the element of play in war and considers reasons for it as an end of war. The second part considers the classical understanding of glory as an end for war. The third part focuses on the just war thinking of early Christians such as Tertullian, Origen, and Eusebius. It shows how the rejection of war by Tertullian and Origen was inadequate to handle the realities of political

---

3. This claim is not as counterintuitive as it appears. For instance, James Turner Johnson argues that the medieval code of chivalry did more to restrain war than the efforts of canonists and theologians did (1999: 37; explicated in Johnson, 1981: 124–50).

power, but Eusebius's articulation of political power wedded Christianity too closely to the empire. The fourth part addresses Ambrose's attempt to incorporate Ciceronian just war thinking into Christianity as a means to avoid the Constantinianism of Eusebius. The chapter concludes with some observations that relate these reflections to contemporary problems in war making.

War and Play

The notion that war is simply evil and that glory (for God or for oneself) cannot be earned through war is relatively new in human history. Jean Baechler argues: "At bottom, one must be imbued with a contemporary pacifist ideology to have forgotten that for millennia men have fought less for political and economic reasons than because they like to, and they like to because it is exciting to risk one's life, and even more exciting to risk it for nothing" (1979: 191). Similarly, Clausewitz includes "the play of probabilities and chance, which make [war] a free activity of the soul" in his "wonderful trinity" of war's predominant tendencies (1968: 1:138). Historically, human beings have fought wars not only for the traditional purposes found in just war theories (for example, self-defense, scarce resources, punishing enemies), but also simply for fun, for play. Play is used here not in a frivolous way, or in a postmodern sense of playfulness in contingency, or simply in the sense of an activity that is engaged in for its own sake or for enjoyment. Play, as Johannes Huizinga describes it, is a "significant" activity that "transcends the immediate needs of life and imparts meaning to the action. All play means something" (1950: 1). While omitting the connection between play and war, Hugo Rahner, S.J., relies on classical and patristic teachings on play and virtue to describe the playful human being as "that beautiful unity of grace and humanity" (1972: 10).[4] Huizinga describes war as a form of play, and the outcome of such wars have been taken to signify the glory of the victor as well as the judgment of the gods (and of God) (1950: 91). Unlike an unlimited war (such as holy war, in which the absolute ends are taken to justify any means to secure them), playful war presuppos-

---

4. He focuses on Aristotle's treatment of *eutrapelia* (literally, "well turned") (Aristotle *Nicomachean Ethics* 4.8 [1128a]).

es the recognition of the rights of others and rules that limit behavior; war becomes unlimited when participants view each other as unequal, whether as heretics, heathens, devils, or simply "lesser breeds without the law." Cicero acknowledges the playful element of war for his ambitious audience when he quotes the verse of Pyrrhus that celebrates Regulus's manly deed of self-sacrifice:

Gold will I none, nor price shall you give; for I ask none;
Come, let us not be hucksters [*cauponantes*] of war, but warriors embattled.
Nay, let us venture our lives, and the sword, not gold, weigh the outcome.
Make the trial by valor in arms and see if Fortuna
Wills it that you shall prevail or I, or what be her judgment.

(*DO* 1.38)

Cicero comments: "A right kingly [*regalis sane*] sentiment this and worthy scion of the Aeacidae." The passage shows the essential characteristics of the play element of war, even while Cicero attempted to persuade his audience that the peaceful activities of the statesman are ultimately more satisfying (Nederman, 2000). It claims that warriors differ from "hucksters" by staking their lives, not their gold, on the judgment of the gods. Playfulness, in this sense, which includes the ability to transcend temporal affairs and ultimately to stand imaginatively in the judgment of God(s), is crucial to just war theorizing. Thus, for war to be playful requires one to combine one's desire for recognition by one's antagonist and by God with an acknowledgment that the higher purposes upon which one stakes one's life demand that only honorable means can be used to secure those purposes. As we shall see, Cicero and Ambrose attempted to channel that sense of play for just purposes.

Huizinga argues that the customs that are internal to play form the basis of international law. Cicero, for instance, followed the Roman custom of viewing oaths, made to enemies and guaranteed through one's honor, as bearing the same obligation as law (*DO* 3.108–11). However, the very emergence of a formal legal system of rules governing combat has the potential to undermine itself when abiding by rules eclipses play as the main motivation; when that occurs, dishonor suddenly becomes too closely wed to injustice and promotes the view that one's enemy is also a criminal. For Huizinga, the eclipse of play as the basis of international law would signal the return to barbarism: "Things have now come to a pass that the system of international law is no longer acknowledged, or observed, as the very basis of culture and civilized living. As soon as one member or more of a community of States virtually denies the binding character of international law . . . as the sole norm of its political behavior, not only does the last vestige of the immemorial play-spirit vanish but with it any claim to civilization at all. Society then sinks down to the level of the barbaric, and original violence retakes its ancient rights" (1950: 101). With that in mind, we turn now to the way classical and early medieval thinkers on just war included glory and honor as goals and attempted to elevate the play element of war to a higher dimension in the consideration of glory. The conclusion of this chapter considers the role that play can perform when barbarism has retaken its "ancient rights."

Polis and Empire, Gaming and Virtuous Imperialism

It is unusual to consider classical just war theory as a means to moderate medieval just war theory, because the reverse was meant to be the case. Classical political philosophers such as Plato, Aristotle, and Cicero thought that the active life (as opposed to the contemplative life) tended to lead people to attempt to become sovereign over others. For the ancients, the active life leads people to seek an ever-expanding sphere of moral grandeur upon which the virtuous could obtain glory from others (Pangle and Ahrensdorf, 1999: 41–44; see Aristotle *Politics* 1324a25–25b31). This is seen in Socrates' famous argument in Plato's *Republic* that the just city (whose every action, by definition, is just) may undermine the security of foreign cities without provocation (423a). It is also reflected in Aristotle's observation that the statesman's primary activity of pursuing despotic powers and honors (*dynasteias kai timas*) is not leisurely (*Nicomachean Ethics* 1177b14). Thus, civic virtue, even in the best city, is prone to create an ever-expanding sphere for virtuous conduct, which justified a kind of virtuous imperialism: "Civic virtue itself offers a powerful inducement to expansion, to more or less benevolent hegemony, and even to conquest" (Pangle and Ahrensdorf, 1999: 42). The classical authors wondered whether the virtuous life could ever be divorced from the desire to rule, as, for instance, Aristotle wonders whether it is nobler to rule alone or to take turns with equals. Thus, the active life is inherently fraught with conflict, as competitors vie for the title of "most virtuous" and of *princeps*. The inner logic of civic virtue toward empire also permitted injustice against those considered unequals (in a manner analogous to the Christian attitude toward heretics in war). For instance, Cicero thought that the general rule requiring faith to be kept with enemies may be broken when one's enemies are enemies of mankind (i.e., pirates) because they have declared war on mankind (*DO* 3.107–8).

Even so, Cicero attempted to channel the unformed passions of the majority of the politically active toward the peaceful activity of the statesman by appealing to their love of honor: "there have been many civic achievements greater and more famous than achievements of war" (*DO* 1.74). By pointing out that the activity of warriors presupposes that of the statesman (who forms the communities that the warriors serve), he attempted to convince them that peace is the purpose of war and that peaceful political community is the best way for human beings to fulfill their humanity as rational beings (*DO* 1.34, 74). Nonetheless, Cicero understood that most of those with grand ambitions would not agree, so he attempted to channel their war-making ambitions toward a more human, civic sense of glory.

Cicero noticed the moderating effects of glory when he argued that wars fought for glory tend to be less bitter than those fought for utility (*DO* 1.38). A closer look at his views on just war and the relationship between the morally right (*honestum*) and expedience (*utile*) show why. As Helgeland, Daly, and Burns observe, the "real context of Cicero's thinking about just war ... was that of honor" (1985: 3). A good regime will go to war only for honor (*fide*) or for safety (1988 [*De republica;* henceforth *DR*] 3.34). Honor here means being faithful to oaths, but Cicero also argues that a healthy republic will see its supremacy over others as a sign of its virtue. Within the rules of just war, officeholders will seek glory for the republic by advancing the republic's imperium, territory, and revenues: "Such service calls for great men; it was commonly rendered in the ways of our ancestors; if men will perform duties such as these, they will win gratitude and glory [*gratium et gloriam*] for themselves and at the same time render service to the republic" (*DO* 2.85).[5] He maintained

---

5. Emerich de Vattel, a modern Ciceronian, explained the importance of national honor and distinguished it from mere pride: "It is of great advantage to a nation and is one of its most important duties to itself to make itself renowned. True renown consists in the good opinion which wise and enlightened men have of us.... Since a nation's renown is a real advantage, it has the right to defend that renown as it would any other possession.... We cannot, therefore, condemn the measures sometimes taken by sovereigns to uphold or avenge the honor

morally stringent ways of waging war, such as the requirement of proclaiming war and keeping oaths to enemies (except to pirates because they are enemies of mankind and because they are unworthy of oaths). In general, Cicero attempted to humanize the rules of war from those of traditional Roman practice, as he extended the laws of treating strangers to the treatment of enemies (whereas he points out that the early Romans reversed this rule by regarding all strangers as enemies) (*DO* 1.38).

The two just causes for war, honor and safety, reflect Cicero's general view that ethics revolves around choosing between the morally right (*honestum*) and the expedient (*utile*). In the same way as his just war thinking is rooted in honor, so too is his ethics, as evidenced by his choice of the term *honestum*, which is related to the word for honorable, *honestus*. The honestum is doing what is right in the right circumstances; an example of a purely expedient action would be committing an injustice for the sake of life or riches.

For Cicero, there ultimately can be no difference between honestum and utile. However, only those with greatness of soul (*magnitudo animi*) will fully appreciate this (*DO* 3.100). A great soul is defined as one who has transcended the vicissitudes of mortal life (including caring for one's own life). Such great souls, however, can cause problems when their souls are not yet sufficiently formed because they are likely to be more tempted than others to act expediently to satisfy their grand ambitions, and their expedient actions can be more damaging than those of people who merely seek goods like wealth. He lists Julius Caesar as such a dangerous great soul (*DO* 1.26). Thus, the quest for glory, characteristic of the highest active life, can also be the most destructive to others and to oneself because it can rob one of one's own liberty (*DO* 1.68). The active life whose goal is glorified virtue is thus beset by an inner tension whereby the quest for glory can deprive the active human being of that very liberty he seeks. Virtue naturally desires glory and honor (*DR* 3.34), and Cicero notes that there is scarcely a man who does not seek glory (or

---

of their crown. They are both just and necessary, and to attribute them to mere pride, except when too lofty pretensions are made, is to be grossly ignorant of the art of ruling, and to undervalue one of the strongest bulwarks of the greatness and safety of the state" (*Law of Nations; or, The Principles of Natural Law Applied to the Conduct and to the Affairs of Nations and of Sovereigns*, 1:191, quoted in Pangle and Ahrensdorf, 1999: 277–79, n. 33). In other words, a nation seeks not simply to preserve itself but must also defend the reasons it deserves to exist: it views its national honor in universalist terms.

recognition, as moderns call and redefine it) for his achievements (*DO* 1.65). Even so, Cicero observes that a war for imperium between equal contestants, as opposed to a war over scarce resources or for survival, will likely be waged more honorably and with less bitterness (*DO* 1.38), which indicates his view of the moderating effect of the quest for glory by the free.

Of the few great souls who seek a glory that transcends pleasure and riches, there are even fewer who do not succumb to the Caesarian temptation of seeking glory at the expense of virtue. Cicero praises Regulus for doing the morally right when he fulfilled his oath to the Carthaginians by returning from Rome to face death by torture. Regulus is the most praiseworthy example of civic virtue because he kept his oath (which Cicero defines as an assurance backed by religious sanctity [*DO* 3.104]) and served Rome by ensuring the return of young Roman soldiers who could benefit Rome further into the future than the aged Regulus could have (*DO* 3.100). Regulus had clearly transcended the vicissitudes of earthly life, and he did not succumb to the temptation to resort to expediency to secure glory. Indeed, he likely manifested the quality of the noblest soul whose virtue consoles him when glory is lacking and, while desirous of glory and honor, does not demand them but receives them gladly if and when they arrive (*DR* 3.40; see also *DO* 1.90). The distinction between the person who demands glory and the person who seeks it and receives it gladly but does not necessarily demand it is crucial for Cicero because such a person understands the tragic nature of the human condition whereby virtue is not a guarantee of securing external goods such as glory. Thus, the noblest soul, while transcending the vicissitudes of life, does so by deepening his awareness of the precariousness of his existence and his ability to receive the gift of glory. Yet, an aporia arises, which Regulus may have considered as he sat wakefully in his torture chamber, and which bothered Cicero as well: is virtue truly self-sustaining? Cicero wondered this when he stated that virtue naturally seeks glory, and that there is scarcely a man who does not seek glory for his achievements. Can one remain happy when one, however virtuously, bears the worst of misfortunes? Indeed, Regulus himself gained glory through the praise bestowed upon him by Rome's best men. This question perplexed the ancient Greek and Roman philosophers and lay at the deepest level of the Christian critique of pagan ethics; Christian thinkers thought that the pagan's wait for glory could be satisfied only by God's glory.[6] For the Christian, virtue, at least that obtained by man's own efforts, does not guarantee happiness. Also, for the early Christians, the pagan attempt to reconcile virtue with happiness was the wellspring that led to their idolatrous war making because, lacking God's glory, the pagans got impatient and instead glorified their warriors. As a result, for Christians, just war theory could not be sufficiently addressed until the relationship between happiness and virtue had properly been established. I now turn to assess the adequacy of their treatment of the problem.

Early Christian Pacifism, Idolatry, and Triumphalism

Most commentators usually distinguish pre-Constantinian from post-Constantinian early Church thinkers on just war. The pre-Constantinian thinkers, such as Tertullian and Origen, are generally taken as pacifists, while the post-Constantinian thinkers, such as Eusebius and Ambrose, are taken to admit that war can be permitted and are often accused of betraying the transcendent aims of Christianity with their support of the Roman emperor. Louis J. Swift argues that this distinction is simplistic: the pre-Constantinian thinkers were not simply pacifists, and the support of the emperor by the post-Constantinian thinkers was more nuanced than their critics allow (Swift, 1983: 26–29).[7] The nuance of the so-called pacifism can be seen in Tertullian, while Ambrose's nuanced affirmation of just war is treated in the next section. This section examines the reasons for Tertullian's near-total rejection of war, and it shows how Origen's pacifism actually shares the same assumptions about Christian providence as Eusebius's support of the emperor.

Tertullian

Tertullian's attitudes toward war can be seen in his treatises *On Idolatry* (c. A.D. 211, although Swift dates it at A.D. 197) and *On the Crown* (c. A.D. 211). The first is a general polemic against the dangers of paganism, which includes the dangers of Christians serving pagan armies. There,

---

6. The locus classicus for this view is Augustine's *City of God*. I have examined this problem in my *Augustine and Politics as Longing in the World* (von Heyking, 2001; see esp. chap. 5).

7. Swift challenges the interpretations of early Christian just war thinking by Paul Ramsey and Roland Bainton.

he argues that Christians ought not to serve in the military because violence is unchristian. His argument is sharpened by the fact that the Roman army was what could be called a "total" institution, which required soldiers to swear oaths (*sacramenta*) that are an affront to Christian sacrament. Tertullian did not absolutely condemn Christian participation in the military, however, because he modified his view in *On the Crown*, where he allows that converts to Christianity may remain in the military so long as they take nonviolent roles.[8] Three points require clarification, however, in order to distinguish Tertullian's pacifism from that of others like Origen. Tertullian did not equate killing in war with murder (see *On the Resurrection* 16.7–8), he did not regard Rome as inherently evil (i.e., as the apocalyptic agent of Satan), and he recognized the need for securing the empire's borders (see *Apology* 30.4); finally, he did not anticipate the imminent arrival of the Parousia that other Christian pacifists thought would eliminate the need for war (*On the Resurrection* 24.18). Thus, Tertullian was generally a pacifist, but he recognized that violence could play a role securing earthly peace. He could not, however, reconcile violence with Scripture.

Origen

If Tertullian was heavily inclined to pacifism, Origen took an absolute pacifist position while actually spiritualizing warfare. He thought that Christians must never take combat positions. Since the Romans prohibited their priests from participating in war, so too should all Christians avoid war because all Christians are priests, strictly speaking. However, he thought that Christians could do battle via prayer in a just war that is led by a just emperor: "Though they keep their right hands clean, the Christians fight through their prayers to God on behalf of those doing battle in a just cause and on behalf of an emperor who is ruling justly in order that all opposition and hostility toward those who are acting rightly may be eliminated. What is more, by overcoming with our prayers all the demons who incite wars, who violate oaths and who disturb the peace we help emperors more than those who are supposedly doing the fighting. . . . We do not go out on the campaign with him even if he in-

---

8. One thinks of pacifists in the twentieth century serving in nonviolent roles to support the war effort, such as retrieving the wounded and digging victims out of bombed-out buildings.

sists, but we do battle on his behalf by raising a special army of piety through our petitions to God" (*Against Celsus* [c. 248 A.D] 8.73).

Origen's pacifism, despite his view that Christian prayers could "eliminate" enemies, is based on his view that the Christian dispensation will put an end to war. War was permitted under the Old Law, but the New Law of Christ's grace and the spread of Christianity will make war obsolete. Yet his eschatological expectations accompanied his view that war is conducted against demons, and so he attempted to reconcile the spiritual missions of Christians with the exercise of political and military power. As Swift observes, "Christian service to the empire, then, must be in the realm of the spirit or not at all" (1983: 56). Origen thus attempted to reconcile Christian obligation with the use of military power by restricting Christian participation to that of offering petitions. While their role would not take the form of physical violence, Origen spiritualized the activity of war to an extent not seen in classical thought, as enemies were not simply barbarians or enemies of mankind but were seen to be tools of demons. War for Origen was the means of carrying out the apocalypse. Yet Origen rejected a violent role for Christians, and left it up to Eusebius to allow Christian priests to join their pagan brethren in violent battle against the devil.

Eusebius

Eusebius developed what could be considered the first Christian philosophy of history, according to which he argued that Roman emperors play active parts in the salvation of mankind. Jesus Christ was born during Octavian's administration, which he interpreted as heralding a new age in the world as it did in the empire. He regarded Constantine as a sign of the end times and as performing God's war. The emperor is to the state as God is to the world. He regarded Constantine as the ensoulment of the cosmic order, as the link between heaven and earth (Helgeland, Daly, and Burns, 1985: 70). This enabled Eusebius to view Constantine as transcending the realm of the traditional rules of war, as he seems to have approved of Constantine betraying Licinius as he expanded the Roman Empire: "There is not the slightest sense of tragedy as Eusebius recounts the destruction of Licinius's army. The Christian apocalyptic crusade had been born and anything in its path was to be swept away in a storm of fire" (ibid.).

While Eusebius wed Christian obligation with political power, and Origen was a pacifist, both spiritualized war to an extent never seen in the classical world because both incorporated war and its outcomes to the Christian drama of salvation. Origen saw Christian prayer as ushering in the end times, while Eusebius regarded Constantine and his armies as the direct hand of God in history. Both had the same eschatological hopes even though they drew different ethical conclusions. In that sense, Swift is correct when he claims that "Eusebius' unsophisticated endorsement of imperial power and authority was as simplistic an answer to the problem as Tertullian's pacifism was" (1983: 97). Coupled with Eusebius's inclusion of Constantine into his apocalyptic narrative is a transformation of the classical understanding of war for the purpose of glory. Whereas Cicero could regard glory as a proper end for a just war, and war's outcome as the judgment of God, Eusebius added onto this the view that glory and judgment are part of the providential story of salvation. Constantine's glory is his and God's glory, and Constantine's victory is a sign of the end times. Conversely, for Cicero, while the great statesman is in some sense the ensoulment of the cosmos, Cicero adamantly points out (in his dream of Scipio) that the statesman's activities pale in comparison to the vistas of contemplation of philosophy; similarly, there is no clear or direct relationship between military glory and historical narrative. For Cicero, glory is for its own sake; it does not herald anything more than that. It does not herald the end times.

Thus, Christian thinking after Eusebius was left at an impasse because its thinkers could not reconcile Christian obligation with the exercise of political and military power. As Swift argues, "What was needed at this juncture was some recognition of the concrete issues involved when Christians had responsibility for living up to the Gospel while at the same time they were directly accountable for managing the affairs of state" (1983: 97). Ambrose, to a large degree, recognized these issues when he translated Ciceronian glory into Christian idiom as a way of taming both pagan warriors and Christians impatient for the apocalypse.

Ambrose and the Transposition of Glory and Just War

Most scholars regard Ambrose's thinking on just war as a continuation of that of Eusebius's Constantinian triumphalism. For instance, Russell argues that Ambrose also transposed the Roman dynamic of empire into his moral theology: "For the older antagonism between Empire and Christianity was substituted the new and more explosive division of heresy and orthodoxy" (1975: 13; see also Helgeland, Daly, and Burns, 1985: 73). This section challenges this interpretation by showing how Ambrose's transposition of classical virtue teaching in his *De officiis ministorum* (self-consciously titled after Cicero's *De officiis*) preserved Christianity's transcendental orientation while emphasizing the glory that informs leadership understood as self-sacrifice for God and community. His thoughts on glory and just war are more nuanced than has been acknowledged, although the success of his transposition of Ciceronian just war theory remains marred by his failure to apply the laws of just war to wars with heretics.[9]

The conventional view of Ambrose has some basis. He was governor of the province of Aemilia-Liguria before being elected bishop of Milan in 374. Thus, he was well ensconced in Roman politics before taking up his duties as bishop, and his political experience undoubtedly colored his thinking on politics and just war. In his sermons, he often described the Roman emperors in Eusebian terms, as he characterized Theodosius as the hand of God for crushing the pagan revolt of Eugenius (*Exposition of Psalm 35*, 25). Elsewhere, he characterized the peace of Augustus as preparing the world for the Gospels (ibid. 45.21). He characterized Gratian's assistance to his uncle, Valens, as the hand of God, and compared his enemy, the Goths, to Gog (*On the Faith* 2.16.136). Yet, as Swift interprets him, Ambrose stopped invoking such apocalyptic symbols after the Roman army was defeated at Hadrianople (378 A.D.): "he undoubtedly came to regret this misplaced enthusiasm of his early episcopacy. At least we never hear talk of this kind in his subsequent writings" (1988: 106).

Therefore, we turn to his great treatise, *De officiis ministorum* (henceforth *DOM*), which was written around 391. The treatise constitutes his general views on the ethics of the Christian life, and naturally includes his views on war, which, Swift points out, follow the traditional Roman teaching on just war. While it does not propound a thoroughgoing just war doctrine, his transposition of Cicero's thought to Christian ethics dis-

---

9. The English version used here is *Nicene and Post-Nicene Fathers of the Christian Church* (Ambrose, 1983). The Latin edition used is the French-Latin bilingual edition in Ambrose, 1984.

tinguishes his treatment of just war from earlier Christians in important ways. The treatise lacks the apocalyptic expectations of his earlier writings. Christian revelation changes politics, as he argues that a Christian society would not exile foreigners in times of famine, as Rome had done (*DOM* 3.7.50). However, while the treatise constitutes an extended commentary on Cicero's treatise, it lacks many direct comparisons between Christian and Roman practice in war, except in praising a Roman general for refusing to poison his enemies (*DOM* 3.15.90–91). While Ambrose emphasizes the differences between Christian and pagan ethics, his direct comparison shows a similarity between the two codes, and, as we shall see, he is in closer agreement with Cicero on the fundamental issues than he lets on.

Because human beings are required to love their neighbors as themselves, Ambrose allows for three just causes for war. Just cause for Ambrose included wars of self-defense (*DOM* 1.35.176–77; 1.27.129), punishing wrongdoers (*DOM* 3.19.110, 116), and securing sacred territory (*DOM* 3.8.54). Unlike Cicero, however, he does not admit of glory in imperium except when he discusses the Israelites' conquest of their enemies to gain entry into the Promised Land; unlike Eusebius, he does not explicitly admit the Romans played a glorious role in God's Providence. He does not deny glory in war but reserves his praise for courage used in defending the *patria* (*DOM* 1.40.206–41.209) and goes so far as to criticize servility and praise fortitude in war, which "bears no light impress on what is virtuous and seemly upon it, for [fortitude] prefers death to slavery and disgrace" (*DOM* 1.41.211). He also mentions the glory of Eleazar's triumph in battle (despite, or because of, his dying) (*DOM* 1.40.206–8), and he mentions the glory of Judas Maccabeus in adversity (*DOM* 1.41.209). He also criticizes Cicero for allegedly claiming that war manifests the best kind of fortitude (*DOM* 1.40.205). Nevertheless, he admired the fortitude of Old Testament figures such as Joshua, Jonathan, and Judas Maccabeus (*DOM* 1.40.195), and, as we shall see, he appreciated the glory of attacks to secure the Promised Land.

Turning to the means of waging war, Ambrose argued for faith to be kept with one's enemy (*DOM* 2.7.33), to avoid unfair advantages (*DOM* 1.29.139), and he placed special emphasis on mercy (*DOM* 3.14.87). Nevertheless, he uses the example of Elisha's espionage against the king of Persia as an example of the most glorious kind of warfare (showing that winning by the grace of God is superior to winning by the strength of one's army) (*DOM* 3.1.5). He also found it acceptable for Joshua and Caleb to spy on the occupants of the Promised Land (*DOM* 3.8.53–56) and pointed to their virtue as the grounds for their authority to lead the Israelites into that land. Ambrose argues that Joshua and Caleb "thought it unseemly to give way before the heathen." Joshua and Caleb would rather be stoned by the cowardly Israelites than to have Israel shrink from taking the Promised Land. Apparently obscuring the difference between glory and virtue, Ambrose observes that the "better part [of the Israelites] . . . preferred glory to safety [*gloriam . . . saluti*]; the worse part safety to virtue [*salutem honestati*]. But the divine judgment approved those who thought virtue [*honesta*] was above what is useful [*utilibus*], while it condemned those who preferred what seemed more in accordance with safety than with what is virtuous" (*DOM* 3.8.56). Those Israelites were glorified, then, who secured the Promised Land, and the spying by Joshua and Caleb appears to be an exception to Ambrose's general rule against taking an unfair advantage over the enemy (the purpose of their mission was restricted to finding out the existence and strength of the enemies). On the other hand, Ambrose cites the example of David's honoring of his enemy, Abner, as the bravest champion as an example of a soldier/statesman who can love his enemy to the extent that he identifies more with his enemy's fortitude than with that of his own countrymen (although Ambrose does not mention that Abner had joined David before being killed by Saul). Ambrose's example of David suggests that he could consider enemies as equal partners in the "play" of war (*DOM* 3.7; see 2 Samuel 3:20).

Ambrose articulated the general principle governing wars against infidels, heretics, and barbarians in his treatise *On Tobias*.[10] One may attack barbarians or infidels on the same principle that one may charge usury. Citing Deuteronomy 23:19–20, he argues: "[Y]ou can legitimately demand interest from someone whom you have every right to wish harm to and against whom you can lawfully wage war. . . . Demand interest from him whom it is no crime to kill. The man who demands interest fights without a weapon; he who exacts interest of an enemy, avenges himself without raising the sword. Thus, usury is legitimate wherever

---

10. Neither Swift nor Romestin provide a date of publication.

war is legitimate. 'Your brother,' in this context is, first of all, everyone who shares the faith and, secondly, every Roman" (*On Tobias* 15.51). It is unclear whether Ambrose still thought this way when he wrote *De officiis ministorum.* Swift argues that "we should be cautious about pressing the point too hard . . . he did not endorse the killing of unorthodox believers and it seems that he learned a lesson from the one instance in which he thought he saw the hand of God assisting the imperial armies against barbarian heretics" (1983: 99).

Ambrose provided a more nuanced articulation of glory than Eusebius did. *De officiis ministorum* lacks the kind of triumphalism found in Ambrose's earlier writings and sermons, and his account of the shining deeds of war, and of the active life in general, is more muted. What is interesting, however, is his attempt to transpose the Ciceronian teaching on glory and play into a Christian theology wherein God glorifies the virtuous, while avoiding the Eusebian triumphalism of explicitly treating great souls as the direct manifestation of the divine will.

Like Cicero, Ambrose's thinking on just war is situated in his account of the morally right and expedient. Like Cicero, he treats duty as threefold: (1) as what is becoming or honorable (*decorum*), (2) as useful (*utile*), and (3) as a mixture of virtue and the useful (*DOM* 1.9.27). He observes that his work differs from that of Cicero in that the morally right for the Christian is understood in reference to eternal life and not simply to the present, which makes it easier to understand the unity of the morally right with the expedient (as Cicero had tried to argue in the case of the great soul) because one seeks eternal rewards (*DOM* 1.9.28). His terminology differs slightly. Ambrose uses *decorum* more than he does *honestum* which, by emphasizing the beauty of virtuous play, arguably makes him more Ciceronian than Cicero himself in his appreciation of the beauty of virtuous action. Another important difference between the two treatises is that Ambrose begins his with some reflections on the necessity of careful speech and writing, going so far as to claim that measure in speaking is the first duty one has as a teacher (*DOM* 1.10.35) and that too much speaking leads to error and sin, much as an overflowing river quickly gathers mud (*DOM* 1.3.12). He explains that careful speech is a sign of the humility that one must practice in discussing sacred Scripture, and it is required because everyone, including the author, is a learner (*DOM* 1.1.3). This restraint becomes significant when Ambrose discusses the difficulty of understanding the relationship between virtue and glory.

As the Latin *decorum* indicates, Ambrose, like Cicero (*DO* 1.27), saw a close relationship between virtue and seemliness: "For it is no light thing in every matter to preserve due measure and to bring about order, wherein that is plainly conspicuous which we call 'decorum,' or what is seemly. This is so closely connected with what is virtuous, that one cannot separate the two. For what is seemly [*decet*] is also virtuous [*honestum*]—and what is virtuous is seemly. So that the distinction lies rather in the words than in the things themselves. That there is a difference between them we can understand, but we cannot explain it" (*DOM* 1.45.228). Emphasizing moderation and modesty, Ambrose also argues that virtue goes hand in hand with seemliness. He does not reveal why he cannot explain the difference between virtue and seemliness. Without knowing exactly the source of this difference, he explains that the way of virtue is to shine out and enlighten the world: "If anyone preserves an even tenor in the whole of life, and method in all that he does, and sees there is order and consistency in his words and moderation in his deeds, then what is seemly stands forth conspicuously in his life and shines forth as in some mirror [*speculo*]" (*DOM* 1.47.234). Ambrose, then, agrees with Cicero's view of the relationship between virtue and glory. He expresses this idea by reversing Paul's metaphor of our knowledge of God as looking through a looking glass. Despite appearances, however, he does not reverse its meaning (1 Corinthians 13:12). Ambrose's statement reflects Jesus's own words to his disciples: "Let your works so shine [*luceant*] before men that they may see your good deeds and glorify [*glorificent*] your father who is in heaven" (Matthew 5:16). Virtuous deeds shine upon others and glorify God. Ambrose did not reject seeking glory, and his association of virtue and glory recalls Cicero's view that virtue naturally seeks glory. Furthermore, his view of a virtuous soul who shines out on the world is close to the Eusebian ensoulment of the cosmos, although Ambrose expresses the idea mutedly with his simple *speculo* comment, and recalls his duty to write carefully.[11] Moreover, glory can also mean keeping the most important aspects of religious life secret: "[i]t therefore belongs to a virtuous life to show mercy and to fast in secret; that you may seem to be

---

11. Augustine makes similar observations in *City of God*, 5.14, 11.18, 22.30.

seeking a reward from God alone, and not from men" (*DOM* 2.1.3). Glory shines forth, as through a mirror but, as Cicero observes, virtue does not strictly demand that it be recognized.

Ambrose also expresses agreement with Cicero's view that the virtuous do not require the judgment of other people: "Blessed, plainly, is that life which is not esteemed at the estimation of outsiders, but is known, as judge of itself, by its own inner feelings. It needs no popular opinion as its reward in any way.... Thus the less it strives for glory, the more it rises above it. For to those who seek for glory, that reward in the shape of present things is but a shadow of future ones" (*DOM* 2.1.2). This statement echoes Cicero's view that the peak of virtue does not demand glory but is self-sustaining, although the Christian Ambrose adds that virtue is sustained by hope in eternal life.

However, honor is useful, as he points out that there is nothing so useful as to be loved and to "give cause for a good estimate and opinion to be formed of us" (*DOM* 2.7.29). Such esteem is gained through service, especially through saving captives from enemies and saving women from shame (*DOM* 2.15.70). He calls the latter two examples the highest form of liberality *(liberalitas)*, and goes on to observe that such deeds are especially excellent when those people are saved from barbarian enemies "who are moved by no spark of human feeling to show mercy, except so far as avarice has preserved it with a view to redemption" (*DOM* 2.15.71). His comment on barbarians' lack of mercy reflects his general attitude toward their inability to practice virtue, although it is noteworthy that Ambrose observes that their vices and self-interest constitute a basic level of behavior whereby their self-interest can produce good outcomes, indicating that they are not simply "beyond the pale" (somewhat in the spirit of Augustine's argument that the inordinate love of honor can produce marvelous deeds of heroism and self-sacrifice).

Turning to Ambrose's view on the most glorious example of war making, we find that he defines good statesmanship and war making in terms of service. David in particular serves as his exemplar because he distinguished himself not only in military glory but also in showing justice toward enemies and toward his people. At the foremost, David took it upon himself to face danger for Israel, and thus willingly offered himself up for sacrifice (*DOM* 2.7.32) which, Ambrose notes, is no small thing for a king to do (*DOM* 2.7.34). In fact, central to Ambrose's teaching on just war is what can be regarded as the third-party principle, whereby one is positively commanded to defend (and kill on behalf of, if necessary) another, which moves beyond simple passive resistance, as it commands one to do for another what is normally prohibited for one to do for oneself. Commenting on Moses's killing an Egyptian in defense of another Israelite, he argues: "For anyone who does not prevent an injury to a companion, if he can do so, is as much at fault as he who inflicts it" (*DOM* 1.36.178).

Ambrose notes that David's service and humility inspired love from the people, and that he was, in fact, loved more for his gentleness than for his actual deeds (*DOM* 2.7.31). He also showed justice toward his enemies as toward his own men (*DOM* 2.7.33). Ambrose observes that David's temporal reward for his efforts was to be loved by his people, and he refers to Cicero's comment on the importance of such love (see *DO* 2.8.30). He observes that his deeds inspired such love that people put him ahead of friends and family (*DOM* 2.7.36).

Ambrose uses the example of David to explain the benefits of suffering that a leader who serves God and community gains. David is an example of a king submitting to God. Ambrose notes that David patiently suffered the scorn of Shimei's son, who charged David with bloodying the house of Saul (*DOM* 1.48.245–46; see 2 Samuel 16:5–14). David, who refused to respond, even when the man physically abused him, left the man unpunished. David did so because Shimei's son's scorn could not harm him (spiritually) and because God had told him to criticize David. David, then, was simply following God's command. Ambrose also uses David to show how the Christian life fulfills the ambitions of the soldier. Like other Christian authors, Ambrose argues that the ultimate battle is with sin, and not simply with human enemies, so he states: "But though perfect, he sought something still more perfect. As a man he grew hot at the pain of his wrongs, but like a good soldier he conquered, he endured like a brave wrestler. The end and aim of his patience was the expectation of the fulfillment of the promises" (*DOM* 1.48.247). He patiently suffered his wrongs and prayed to understand their purpose, the purpose of his suffering. Ambrose argues that David's gentleness and humility, what distinguishes him from other kings, derived from his having sought eternal reward for his tribulations (*DOM* 1.48.247): "For when the kingdom is delivered up to God, even the Father, and all the powers are put down, as the Apostle says, then perfection begins. Here, then, is the hindrance, here the weakness of the perfect; there full perfection. Thus it is he asks for those days of eternal life which are, and not for those which pass away, so that he may know what is wanting to him, what is the land of promise that bears everlasting fruits, which is the first mansion in his Father's house, which the second, which the third, wherein each one will rest according to his merits" (*DOM* 1.48.247).

The source of David's humility and strength was his "weakness of the perfect," which was structured by his hope in redemption. This is Ambrose's, and Christianity's, response to the aporia in Ambrose's wondering whether seemliness differs from virtue, and to the question of whether Regulus truly was self-sufficient inside his torturer's box. For Ambrose, the human mind cannot adequately articulate the difference between glory and virtue; it can know that the human soul seeks a unity between virtue and its good effects, which it expresses with terms like *gloria* and *honestum*. However, it cannot explain the mystery of iniquity in a world where the virtuous and vicious suffer alike (and whose iniquity sometimes leads the great-souled to slip and to demand glory when it is not forthcoming from where they expect it). The glory that the suffering servant David seeks is intimated in Cicero's observation that there is scarcely a man who does not seek reward for his exertions; but faith for Ambrose fulfills those ambitions.

Ambrose, as a Christian, further explicates the tension between virtue and glory by arguing that faith in eternal life constitutes the "achievement" (by God's grace alone) of one's solitary suffering and, therefore, seemingly implies that Cicero's argument for the self-sufficiency of virtue is prideful. On the other hand, would not the pagan Cicero respond that Ambrose is simply expressing the sentiment of a less than great soul who demands glory (rather than simply accepting it with gratitude when and if it is forthcoming), except that it now seeks it in the afterlife? The two alternatives are not so easily distinguished, however. Cicero himself argued that virtue naturally seeks glory and that there is scarcely a man who does not seek glory. Further, one cannot claim that Regulus lacked glory despite his lonely and torturous death, as he undoubtedly knew the future esteem he would receive from the Romans. (Whether such esteem actually constitutes happiness is another issue.) Virtue, at least in the active life, lacks self-sufficiency for Cicero as much as for Ambrose, as Cicero observed that the great soul receives glory with gladness even though he does not stringently demand it. Thus, Cicero, like Plato and Aristotle, regarded the contemplative life as the only self-sufficient life and one that ultimately satisfies political ambition. Ambrose perhaps would not disagree, but would add that the religious life also fulfills the active life (and, importantly, transforms the active life through the practice of *caritas*, as shown in the example given above of Rome's treatment of foreigners during famine). His view that the religious life fulfills the active life, including the military life, was seen above in his use of military analogies to describe the battle with sin. Thus, both Cicero and Ambrose are in substantial agreement about the peak of active virtue, and both express doubt about the self-sufficiency of virtue.

Conclusion

Ambrose attempted to reconcile Christian love with the duties of political power and was nearly successful in achieving a synthesis of Christian and Ciceronian ethics. Specifically, he articulated rules for war making and incorporated a Ciceronian understanding of military glory into Christianity. He surpassed the disastrous efforts of Eusebius and his own earlier efforts of glorifying leaders like Constantine as the ensoulment of the cosmos, while acknowledging a limited role that glory can play as an end of just war that also moderates its means. Ambrose shared Cicero's view (and that of the later chivalric code) that military leaders are usually motivated by the desire for glory, and adopted a similar strategy to that of Cicero in channeling their ambitions to more constructive ends. Cicero tried to convince them of the superiority of peaceful statesmanship (which he admitted was not the highest way of life), while Ambrose attempted to persuade them of the superiority of peaceful statesmanship formed by the love of and service to God and neighbor. Both could appeal to the warrior's love of glory and his sense of playfulness because both acknowledged that such playfulness is rooted in the insufficiency of the warrior's life and that true freedom and glory, true play, resides in the higher pursuits of statesmanship, philosophy, and faith. Moreover, Ambrose's skepticism toward glory and play provides a way of moderating the fervor of those seeking apocalypse.

Glory is a primary concern in discussions of contemporary war making, despite the lack of opportunity for personal virtue on the modern battlefield. One need only consider glory sought by apocalyptic terrorists, including those among the al-Qaeda who are drawn from Arab nations where honor and glory play a larger political role than in the liberal bourgeois West. Michael Ignatieff argues that our fragmented international condition, where international anarchy is coupled with nation-states that themselves lack moral and social cohesion, provides little ground for conventions governing the conduct of war. This fragmentation raises once again the issue of glory and honor. The lack of overarching narrative exacerbates the tendency to regard enemies as the "enemies of humanity" who require destruction at any cost. Postmodern difference extends the medieval disregard of heretics and infidels to all enemies; postmodern difference does not make distinctions between enemies one treats justly from others who are beyond the pale. Honor, Ignatieff argues, echoing Cicero, is ultimately the ground of convention (1998: 116). Thus, the lack of honor codes makes legal conventions unsupportable, and thus makes just war thinking impossible. Despite these problems, though, he holds out the possibility that honor may be the only (thin) ground on which to reconstruct a public recognition of just war in our fragmented world. For instance, he describes television commercials produced by the International Committee of the Red Cross that attempt to teach combatants in the Balkans why it is dishonorable to kill prisoners and children and to rape women: "[The voice-over] did not appeal to any notion of compassion or decency. It did not appeal to anyone as a human being. It appealed solely to the combatants as warriors" (ibid.: 157) Echoing Johnson's comment that the internal chivalric code did more to govern the conduct of war during the medieval ages than did the Church or the arguments of theologians and canonists, Ignatieff points out that the Red Cross has the most success in promulgating the laws of war when its members appeal directly to warriors' sense of honor, be they Serbian, Croatian, Hutu, Tutsi, or fighting for the Taliban.

The efforts of the Red Cross demonstrate the importance of Cicero's and Ambrose's reflections on just war and on the relationship between virtue and glory. These efforts show that Cicero's and Ambrose's reflections are communicable to non-Westerners and non-Christians even if they themselves failed to extend the laws of war to pirates and heretics, respectively. (Indeed, neither Cicero nor Ambrose advocated the kind of ruthlessness toward pirates and heretics that Ignatieff describes of today's warriors who lack honor.) Both understood the motivations of warriors and both provide a way to channel their ambitions to higher ends because they appeal to the warrior's sense of play—a longing for free activity that is simultaneously conducted for its own sake as well as for the sake of glory—as an intimation of the free activity that better clarifies the gulf between virtue and glory, the mystery of iniquity, as the Christians called it, and which better enables one to experience that gulf as inherent to our mortal lives. Ambrose is of especial contemporary relevance because he provides us with the means to understand how the love of apocalyptic glory, as in the case of al-Qaeda, can be moderated and, more important, can be moderated on its own terms. Cicero and Ambrose also show how appeals to honor and glory can provide the groundwork for more formal rules that govern war making that speak to the fundamental motivations of warriors and to the desire of human beings generally to understand the goal of their suffering, as Regulus and David sought theirs. Ignatieff perhaps overestimates the lack of narrative in the postmodern world, as descending into the pit of suffering is certainly common to all sides. Questioning the meaning of suffering is a good starting point to develop honor codes and rules of war where no other customs exist, and Cicero's and Ambrose's reflections on honor, glory, just war, and suffering, as parts of their overall critique of the active life, constitute excellent entry points into rebuilding these customs.

REFERENCES

Ambrose of Milan. 1952 (1890). "On the Duties of the Clergy." In *Ambrose: Selected Works and Letters.* In Philip Schaff and Henry Wace, eds., H. de Romestin, trans., *Nicene and Post-Nicene Fathers of the Christian Church,* 2nd ser., vol. 10. Grand Rapids, Mich.: William B. Eerdmans, 22–155.
———. 1984. *Les devoirs.* 2 vols. Ed. Maurice Testard. Paris: Société d'Édition.
Baechler, Jean. 1979. *Suicides.* Trans. Barry Cooper. Oxford: Basil Blackwell.
Bloch, Marc. 1964. *Feudal Society.* Trans. L. A. Manyon. Chicago: Phoenix Books, University of Chicago Press.
Cicero. 1983. *De officiis.* Trans. H. Rackham. Loeb Classical Library. Cambridge: Harvard University Press.
———. 1988. *De republica. De legibus.* Trans. C. W. Keyes. Loeb Classical Library. Cambridge: Harvard University Press.
Clausewitz, Karl von. 1968. *On War.* Ed. Anatol Rapoport. New York: Penguin.
Helgeland, John, Robert J. Daly, and J. Patout Burns. 1985. *Christians and the Military: The Early Experience.* Philadelphia: Fortress.
Heyking, John von. 2001. *Augustine and Politics as Longing in the World.* Columbia: University of Missouri Press.

Huizinga, Johannes. 1950. *Homo Ludens: A Study of the Play-Element in Culture.* Boston: Beacon.
Ignatieff, Michael. 1998. *The Warrior's Honour: Ethnic War and the Modern Conscience.* Toronto: Penguin.
Johnson, James Turner. 1981. *Just War Tradition and the Restraint of War: A Moral and Historical Inquiry.* Princeton: Princeton University Press.
———. 1999. *Morality and Contemporary Warfare.* New Haven: Yale University Press.
Nederman, Cary. 2000. "War, Peace, and Republican Virtue: Patriotism and the Neglected Legacy of Cicero." In Norma Thompson, ed., *Instilling Ethics.* Lanham, Md.: Rowman and Littlefield, 17–29.
Pangle, Thomas L., and Peter J. Ahrensdorf. 1999. *Justice among Nations: On the Moral Basis of Power and Peace.* Lawrence: University of Kansas Press.
Rahner, Hugo. 1972. *Man at Play.* New York: Herder and Herder.
Russell, Frederick H. 1975. *The Just War in the Middle Ages.* Cambridge: Cambridge University Press.
Swift, Louis J. 1983. *The Early Fathers on War and Military Service.* Wilmington, Del.: Michael Glazier.

3

Augustine and Just War

Between Virtue and Duties

HENRIK SYSE

Augustine is often referred to as the founder of just war doctrine. While that is not quite accurate, since Cicero and several of the earlier Church Fathers had already formulated the basic elements of the just war idea,[1] it is certainly true that Augustine would become the most influential of the early Christian teachers writing on the morality of war. He formulated his ideas at a crucial time in Church history, just when the Western Roman Empire was crumbling and Christianity had to accommodate to life in the world — a world that was showing few signs of an imminent end, in spite of the eschatological expectations of the early Church.

Augustine's teaching on the justice of war has been the object of a rich array of commentaries. Therefore, I will give no more than a brief summary of its main tenets here. (Also, my account is very much complemented by the interesting insights of Phillip Gray in chapter 4 and Gerson Moreno-Riaño in chapter 7 of this volume.) My chief aim is to give an interpretation of certain aspects of the Augustinian doctrine in light of some present-day challenges in ethics and political theory, hope-

---

1. See, particularly, Cicero's *De officiis* 1.34–40 and 3.107–15, in Cicero, 1991: 14–18 and 141–45, and early Christian theologians (such as Tertullian, Clement of Alexandria, Origen, and Ambrose), in Swift, 1983: 32–110. For a useful discussion of pre-Augustinian Christian attitudes to war and the roots of the just war doctrine, see Johnson, 1987: 3–56, and Reichberg, Syse, and Begby, 2006: 60–69. See also John von Heyking's contribution to this volume, chapter 2.

fully throwing more light on its original intention and current import. I believe that Augustine, as well as his medieval readers, understood just war doctrine differently from the modern, post-Westphalian expositors of just war and international law. Whereas the latter—and this is clear even from the literature today—understood (and understand) the just war idea as a moral doctrine emphasizing rules and consequences, thus constituting a mixture of deontology and consequentialism, Augustine himself was more concerned with what we today would call "virtue ethics" in his approach to war. (I certainly acknowledge the anachronistic ring of using these terms about Augustine's thought, since these are theoretical divisions of a later date. Yet I believe they are useful in gaining a perspective on the Augustinian just war teaching.)

Furthermore, Augustine's perspective on war is rather different from the modern, mainly post–World War II emphasis on self-defense and the avoidance of offensive war. As James Turner Johnson, among others, has pointed out, the Augustinian just war doctrine does not primarily exhibit a presumption against war per se, but rather a presumption against injustice (see Johnson, 1996; Winwright, 1998; see also Gregory M. Reichberg's contribution to this volume, chapter 5). The latter does not categorically exclude an idea of offensive war, provided morality and the pursuit of justice call for it. Whether this is a strength or a weakness of the Augustinian doctrine—whether it, for instance, contributed to the ruthless exploitation of just war ideas in the excesses of the Crusades and the Reformation-era religious wars—will not be judged here. That we see a return, albeit largely unacknowledged, to the Augustinian framework with the growing currency of the idea of "humanitarian interventions" is, however, beyond doubt.

Augustine on the Moral Criteria for a Just War

It may be something of an exaggeration to entitle Augustine's ideas on the justice of war a "doctrine." His remarks are scattered, and nowhere do we find a fully developed and systematic discussion of the criteria for the justice of war. His attitudes even seem to change in the course of his life, and thus a consistent Augustinian theory does not really exist.[2]

---

2. Among the many available expositions of Augustinian just war ideas, I mention here Ramsey, 1961: 15–33; Stevenson, 1987: 11–113; Johnson, 1987: 56–66; Holmes, 1989: 114–45;

Yet in several places Augustine discusses the defensibility of fighting just wars, and in at least two passages he outlines the main moral criteria justifying the undertaking of armed combat. In the first, he writes: "As a rule, just wars are defined as those which avenge injuries, if some nation or state against whom one is waging war has neglected to punish a wrong committed by its citizens, or to return something that was wrongfully taken" (*Quaestiones in Heptateuchum* 6.10, in Reichberg, Syse, and Begby, 2006: 82; see also Holmes, 1989: 132). The second passage reads: "The natural order, which is suited to the peace of mortal things, requires that the authority and deliberation for undertaking war be under the control of a leader, and also that, in the executing of military commands, soldiers serve peace and the common well-being" (*Contra Faustum* 22.75, in Augustine, 1994: 222). There is also—discussed, for instance, before and in the continuation of the passage from the *Contra Faustum* here cited—the case where war is expressly commanded by God.[3] The most obvious instances of such "wars commanded by God" are the Old Testament wars. It is a hotly debated topic, however, whether Augustine's ideas on this topic can be extended into a doctrine of *holy war*, according to which a ruler can lay claim to a divinely ordained justice. There is no doubt that Augustine held the Old Testament wars for Yahweh to be just. But I agree with Stevenson that, given Augustine's view of the particularity of the biblical "messengers of God" (for instance, Moses and Joshua), and not least his pessimistic view of the possibility of a human realization of justice in this last age (the *saeculum senescens*), it is unlikely that Augustine was (or would have been) a supporter of purportedly holy wars undertaken in his own time, that is, wars fought purely for religious purposes, with divine justice claimed to be squarely on one's own side.[4] I will, however, leave that question aside here and concentrate on what is

---

Elshtain, 1995: 105–12; Russell, 1999: 875–76; and Pangle and Ahrensdorf, 1999: 73–80. Useful collections of Augustine's most important (and very scattered) remarks on war can be found in Swift, 1983: 110–49; Augustine, 1994: 26–27, 32, 130–31, 148–55, 205–29; and Reichberg, Syse, and Begby, 2006: 70–90. These works include excerpts from *De libero arbitrio*, *De civitate Dei*, and several other works.

3. Indeed, *all* war is in a sense commanded by God, since all wars serve a purpose in God's plan. This also means that serving in the army under an unjust king is not a sin, because the acts of war then undertaken—when committed out of rightful deference to authority and not from lust—cannot be imputed as sinful to the individual soldier. However, Augustine insists that *the unjust king* is acting sinfully, even if his wars are part of God's greater scheme, since he is acting from impure motives. See Ingierd and Syse, 2005.

4. See Stevenson, 1987: 42–44, with references to, among others, Frederick Russell, John Langan, and Christopher Dawson. See also Syse, 2000, for more on the Augustinian pessi-

most often the topic of discussions of just war, namely, wars fought for the sake of (some sort of) earthly justice.

The criteria most clearly delineated in the quotes above are "just cause" (avenging of injury or restoration of what has been unjustly taken), "rightful authority," and "right intention." The last of these encompasses two senses of intention: both the rightful aim (the aim of peace) and that which later in the tradition becomes known as the *ius in bello* (the right attitude and behavior not only in the taking up of arms but also in the fighting of war). Johnson remarks that ideas of "last resort" and "proportionality," both derived from similar ideas in Roman and early Christian thought, are also present in Augustine, if only indirectly (1987: 60).

In short, war, according to Augustine, must be justified before the court of morality. The primary and incontrovertible criterion is that a wrongful action must have been committed prior to the start of hostile, violent action. A just war is always a reaction to wrongdoing.[5] Closely attached to this criterion is Augustine's firm belief that war is no truly noble undertaking. In sharp contrast to later chivalric ideas of warfare, as well as earlier (especially Spartan) ideals of military virtue, Augustine has no illusions about the essential morality or nobility of war. War inspires violence, greed, and lust and stands in sharp contrast to that peaceful atmosphere which fosters piety and decency. Therefore, war should be avoided whenever possible and should be concluded as soon as morally feasible.

Furthermore, war is no private matter and should be under the con-

---

mism with regard to historical progress, as well as Ernest Fortin's trenchant analysis of Augustine's warnings against a fully *political* theology, in his introduction to Augustine, 1994. Whether the conflict with the Donatists was a "religious war" is an interesting and difficult question. I believe that Augustine himself did not see it that way, although religious issues lay at the heart of the controversy. That Augustine, in the course of his struggle with the Donatists, came to see it as rightful to somehow "force" heretics back into the Church (see, for instance, *Ep.* 93, to Vincentius, in Augustine, 1994: 232–45) is beyond doubt. But I doubt that we can define the violence against the Donatists as "holy war" in the later medieval sense or in the sense of aggressive coercion in matters of faith. For Augustine, the violent action against the Donatists—while sometimes certainly blameworthy by later Christian standards—was defensive in nature. See, however, Phillip Gray's penetrating essay in this volume (chapter 4) for an argument that Augustine's logic vis-à-vis the Donatists was a different one from that pertaining to "ordinary" just war.

5. Whether this, according to the Augustinian just war idea, includes planned wrongdoing that has not yet taken place—that is, the problem of preemptive strikes—is a debated point. For interesting discussions of the general problem of preemptive strikes, see Walzer, 1977: 80–85; Tuck, 1999: 18–31; and for the relationship between self-defense and preemptive or preventive strikes, see Dinstein, 2001: 159–91.

trol of a leader responsible for the good of the community. This is closely correlated with the idea that right intention should guide all war making. It is, namely, the common good, not private concupiscence, that should provide the aim of warfare. This perspective betrays what we may call a cosmopolitan view of the common good, where the good of both (or all) belligerents should ideally be taken into consideration.[6] This can best be understood in light of Augustine's general view that no earthly society is the full "beholder" of justice. Thus, the (earthly) good of peace should not be the sole possession of one side only. One should, as far as is possible, aim at the peace and common good of *all* mankind, making the pilgrimage of the citizens of the City of God (who can be found in all societies) easier and facilitating a better approximation, however imperfect, to that peace which God in his goodness has intended for his creation.

I realize that my language here, talking about authority serving the "common good" rather than being a "necessary evil," rings more of Thomas Aquinas than of Augustine. Yet, the latter's negative views regarding the naturalness and efficacy of human authority does not take away the fact that he saw authority and political rule as serving an important, positive function in God's dispensation (cf., for instance, *Epistles 91* and *138*, in Augustine, 1994: 202–12). And exactly because this function is limited, and not in itself linked to transcendent perfection or fulfillment, it rightly belongs to *all* of the earthly city. Thus, the aim of peace should encompass both (or all) fighting parties.

This is also a result of another facet of Augustine's concept of authority. As William Stevenson usefully points out, fully just authority belongs only to God (1987: 66). Human political authority is a result of and a remedy for sin, and while legitimate and necessary, it can never be completely just. The morality of authority must always be seen in reference to God and obedience to him. In this respect, all cities and nations are equally responsible to God, and they can all be God's instruments in history. The hierarchy of authority clearly puts no earthly city or prince at the apex; only God is supreme.

The gist of Augustine's just war teaching is that war is undertaken to punish and correct wrongdoing so that peace may follow. War making is necessary, but not really noble—it can be moral, but is too often a pretext

---

6. This can be contrasted with Cicero's republican "civic humanism"; see Tuck, 1999: 10–11.

for immorality. It is with this short summary of Augustine's stand in mind that we will now discuss the proper role of virtue in war and the other-regarding quality of Augustine's teaching on the right use of violence.

Augustine and Virtue Ethics

In recent debates about ethics, not least following the publication of Alasdair MacIntyre's *After Virtue* in the early 1980s, the concept of virtue figures prominently. The complaint—voiced by, among others, MacIntyre, but with roots back to Elizabeth Anscombe's essay "Modern Moral Philosophy" (originally published in *Philosophy* 33 (1958), reprinted in Crisp and Slote, 1997: 26–44)—is that modern deontology, consequentialism, and emotivism do not offer a complete and coherent language to describe and make sense of morality. The first two are action-centered, not agent-centered, and thus fail to take into account the qualities and attitudes of the agent. The last, although focusing on the agent, is by necessity subjectivist and opportunistic, relying on sentiments and whims of the moment rather than tradition and argument. The more general claim is that the virtues have been neglected in recent moral philosophy, whether deontological, consequentialist, emotivist, or of whatever other stripe, and that they need to be reintroduced if a good ethical discourse is to exist at all.[7]

I will not enter into the general debate about virtue ethics here. I do believe, however, that the virtue perspective complements and enriches the more standard deontological and consequentialist approaches. Furthermore, a renewed attention to virtue perspectives can help us understand the concerns of many premodern thinkers, who cannot so easily be categorized according to modern, post-Kantian labels.

And this is the point I will focus on in the following. In most recent literature on just war, a lot of emphasis has been placed on the criteria for a just war. Thereby, a decidedly deontological emphasis has been achieved. This tendency has been strengthened by the fact that, since the

---

7. Useful introductions to virtue ethics, and its relationship to other approaches to ethics, can be found in Baron, Pettit, and Slote, 1997; and Crisp and Slote, 1997. It is, however, striking that the authors found in these volumes, including Anscombe, seem to downplay the Christian case for virtue ethics. Indeed, to the degree that Christianity is discussed at all, its ethics is mainly described as being squarely of the "divine command" type. A fine and balanced defense of Christian ideas of virtue can be found in Kotva, 1996.

time of Suarez and Grotius in the early seventeenth century, just war has developed into a theory of international law, that is, of the rights and duties of states and their rulers. While there are many good reasons why this originally happened, and many ways in which it helped create a more peaceful order of states after the horrors of the religious wars, it may also be that central aspects of premodern just war ideas were lost on the way.[8]

It must be emphasized that there is not only deontology to be found in recent writings on just war. Consequentialism features heavily as well, and for a good reason. Concerns of proportionality are among the most important in any discussion of the justice of war. Consequences of alternative courses of action have to be weighed, and the stakes are indeed high. One of the most famous and fateful examples in recorded history of a consequentialist calculus was connected with war: President Truman's decision as to whether to drop the atomic bomb on Hiroshima and Nagasaki. And the whole debate about "double effect" and the responsibility for side effects in war, dating back to Thomas Aquinas, certainly invokes the weighing of consequences (more about this below).

I am not denying, then, that the formulation of rules and the calculation of consequences have a pivotal role to play in a doctrine of just war. My claim is rather that for Augustine, and the medieval tradition of just war bearing his name and ancestry, neither deontology nor consequentialism constitutes the primary perspective. Augustine's just war teaching is what we today would call virtue-ethical. This is not only because Augustine in general emphasizes virtues and vices over steadfast rules or rights; it owes as much to the nature of war itself. Early Christian pacifism and Augustinian just war doctrine share a deep fear of the effects of war on the human soul.[9] Indeed, it seems clear that this, rather than any total rejection of war as such, was what animated much of pre-Augustinian pacifism.[10] And this shines through even more clearly in Au-

---

8. See Fortin, 1996: 283–94, for an argument that insights from the Augustinian just war perspective have indeed been lost in much of modern theorizing on war.

9. Inner dispositions and virtues certainly play an important role in Augustine's overall argument for the possibility of just wars and more generally participation in political life, since he insists that injunctions such as "Turn the other cheek" (from the Sermon on the Mount) should be read as applying to inner dispositions rather than to outward action. Thus he opens up a field for political, even violent action in the service of peace, performed by believers who strive to keep their hearts pure. (I am grateful to one of this book's referees for reminding me of this crucial point in Augustine's argumentation.)

10. Both Swift, 1983, and Johnson, 1987, support this conclusion.

gustine himself. The most striking indication can be found in a famous passage from the *Contra Faustum*, where Augustine inquires about the evils of war. We may expect—from the author who, in *De civitate Dei*, demonstrates such a keen and compassionate sense for describing disaster and suffering—a list of the inevitable external ills attendant upon war. Instead, we find Augustine turning his attention toward the "internal" dogs of war: "The desire for harming, the cruelty of revenge, the restless and implacable mind, the savageness of revolting, the lust for dominating, and similar things—these are what are justly blamed in wars" (*Contra Faustum*, 22.74, in Augustine, 1994: 221–22). Both here and elsewhere, it seems that what truly worries Augustine is what happens to the human soul. All human beings will eventually die, and while he never idealizes suffering (cf. his ridicule of the Stoics in *De civitate Dei*, e.g., 19.4), he does not believe that suffering can be eradicated, or that eternal and harmonious peace can ever be achieved on earth. Indeed, suffering can even serve a good purpose in God's providential plan. However, war is dangerous because it poses a huge challenge to the soul that strives to live virtuously. A war can hardly be imagined in which cruelty and lust are not given far too free rein. Therefore, even just wars should be regretted, as the truly just man would much rather avoid the necessity of violent fighting than resort to arms (cf. *De civitate Dei*, 19.7, in Augustine, 1972: 861–62).

To put this in more systematic terms, we may pose a comparison between a deontological, a consequentialist, and what I claim to be an Augustinian virtue-ethical perspective on the justice of war.[11] A deontological approach will emphasize both that certain *general* rights and duties are obligatory for all human beings, even in war, and also that there are rights and duties *specifically pertaining to war*, such as those associated with prisoners of war or the use of certain weapons. From this approach follow legal regulations intended to determine jurisdiction (whose rights and duties apply where and when) and to help adjudicate in hard cases. This is the gist of modern (Grotian and post-Westphalian) international law, which is based on the importance of sovereign jurisdictions and on deontological rules intended to avoid war or, if war nonetheless takes place, ameliorate it.

---

11. For a general account of the meaning of "virtue" in Augustine, see Lavere, 1999.

There is little doubt that the development of international law, although still very much a work in progress, constitutes one of the most important achievements of the modern age. While sovereignty may currently be under fire, and while international law has been proven far too weak on many occasions—not least in the years before World War II—huge gains have been made in codifying rules of warfare, thus disallowing wanton violence and brutal slayings, or, in the extreme case, genocide.

However, there is no available evidence to show that the horrors of war are about to disappear. A certain comfort can be taken from the fact that the Western world (now being enlarged eastward) has largely avoided internal wars totally since World War II (Northern Ireland is possibly an exception), and that established democracies tend not to fight each other (see, i.e., Gleditsch, 1999). In addition, the number of armed conflicts has been steadily declining more or less since the end of the cold war.[12] However, wars result in far more civilian casualties today, relatively speaking, than a hundred years ago. And, to be sure, totalitarian disasters abounded in the twentieth century, the century in which international law documents were developed to an unprecedented degree, only to be followed by the grave threat (and reality) of terrorism—by definition directed against civilians—in the early twenty-first century.

Augustine would not have been surprised. First, he would not have expected any radical changes in human behavior, given his pessimistic view of the fallen state of man. Second, and more important in our context, he would have lamented a development that establishes rules without instilling the virtues needed to uphold them. In the Augustinian perspective, rules as such are of little consequence or avail if human beings do not appreciate and foster the virtues needed to maintain them, and that can (for Augustine) happen only within the community of faith. As Augustine sees it, we need rulers who resist the temptations to conquer and rule. We need soldiers imbued with charity, not only obedience. We need societies that aim at peace, not only in this world but with God—a peace possible in the end only among true believers. Thus, Augustine's judgment is seemingly the very opposite of Kant's, who in his *Eternal Peace* said that the task of achieving peace "does not involve the moral improvement of man" and that the problem of setting up a peaceful or-

---

12. See the yearly overviews of armed conflict in *Journal of Peace Research*, based on figures from the University of Uppsala and PRIO (International Peace Research Institute, Oslo).

der (i.e., a republican state) "can be solved even by a nation of devils (so long as they possess understanding)" (1991: 112–13). I am not thereby claiming that the development of human virtue is not important to a deontological thinker such as Kant. But his project of eternal or "perpetual" peace solves the problem of war by putting "principle over end" (Shell, 2005: 96) and thus by inculcating honor and morality through mutually binding expectations rather than through the pursuit of a highest moral and religious goal, leading in the end to the construction of institutions that will prevent war. This is different from the "profound analysis of the human soul" (Fortin, 1996: 293) on which the Augustinian just war approach is founded. The Kantian approach is, oddly enough, at once more pessimistic and optimistic than Augustine's virtue-centered perspective: pessimistic because skeptical of the possibility of a Christian morality informing politics (including warfare) but optimistic in its belief that there do exist institutional solutions that, when fully respected and adhered to, will actually abolish war. Augustine, while more adamant—and optimistic—about the possibility of fighting war justly even in this sinful world, was never so optimistic that he envisioned a total, institutional solution to the problem of warfare.

A thoroughgoing consequentialist perspective, on the other hand, would be one that in all cases would employ a calculus of consequences, measured in human lives and/or material goods, to determine the relative rightness of actions. This is also different from the Augustinian approach. While a consequentialist perspective must certainly play a part in any just war thinking, with its aim of reducing suffering, it can never explain the whole field of justice or morality in war, according to an Augustinian point of view. For instance, the rule of double effect, developed by Thomas Aquinas but surely inspired by Augustine's idea of right intention, presupposes a virtue-ethical perspective to complement its consequentialist meaning.[13] The rule says that if an action produces two effects, one good and one bad, and both are foreseen, the action can be deemed just if (1) the bad effect is not the one intended, (2) it is unavoidable, (3) one strives to mitigate and limit it,[14] (4) its badness is not out of

---

13. See *Summa theologiae* II-II, qu. 64, art. 7, in Thomas Aquinas, 1988: 225–27, which is often (though not entirely accurately) cited as the main source of the double effect doctrine.
14. This constitutes the famous teaching of "double intention" developed in Walzer, 1977: ch. 9.

proportion to the good produced by the action, and (5) the good effect is of decisive significance to the (legitimate) war effort. From a purely consequentialist standpoint, however, intention and frame of mind would not figure as elements in the ensuing calculus, something that stands in stark contrast to the Augustinian and later Thomist perspective and to the entire meaning of the doctrine of double effect.

To sum up, I claim that the Augustinian approach to just war cannot be understood purely according to deontological and/or consequentialist categories. It is to a significant extent developed within the framework of what we today would call an agent-centered, virtue-ethical approach. Arguably this also constitutes one of its main strengths as a theory that aims at mitigating the devastating effects of war. It is Augustine's view that war is sometimes necessary because of sin, but it is also a tragedy because of sin.[15] In war, vices are unavoidably let loose, and so war is rarely a desirable course of action, and never to be joyfully accepted, even though it may often be morally defensible according to human perspectives, rules, and customs (i.e., deontologically speaking), and even though it may produce, materially speaking, the best of consequences.

Finally, it must be emphasized that the kind of natural virtue called for in mitigating war between nations is not necessarily true virtue in the Christian sense. While the pagan virtues are better than no virtues, according to Augustine, they are limited and imperfect (see Lavere, 1999: 872, with reference to *De civitate Dei* 5.19). And, as was emphasized above, Augustine nowhere considers war as such to foster true virtue—quite the opposite. However, virtues such as courage and temperance, especially when given their true direction by the Christian virtue of charity, can help limit the ravages of war and make it possible for the war maker—from the highest-ranking officer to the lowliest soldier—to engage in war without the destruction of one's soul.

Defense of Self and Others

The paradigm of a just war in modern international law is quite clearly war in self-defense. Interestingly, however, Augustine and the Augustinian tradition never put forth self-defense as the most clear-cut case

---

15. I thank my colleague Gregory Reichberg for discussing this point—and several other important points in this chapter—with me.

of a just war. Indeed, in *De libero arbitrio* (see 1.5–6, in Augustine, 1994: 213–17). Augustine suggests that self-defense is not in accordance with eternal law, since one defends that "which one may lose against one's will"—that is, noneternal goods (even though self-defense must be allowed according to temporal law, since the latter needs to defend in a reasonable way the goods and peace of earthly society). Some have held this to constitute all but a denial of the justifiability of self-defense, even war.[16] This, however, is going too far, since the passage in *De libero arbitrio* primarily addresses *individual* self-defense. The rightful (legitimate) sovereign who acts on behalf of the common good is certainly not acting in pure and "egoistic" self-defense in going to war, but fulfills his duty as an earthly sovereign.[17] Nonetheless, it is quite certain that the concept of just cause in Augustine is not centered around a purely defensive stance. It is the pursuit of justice and the punishment of wrongdoing that lie at the heart of his case. Defending persons or parties not able to defend themselves is nobler than narrowly defending one's own cause, however one should define "one's own."

This makes Augustine's just war doctrine in a very real sense "other regarding." Therefore, it is not at all unreasonable to say that the modern, liberal idea of humanitarian interventions, held up against the realist view of competing, egoistic powers, is as Augustinian as its rival view. That the realist perspective has clear and deep-seated Augustinian roots is well known, not least from the thought of Reinhold Niebuhr, who stated so clearly that political morality represents "the most uncompromising antithesis to religious morality" (1932: 259, quoted in Stevenson, 1987: 142).[18] In other words, Augustine has inspired a view of international politics as a competition between interests and antagonistic forces. But the denial of decisive significance to sovereignty, the pursuit of a better world order, and the admission of other motives than self-interest are *also* Augustinian motifs. Indeed, the true purpose of war, according to the Augustinian perspective, is moral in character: to hinder and punish wrongdoing that cannot be hindered and punished in any other way.

16. This seems to be the interpretation in Regan, 1996: 17.
17. A tyrant, on the other hand, who narrowly rules for his own good and who comes to defend himself against armed attack by using military force, would not be defending himself justly according to the Augustinian just war perspective, even though he would indeed be acting in self-defense.
18. He would come to see the dropping of the atomic bomb in 1945 as the ultimate example of this tension between political and religious morality.

While he would not trust any one institution to have the necessary virtue and moral competence to do this in a perfect manner—thus, he would certainly oppose the view that one could erect a world government and create a lasting world peace—he would also deem it necessary for virtuous rulers to help oppose wrongdoing and injustice when possible and feasible. Indeed, that is the very reason why he deems war to be just in certain cases.

This points to a more general fact about the premodern just war tradition. While modern international law operates on the assumption of a relatively clear-cut distinction between offensive and defensive use of force, prohibiting the former except in cases of U.N.-mandated interventions for the sake of maintaining peace and security, the just war tradition is less absolute. While the entire tradition, from Augustine to Grotius, makes clear that resort to armed force must be a reaction to prior wrongdoing—and thus must be defensive in a general sense of the term—there is no real opposition to *initiating* warfare for the sake of repelling injustice (see Reichberg and Syse, 2002: 310–14; see also Francisco de Vitoria, *On the Law of War*, in Vitoria, 1991: 293–327). The emphasis thus being on justice rather than on the institutional fact of sovereignty, the just war tradition naturally becomes more open to embracing just causes for war that are not immediately recognized by the modern states system and the U.N. charter. The recent debates in the international community on exactly this issue can therefore usefully be seen as a corollary to a much older set of views nested within the just war tradition.

Conclusion

Augustine's ideas about war are many faceted, and I have concentrated only on a few, limited points here. However, I believe these points make Augustine's just war teaching distinctive and worthy of renewed attention. Augustine challenges us to think through the ramifications of human sinfulness and depravity for warfare in a way that certainly poses challenges to military training as well as political ideas about warfare.[19] If what is truly to be feared in war is our own fallibility and lust for domination, we must see to it that tenets of justice and love of the other are em-

---

19. For a trenchant analysis of the relevance of virtue for military training and practice, see Osiel, 1999.

phasized and fostered as the basic premise and groundwork of the military order. This may seem naïve, even impossible, since warfare is about taking lives and obeying orders, no matter how harsh they may seem. However, it is a perennial lesson of warfare that when cruelty is encouraged and institutionalized—such as in many medieval armies, where just war ideas were known but scarcely adhered to; or in the armies of totalitarian states, where cruelty and brutality are applauded—atrocities (not least against civilians) are much more widespread than when ideals of military honor and respect for the enemy are inculcated. The latter was, after all, the case among several medieval knightly orders, or—to draw the point closer to our own time—in World War II, for instance, among the soldiers and officers of the German Luftwaffe as compared to those of the SS. While these more "noble" examples may valorize military honor to a degree that Augustine would not—or they may be seen, negatively speaking, as glorifying the use of force for unjust reasons—they certainly adhere to Augustine's intention of mitigating cruelty through the inculcation of virtue.

In other words, virtue matters, according to Augustine. And so, obviously, does justice. A just war is all about rectifying wrong when rectification cannot be ensured in any other way. Following the general tenor of Augustine's ethical thought, defending the just cause of others, of those who are (relatively speaking) innocent and cannot fend for themselves, is even more noble than defending one's own cause. Therefore, the concept, if not the practice, of humanitarian intervention in our own time would seem to fall within the general intention of Augustine's just war ideas.

REFERENCES

Augustine. 1972. *City of God*. Trans. Henry Bettenson. London: Penguin.
———. 1994. *Political Writings*. Ed. Ernest L. Fortin and Douglas Kries. Trans. Michael W. Tkacz and Douglas Kries. Indianapolis: Hackett.
Baron, Marcia W., Philip Pettit, and Michael Slote. 1997. *Three Methods of Ethics*. Malden and Oxford: Blackwell.
Cicero. 1991. *On Duties*. Ed. M. T. Griffin and E. M. Atkins. Trans. E. M. Atkins. Cambridge: Cambridge University Press.
Crisp, Roger, and Michael Slote, eds. 1997. *Virtue Ethics*. Oxford: Oxford University Press.
Dinstein, Yoram. 2001. *War, Aggression, and Self-Defense*. Cambridge: Cambridge University Press.
Elshtain, Jean Bethke. 1995. *Augustine and the Limits of Politics*. Notre Dame: University of Notre Dame Press.

Fortin, Ernest L. 1996. *Human Rights, Virtue, and the Common Good*. Lanham, Md.: Rowman and Littlefield.
Gleditsch, Nils Petter. 1999. "Peace and Democracy." In Lester Kurtz and Jennifer Turpin, eds., *Encyclopedia of Violence, Peace, and Conflict*, vol. 2. New York: Academic Press.
Holmes, Robert L. 1989. *On War and Morality*. Princeton: Princeton University Press.
Ingierd, Helene, and Henrik Syse. 2005. "Responsibility and Culpability in War." *Journal of Military Ethics* 4(2): 85–99.
Johnson, James Turner. 1987. *The Quest for Peace*. Princeton: Princeton University Press.
———. 1996. "The Broken Tradition." *National Interest* 45 (Fall 1996): 27–36.
Kant, Immanuel. 1991. *Political Writings*. Ed. Hans Reiss. Cambridge: Cambridge University Press.
Kotva, Joseph J. 1996. *The Christian Case for Virtue Ethics*. Washington, D.C.: Georgetown University Press.
Lavere, George J. 1999. "Virtue." In Allan D. Fitzgerald, ed., *Augustine through the Ages: An Encyclopedia*. Grand Rapids, Mich. and Cambridge: William B. Eerdmans.
Niebuhr, Reinhold. 1932. *Moral Man and Immoral Society*. New York: Charles Scribner's Sons.
Osiel, Mark. 1999. *Obeying Orders*. New Brunswick, N.J.: Transaction.
Pangle, Thomas L., and Peter J. Ahrensdorf. 1999. *Justice among Nations*. Lawrence: University Press of Kansas.
Ramsey, Paul. 1961. *War and the Christian Conscience*. Durham: Duke University Press.
Regan, Richard J. 1996. *Just War—Principles and Cases*. Washington, D.C.: The Catholic University Press of America.
Reichberg, Gregory, and Henrik Syse. 2002. "Humanitarian Intervention: A Case of Offensive Force?" *Security Dialogue* 33 (3): 309–22.
Reichberg, Gregory, Henrik Syse, and Endre Begby, eds. 2006. *The Ethics of War: Classic and Contemporary Readings*. Oxford: Blackwell.
Russell, Frederick. 1999. "War." In Allan D. Fitzgerald, ed., *Augustine through the Ages: An Encyclopedia*. Grand Rapids, Mich. and Cambridge: William B. Eerdmans.
Shell, Susan. 2005. "Kant on Just War and 'Unjust Enemies': Reflections on a 'Pleonasm.'" *Kantian Review* 10:82–111.
Stevenson, William R. 1987. *Christian Love and Just War*. Macon: Mercer University Press.
Swift, Louis J. 1983. *The Early Fathers on War and Military Service*. Wilmington, Del.: Michael Glazier.
Syse, Henrik. 2000. "Augustinian History and the Road to Peace: Perspectives from Two Latter-Day Augustinians." *Augustinian Studies* 31(2): 225–39.
Thomas Aquinas. 1988. *On Law, Morality, and Politics*. Ed. William P. Baumgarth and Richard J. Regan. Indianapolis: Hackett.
Tuck, Richard. 1999. *The Rights of War and Peace*. Oxford: Oxford University Press.
Vitoria, Francisco de. 1991. *Political Writings*. Ed. Anthony Pagden and Jeremy Lawrance. Cambridge: Cambridge University Press.
Walzer, Michael. 1977. *Just and Unjust Wars: A Moral Argument, with Historical Illustrations*. New York: Basic.
Winwright, Tobias L. 1998. "Two Rival Versions of Just War Theory and the Presumption against Harm in Policing." In John Kelsay and Summer B. Twiss, eds., *The Annual of the Society of Christian Ethics*, vol. 18. Chicago: Society of Christian Ethics, 221–39.

4

Just War, Schism, and Peace in St. Augustine

PHILLIP W. GRAY

In the scholarly literature on Augustine's writings, few topics have instigated more discussion or debate than his belief about the use of coercion against schismatics and heretics. Many scholars see his choice to use coercion against the Donatists as a deviation from his usual way of thinking. For instance, as Ernest Fortin wrote about the matter: "The peculiar intractability of Donatists, their continued agitating, and the methods of terrorism to which they frequently resorted, had made of them a persistent threat not only to the religious unity but to the social stability of the North African provinces. Reluctantly and only after having exhausted all other resources, Augustine agreed to turn the matter over to the local civil authorities.... What was, for him, a mere concession to necessity or at most an emergency measure designed to cope with a specific situation was later invoked as a general principle to justify the church's reprisals against heretics and apostates" (1987: 198). Fortin's interpretation of Augustine's request for coercion against the Donatist schism in the 390s A.D. has commanded considerable agreement. But this explanation does not seem to take into account the bishop's nuanced accounts of peace and the place of the Heavenly City. Indeed, he believed, thanks to the evil of man, that it was necessary to teach humanity *per molestias eruditio*, "teaching by inconveniences" (Brown, 1967: 237). This is the underlying source for Augustine's apparently different views on coercion used in just wars and his ideas about the Donatists, where the main point of coercion is to save the schismatic or heretic from his own weakness and damnation by forcing him into the Church (taking note that forcing someone physically into a church to hear the Good News is different from forcing *conversion*). But this, too, seems incomplete. Why would Augustine take such a different stand against Donatists and other such schismatics, which seems to go against his ideas both about conversion and about just war (for, to all intents and purposes, the conflict with the Donatists was a war)?

The answer lies in Augustine's views of peace regarding the two cities. How so? The bishop, as part of his justification for just war, declared that an earthly peace allows the Church, as the agent of the Heavenly City on earth, to perform its mission of saving souls. Thus we can derive Augustine's notions of a just war. But peace is not enough when it comes to schismatics, because the Church cannot pursue its mission so long as they exist. Peace in the earthly city is irrelevant if there is conflict among the agents of the heavenly one. By allowing schismatics to coexist peaceably (or as peaceably as possible) with the true representatives of God, there is no peace conducive to the Heavenly City, and the Church is stymied. For this reason, and not merely for the timely practical convenience Fortin ascribes to him, Augustine may have wished to see the Donatists taken care of in a way the bishop would find disagreeable as regards nations in a just war.

In order to bring out these views of Augustine's, several of his writings will be reviewed in this chapter, especially his seminal *City of God* and a letter he wrote (in the year 417 A.D.) to the tribune Boniface concerning the Donatists (referred to as *Epistle 185*). By comparing these two texts, one can see the similarities and differences in Augustine's views toward schismatics and toward warring nations. From this, along with supplemental information from other works, a coherent perspective on the differences for Augustine between the types of war will emerge.

The Setting

First, one needs to know something about the setting of the conflict and the societal context in which Augustine lived and wrote these two works. When Augustine wrote *City of God*, it was in response to the events of "August 24th, 410, [when] the inconceivable happened: a Gothic army, led by Alaric, entered Rome . . . Rome was sacked for three days; and parts of it were, inevitably, burnt" (Brown, 1967: 288). The chaos caused some to question whether the separation from the old gods resulted in the disaster. As such, Augustine used *City of God* to point out how "the influence of Christianity" had actually made changes for the better, such as how it "established a new custom ... the savagery of the barbarians took on such an aspect of gentleness that the largest basilicas were selected and set aside to be filled with people to be spared by the enemy. No one was to be violently used there, no one snatched away" (Augustine, 1984: 13, 12). Augustine used the book to defend Christianity in Rome after the sack of Rome as well as to describe the place of Christians in society in general (among a plethora of other issues). The sections of *City of God* that are of particular concern to our topic—coercion and peace—were finished around the year 420. At the time Augustine wrote *Epistle 185* to Boniface, three years prior to the relevant sections of *City of God*, a different conflict was afoot in North Africa, which had been a difficulty for Augustine and the Catholic Church for some time before this letter. The enemy was the Donatists, a schism of the Catholic Church. Donatism began early in the fourth century, when

> [t]oo many bishops, it was thought, had "collaborated" during the last, the Great, Persecution of Diocletian, in 303–305. They had handed over copies of the Holy Scriptures to be burnt by pagan magistrates. This craven act, the *traditio*, the "handing-over" of the Holy Books, would have deprived the guilty bishop, the *traditor*, of all spiritual power. It was believed that Caecilian, bishop of Cathage, had been ordained by such a *traditor*. It was a simple matter for 80 Numidian bishops, in 311, to declare his ordination invalid, and to elect another bishop in his place. This "pure" bishop was soon succeeded by another, Donatus: and, it was he, who, as rival bishop for Carthage, gave his name to what we call "The Donatist Church"—the *pars Donati*, "the party of Donatus." (Brown, 1967: 215)

Their numbers were great, and "[i]n Hippo, the Catholics were in a minority ... Donatism, not Catholicism, was the established church of Numidia" (Brown, 1967: 226). Although there had been relative peace between the Donatists (remaining loyal to the empire) and Catholics for some years, by the 390s "[p]rovincial loyalties began to turn, at least in part, from the empire to local leaders" among the Donatists, and among both sides there "was the transformation in ecclesiastical leadership. The Donatist side saw the rise of several new bishops, men both blunt and strict" while the "new Catholic leaders [were] far more capable and aggressive than their predecessors" (Tilley, 1997: 132–33). As such, with more parochial concerns on the minds of the Donatists and the strong personalities on both sides (including Augustine) ready to confront each other, conflicts became imminent. Moreover, it appeared the Donatists were placing themselves so "that only a few concessions needed to be made to complete the absorption, by their 'purified' church, of the despised and weakened 'church of the *traditores*.' [i.e., the Roman Church]" (Brown, 1967: 226). Therefore, Augustine sought help from the imperial government in order to force the Donatists into the Catholic Church. Help came through the tribune Boniface, and he in turn looked for guidance from Augustine on the issue of coercion. To follow the chronological order of events, first Augustine's letter to Boniface will be examined, followed by an analysis of the relevant text from *City of God*.

Teaching by Inconveniences

In the letter from St. Augustine to Boniface, tribune and count in Africa (also known as *Epistle 185*), St. Augustine took a much different view as to the motivating force for coercion than he had in *City of God*. In this case, he supported the idea of *per molestias eruditio*, "teaching by inconveniences" (Brown, 1967: 237). The act of coercion is not a vicious one, but rather shows, as Augustine wrote, "[B]oth our faith and our love may be more approved — our faith, namely, that we should not be deceived by [heretics]; and our love, that we should take the utmost pains we can to correct the erring ones themselves." (1999: 633–34). The end of coercion, in this piece, was to bring heretics into the Church, even if against their own will, because it was better to cause discomfort and/or pain now and save their souls than let them die and suffer eternal damnation. Coercion was part of the solution, "not only watching that [heretics] should do no injury to the weak, and that they should be delivered from their wicked error, but also praying for them, that God would open their understanding, and that they might comprehend the Scriptures" (ibid.: 634). In this way, Augustine wanted physically to move the heretics into the Church to make them listen to Catholic views on the faith, with the hope that at least some of the Donatists would reconsider their beliefs and perhaps even renounce their old ways for the ways of the Catholic Church. Moreover, Augustine argued for scriptural backing to the use of force, employing one of the most influential writers in the Bible as his example. Using the conversion story of Paul (Acts 9:1–18), Augustine argued that coercion can make a good Christian, even the best Christian, for "it is wonderful how he who entered the service of the gospel in the first instance under the compulsion of bodily punishment, afterwards labored more in the gospel than all they who were called by word only.... [W]e have shown that Paul was compelled by Christ; therefore the Church, in trying to compel the Donatists, is following the example of her Lord" (ibid.: 641–42). Augustine also wrote that, in the past "a religious and pious emperor, when such matters were brought to his knowledge, thought it well, by the enactment of most pious laws, entirely to correct the error of this great impiety, and to bring those who bore the standards of Christ against the cause of Christ into the unity of the Catholic Church, even by terror and compulsion, rather than merely to take away their power of doing violence, and to leave them the freedom of going astray, and perishing in their error" (ibid.: 644). It seems clear that Augustine believed, in this work, that to bring heretics back into the faith (or at least into the church building), even with force, is better than letting them continue in their error and sin.

Coercion and Peace

In *City of God*, St. Augustine deals with the issue of coercion under the heading of peace. One must first understand the duality of the earthly city and the Heavenly City. In Augustine's understanding, "the former looks for glory from men, the latter finds its highest glory in God, the witness of a good conscience" (1984: 593). On earth, Augustine deduces a relation between "the City of God" and "the holy Church" (ibid.: 335), One must be careful not to extend this too far, for "[t]he Church is not the heavenly city but prefigures it"(Elshtain, 1995: 21). While Augustine covers many aspects of these two cities, one of the most important is his idea of peace as regards both of these cities. Specifically, he believed "peace is the desired end of war. For every man is in a quest of peace, even in waging war, whereas no one is in quest of war when making peace" (1984: 866).

What exactly is peace? Augustine saw it as "tranquillity of order," where order is "the arrangement of things equal and unequal in a pattern which assigns to each its proper position" (1984: 870). Peace is desired by both cities, for "[the earthly] city desires an earthly peace, for the sake of the lowest goods" as does the Heavenly City, but "if the higher goods are neglected, which belong to the City on high . . . the inevitable consequence is fresh misery, and an increase of the wretchedness already [in the earthly city]" (ibid.: 599, 600). The key to war, and coercion, is peace, for both cities understand it as a good and aim for it.

But why is earthly peace of importance to the higher Heavenly City? Augustine wrote that the "Heavenly City . . . makes use of the earthly peace . . . [and] relates the earthly peace to the heavenly peace, which is so truly peaceful that it should be regarded as the only peace deserving the name" (1984: 878). So, in summation, war or coercion can be a good because it brings about earthly peace. This earthly peace is a good, because it can be used by the Heavenly City, through its agent on earth (the Church), to bring about the heavenly peace. Thus, the use of coercion is good when it can bring a just peace inasmuch as the agents of the Heavenly City (the Church) can use said peace to bring about the "higher goods" of heavenly peace.

There are definite differences of opinion between Augustine's works as to what the major purpose of coercion should be. In *City of God,* coercion (usually in the style of war) is used to make earthly peace. One needs to keep in mind, however, that "Augustine acknowledges that peace may be truly just; but it may not be, for peace is more inclusive than justice . . . [a]greement may be the peace of conspirators or brigands; there can be unjust peace" (TeSelle, 1998: 110). From that peace, just or no, there can be a better opportunity for heavenly peace. One reaches this peace through the Heavenly City with its earthly representative/agent, the Church. Moreover, "this peace is grounded on an order given by nature . . . [a]ll conflicts, even small ones, are waged to restore this order or to reorganize it according to the ideas of the warring factions" in order to bring peace (Reventlow, 1994: 166–67). The Church's involvement in coercion, by making use of earthly peace for the sake of heavenly peace, is rather passive. This does not mean that God is not involved with the outcome of wars, for "[i]t rests with the decision of God in his just judgment and mercy either to afflict or console mankind, so that some wars come to an end more speedily, others more slowly" (Augustine, 1984: 216–17). Although war is fought to reach peace, Augustine did not hold any false notions about how "war and strife, however just the cause, stir up temptations to ravish and to devour, often in order to ensure peace" (Elshtain,

1995: 111). Moreover, there is a punishment element to the idea of a just war. Augustine thought that "just war is the punishment imposed upon a state and upon its rulers when their behavior is so aggressive or avaricious that it violates even the norms of temporal justice. Other states then have not merely the right but *the duty to punish these crimes* and to act in the same fashion as the judge, policeman, jailer, and executioner act within the state" (Deane, 1963: 156; emphasis added).These acts of punishment are between states, and "the punishment can only be rough justice; the innocent will suffer with the guilty" (ibid.). But these are the matters of states. The *City of God,* then, does not seem to reflect a heavy, active involvement of the Church in coercion.

The opinion in *Epistle 185* seems markedly different. There, the main point of coercion is to save the schismatic or heretic from his own weakness and damnation by forcing him into the Church. Augustine "became convinced of the rightness of coercion when he saw how grateful former Donatists were for being freed from long-standing custom and being brought to their right minds.... He was sure that love cannot go wrong, even if the means seem harsh, when it begins to correct error" (TeSelle, 1998: 118–19). The motivation, then, becomes much more proactive. On the issue of the imperial decree against the Donatists, "Augustine explained [to Boniface] that... [t]he emperor has the responsibility for maintaining peace within the empire and a Christian ruler should suppress a schism in the church, which is rebellion against his Lord, in the same way he would deal with insurrection in the empire" (Burns, Daly, and Helgeland, 1985: 84). One reason for this might be Augustine's idea that humanity suffers from a "disordered love" thanks to original sin, and as such "transforms man's natural sociability into the will to dominate" (Parel, 1990: 77). However, thanks to some "vestiges" of true justice in the soul, a type of civil order remains, but "these vestigial traces of justice are at the mercy of disordered love to such an extent that whatever civil society achieves, it achieves only if one presupposes coercion. Coercion is, as it were, the price that one has to pay for self-love" (ibid.). Also, he "returns to the theme of loving punishment... in order to reconcile violence on behalf of religion with the evangelical commands" (Cahill, 1994: 77). Having said all of this, Augustine is not seeking utter annihilation of these schismatics, for he believes the Church "desires not the death of her enemies but rather their deliverance from error and from the penalty of eternal punishment; so, while she wishes her errant children to be corrected with suitable discipline, she is unwilling that they should suffer the more severe punishments that they deserve [i.e., capital punishment]" (Deane, 1963: 209). Violence for the faith is done in love, as the stern father loves his rebellious son.

Augustine's "Realism"

Augustine's view of coercion, then, does seem different depending upon where one looks, *City of God* being more passive, while *Epistle 185* is proactive. However, both rely on the same underpinning logic: "the elemental bedrock of the ideas that [Augustine] had crystallized in justifying the 'controlled catastrophe' of the coercion of the Donatists: the human race needed discipline, by frequent, unwelcome impingements" (Brown, 1967: 293). Augustine, through his beliefs in original sin and habit, held in very low esteem the potential for humanity to do good on its own. As such, "impingements" were required to bring people to the faith. This is alluded to in *City of God* during a discussion on the removal of temporal goods, for Augustine wrote, "we might say that torture conveyed the lesson that what is to be loved is the incorruptible good," for "not even the saints and the faithful worshippers of the one true and supreme God enjoy exemption from the deceptions of the demons and from their multifarious temptations" (1984: 19, 864).

This is often regarded by those who study Augustine's political ideas as evidence of Augustine's "realism," given his emphasis (especially in *City of God*) "on the limitations that sin imposes upon governments, dreams of world peace, and enduring earthly solutions to collective problems" (Fowler, 1994: 175). In political science, "realists" generally "maintain that, by nature, humans are motivated to seek domination over others, making politics among nations a struggle for power, and *realpolitik* policies the necessary prescription for survival" (Allison and Zelikow, 1999: 26–27). One hears an echo of "Augustine's famous phrase *libido dominandi*, the lust for domination" in that definition, very much in line with Augustine's view that "man's tendency to follow his own selfish interests and lower appetites remains all but irresistible" (Swift, 1983: 111). For a man who brought the concept of original sin to the fore, realism would have been a very comfortable political paradigm.

One could argue that the example of the Donatists in *Epistle 185* fits into Augustine's views on earthly peace in *City of God*. After all, what better way to bring an earthly peace than to draw the dissenting group (i.e., the Donatists) within the Church, thus instituting an earthly peace that the Church can use to bring about the Heavenly Peace? As such, one could say that Augustine's position on the specific case of the Donatists fits in rather well within his views on peace expressed in *City of God*. While it is certainly a reasonable idea, one reaches this conclusion by focusing on the intrinsic need for discipline rather than on the external motivation for coercion. Keep in mind that what Augustine left out of *City of God* is in some ways almost as important as what he included. Augustine argued that the aim of war was peace, and that through earthly peace the "Heavenly City ... makes use of the earthly peace ... [and] relates the earthly peace to the heavenly peace, which is so truly peaceful that it should be regarded as the only peace deserving the name" (1984: 878). But note also that Augustine did allow for an unjust peace on earth, that such a peace could still be used. He did not dictate that the peace necessarily had to be explicitly conducive to the Church; in other words, the Church coming out "on top" in a war is not mentioned as being necessary in the aim of earthly peace. However, in *Epistle 185*, Augustine advised "not only watching that [heretics] should do no injury to the weak, and that they should be delivered from their wicked error, but also praying for them, that God would open their understanding, and that they might comprehend the Scriptures" (1999: 634). One gets the impression that Augustine believed that bringing about a heavenly-oriented peace was necessary—that it was important not only to bring peace (even if possibly involving compromise) but also to bring the opponent into the Church to hear the Catholic (heavenly) truth. While both do have similarities in that they come from the same conception of the need for discipline (one for peace, the other for Church entry), at the level of motivation the rationales behind *City of God* and *Epistle 185* are not the same.

Pagans and Schismatics

But if this is so, then what factor accounts for the difference? Even given Augustine's pastoral way of dealing with philosophical questions, one would expect on these two similar topics—war and dealing with schismatics—that the bishop would hold rather consistent views. The difference in time between the texts was minimal, and both situations, as they dealt with the use of coercion by the state, did indeed have great similarity. What, then, is the explaining variable? The main difference, it appears, is with the schism itself. Specifically, it appears that something about schismatics, especially as regards the religious life on earth, brings about a particular agitation and feeling of danger to Augustine. But why are schismatics such a danger, requiring such a response, when much more powerful pagan forces may present a greater challenge to the faith of peoples? The danger, Augustine may say, is in the similarity between the true Church and the schismatic interlopers. To Augustine, the danger of pagans may have seemed less serious in two regards. First, their numbers were fewer than in days past and could not present the same coercive threat as in those days, especially after they had been coerced to give up these beliefs (with Augustine's approval). Second, and more important, perhaps Augustine found them easier to refute. The pagans' gods could not hold up to truth nor to adversity, as Augustine points out that "[t]o worship 'vanquished' gods as protectors and defenders is to rely not on divinities but on defaulters. It is not sensible to assume that Rome would have escaped this disaster [being sacked] had these gods not first perished; the sensible belief is that those gods would have perished long before, had not Rome made every effort to preserve them" (1984: 9). As these gods were so easily destroyed, the Church can do its duty in a somewhat easier fashion against pagans simply because it can present to people with a clear (or at least clearer) contrast between the pagans and the true faith. Therefore, an earthly peace was all the Church needed among the pagans to do its duties to the Heavenly City.

Here, however, the main difference between the pagan armies and schismatics comes into play. While the pagans were not a significant enough threat, either politically or theologically, to make anything more than an earthly peace necessary, schismatics are a different matter. Clear-cut contrasts were not nearly as simple with schismatics. Nor could Augustine claim that their God could be vanquished (as he shared with them the same God). Again, Augustine is concerned about those "who bore the standards of Christ against the cause of Christ," those who would claim the true faith while practicing the false type (1999: 644). With schismatics, there is much greater theological nuance, which may be confusing or seem irrelevant to the average potential churchgoer, but which could in fact lead a well-meaning potential (or even actual) Christian to turn to the darkness of schism. And in the case of the Donatists, this danger was present for the Church all the more: for while the Catholic Church recognized the baptism of the Donatists (although it was not as valid), Donatists considered all baptism other than theirs as worthless. A pragmatic parishioner may then go to the Donatists, thinking that it would be a safer bet to receive a baptism accepted by both instead of a baptism acceptable only to one.[1] This is a very clear example of the kind of war within which the agents of the Heavenly City on earth are embroiled, which makes earthly peace irrelevant and presents a daunting challenge to the Church. If such a war is going on within the Church, then perhaps the same notion of punishment from the just war comes into play here, for leaders of the Church (or more specifically their political associates) "have not merely the right but the duty to punish these crimes and to act in the same fashion as the judge, policeman, jailer, and executioner act within the state" (Deane, 1963: 156). Not only *can* the Church (or the political leaders associated with it) punish schismatics, but it is *required* to do so.

Were the Donatists' beliefs so dangerous, in reality? Their numbers were quite large in North Africa at that time, but even with this, why did Augustine believe the schismatics presented such a danger as to require escalation from persuasion to a directly coercive route? Admittedly, he did support moves to persuade at first and agreed with the actions of the other Catholic bishops who "wanted to conduct the struggle *more ecclesiastico*, by preaching, by discussion and in public debate" (Markus, 1970: 137). And yet, for some reason Augustine decided to take the hard line. Why? There are various possible explanations. The quotation by Fortin above is one explanation: the Donatists were just becoming too much of a security concern. Similarly, perhaps Augustine was especially fearful because of the actions of the vicious Donatist *circumcelliones*, whom he "charged with moral depravity on the basis of their heinous crimes against the lives and properties of upright men and women, their sinful way of life and refusal to adhere to the sacred precepts of Christian morality" (Wood, 1986: 43). Augustine's reaction, then, results from being "[h]aunted by the spectre of disintegration of spiritual unity" (ibid.:

---

[1]. Thanks to Dr. Maureen Tilley of the University of Dayton for this point.

49). Another reason comes from a sociological angle, as TeSelle points out (paraphrasing René Girard): "The real difficulty arises when this differentiation—and hence the social body as a whole—is threatened. Rather than ascribe the threat to the social body itself, which would be destructive of its tenuous order, the guilt for the breakdown of difference is ascribed to someone whose difference seems to come from outside the body social... or to someone whose *abnormality and deviance* so symbolize the disturbances as to be their cause" (1998: 119–20; emphasis in original). If this is the case, then the main source of motivation is a fear of difference. Augustine certainly could not fault the Heavenly City itself, for this was indeed the City of God. Nor could he probably blame the agent of that city, the Church. Rather, schismatics against the true Word were threatening the peace of the Heavenly City's agent to do its work, and thus must be suppressed. Similarly, perhaps William Connolly is correct in using an identity/difference paradigm to address Augustine's views. Specifically, Connolly holds that "[a]n Augustinian heresy is a *temptation* within his own faith in that its declarations receive their impetus from uncertainties and ambiguities floating within the authoritative doctrine itself; it is a *political* threat in that its articulation disturbs the highest hope the authoritative doctrine is designed to sustain; it is politically indispensable in that its constitution as heresy stills the threat within the doctrine and the self through exclusion of those giving voice to it" (2000: 78; emphasis in original). Thus, the heretics and schismatics become a large, and indeed required, threat.

Or perhaps the matter is merely biographical. Augustine himself spent many years in the embrace of the Manichean heresy and would later say "I had wandered on along the road of vice in the sacrilegious superstition of the Manichees, not because I thought that it was right, but because I preferred it to the Christian belief, which I did not explore as I ought but opposed out of malice" (1961: 169). Perhaps his own revulsion at being involved in this "sacrilegious superstition" for so long translated into a belief that others would similarly appreciate being freed from such sin, especially on seeing "how grateful former Donatists were for being freed from long-standing custom and being brought to their right minds" (TeSelle, 1998: 118–19). But these notions of difference or biographical data do not, in fact, provide the best answer to this question.

Rather, the issue for Augustine seems to be one of peace. Consistent with his views in *City of God*, peace is of primary importance and is indeed (when put in the heavenly context) seen as the greatest good. He explicitly makes this point about earthly peace. By looking at his activities against the Donatists from this same perspective, we may find consistency and indeed illumination of the deeper currents of Augustine's thoughts about coercion. As Augustine does not use the same terminology in the two cases, it makes explicit comparisons difficult, but this does not mean it cannot be hypothesized. While schismatics, as a disruptive force, cannot be said to be to the Heavenly City like armies are that disturb peace in the earthly city, perhaps we can say they do indeed act as disruptive forces in some middle ground between the earthly city and the Heavenly one: that as these two are "mixed" in our view as mortals, the disruption is not of merely earthly peace but of a peace that affects pilgrims on earth headed to the Heavenly City. Something had to be done, for "[h]ad the Catholics done nothing to alarm and correct them [the Donatists] by this wholesome fear of temporal punishment, they would not have been good or merciful towards them but rather would have rendered unto them evil for evil" (Deane, 1963: 196). As these disruptions touch on the one eternal and true peace, this appears to be why Augustine believes more stringent measures are needed to deal with them. As with the just war, the *attitude* is everything: if such coercion is done with Christian love in the heart of the persecutors, the prosecutors avoid "the sins which would make war blameworthy: love of violence, vengeful cruelty, strife and implacable enmity, savagery, lust for power and so forth" (Markus, 1983: 5). If love is the motivating force behind force, then war and coercion can both be justified. "Although we are commanded to love our enemies, yet we must also, in the spirit of love, correct their errors" (Deane, 1963: 197).

The "impingements" mentioned earlier shed some light on this issue. Augustine did, at the basic level, hold a similar idea about both just war concerns and schismatics as concerning the idea of *per molestias eruditio* and what actions need to be taken reflect this. In other words, he believed that humans, as sinful creatures, need to learn by inconveniences and impingements — and war could serve such a purpose. But as the levels in conflict (i.e., the higher Heavenly City versus the lower earthly one) are markedly different, so, too, are the methods needed to rectify the situation. After all, Augustine's views of the human condition play an exceptionally pivotal role in his opinions about war and coercion, stemming from his gradually formed notion that "[s]alvation is no longer ... an ordered progression towards a distant goal; it involves sharp conflict between sin and grace" (Markus, 1983: 7). This applies to schismatics even more than war itself, for "Augustine saw *the lack of worship of God* as the root of all evil" (Adeney, 1988: 29; emphasis added). How much worse is this lack of worship when it is by those "who bore the standards of Christ against the cause of Christ" (Augustine, 1999: 644)? In addition, believers are required to do *something* about these schismatics, since "[j]ust as it is possible—and right—to take action against those who do evil, by admonishing, punishing, or even killing them [as in just war], while retaining benevolence and love towards them in our hearts, it is possible—and wrong—to refrain from action intended to correct and discipline the evil, while cherishing anger and hatred toward them within ourselves" (Deane, 1963: 165). There comes into question how exactly the pilgrimage toward the Heavenly City can be aided when rebels are within its very gates. Or more specifically, at what point does mere theological difference become in fact a dangerous schism?

The *Saeculum*

It is appropriate to compare my view to the interpretation provided by eminent Augustine scholar R. A. Markus (1970). The previous comments should be compared to what Markus describes as Augustine's views on history and society, which he labels the *saeculum*. This saeculum entails "the whole stretch of time in which the two cities are 'inextricably intertwined'; it is the sphere of human living, history, society, and its institutions, characterized by the fact that in it the ultimate eschatological oppositions, though present, are not discernible" (133). In his discussion, Markus rightly points out that Augustine was initially skeptical about using coercion, since "what, he had thought, was the use of legislation to convert heretics into 'feigned' (*ficti*) Catholics?" (ibid.: 137). Markus gives various reasons why Augustine decided to overcome these fears and to start approving of coercion against the Donatists. One is that he always supported coercion as a pastoral means, with this coercion "as an exercise of this *severitas*, as an infliction of *disciplina* for the education of the coerced" (ibid.: 144). Another reason, though lesser and shorter lived, is Augustine's "theology of the Roman Empire as a divinely willed instrument of the Gospel," (ibid.:

145) but this phase of his thinking probably ended with the sack of Rome. A final way that Markus believes Augustine shielded himself from what may seem inconsistencies in his theology (although Markus does seem to imply that it may be more what perspective one takes) is through the terminology and conceptions he used to discuss Christian rulers. Even after he distanced himself from his earlier ideas on Rome as God's instrument, "Augustine continued to speak of Christian rulers and officials owing specific service to God in their public official capacity" (ibid.: 147).

In this regard, Augustine seemed to give rulers a great deal of leeway regarding the areas of life that could be under governmental observation and regulation. Indeed, "[t]here is no trace of any reservation about the scope of imperial or royal authority in such statements [about how Christian emperors should use their position to serve God and increase the worship of him], no suggestion that it is in any way restricted to 'temporal' matters. . . . Neither in his dealings with imperial officials nor in his writings in defence of religious coercion did he ever consider Christian rulers and civil servants as parts of a governmental machinery, of the 'state.' He thought of them as members of the Church. Through them, it is the Church that 'uses power'" (ibid.: 148). While all these points are insightful and useful, this last view may hold the key to the problem Markus has in reconciling Augustine's ideas about coercion with the rest of his theology. Specifically, Markus worried, "the truth of the hypothesis [of saeculum] threatened, by an aspect of Augustine's mind . . . his readiness to endorse religious coercion by the authorities of the state." Moreover, he was concerned whether this particular aspect of Augustine's thought would "invalidate the interpretation of his theology of saeculum which has disclosed a very direction in his thought?" (ibid.: 134). But perhaps reconciliation is easier than Markus believed.

As Markus notes, Augustine saw Christian rulers and civil servants as being of the Church, not of the state. With this notion of rulers in mind, a great deal of the difficulty in understanding Augustine's view is eliminated: if these officials are first and foremost part of the Church, the agent of the Heavenly City, then the fact that they would use the machinery of government coercion to bring schisms to an end makes sense. After all, as Markus explained in a later piece on just war, "Augustine . . . offers us a vision of the social order which springs from a vivid sense of conflicting purposes, of uncertainties of direction, of divergent loyalties and irresolvable tensions. Political power has become a means of securing some minimal barriers against the forces of disintegration. In this 'hell on earth' all the institutions of political and judicial authority serve to keep conflict within check, to secure breathing space" (1983: 9–10). If the political authorities must keep disintegration and conflict in check, why would it only be on matters purely of the earthly city? Especially for Augustine, who always keeps the concerns of heaven in mind, it would seem even more important for these officials to keep conflicts that prevent access to the Heavenly City at bay. This appears consistent with Augustine's ideas about secular authority, for "the secular authorities have not only the right but the duty to act with severity and with love toward those who are guilty of heresy and schism. When they act this way, they are serving as agents and ministers of God, who through them corrects and emends the conduct of those who have gone astray and scourges with punishment those who refuse to turn from their wickedness. Compulsion and punishment serve as a warning and as an entering wedge to permit instruction and persuasion to go forward once the hindrances of violence, long-continued habit, and slothful indifference have broken down" (Deane, 1963: 204). But more important, this line of thought shows why the way to deal with schismatics is more severe than one would consider consistent with Augustine's just war views. Indeed, by examining this way of thinking, one can see that Augustine is still using the same underlying logic for both cases. There is a need for peace, but a peace of a different order than the one dealing exclusively with the earthly city. Augustine is very clear about his views of heretics and schismatics. As he wrote,

> even when those who are outside [the Church,] and there seems to be, and really is, tranquillity, which brings great consolation, especially to the weak, even so there are always some, inside indeed there are many, who by their undisciplined behaviour torment the feelings of those who live devout lives. For such people cause the name of "Christian" and "Catholic" to be defamed. And the dearer this name is to those who want to live a devout life in Christ, the more they grieve that evildoers within the Church make that name less beloved than the hearts of the devout long for it to be... those who want to live a devout life in Christ suffer persecution... they suffer this persecution not in their bodies but in their hearts. (1984: 834)

In this way, Augustine sees the matter as indeed a lack of peace within the Church, the agent of the Heavenly City itself. And the true pilgrims to the City of God are "persecuted" in their hearts by the deceit and falsehoods of these schismatics and heretics. If there is such discord within the very agent of the Heavenly City itself, then what is to be done?

It appears that the solution is to rely on the agents of the agent—that is, for the Church to use its members who hold political office to bring about a peace through the use of religious coercion. The benefits are twofold. First, bringing these schismatics into check frees the devout from the persecution in their hearts and frees the Church to do its business. Second, banning such schismatic evil "also can be the means of releasing others from the fear of the violence of the fanatics; once the timid followers are freed from this fear and from the bonds of habit, it may be possible to convince them by rational arguments and scriptural authority" (Deane, 1963: 194). In doing this, the Heavenly City's agent gains peace for those already on the pilgrimage to God and also gains a peace that allows the "timid followers" to go in the right direction. Augustine, both for just war and dealing with schismatics, uses "[t]he language of 'necessity'" to explain why officials must do these things (Markus, 1983: 10). He appeals to these leaders to act when "he speaks of public duty [as] 'compelling' or 'constraining' a man. These are the 'necessities' the just man may not avoid, but will pray to God to be delivered from" (ibid.: 11). Additionally, "Augustine insists that it is not only right for public authorities to punish wrongdoing, since in doing so they are acting as ministers of God, but that such punishment is an act of love which is intended to lead to the correction and reform of those who are punished" (Deane, 1963: 189). Peace is still the aim, and love is still the motivation, but the battlefield has changed, and with it so, too, have the rules of engagement.

This conclusion is not extreme. Indeed, it can mesh rather well with Markus's view of Augustine's saeculum theology. The world we all live in, the world before the return of Christ, is "mixed" or, in other words, while the earthly city and the Heavenly one are separate and distinct groups, "in their historical existence they can never be discerned in their unmixed state" (Markus, 1970: 151). Thanks to this mixed state of affairs, one cannot easily divide the wheat from the chaff and have a clear view of each city within its own confines. So here is where attention must be paid to religious coercion. Were the world in a clearer state, the Heavenly City and the Church would be one and the same, and therefore all who were in the Church could be guaranteed to be with God. But as it is mixed, there are those "evildoers within the Church" who make the work of the Church difficult. This creates problems, as "the visible Church was—and always would be—a mixture of good and evil men, it was impossible and blasphemous to attempt to make a final separation of the good and the wicked before the end of the world and the Last Judgement. Of course, *church discipline had to be maintained,* and overt and notorious sinners had to be corrected and, if necessary, expelled from the Church" (Deane, 1963: 183; emphasis added). It is not that there is a war going on within the Heavenly City, but rather that since the two cities are currently difficult to discern from one another, the agent of the Heavenly City must deal with barbarians within its gates who would prevent the Word reaching the devout and possible converts. Church discipline had to be maintained. As such, instruments of the agent of the Heavenly City, the Christian rulers, are to bring a forced peace to this mixed realm to ensure the good operation of the Church in the world. In a way, then, it is almost as if dealing with schismatics is somewhere in between bringing earthly peace and heavenly peace: what would be an acceptable peace for the former is not tolerable with schismatics, but at the same time the battlefield is not directly the City of God, as it cannot have such dissention within it. In this way, Augustine's views on religious coercion may actually be the fullest expression of his saeculum theology: as we have a view that makes the two cities mixed, it is necessary that the one clear sign of the City of God, the Church, be as true and obeyed as can be done, be it with persuasion or by other means.

Conclusion

One might reasonably ask what, if anything, this explanation of Augustine's views has to do with the modern world and its ideas of war and conflict. On a historical level, it most certainly helps develop and flesh out Augustine's views on just war. And as such, there may be a connection to our times. If the view above is correct, then there are certain times when something more stringent than a just war is required. For most secular states, this presents no problem. In fact, one could even question whether the modern secular state, thanks to its separation from Church and faith, is by nature capable of waging just wars in any consistent way. This is an issue for another time. But this chapter's idea may present an issue for consideration by the Catholic Church as regards what kinds of wars it supports, and it could also affect those of faith who occupy seats of political/military power who want to know whether a just war—or something greater than that—should be fought.

In terms of the Catholic Church, the importance of Augustine's views may not seem immediately obvious. Certainly, much has changed since Augustine's time, such as the nature of Church-state relations, the Protestant Reformation, and the general acceptance of pluralism in the world and within Church doctrine. Indeed, one might question whether the Church could, or even should, take to heart the idea of per molestias eruditio against those who could be considered schismatics. In considering the importance of religious freedom, both in Vatican II and in the encyclicals of Pope John Paul II, forcing others to come into the Church is effectively forbidden. As such, what Augustine advocated—bringing in those who use "the standards of Christ against the cause of Christ"—is no longer a viable policy, in terms of belief as well as ability, for the Catholic Church. In these matters, then, one could conclude that Augustine has nothing to say to the Church today.

But in terms of the just war, such a dismissal of Augustine's thought is unwise. Augustine's views can help the Church determine what wars would be just and unjust, at least within the "just cause" requirement for the doctrine. Augustine recognized the deep importance of ideas, how they can act as chains to those caught within them, and how they can interrupt the peace on earth conducive to the propagation of the faith in the saeculum. Pluralism, like all things under heaven, is at best a mixed blessing. While the current configuration of relations between Church, state, and culture prevent a more active role by the Church (perhaps more reflective of Augustine's views in *City of God*), following Augustine's views would save the Church from falling into the opposing mistake: laxness against ideas fundamentally incompatible with the spread of the Gospel. When considering whether a war is just, the Church would be wise to consider the problems that Augustine contended with during the Donatist schism. By considering the various belligerents' views on life, existence, and faith, the Church might be better prepared to see where justice lies. This is directed, primarily and most strongly, by what is required of the earthly peace for heavenly work. In considering which side(s) of a war might be just, the Church would be wise to consider whose victory will be the most conducive to the faith. In this way, pluralism is at best an instrumental good and cannot be held as higher than that in the extremes of warfare.

To the secular state, however, there may indeed be a further connection with Augustine's thought: to democracy. In recent military conflicts, Western democracies fight wars (be it under the name of "police action," "peacekeeping," or any other designation) that are claimed to be just according to a secular notion of just wars, and yet at the same time seem to contravene the very precepts of such a concept, most especially on the principle of not killing noncombatants. From a purely objective point of view, it would seem that Western states are contradicting their own principles. But if one transposes Augustine's ideas about schismatics into the situation, replacing faith with the secular creed of democracy, a more coherent pattern is formed. In wars where democracy is concerned, especially those in which an established democracy wants to bring "true" democracy to the people of another state, these established democracies will fight their opponents in ways reminiscent of the views of Augustine toward schismatics: some just war rules may have to be negated for the protection of the true faith of democracy in the face of authoritarian rulers or tyrants like Slobodan Milosevic. Whether this parallel between Augustine and the secular states rings true is a matter for further development elsewhere—it certainly and admittedly has its problematic aspects, morally and politically. But it also shows that Augustine's influential and important ideas from what was clearly a more *theological* context have relevance and challenge us even in our *secular* setting.

Augustine is constantly concerned with peace. But peace can mean many things, as is illustrated by the metaphor of the two cities. Peace in the earthly city can simply be order, and by using the notions and attitudes of the just war, one can bring about peace rightly. But when one delves into the mixed realm of the earthly city and the Heavenly City, peace requires something more stringent and more coercive. Peace in the earthly city brings about a positive environment for the Church as the agent of the Heavenly City to perform its mission of saving souls. Peace within the agent itself, however, is key: for if there is conflict within the Church (due to schismatics), then earthly peace cannot be enough for the Church to commit to its mission as it must. For Augustine, peace is needed for the earthly environment where pilgrims are heading toward God as well as in the agent that will guide these souls onto the correct path. Schismatics distort the true way, and thus the political instruments of the Church, Christian rulers, must (Augustine believes) bring schismatics back into the fold. It is not, in my view, that Augustine chose this out of dire need, and thus, in a way, out of his intellectual character. Rather, Augustine simply was extending his notions of peace and salvation to their logical fulfillment.

REFERENCES

Adeney, Bernard T. 1988. *Just War, Political Realism, and Faith.* ALTA monograph series 24. Metuchen, N.J.: Scarecrow.
Allison, Graham, and Philip Zelikow. 1999. *Essence of Decision—Explaining the Cuban Missile Crisis.* 2nd ed. New York: Addison-Wesley.
Augustine. 1961. *Confessions.* Trans. R. S. Pine-Coffin. London: Penguin.
———. 1984. *City of God.* Trans. Henry Bettenson. London: Penguin.
———. 1999. "A Treatise concerning the Correction of the Donatists; or, Epistle CLXXXV." In Philip Schaff, ed., and J. R. King, trans., *Augustine: The Writings against the Manichaeans, and against the Donatists.*. Vol. 4 of *Nicene and Post-Nicene Fathers.* Peabody, Mass.: Hendrickson, 633–51.
Brown, Peter. 1967. *Augustine of Hippo: A Biography.* Berkeley: University of California Press.
Burns, J. Patout, Robert J. Daly, and John Helgeland. 1985. *Christians and the Military—The Early Experience.* Ed. Robert J. Daly. Philadelphia: Fortress.
Cahill, Lisa Sowle. 1994. *Love Your Enemies—Discipleship, Pacifism, and Just War Theory.* Minneapolis: Fortress.
Connolly, William E. 2000. *The Augustinian Imperative: A Reflection on the Politics of Morality.* Modernity and Political Thought 1. Walnut Creek, Calif.: AltaMira.
Deane, Herbert A. 1963. *The Political and Social Ideas of St. Augustine.* New York: Columbia University Press.
Elshtain, Jean Bethke. 1995. *Augustine and the Limits of Politics.* Notre Dame: University of Notre Dame Press.
Fortin, Ernest. 1987. "Augustine." In Leo Strauss and Joseph Cropsey, eds., *History of Political Philosophy,* 3rd ed. Chicago: University of Chicago Press, 176–205.
Fowler, Robert Booth. 1994. "Augustine's Political Theory: 'Realism' Revisited." In Christopher Kleinhenz and Fannie LeMoine, eds., *Saint Augustine the Bishop—A Book of Essays.* New York: Garland, 75–176.
Markus, R. A. 1970. *Saeculum: History and Society in the Theology of St. Augustine.* New York: Cambridge University Press.
———. 1983. "Saint Augustine's Views on the 'Just War.'" In *The Church and War: Studies in Church History 20.* London: Ecclesiastical History Society, 1–13.
Parel, Anthony J. 1990. "Justice and Love in the Political Thought of St. Augustine." In H. A. Meynell, ed., *Grace, Politics, and Desire: Essays on Augustine.* Calgary: University of Calgary Press, 71–86.
Reventlow, Henning Graf. 1994. "The Biblical and Classical Traditions of 'Just War.'" In Yair Hoffman, Henning Graf Reventlow, and Benjamin Uffenheimer, eds., *Politics and Theopolitics in the Bible and Postbiblical Literature.* Sheffield: JSOT Press, 160–75.
Swift, Louis J. 1983. *The Early Fathers on War and Military Service.* Ed. Thomas Halton. Message of the Fathers of the Church 19. Wilmington, Del.: Michael Glazier.
TeSelle, Eugene. 1998. *Living in Two Cities: Augustinian Trajectories in Political Thought.* Scranton: University of Scranton Press.
Tilley, Maureen A. 1997. *The Bible in Christian North Africa—The Donatist World.* Minneapolis: Fortress.
Wood, Neal. 1986. "*Populares* and *Circumcelliones*: The Vocabulary of 'Fallen Man' in Cicero and St. Augustine." *History of Political Thought* 7 (1).

5

Is There a "Presumption against War" in Aquinas's Ethics?

GREGORY M. REICHBERG

Over the past few years a debate has arisen among proponents of just war thinking about the correct starting point for moral reflection on war. The debate concerns how moral reasoning should proceed when the just war criteria of legitimate authority, just cause, and right intention are made to inform decision making about resort to military force *(ius ad bellum)*.

Some authors have maintained that moral reasoning about war should begin with a reflection on the obligation "Do no harm." From this obligation there derives, they argue, a strong presumption against the use of force, a presumption that can be overridden only in "exceptional circumstances" (Miller, 1991: 16; cf. Childress, 1980). On this understanding, as articulated inter alia by the American National Conference of Catholic Bishops, "Just war teaching has evolved . . . as an effort to prevent war; only if war cannot be rationally avoided does the teaching then seek to restrict and reduce its horrors. It does this by establishing a set of rigorous conditions which must be met if the decision to go to war is to be morally permissible. Such a decision, especially today, requires extraordinarily strong reasons for overriding the presumption *in favor of peace and against war*" (1983: 27). By contrast, other authors have argued for a more proactive conception of military force. Moral thinking about war should begin, they argue, with a reflection on the duty of civic leadership to oppose grave wrongdoing. Its starting point, in the words of James Turner Johnson, is a presumption against *injustice*.

[T]he development of Christian just-war tradition follows a line of reasoning focused on the rightness of the resort to force to combat the evil of injustice, and that development did not construe at any point the use of force to be a moral problem in itself. In classic just-war theory the use of force is morally problematical only when it is the source of injustice. But even then, wrong uses of force do not call force itself into question, but instead justify the resort to force to set matters right. What Christian just-war doctrine is about, as classically defined, is the use of the authority and force of the rightly ordered political community . . . to prevent, punish, and rectify injustice. There is, simply put, no presumption against war in it at all. (1996: 30)

Significantly, each of these rival versions of just war theory appeals to Thomas Aquinas as a source for its respective views. Thus, we read in the American Catholic bishops' pastoral letter that "in the twentieth century, papal teaching has used the logic of Augustine and Aquinas to articulate a right of self-defense for states in a decentralized international order and to state the criteria for exercising that right" (NCCB, 1983: 27). From the opposing perspective, Johnson writes that "the position of Thomas Aquinas looms as especially important [for the development of just war thinking along the lines of a presumption against injustice]. . . . What is morally condemnable in war [for Aquinas] . . . is not force itself but the use of force with the wrong intention (1996: 29).

Thus, on the one hand, we have those who view participation in war as morally suspect, and hence as standing in need of the most stringent justification if it is to have any ethical warrant at all. Recourse to military force should be restricted as much as possible, resorted to only in the most pressing circumstances. It should not be thought of as part of the ordinary functioning of political leadership. On this understanding, pacifism and just war "share a common starting point: a moral presumption against the use of force" (Miller, 1991: 16).[1] This "point of contact" between the two moral traditions is "both substantive and heuristic" (ibid.:

---

1. In arguing his case that in Thomas there may be found "a bias against violence," Miller (23–27) attempts to document a "Thomistic convergence" between the pacifist and just war traditions, "which foreshadows Childress's insight" that these traditions share a common root in the presumption against violence. Miller credits Childress (1980) with first articulating the convergence thesis. Miller presents his book as an expansion (historical and systematic) on

18).² Opponents of this view make the case that it underestimates the weight of injustice in human affairs, hindering the ability of moral leaders to counter it effectively.³ Moreover, it is argued that this view unduly limits the legitimate scope of the ius ad bellum to self-defense; it thereby "trammels action and initiative in foreign policy" (Ramsey, 1968: xv).

How might we situate Aquinas in this debate?⁴ In what follows, I will examine the context for his treatment of war in the *Secunda secundae*,⁵ wherein *bellum* is listed as one of the sins opposed to *caritas*, to see whether this indicates a preference in favor of a presumption against war. I begin with Aquinas's construal of just cause, for in this respect he shows a clear-cut preference for a presumption against injustice. Never, in effect, does Thomas restrict the legitimate scope of the ius ad bellum to the purely defensive posture of repelling armed attack. Unlike many "presumption against war" theorists, therefore, Aquinas appears to think that occasions may arise when offensive war may justified: to regain stolen goods, to thwart and to punish organized evildoing, or to protect innocents from harm. Just war, on this understanding, is a means for setting right the violated order of justice.⁶ Thomas thus writes that there is "just cause" *(iusta causa)* for war only when "those who are attacked deserve attack on account of some fault."⁷

Childress's earlier statement of this thesis. More recently, he has sought to defend his reading of Aquinas from the objections of several critics (Miller, 2002). This article amplifies the same set of arguments that were earlier presented in Miller, 1991.

2. Upon claiming that "each [of these traditions] presumes a bias against violence," Miller tells us that the chief aim of his book is to show "how this presumption ought to affect the manner in which the *ad bellum* and *in bello* criteria are interpreted and ordered" (ibid.: 13).

3. Ramsey (1968: xv) in particular is very critical of the notion that war is an activity that stands apart from the ordinary and expected tasks of political governance: "Thus, the typical Western liberal holds a tame version of the limited-war doctrine. This view concedes the use of force as an 'exception'; at all other times politics is being rightly conducted. This view has not let the constant function of force or the threat of force in the nation-state system sink deeply into consciousness. . . . [I]t is prone to delay, waiting for the rare 'exceptional' case which it falsely identifies with the proviso in the just-war doctrine that a use of armed force should be in the last reasonable resort."

4. A useful summary of the contemporary debate on the presumption against war may be found in Winwright, 1998.

5. All references are taken from Thomas Aquinas, 1895.

6. Johnson (1996: 29) notes that Aquinas, in elaborating his notion of legitimate war-making authority in *STh* II-II, q. 40, a. 1, was inspired by Romans 13:4 ("The sovereign beareth not the sword in vain: for he is God's minister, an avenger to execute wrath upon him that doth evil"). This underscores the extent to which the idea of punishment (understood as a remedy for injustice), and not merely defense against actual attack, was integral to Aquinas's construal of just cause for war. It remains true, however, that Aquinas is exceedingly sparing in his account of what might count as *iusta causa*. He seems more intent on delimiting the formal characteristics of the belligerent who has the right to make war: the prince without a superior who has care of the political community.

7. "[R]equiritur causa iusta: ut scilicet illi qui impugnantur propter aliquam culpam im-

In fact, the requirement of proper authority, the first of the famous three criteria listed in *STh* II-II, q. 40, a. 1, suggests that offensive war,[8] not simply defensive protection from attack, is most at issue in Aquinas's *Summa theologiae* treatment of iustum bellum.[9] For, as he argues in another passage of the same work (*STh* II-II, q. 64, a. 7), using enough force to ward off an (unjust) attack necessitates no special appeal to legitimate authority. This is an option open even to private individuals. Only when initiative is taken to use lethal force for the repression of wrongdoing — especially where there is a direct intent to cause serious harm or even to kill — does legitimate authority become a necessary (although not a sufficient) condition for a morally justified employment of armed force.[10] A particularly clear restatement of this view may be found in Suarez. De-

---

pugnationem mereantur" (*STh* II-II, q. 40, a. 1). Finnis (1998: 284) explains that "just cause," as used in this context, means very much the same as the phrase "cause of action" in Anglo-American law, "i.e. a wrong giving ground for complaints and just claims for redress."

8. Among the Scholastics, the term *bellum offensivum* seems to have made its first appearance in Francisco de Vitoria's *De iure belli*. See, for instance, Vitoria, 1981: 106 and 126-28. Earlier authors, Aquinas included, employ equivalent expressions such as *movere, inferre, indicere bellum*.

9. Cajetan interprets Thomas this way in his commentary on *STh* II-II, q. 40, a. 1 (in Reichberg, Syse, and Begby, 2006: 242): "In order to ascertain the authority needed to wage war, it should be understood that this is not a discussion of defensive war, namely when someone makes a war in defense against a war made on himself; for any people has a natural right to do this. But here the concern is with declaring war: what authority is required for this?" Suarez (*De bello*, in Reichberg, Syse, and Begby, 2006: 342) likewise interprets the just war tradition as holding that legitimate authority is needful only for the waging of offensive, not defensive, war. It must be admitted, however, that Aquinas does not explicitly draw out a distinction between offensive and defensive war. He uses a single concept to cover both types of war.

10. After explaining that it is lawful for private individuals to repel force by force, as long as due moderation is shown, Aquinas adds that such individuals are not allowed to intend the death of the attacking party: "illicitum est quod homo intendat occidere hominem ut seipsum defendat, nisi ei qui habet publicam auctoritatem" (*STh* II-II, q. 64, a. 7). This exclusion of intentional killing from the sphere of self-defense has been diversely understood by Aquinas's commentators. Some (e.g., Boyle, 1978) take this to mean that, in legitimate self-defense, the death of the attacker is allowable only as a side effect; such an effect should be never be deliberately aimed at, either as an end or as a means. For others, by contrast, the restrictions placed on self-defense do not exclude all intentional killing whatsoever, but only killing that is carried out with the intent of *punishing* the assailant (see Reichberg, 2005). Along similar lines, Vitoria (1981: 116) notes that while private persons have the right to defend themselves from immediate attack ("defensio oportet ut fiat in praesenti"), they are not allowed to avenge and punish injuries. By contrast, commonwealths are entitled not only to defend themselves from attack; they may also punish wrongdoing and seek redress for offenses. To this formulation, Suarez adds that "more things are allowable to a given state or commonwealth with regard to its own defence than to a given individual; because the good defended in the former case is common to many, and is of a higher grade, and also because the power of a state is by its very nature public and common; therefore it is not strange that more things are permissible to a state than to an individual" (*De bello*, in Reichberg, Syse, and Begby, 2006: 345). He does not spell out in detail what broader limits on self-defense states may be held to possess. And presumably, the more offensive these tactics become, the more they will require authorization from the sovereign political authority and the less they can justifiably be carried out by the individual's — or local authority's — own initiative.

fensive force should be distinguished from offensive force, he notes, insofar as the former seeks to counter unjust violence that is already under way (or on the verge of taking place), while the latter seeks redress for an injustice that has already been committed. Since offensive war[11] appears to be the sort of undertaking that is primarily envisioned by Aquinas in *STh* II-II, q. 40, a. 1, Johnson is doubtless correct in his assessment that the recent trend in both international law and the Roman Catholic magisterium to condemn "any offensive use of force, whatever the justifying reason" (1996: 31),[12] represents a departure from the teaching of Aquinas and other eminent representatives of the classical just war tradition.[13]

The Ethics of War in Thomas Aquinas

Although allusions to war occur throughout Aquinas's writings,[14] the *Secunda secundae* of the *Summa theologiae* contains his sole explicit treatment of this theme (*STh* II-II, q. 40). With the exception of Alexander of Hales, whom he does not mention in this connection, Aquinas appears to have been one of the first theologians (as distinct from the can-

---

11. Some of the later Scholastics (Cajetan and Suárez in particular) viewed offensive war as necessarily punitive in character. It is precisely because such war involves punishing wrongdoing that it can be waged only with a special mandate from legitimate authority. By contrast, other Scholastics (Vitoria and especially Molina) did not consider punishment as inherent to the very *ratio* of offensive war. This kind of warfare they define by reference to the broader idea of redressing wrong (which may or may not involve attributions of guilt and the attendant imposition of punishment). Given the extreme brevity of Aquinas's comments on just cause for war, there is uncertainty on how to read him on this issue. For a close analysis of this topic, see Haggenmacher, 1983: 407–25. In presenting Scholastic views on the link between offensive war and punishment, Haggenmacher argues that for early thinkers such as Gratian and Aquinas, "ce n'est pas [l'élément penal] qui fait l'object principal de la guerre; celle-ci vise avant tout à rétablir le droit, à effacer l'*iniuria;* la *culpa* n'a qu'une function latérale" (418). Haggenmacher notes (124) that Aquinas seems to avoid using the term *bellum* when describing the prince's exercise of *vindicatio* (apropos the virtue of justice in *STh* II-II, q. 108). This leads Haggenmacher to speculate (129) that while Aquinas did not exclude *vindicatio* as a just cause for war, he seems to have favored defense as the most appropriate reason for waging war.

12. Indeed, in the opening summary to NCCB (1983: iii) it is stated: "Offensive war of any kind is not morally justifiable."

13. See Johnson, 1973 for a more ample discussion of this trend. Further elaborations may be found in Coste, 1962: 272–88. Coste concludes that for Pope Pius XII (the pivotal figure in the development of contemporary Catholic just war doctrine), offensive war, in the juridical and moral sense of the term, must be entirely excluded (288). This represents, Coste acknowledges, "une divergence importante avec la doctrine traditionelle" (ibid.).

14. See Synan, 1988, for a survey of Thomas's comments on war and military service, especially as found in his biblical commentaries.

on lawyers) of the thirteenth century to have expressly thematized the topic of war. No parallel to question 40 may be found in the writings of Albert the Great, Bonaventure, or Duns Scotus, for instance.[15] Yet not until the sixteenth century, when Aquinas's *Summa theologiae* began to replace Lombard's *Sentences* as the main textbook for theological studies in the West, did war become a standard topic in treatises devoted to ethical questions.

Two general considerations, both relating to the basic structure of the *Secunda secundae*, seem to have prompted Thomas to reserve an entire quaestio to war. First of all, he intended the exposition of the different virtues and vices to be as exhaustive as possible. The aim, of course, was not to say all that could be said about each of these moral dispositions, but to say just enough about each virtue and vice so that all the main categories of human acts (i.e., acts issuing from deliberation and choice) would be identified in their moral kind. Aquinas's attempt at providing a complete typology of human acts contributed some novel developments to medieval thought, of which his treatment of war is but one instance (cf. his treatment of *studiositas* in *STh* II-II, q. 166). The project of cataloguing moral acts is particularly visible in questions 37–42, where he singles out the genus of conflict-causing behavior and several species within it: discord, contention, schism, war, strife, and sedition.

The other reason that may have motivated Aquinas to set aside space for the ethical analysis of war was his focus upon the different "states of life" in questions 171–89 of the *Secunda secundae*. Although that series of questions includes no express mention of the profession of arms, it is undeniable that consideration of military life as a particular calling was present in his mind in the discussion of war in question 40, especially article 2, where he compared the activity of soldiers to those of businessmen and clerics. Whether soldiering might be deemed compatible with the moral demands of the Christian life is a question implicitly raised by much of question 40. In this connection, Edward Synan has done well to remind us that military life was a vital aspect of the "human and cultural

---

15. While not as systematic as Aquinas, Albert the Great did discuss war in his commentary on Aristotle's *Politics* 7.2.1325a (*Commentarium Politicorum VIII*, in Albert the Great, 1890–99: 8:636). Thomas may also have benefited from the work of his fellow Dominican Vincent of Beauvais, who, in the *Speculum Doctrinale* (II, 36), "assembled various theological opinions to show that war was sometimes necessary to preserve liberty and territory and to increase dignity" (Russell, 1975: 264).

matrix within which St. Thomas was born and which, in important ways he never left" (1988: 404). After all, the saint's father, and most likely all three of his full brothers, were knights. "He had come to consciousness of brothers and sisters in a feudal castle. Abundant evidence establishes that he had witnessed his brothers' exercises with their weapons, and that he absorbed their discussions of knighthood and its preoccupations. . . . military life . . . dominated the Aquino clan. In that exposure," Synan conjectures, Thomas "hardly saw knighthood at its best and, although his writings may encourage high standards for the military, his realistic evaluations of knights border on cynicism" (ibid.: 407). "Knights are rapacious" is a cutting phrase that escaped Thomas's lips on at least one occasion (*Sermo 41*, cited in ibid.: 424n83).

Does Thomas's decision to locate his discussion of war within a section of the *Secunda secundae* devoted to sins against charity manifest a skepticism toward the moral foundations of military life? Since earlier writings of the theological tradition did not dictate such a choice, this may tell us something significant about Thomas's own distinctive orientation to the ethics of war.[16]

The Dominican theologian could have linked his *ex professo* discussion of war to one or other of the virtues. He seems to have been alert to this possibility, since on at least two occasions the question of war is taken up within the context of virtue. Thus, regarding the prudence of political leadership (*prudentia regnativa*), we find an article devoted to the special conditions that attach to military command (*STh* II-II, q. 50, a. 4). Against the second objection, which maintains that there is no need to assign a distinct mode of political prudentia for military affairs, no more than there need be a special prudence for commerce or craftsmanship, Thomas responds that this analogy does not hold: while the latter activities are chiefly directed to the profit of private individuals, and only indirectly to the good of the political community (*civitas*), military activity is

---

16. Alexander of Hales's treatment of war in his *Summa theologica* (1948: 4:683–86n.466) is situated in a section on the laws of punishment (*De legibus punitionis*). This juridical perspective (*de sententia iudiciali* is in fact the heading for the broader sequence of questions) remains much closer to the writings of the canon lawyers than the virtue-centered approach followed by Aquinas some decades later in the *Secunda secundae*. The same may be said of Raymond of Peñafort, whose *Summa de casibus* included a discussion of war and self-defensive war (for a translation of the relevant passages, see Reichberg, Syse, and Begby, 2006: 131–47). However, it is nonetheless significant that this treatment of war arises in a section of the work that is devoted to sins against the neighbor (see Ehrlich, 1961: 217), and in this respect it may have served as a model for Aquinas's later treatment of this theme.

ordered immediately to the protection of the entire common good (*totius boni communis*). Military command thus requires a distinct form of morally directive prudence.

Question 123 on courage (*fortitudo*) likewise speaks of military service from the standpoint of virtue (a. 5, "Utrum fortitudo proprie consistat circa pericula mortis quae sunt in bello"). Thomas notes that courage is virtuous only when a man risks death in the pursuit of a worthy good, for *virtus* names a disposition always tending to what is good, never to what is evil. To protect the common good by a just combat (iustum bellum) is unambiguously a good. Hence moral virtue is found in "the genus of courage that regards warlike actions" (ad 1). This point is reinforced with respect to the third objection, where, in reply to the complaint that the peace of the temporal city is a good mixed with much evil, for which reason it does not merit that we should expose ourselves to death for its sake, Thomas affirms that the peace of the commonweal (*pax reipublicae*) is something inherently good, *secundum se bona*. Thus here, too, the implication is that the (lay) Christian's participation in war is not merely permissible but, if carried out for the common good, and with due restraint, it represents an exercise of true virtue.

Another text worthy of mention in this connection is Thomas's discussion of retribution (*vindicatio*) in *STh* II-II, q. 108. After assuring the reader that the punishment of evildoers is indeed licit, provided that certain conditions be met (in particular the avoidance of improper sentiments such as hatred [a. 1]), he then asks whether the infliction of just retribution falls within the purview of a distinct virtue (a. 2). Vindicatio names such a virtue, Thomas maintains, when private individuals use force to repulse harm (*iniuria propulsatur*) from themselves or others (a. 1, ad 2). By contrast, when punishment is meted out by public authorities serving as guardians of the commonweal, it falls under the virtue of commutative justice.[17] In either case, the primary root of virtuous retribution is a zeal (*zelus*) inspired by love: "a man avenges the wrong

---

17. *STh* II-II, q. 108, a. 2, ad 1: "[P]unitio peccatorum, secundum quod pertinet ad publicam iustitiam, est actus commutativae iustitiae; secundum autem quod pertinet ad immunitatem alicuius personae singularis, a qua iniuria propulsatur, pertinet ad virtutem vindicationis." See Haggenmacher, 1983: 409-17, for a nuanced discussion of Thomas's placement of public punishment within the category of "commutative justice" and the significance of the shift (in Scotus, Cajetan, and especially Suarez) to specialized categories of "punitive justice" and "punitive war."

done to God and neighbor, because charity makes him regard them as his own" (a. 2, ad 2).[18] Although just war is not referred to here,[19] we can adduce from Thomas's earlier comment (*STh* II-II, q. 40, a. 1) on the vindicative character of such fighting—"those who are attacked, should be attacked because they deserve it on account of some fault [*propter aliquam culpam*]"—that soldiering may indeed spring from well-ordered inner dispositions of justice and charity.[20]

I have now alluded to several virtues—prudence, courage, retribution, justice, and charity—each of which could have served as the setting for Thomas's systematic elaboration on war. This shows how distant he was from the pacifism of a Tertullian or a Lactantius, for whom active participation in war could never serve as a context for positing true acts of virtue. However, the fact remains that Thomas chose vice, not virtue, as the locus for his ethical analysis of war. This is what we need to look at more closely.

The preface to question 37 (*De discordia*) outlines the sequence of quaestiones concerned with conflict-causing sentiments and deeds. "We must now consider the sins contrary to peace, and first we shall consider discord [*discordia*] which arises in the heart, secondly contention [*contentio*], which arises in words, thirdly, of those [conflict-causing sins] which consist in deeds, namely schism [*schisma*], strife [*rixa*], and war [*bellum*]."[21] This group of quaestiones is organized under the rubric of sins against charity. Thus, corresponding to each of the acts or effects of charity—love (*dilectio*), joy (*gaudium*), peace (*pax*), mercy (*misericordia*), and beneficence (*beneficentia*)—are the opposing vices. Hatred is

---

18. See *STh* II-II, q. 60, a. 6, ad 2, where Thomas cites approvingly the famous words of Ambrose (*De offic.* 1.36): "whoever does not ward off a blow from a fellow man, when he can, is at much at fault as the striker."

19. It is difficult to know what to make of Aquinas's silence in this regard. Haggenmacher (1983: 124) speculates that it was deliberate ("Thomas évite par ailleurs soigneusement le term *bellum* en parlant, sous la virtue de justice, de la *vindicatio*") and that Aquinas meant thereby to downplay (yet not altogether excluding) *vindicatio* as a motive for war. In the absence of any explicit comment by Aquinas on this score, it is impossible to know with certitude whether this was in fact his intent.

20. Apropos the question "whether there was anger in Christ?" Aquinas notes affirmatively that the desire to avenge wrongs may indeed spring from sinless passion: "[Q]uandoque [appetitus vindicate] est sine peccato, immo est laudabilis: puta cum aliquis appetit vindictam secundum ordinem justitiae" (*STh* III, q. 15, a. 9).

21. In this passage, Aquinas seems to have inadvertently omitted sedition (*seditio*) from the list of conflict-causing sins. He nevertheless clearly intends to include it in his enumeration, as is indicated by the short preface to q. 39 (*De schismate*): "We must now consider the vices contrary to peace which pertain to deeds: such are schism, strife, sedition, and war."

opposed to love, sloth and envy to joy, scandal to mercy and beneficence. In opposition to peace stand discord, contention in words, schism, war, strife and sedition.

Taken as an effect of charity, peace is twofold (q. 29, a. 1): first, it consists in the inner harmony of an individual's will and sensible appetites, when these are rightly ordered to the due end. Peace, second, consists in the union of appetites (desires and choices) among various persons; in this respect it goes by the name "concord" (*concordia*). Understood in this way, two basic forms of conflict (*dissensio*) are opposed to peace: the conflict a person experiences within himself and the conflict that arises when one or several persons are pitted against others. The latter sort of conflict is what stands contrary to concord (q. 29, a. 1, ad 3). Thomas takes care to point out (q. 29, a. 3, ad 2) that not just any sort of conflict is opposed to the concord of charity. Nothing hinders those who have charity from holding different opinions, nor, by consequence, is charitable concord disrupted by the incompatible desires that flow from these differing opinions.[22] Only disagreement about fundamental truths and a clash of wills regarding truly important projects are inconsistent with the demands of charity in this life.[23]

Thus, the vices listed in opposition to peace (*de vitiis oppositis paci*) represent causes of *destructive* conflict: inner sentiments or deeds that divide people with respect to fundamental goods. Each of these vices is defined by reference to the specific type of concord that it vitiates. Schism is "opposed to the spiritual unity of the multitude, namely ecclesiastical unity" (q. 42, a. 1, ad 2); strife is opposed to the private good (*bonum privatum*) by which several persons are joined together (q. 42, a. 2), while sedition is "opposed to the temporal or secular unity of the multitude, for instance of a city or a kingdom" (q. 42, a. 1, ad 2), which is "a fellowship recognized by law and for the common good" (q. 42, a. 2, citing St. Augustine, *De civitate Dei* 2.21). War, finally, disrupts the bond that unites

22. Similarly, Aquinas distinguishes (*STh* II-II, q. 42, a. 2, ad 2) between "discord from what is not evidently good" and "discord from what is evidently good." The first, he says, "may be without sin" and hence is compatible with the spiritual union of those who have charity, while the second "cannot be without sin" and is thus destructive of true concord. Cf. *STh* II-II, q. 37, a. 1.

23. Aquinas distinguishes between the "imperfect peace of the wayfarer" and the "state of perfect peace" in the next life ("wherein the truth will be known fully"). The first is consistent with a clash of opinions, the latter not (*STh* II-II, q. 29, a. 3, ad 2). The suggestion, then, is that we should not seek to achieve a total elimination of conflict in this life. That is attainable only in the next.

"one people to another [*quasi multitudinis ad multitudinem*]" (q. 42, a. 1), that is, the interrelationship of independent nations.

Adopting concord as the point of reference for the definition of conflict-causing vices is the methodological principle that explains why Thomas situates these vices in opposition to theological charity. A virtue that promotes friendship based on shared goods of the highest order (natural and supernatural), "charity directs many hearts together to one focal point, which is chiefly the divine good, secondarily the good of our neighbor." Hence, "concord results from charity [*concordia ex caritate causatur*]" (q. 37, a. 1). Drawing out the political implications of this view, Thomas affirms with Aristotle that civic friendship is the bond that holds political communities together (Aristotle, *Nicomachean Ethics* 8.1.1155a23–24; Aquinas, VIII *Ethic.* 1). Since concord (both within and among political communities) is akin to friendship, and because the chief cause of concord is charity ("secundum propriam rationem caritas pacem causat" [q. 29, a. 3, ad 3]), it follows that actions that intentionally disrupt concord are themselves opposed to charity.

The idea that peace (*qua* concord) is a positive reality that follows upon a shared sense of belonging, a union of the affections directed toward the common good, is what leads Aquinas to situate the opposing vices (war, sedition, strife, etc.) within the section of the *Summa* that deals with charity, rather than in the section on justice.[24] "Peace," he writes, "is the 'work of justice' *indirectly*, insofar as justice removes the obstacles to peace: but it is the work of charity *directly*. . . . For love is a unitive force" (q. 29, a. 3, ad 3).

Justice, focused as it is on what is due to the neighbor, hence upon the other precisely as *other*, is itself an insufficient ground for holding people together in political community. Union of the affections, an endur-

---

24. Aquinas's decision to discuss war within the treatise on charity has been criticized for overlooking the "objective" character of public right in favor of an emphasis on the "subjective" dimension of intention and conscience. Solages (1946: 18) writes, for instance, that Aquinas "se place au point de vue individual, subjectif, alors que le point de vue primordial est ici [le problème moral de la guerre] le point de vue social, objectif. Problème de droit naturel et, indirectement seulement, casuistique de péché." To emphasize the overarching importance of *ius naturale*, Solages recommends placing war within the treatise of justice, where the non-confessional (i.e., natural) and public dimension of decision making about war would be better recognized. In my judgment, however, this objection misidentifies Aquinas's reason for situating the question on bellum within the treatise on charity. The aim is not so much to consider how war making is a matter of personal conscience (for political leaders and soldiers), but rather to show how the highest good of the temporal order (civic communion within and among nations—a fruit of charity) is endangered by unjust resort to violence.

"Presumption against War" in Aquinas? 83

ing commitment to a shared project, is what makes possible the maintenance of civic concord over time. Whether such a civic *communio* is possible on a scale broader than an individual polity seems not to have been explicitly raised by Aquinas within the *Summa theologiae*.[25] However, the way that he sets up the respective definitions of sedition and war—the first violating the just concord of citizens within a single political community (an independent city or kingdom), the second violating the concord of two or more independent political communities—suggests that a certain idea of international order lies behind Thomas's theory of just war. It would not be long before such an idea received ample development at the hands of Dante, author of the *Monarchia*, albeit from a perspective very different from the one adopted by Thomas.[26]

In any event, we do occasionally find Aquinas drawing out practical implications from the view that civic concord results more formally from caritas than from justitia. For instance, he approves the practice of legislators who "have greater zeal for maintaining friendship among citizens than even justice itself which is sometimes omitted, for example, in the infliction of punishment, lest dissension be stirred up" (VIII *Ethic.* 1).[27] In so doing the aim, of course, is not simply to sacrifice the requirements of justice to charity but instead to remember how in the last analysis the first is ultimately ordained to the second: "lawmakers especially want this concord and eliminate from the citizenry the contention inimical to the well-being [*salutis*] of the civitas" (VIII *Ethic.* 1).

Richard Miller finds in this teaching on the subordination of justice to civic concord evidence for a "presumption against violence" in Thomas's doctrine of the just war. The author of *Interpretations of Conflict* explains that "the effect of this argument is to *restore* the presumption against vi-

---

25. Yet in his youthful *Commentary to the Sentences of Peter Lombard* (IV, d. 24, q. 3, a. 2, qc. 3co), Aquinas does allude in passing to this idea: "and between a single bishop and the Pope there are other grades of dignities corresponding to the grades of unions insofar as one congregation or community includes another one, as the community of a province includes the community of the city, and the community of the kingdom includes the community of the province, and the *community of the whole world* includes the community of a kingdom [*et communitas totius mundi communitatem unius regni*]."

26. The novelty of Aquinas's conception of international order is discussed by Haggenmacher (1983: 122–25). For a comparison between Aquinas and Dante on the question of war among nations, see Reichberg, 2002.

27. Aquinas's argumentation is reminiscent of the reasoning behind the establishment of a "Truth and Reconciliation Commission" in South Africa. The stated aim of the commission was to forgo strict criminal justice against persons implicated in the violent struggle for and against the apartheid regime, precisely in the interests of furthering civic reconciliation (on this, see Villa-Vicencio, 2000).

olence that is apparently compromised when Thomas grants the soldier the right to intentionally injure an opponent" (1991: 26). Without doubt, Miller has good reason to point out that just punishment is not for Thomas an unconditional good. Rather, in its application, this form of justice must be regulated in view of higher, more overarching goods—most especially the good of civic communion within and among nations. This would seem to be an elaboration on the standard criterion of *right intention* (already advanced by Augustine, Gratian, and Alexander of Hales). Taken alone, this does not indicate a special affinity between pacifist thinking and the just war tradition.

Miller's contention that the subordination of punishment to the broader goal of peace deserves to be called a "presumption against violence" hinges on his ancillary claim that, for Aquinas, just war is modeled on the idea of self-defense. Given the restrictions that medieval authors placed on self-defense (as opposed to offensive employments of force),[28] this interpretation has the effect of moving Aquinas toward the camp of the "presumption against war" theorists.

While conceding the faulty analogy between the two ideas of just war and self-defense—the former permits intentional killing while the latter does not—Miller nevertheless maintains that just war is, in Aquinas's view, an extension of the more basic idea of legitimate defense. In support of this, he cites *STh* II-II, q. 64, a. 7, where Aquinas writes that intentional killing may be allowed as a mode of self-defense when it is carried out by duly authorized representatives of the community (soldiers, for instance), acting for the benefit of the common good.[29] Miller takes Aquinas to be saying that "intentional harm must be ordered to the defense of the community, not the vindication of justice alone" (1991: 40).

Miller, however, extracts more from Aquinas's *articulum* than the text itself warrants. The comment that soldiers may deliberately kill in self-defense does not of itself imply that this is the sole basis on which they may be given moral license intentionally to harm enemy combatants. As Thomas later explains in question 108 on vengeance (*De vindicatione*), force may be used by civil authorities, not only that malefactors may be

---

28. See Reichberg, 2005: 341–70 for a presentation of the thirteenth-century canonists (Raymond of Peñafort and Innocent IV, in particular) on the limits of self-defense. These thinkers provided the theoretical background to Thomas's own treatment of this theme.

29. *STh* II-II, q. 64, a. 7: "[O]ccidere hominem non licet nisi publica auctoritate propter bonum commune."

restrained from disturbing the peace (legitimate defense narrowly defined), but for other purposes as well: correcting evildoers, restoring the order of justice, and so forth.[30] In sum, the treatment of self-defense in question 64, article 7 provides an insufficient foundation on which to build the claim that "killing another in self-defense, individual homicide, provides an analogy for evaluating the acts performed by the [legitimate] *authority*—the formal cause—in a just war" (Miller, 1991: 26).

Presumption for or against Armed Force?

Having considered Aquinas's rationale for raising the question of war in the context of sins opposed to charity, we need now to consider whether taken in itself this bespeaks an ethical presumption against the use of armed force. If bellum names a sin—and not a minor sin at that, but one standing in direct opposition to the highest and best of the virtues—then it would seem that any participation in war, even for the best of motives, would bear the stigma of moral disapprobation. This point of view seems reinforced by the title to the opening (and central) article of question 40 (*De bello*), which asks "whether waging war [*bellare*] is always [*semper*] a sin," thereby suggesting that those who engage in warlike conduct are nearly always in the wrong, and that the onus is on them to prove otherwise.

We have seen, however, that Aquinas does countenance the possibility of a just and even virtuous resort to arms; hence, the term *bellum* cannot of itself designate sinful behavior. By the same token, we should not be misled by the rather emphatic tone of the article's title, which was in fact introduced by an editor simply as the interrogative form of the first line of the article's first objection: "Videtur quod bellare semper sit peccatum."[31] A more accurate representation of the article's content may be gleaned

---

30. This is the list that appears in *STh* II-II, q. 108, a. 1: "Si vero intentio vindicantis feratur principaliter ad aliquod bonum, ad quod pervenitur per poenam peccantis, puta *ad emendationem peccantis,* vel saltem *ad cohibitionem eius et quietem aliorum,* et *ad iustitiae conservationem* et *Dei honorem,* potest esse vindicatio licita, aliis debitis circumstantiis servatis." It is true that Aquinas sometimes speaks of just war in terms of *"defending* the common good," as, for instance, in *STh* II-II, q. 123, a. 5: "Sed pericula mortis quae est in bellicis directe imminent homini propter aliquod bonum: inquantum scilicet *defendit bonum commune per iustum bellum."* Cf. *STh* II-II, q. 40, a. 1: "Ad [principes] pertinet rempublicam . . . tueri; licite *defendunt eam."* In these cases, however, *defensio* is construed broadly to include any use of force that promotes the common good, including the various motives for punishment mentioned above.

31. The original text of the *Summa theologiae* did not carry titles for each of the individual

from Thomas's own prologue to question 40, which tells us (less provocatively) that this article will discuss "whether any war can be permissible [*utrum aliquod bellum sit licitum*]." More specifically, from the context it is clear that the kind of war that Thomas has in mind is offensive, not defensive. He is asking whether it is ever licit to take the initiative in recurring to the sword. Here *licitum* refers to permissibility under divine and natural law; it was the standard term used by theologians and canon lawyers in evaluating actions with negative connotations.[32] To say without further qualification that a given act is permissible would express a minimal approval, not a strong endorsement, of the act in question. The "permissible" was thereby distinguished from the "meritorious."[33]

A question raised under the heading of licitum usually aimed to determine whether the act in question should, given its unfavorable connotations, be deemed morally wrongful in kind. To perform such a wrongful act would be sinful, hence impermissible, whatever the circumstances, consequences, or good intentions of the agent. Inversely, determination that a certain act is permissible (taken abstractly in its moral species) does not bring its ethical evaluation to a close, since *concretely*, in its actual performance, such an act will be further specified as good or bad by the end for the sake of which it is done (i.e., the end intended by the agent) and the circumstances under which it is carried out.[34]

---

articles. These titles were added by an early editor who simply reformulated as a question the first objection appearing in each article.

32. Alexander of Hales's *Summa* discussion of war begins with exactly the same question "utrum bellare sit licitum," but takes the "licitum" to cover divine and human positive law ("Bellare iuste secumdum legem divinam licitum est et etiam in praecepto regibus et principibus terrae," in Alexander of Hales, 1948, 4:683). This contrasts with Aquinas's subsequent discussion, which takes Scripture (divine law) and especially the natural moral law as its focus, with little or no reference to human laws. (Still, it must be admitted that Aquinas does not *expressly* refer to *ius naturale* or *ius gentium* in connection with the moral problem of war; Vitoria appears to have been the first explicitly to establish that link.)

33. An example would be Thomas's ethical analysis of trading for profit. In an article devoted to the question "whether it is ever permissible in trading to sell a thing for a higher price than was paid for it" (*STh* II-II, q. 77, a. 4), he points out that "gain [*lucrum*—earning a profit above costs] which is the end of trading, though not implying, by its nature, anything virtuous or necessary, does not, in itself [*in sui ratione*] connote anything sinful or contrary to virtue."

34. While Aquinas can acknowledge that certain acts are morally neutral in *kind* (*indifferens secundum suam speciem*—see *STh* I-II, q. 18, a. 8), he denies that any deliberate action actually instantiated in the world can be neutral with respect to its morality. On this, see *STh* I-II, q. 18, a. 9, especially ad 1, where he notes that although an act may be neutral in kind ("quia non habet ex sua specie quod sit bonus vel malus"), some other reason will nevertheless supervene to render it concretely good or bad ("unde per aliquid aliud potest fieri bonus vel malus"). Hence (*STh* I-II, q. 18, a. 9, ad 3), whenever "an end is intended by deliberate reason, it belongs either to the good of some virtue, or the evil of some vice." Cf. *De malo*, q. 2, aa. 4–5, for Aquinas's most detailed treatment of the technical distinctions between acts good and evil *ex genere*, *in specie*, and *secundum individuum*.

As we have seen, the acts evaluated in *STh* II-II, qq. 38–43 (contention, schism, war, strife, and sedition) are alike in that each involves the intentional disruption of concord. Of these, three—schism, strife, and sedition—are deemed wholly impermissible and hence evil in kind (*mala in sua specie*), because they entail direct opposition to legitimate authority, the condition sine qua non of concord. *Schism* violates the authority vested in St. Peter and his successors, *strife* usurps secular authority's exclusive prerogative vis-à-vis the imposition of punitive violence, while *sedition* severs the bond that unites the members of a civic multitude under their rightful rulers. Each of these three terms unequivocally names a sin; thus a negative moral appraisal is implied in their very meaning. In this sense there is a strong presumption against them. Hence, in contradistinction to the proper denotation of the term *war*, it would be oxymoronic to speak of a *just* schism, a *just* sedition, or a *just* strife. Schism divides the common spiritual good of the Church, sedition the common good of a temporal community, and in strife individuals wage a "kind of private war [*quoddam privatum bellum*]" (q. 41, a. 1)—which, since legitimate authority is lacking, is always sinful (*semper importat peccatum*). The positive counterparts recognized by Thomas for two of these terms go by other names: the forcible removal of tyrannical rulers (just insurrection), and legitimate self-defense.[35] Significantly, he refuses to acknowledge that just revolt and sedition are contraries within the same moral genus (the one commendable, the other bad). Instead he affirms that these are generically different kinds of moral acts: "[Seditio] ex suo genere est peccatum mortale" (q. 42, a. 2). In other words, he admits of no common genus that would be the referent for the single word *insurrectio*, a genus that could be further subdivided into the distinct species of just and unjust revolt. Likewise for strife.[36] Although Aquinas does not

---

35. "Illi vero qui bonum commune defendunt, eis resistentes [eos qui seditionem procurant], non sunt dicendi seditiosi: sicut nec illi qui se defendunt dicuntur rixosi" (*STh* II-II, q. 42, a. 2). Thomas explains in the response to the third objection that there is no sedition in disturbing (*perturbatio*) a tyrannical government, because "it is the tyrant rather who is guilty of sedition, since he encourages discord and sedition among his subjects, that he may lord over them more securely" (*STh* II-II, q. 42, a. 2, ad 3).

36. It is worth noting that Thomas presents his moral evaluation of theft along similar lines as strife and sedition. After explaining why it is that "every theft is a sin" (*STh* II-II, q. 66, a. 5), he goes on to say (*STh* II-II, q. 66, a. 7) that in moments of urgent and manifest need "it is permissible for a man to succor his own need by means of another's property; by taking it openly or secretly: nor is this properly speaking theft or robbery." In response to the third objection, Aquinas explains why "taking" in such circumstances does not count as "theft": "because that which a man takes for the support of his life *becomes his own property*

elaborate on the reasons for this semantic nuance, it would seem that this has something to do with the very exceptional character of the just revolt and private self-defense. The latter acts, while sometimes allowable in Thomas's eyes, still lack the sort of institutional recognition that had long been conferred upon preparedness for, and participation in, war. Moreover, in the few instances in which Aquinas acknowledges the permissibility of resort to arms against tyrannical rule,[37] he shows himself considerably more reserved than in his pronouncements on the just use of force against foreign enemies. In this respect Miller rightly points out that "Aquinas's order of charity entails a greater caution about resort to force *ad intra* than *ad extra*" (1991: 61).

Thus, unlike sedition and strife, in the manner of its signification "waging war" (bellare) is not inherently evil. What determines its specific morality is the existence or nonexistence of prior wrongdoing committed by another polity. War is evil in *species* when undertaken without a just warrant. In this respect the term functions in very much the same way as *sedition* or *strife*. Inversely, however, *war* may also be denoted good in *species* ("iustum bellum") when it is undertaken with due cause as a response to manifest injustice. Nevertheless, like all other acts good in kind (e.g., exercising professions such as teaching or healing), waging *just war* may become bad concretely (*secundum individuum*) by reason of the agent's wrongful intent, use of prohibited means, lack of due restraint, or in connection with improper circumstances.

Thus, if "presumption against" is taken to mean the recognition that an act is inherently wrongful in kind (i.e., it represents the violation of an exceptionless moral norm), then for Thomas there is no presumption against war, as there is a presumption against schism, strife, and sedition. On the other hand, if "presumption against" is taken to mean that the act in question requires justification, since it entails the deliberate infliction of pain and even death, then Thomas would acknowledge that there is a presumption against war, just as there is a presumption against the administration of any sort of penalty. Whenever punishment is meted out it must antecedently be established that it is in fact merited. In this respect

---

by reason of that need." Hence "theft," like "sedition," denotes an inherently wrongful act of which there can be no good kind.

37. Aquinas discusses rebellion against tyrannical rule on at least three occasions: in the *Sentences* commentary (II *Sent.* d. 44, q. 2, a. 2), in *De regimine principum* I, c. 6, and in *STh* II-II, q. 42, a. 2.

war stands apart from those acts of governance—giving speeches, setting up schools and hospitals, holding elections, reaching trade agreements, and so on—that do not presuppose prior wrongdoing by another party.

The conceptualization of just cause as a *response to prior wrongdoing* appears to be the factor that prompted Thomas to treat of war—including just war—within the context of sin. War springs from sin and is itself always sinful on the part of at least one of the belligerents involved in the conflict. Thus, if *war* is understood to signify a situation of violent conflict in which two (or more) polities contend violently against each other, then by its very meaning it connotes a sinful state of affairs. For this reason Thomas classifies war under the heading of sin or vice, and in this respect he would agree that there is a strong presumption against it.[38]

If, by contrast, the term *war* is no longer taken to denote the situation in which two or more belligerents direct armed force against each other (bellum), but instead designates one side's engagement in the war (bellare), then it can serve to signify a meritorious pursuit.[39] Such an activity will be justifiable only when undertaken as a response to the other party's violation of a true concord.[40] For this reason even the notion of a just

---

38. Cf. Miller, 1991: 60: "For both Aquinas and Augustine the notions of tranquillity and concord establish a presumption against conflict, for conflict is a symptom of unsatisfied ambition, contrary to the elementary inclinations of nature and the infusion of charity." Correct in the main, Miller does, however, overstate this point somewhat, since for Thomas it is not true that all conflicts arise from personal sin but only those conflicts in which "a man knowingly and intentionally dissents from the Divine good and his neighbor's good, to which he ought to consent" (*STh* II-II, q. 37, a. 1). Hence, a certain amount of conflict can arise between even good and virtuous individuals: "such like discord is neither sinful nor against charity, unless it be accompanied by an error about things necessary to salvation, or by undue obstinacy" (*STh* II-II, q. 37, a. 1). On the other hand, Miller is correct in his assessment that for Augustine and Aquinas "[c]onflict does not structure historical change or social relations as it does for more radical thinkers in modern Catholicism" (1991: 60).

39. In the course of explaining why active participation in war is not permitted of clerics, Thomas remarks that this *activity*, when undertaken by laymen, may, in fact, be virtuous: "Ad quartum dicendum quod, licit *exercere bella iusta sit meritorium*, tamen illicitum redditur clericis propter hoc quod sunt ad opera magis meritoria deputati" (*STh* II-II, q. 40, a. 2, ad 4). He goes on to compare the waging of just war to matrimony: although the latter, like the former, is meritorious, "it becomes reprehensible in those who have vowed virginity, because they are bound [*obligationem*] to a greater good" (*STh* II-II, q. 40, a. 2, ad 4).

40. Thomas distinguishes between true concord and the appearance of concord: it is always wrong to disturb the first, but sometimes right to oppose the second. Thus, "those who wage war justly aim at peace; thus they are not opposed to peace, except to an evil peace [*ita paci non contrariantur nisi malae*]" (*STh* II-II, q. 40, a. 1, ad 3). Cf. *STh* II-II, q. 29, a. 2, ad 3: "[P]ax vera non potest esse nisi in bonis et bonorum. Pax autem quae malorum et, est pax apparens et non vera." In saying that peace is "only in good men and about good things," Thomas is thereby indicating that (1) peace is a positive reality, hence much more than the simple absence of armed conflict, and (2) peace is a normative, not merely an empirical concept—it describes a state of societal agreement about goods that truly befit human dignity.

war receives treatment within a set of questions devoted to sins against concord. Understanding this point defuses the seeming paradox of a *De bello* purportedly about sin (given its positioning in the *Summa theologiae*), but which in fact concentrates upon the characteristics of the just war. Consequently, taken in itself, Thomas's decision to discuss military might within the context of sins against charity evinces no special presumption against the justified use of such force within the temporal sphere.[41]

It is true that the doctrine of *raison d'état* (present in ancient Rome and again in late Renaissance and early modern Europe)[42] fostered a conception of war severed from any necessary link with just cause; war was viewed as simply another way to advance the national interest, subject only to narrow prudential concerns, and thus required no special moral justification. Yet this is not a view endorsed by any just war theorists today, certainly not Paul Ramsey or Johnson, who would agree that there is indeed a "presumption against war" if this expression is understood to mean that war is warranted only as a response to another state's wrongdoing. Much of the debate regarding whether there is a presumption against war accordingly centers on the question of how broadly or restrictively the notion of just cause ought to be construed. All just war theorists, whichever side of this debate they happen to be on, concur that *in se* the use of armed force by legitimate governments is not morally wrongful.[43] This is what divides just war thinking from the various forms

---

41. In his recent treatment of this theme Miller (2002: 183) maintains that the precise list of objections selected by Aquinas in II-II, q. 40, a. 1, indicates how the "value of non-violence, not the virtue of justice, generates the intellectual clearing within which he develops his inquiry." By contrast, I would prefer to say that Aquinas's selection of objections in the *De bello* is oriented around the need, given its placement in the *Summa*, to show how participation in war is not fundamentally incompatible with the inner dispositions required of us by the virtue of charity. Given this task, it was natural that Aquinas would look to the sort of claims advanced by Christian pacifists. Of itself, this argumentative strategy evinces no special presumption against participation in war.

42. On the similarities between ancient Roman and Renaissance political realism, see Tuck, 1999.

43. Johnson seems to attribute to his opponents in the "presumption against war" debate the view that the current use of military force is intrinsically wrongful (and hence a tacit pacifism) when he writes that for them "war in its contemporary form is inherently suspect" (1996: 30). Since none of the proponents of the presumption thesis actually embrace this view, in this regard Johnson would appear to have created a straw man. However, if by "war" Johnson is referring most especially to *offensive* (not defensive) military engagements (this is suggested by the overall context of his argument), then he does appear to have given an accurate representation of the other side's position. Many "presumption against war" theorists do in fact restrict the valid use of military force to defensive operations only, thereby banning as *per se mala* all offensive operations (see 31–33).

of principled pacifism, just as, inversely, the moral requirement of just cause sets it apart from all forms of realpolitik.

I have now discussed two versions of the "presumption against war" thesis: first, the view that waging war is evil per se; second, the view that it is legitimate only when undertaken as a limited response to another regime's wrongdoing. The first is equivalent to pacifism and is rejected by Thomas. The second is accepted by all just war theorists, including Thomas, and is not under contention in the presumption debate. A third view, according to which war is a sinful state of affairs that arises from a violation of justice and charity, may also be found in Thomas. To his mind, this is fully compatible with the idea of a just war, since it is altogether possible for the burden of guilt to rest squarely with one of the belligerents and the cause of justice squarely with the other. However, for some recent just war theorists, the equation of war with a sinful state of affairs has called into question any clear-cut distinction between just and unjust protagonists in war. This has led to the introduction of a criterion of "comparative justice," according to which "neither side has a monopoly on absolute justice in defense of its claims" (Miller, 1991: 105). Emphasizing the distortions that result from "partisan perceptions,"[44] proponents of this criterion present it as a much-needed corrective to the national self-interest of statesmen. Placed among the list of ius ad bellum criteria, the admonition to relativize one's own claims to justice will certainly function as a presumption against war, since "if both sides in a conflict appear to have just cause, then the tradition would enjoin them not to fight; that is, it would see ambiguity itself as a restriction on *ius ad bellum*, the very right to go to war" (Johnson, 1996: 30).

Johnson argues that the idea of simultaneous ostensible justice—the *perception* of justice at both sides at once—was never intended in classical just war teaching to serve as a criterion to be adverted to in deliberations over the resort to force (ius ad bellum). Rather, it was a rule to be applied within the context of an armed conflict already under way, "as a base for more attention to restraint in war, thus feeding the development of the *ius in bello*."[45] Johnson accordingly finds in this doctrine no theoretical basis for a presumption against war.

---

44. This expression is borrowed from Fisher and Brown, 1988: 25–26.
45. In NCCB, 1983: 29, the American Catholic bishops do in fact place their discussion of comparative justice within the section of their pastoral letter entitled "Ius ad Bellum."

It goes without saying that Aquinas himself never spoke in terms of "simultaneous ostensible justice." This doctrine has a more recent provenance; it appears to have been first articulated by Vitoria in his *De Indis*.[46] It is a matter of some dispute whether this innovation is consistent with Thomas's normative discussion of war.[47] At the very least, the logic of Thomas's argumentation leaves little doubt that he would have denied the possibility of simultaneous *objective* justice in war, at least within the order of (what we now call) the ius ad bellum. Whether Thomas exhibited greater optimism than his successors in the just war tradition (who embraced the idea of simultaneous *ostensible* justice) regarding the ability of political and military leaders to make objective judgments about matters of right and wrong, especially where the well-being of their own polity is at stake, cannot be decided here.[48]

Contemporary writers who approach the ethics of war from a pacifist outlook often express a deep skepticism about the readiness of political decision makers to pay more than lip service to objective justice. It is taken for granted that the moral judgments of statesmen are inherently biased in favor of their nations' interests, so that the language of just war, while perhaps abstractly meaningful, in the heat of action does little more than express self-serving views about what is right and wrong. To its opponents (e.g., Johnson), the addition of "comparative justice" to the list of just war criteria, in support of an alleged presumption against war, thus smacks of a misguided compromise with a traditional plank in the pacifist argumentation—the so-called venality of princes (or later, the venality of the nation-state).

Aquinas was not unaware of the dynamics of bias in human judgment. Commenting on the Aristotelian adage "such as a man is such does the good appear to him" (*qualisquidem igitur sibi unusquisque est, talis et fi-*

---

46. See in particular his *Relectio de Indis*, I.3.5 (in Vitoria, 1967: 85). Cf. Johnson, 1975: 185–95. Disagreeing with Johnson's reading of Vitoria, Haggenmacher (1992: 442) argues that Vitoria's recognition of simultaneous justice "remains marginal and does not really affect the unilateral character of the rights conferred by just war. Attempts to see a humanization of war in this limited recognition of bilateral rights of war are misguided."

47. Some authors (e.g., Vanderpol, 1925: 255–85) have held that the doctrine of simultaneous ostensible justice ("probabilism") is at bottom incompatible with Aquinas's argumentation on the punitive character of just war. Others (e.g., Regout, 1935: 25–30, 91–93, 182–85) maintain that this doctrine represents an organic development, not a repudiation of Aquinas's earlier views.

48. For some indications on how such a comparison might proceed, see Reichberg, 2002: 32–34.

nis videtur ei), he recognized how interests, particularly self-interest, can distort our moral perceptions of right and wrong, particularly when those perceptions are made to inform our concrete choices.[49] His remedy to the problem of bias was not to recommend a process of moral judgment purged of all passion, desire, and self-interest but rather to insist on the importance of educating the passions rightly, since well-ordered passions conduce to true judgments. This obtains most especially within that exercise of practical reason that he terms *deliberation:* the process of mental reflection that terminates in a decision about what ought to be done. Deliberating well, such that the choices one makes reflect the true order of justice, is, in his view, the combined fruit of mental skill and moral uprightness (well-ordered passions). This, in his lexicon, goes by the name *prudentia,* of which *prudentia regnativa* is the special variant for individuals holding positions of political authority.

The prudence of governance will be particularly needful whenever decisions are made concerning the resort to armed force, because in this instance statesmen encounter demands, interests, and passions of the most intense sort. It is easy for a political leader to reach the conclusion that justice is on his side; even corrupt leaders sometimes believe that, perhaps even sincerely. For this reason, Aquinas challenges politicians to cultivate the inner virtues of character from which *sound* moral judgments about war can spring.

In this connection he remarks that taking due care to judge fairly (inwardly in thought, outwardly in words) of someone else's character and actions (including, presumably, the character and actions of another polity and its leaders) is itself an obligation of justice.[50] Thomas warns against being overly suspicious, as "when a man, from slight indications, esteems another man's wickedness as certain" (*STh* II-II, q. 60, a. 3). "Consequently, unless we have evident indications of a person's wickedness, we ought to deem him good by interpreting for the best whatever is doubtful about him" (*STh* II-II, q. 60, a. 4). Thomas tempers this

---

49. III *Ethic.* 13., to Aristotle, *Nicomachean Ethics* 3.13.1114b. Cf. *STh* II-II, q. 60, a. 3: "everyone easily believes what he desires [*unusquisque faciliter credit quod appetit*]."

50. Judgment (*iudicium*), which denotes a determination about what is just, is itself an act pertaining to the virtue of justice; see *STh* II-II, q. 60, a. 1, ad 4. In article 2 of the same question, Thomas lays out three conditions that are requisite for a judgment to be an act of justice: "first, that it proceed from the inclination of justice [*ex inclinatione justitiae*], second, that it emanate from one who is in authority; third, that it be pronounced according to the right ruling of prudence. If any of these be lacking, the judgment will be faulty and illicit."

comment, however, by noting that "when we have to apply a remedy to some evil, whether our own or another's, in order for the remedy to be applied with greater certainty of a cure, it is expedient to take the worst for granted, since if a remedy be efficacious against a worse evil, much more is it efficacious against a lesser evil" (*STh* II-II, q. 60, a. 4, ad 3).Significant here is the importance Aquinas attributes to an ethics of judgment within his theory of prudence. Presumably this ethics obtains not just in private life but also within that part of prudentia that is concerned with statecraft. Although he does not necessarily recommend the cultivation of self-doubt vis-à-vis one's own claims to justice (in this respect the proponents of "comparative justice" go well beyond what he would demand), Thomas does nevertheless affirm that these claims should always be weighed by reference to the moral dictates of natural and positive law (*STh* II-II, q. 60, a. 5). To judge otherwise would amount to an arbitrary usurpation of authority (*STh* II-II, q. 60, a. 6). Thus, the moral virtue of justice—"the perpetual and constant will to render to each one his law"—should inform political decision making, most particularly in those heated moments when political leaders formulate their grievances against other states.

We have just seen how one line of "presumption" reasoning emphasizes the inherently biased character of political decision making about war. Another line of argument, by contrast, emphasizes the grave pressures that ordinary soldiers undergo in the heat of battle. It is alleged that the violent nature of military combat renders such action a poor instrument for the prosecution of justice. The point is not so much that the resort to lethal force is inherently wrongful in itself. Rather, it is held that even when its use is justified, the application of lethal force initiates a dialectic of violence that undermines the very goal of justice it purports to serve. Hence, resort to armed force is deemed illicit in all but the most egregious circumstances. Johnson objects to this kind of argumentation on grounds that it "effectively destroys the logic of just-war theory by putting *ius in bello* above *ius ad bellum*" and in so doing "it gives pride of place to judgments about contingent conditions over obligations inherent in moral duty" (1996: 33).

What of Thomas Aquinas? Did he believe that warfare (by its very nature) bears an inherent tendency to excess—even when undertaken with the best of intentions for the sake of a just cause? In the context where one would most expect him to raise the issue of participation in wartime violence—*STh* II-II, q. 40, a. 2, "Whether it is lawful for clerics and bishops to fight"—he is surprisingly silent on this score. Only two arguments are given to support the conclusion that warlike pursuits are incompatible with the priestly calling. First, such pursuits "are full of unrest [*maximas inquietudines habent*], so that they greatly hinder the mind from the contemplation of divine things." This impediment is not proper to war, for, as he points out, commercial enterprises (*negotiationes*) are forbidden to clerics for the very same reason. Second, since wars are directed to the shedding of blood (*ordinantur ad sanguinis effusionem*), fighting in them is incompatible with the sacramental imitation of Christ (who freely gave himself up as a victim) incumbent upon the priestly function. Nowhere in this article does Thomas emphasize the special moral dangers attendant upon an active engagement in the violence of war. On the contrary, he makes a point of stating that "clerics are forbidden to take up arms, not as though it were a sin [*non enim interdicitur eis bellare quia peccatum sit*], but only because it is incongruent with the requirements of their profession" (*STh* II-II, q. 40, a. 2, ad 3). Indeed, the obligation of clerics to abstain from actual fighting does not preclude any participation whatsoever in war: prelates may utilize "spiritual weapons" (*spiritualibus armis*) to oppose the pillagers (*raptoribus*) and tyrants (*tyrannis*) who wreak bodily harm on their flock (*STh* II-II, q. 40, a. 2, ad 1); "as they may direct [*disponere*] and urge [*inducere*] other men to wage just wars [*ad bellandum bella iusta*]" (*STh* II-II, q. 40, a. 2, ad 3).

Thomas seems more worried about the spiritual dangers endemic to the life of the tradesman than about the moral risks of the military profession. While acknowledging that a profit may legitimately be earned in the exchange of goods, and hence that such trading is not inherently wrongful, he nevertheless contends that to devote one's life to this pursuit "has a certain debasement attaching thereto [*quandam turpitudinem habet*]" (*STh* II-II, q. 77, a. 4). Because commerce for profit lacks a virtuous or necessary end, it carries a built-in propensity to immoderation: "it satisfies the desire for gain which knows no limit and tends to infinity [*in infinitum tendit*]" (*STh* II-II, q. 77, a. 4).

Responding affirmatively to the question whether trading should be forbidden to clerics (*STh* II-II, q. 77, a. 4, obj. 3), Thomas makes the already familiar point about this activity being an obstacle to contemplation ("engages the mind too much in worldly cares") and then provides two additional arguments: "Clerics should abstain not only from things that are evil in themselves, but even from those that have an *appearance of evil*. This happens in trading, both because it is directed to worldly gain, which clerics should despise, and because *trading is open to many vices*." Significantly, no such reasons are advanced in his earlier (*STh* II-II, q. 40) treatment of the military calling. Thomas seems to exhibit much less worry about the spiritual dangers of war than does, for example, St. Augustine.[51]

Conclusion

I began this chapter by asking whether support could be found in the writings of Thomas Aquinas for the idea that there is a presumption against war. This led me to analyze the different meanings that this idea has come to have in the eyes of its contemporary exponents. I have been most intent on highlighting those meanings of the presumption thesis that render it a distinctive trend within present-day just war thinking. Seeking points of dialogue with the pacifist tradition, presumption theorists emphasize (1) a restrictive reading of the ius ad bellum, a reading that by and large limits it to defensive war; (2) the priority of interstate reconciliation over the punishment of injustice; (3) a skepticism regarding the ability of statesmen to make objective determinations of justice; (4) an endorsement of the criterion of "comparative justice"; and (5) the inherent propensity of violence, even when it is used for the sake of a just cause, to exceed the measure of moral virtue. Friends of the "presumption against injustice" thesis generally seek to establish points of contact with the tradition of political realism, and in so doing reject most of the points just mentioned, with the exception of (2).

My review of Aquinas's writings has revealed numerous affinities with the "presumption against injustice" side of the contemporary debate. Proponents of this view have found in his treatment support for the idea that military preparedness, even in peacetime, should be part of the nor-

---

51. For an illustration of Augustine's rather somber assessment of the moral hazards of participation in war, see *Contra Faustum* 22: "What is it about war that is to be blamed? ... The desire for harming, the cruelty of revenge, the restless and implacable mind, the savageness of revolting, the lust for dominating, and similar things—these are what are justly blamed in war" (in Augustine, 1994: 221–22).

mal functioning of government. Likewise, Thomas's idea that just war provides a setting for the exercise of moral virtue gives impetus to those who would view military life as an authentic profession. And finally, his allowance of offensive war, undertaken to repair the violation of justice, has provided inspiration to those who would apply military force not only for national self-defense, but for humanitarian purposes as well.[52]

52. The 1990s showed a resurgence of support for military initiatives ("humanitarian interventions") on behalf of third parties, of the sort undertaken in Somalia, Bosnia, and Kosovo. For an argument in favor of this mode of military action, considered precisely as a form of offensive war, see Reichberg and Syse, 2002. A review of ethical debate on this topic, with reference to Aquinas and other Scholastics, may be found in Fixdal and Smith, 1998.

REFERENCES

Albert the Great. 1890–99 *Opera Omnia.* 38 vols. Ed. A. Borgnet. Paris: Vives.
Alexander of Hales. 1924–48. *Summa theologica.* 4 vols. Florence: Quaracchi.
Augustine. 1994. *Political Writings.* Ed. E. L. Fortin and D. Kries. Trans. M. W. Tkacz and D. Kries. Indianapolis: Hackett.
Boyle, Joseph M. Jr. 1978. "*Praeter Intentionem* in Aquinas." *Thomist* 42: 649–65.
Childress, James F. 1980. "Just-War Criteria." In Thomas A. Shannon, ed., *War or Peace? The Search for New Answers.* Maryknoll, N.Y.: Orbis, 40–58.
Coste, René. 1962. *Le problème du droit de guerre dans la pensée de Pie XII.* Paris: Aubier.
Ehrlich, Ludwik. 1961. "Guillaume de Rennes et les origines de la science du droit de la guerre." In *Mélanges Gidel.* Paris: Sirey, 215-27.
Finnis, John. 1998. *Aquinas: Moral, Political, and Legal Theory.* Oxford: Oxford University Press.
Fisher, R., and S. Brown. 1988. *Getting Together: Building Relationships as We Negotiate.* New York: Penguin.
Fixdal, M., and D. Smith. 1998. "Humanitarian Intervention and Just War." *Mershon International Studies Review* 42: 283–312.
Haggenmacher, Peter. 1983. *Grotius et la doctrine de la guerre juste.* Paris: Presses Universitaires de France.
———. 1992. "Just War and Regular War in Sixteenth Century Spanish Doctrine." *International Review of the Red Cross* 290: 434–45.
Johnson, James Turner. 1973. "Toward Reconstructing the *Ius ad Bellum.*" *Monist* 57: 461–88.
———. 1975. *Ideology, Reason, and the Limitation of War: Religious and Secular Concepts, 1200–1740.* Princeton: Princeton University Press.
———. 1996. "The Broken Tradition." *National Interest* 27–36.
Miller, Richard B. 1991. *Interpretations of Conflict: Ethics, Pacifism, and the Just-War Tradition.* Chicago: University of Chicago Press.
———. 2002. "Aquinas and the Presumption against Killing in War." *Journal of Religion* 82: 173–204.
NCCB (National Conference of Catholic Bishops). 1983. *The Challenge of Peace: God's Promise and Our Response.* Washington, D.C.: United States Catholic Conference.
Ramsey, Paul. 1968. *The Just War.* New York: Scribner.
Regout, Robert. 1935. *La doctrine de la guerre juste de saint Augustin à nos jours d'après les théologiens et les canonistes catholiques.* Paris: A. Pedone.
Reichberg, Gregory M. 2002. "Just War or Perpetual Peace?" *Journal of Military Ethics* 1: 16–35.

———. 2005. "Aquinas on Defensive Killing: A Case of Double-Effect?" *Thomist* 69: 341–70.
Reichberg, Gregory M., and Henrik Syse. 2002. "Humanitarian Intervention: A Case of Offensive Force?" *Security Dialogue* 33: 219–33.
Reichberg, Gregory M., Henrik Syse, and Endre Begby, eds. 2006. *The Ethics of War: Classic and Contemporary Readings*. Oxford: Blackwell.
Russell, Frederick. 1975. *The Just War in the Middle Ages*. Cambridge: Cambridge University Press.
Solages, Bruno de, Mgr. 1946. *La théologie de la guerre juste*. Paris: Desclée de Brouwer.
Synan, Edward A. 1988. "St. Thomas Aquinas and the Profession of Arms." *Medieval Studies* 50: 404–37.
Thomas Aquinas. 1895. *Sancti Thomae Aquinatis Doctoris Angelici Opera Omnia iussu impensaque Leonis XIII*. Rome: Editori di san Tommaso.
Tuck, Richard. 1999. *The Rights of War and Peace*. Oxford: Oxford University Press.
Vanderpol, Alfred. 1925. *La doctrine scolastique du droit de guerre*. Paris: A. Pedone.
Villa-Vicencio, Charles. 2000. "Restorative Justice: Dealing with the Past Differently'" In C. Villa-Vicencio and W. Verwoerd, eds., *Looking Back, Reaching Forward: Reflections on the Truth and Reconciliation Commission of South Africa*. Cape Town: University of Cape Town Press, 68–76.
Vitoria, Francisco de. 1967. *Relectio de Indis*. Ed. L. Pereña and J. M. Pérez Prendes. Corpus Hispanorum de Pace 5. Madrid: Consejo Superior de Investigaciones Científicas.
———. 1981. *Relectio de iure belli; o, Paz dinámica*. Ed. L. Pereña, V. Abril, C. Baciero, A. García, and F. Maseda. Corpus Hispanorum de Pace 6. Madrid: Consejo Superior de Investigaciones Científicas.
Winwright, Tobias L. 1998. "Two Rival Versions of Just War Theory and the Presumption against Harm in Policing." In J. Kelsay and S. B. Twiss, eds., *The Annual of the Society of Christian Ethics*, vol. 18. Chicago: Society of Christian Ethics, 221–39.

6

Poets and Politics

Just War in Geoffrey Chaucer and Christine de Pizan

KATE L. FORHAN

> *There never was a good war, or a bad peace.*
> Benjamin Franklin

During the Middle Ages, traditions of blood feud, desires for conquest and power, and even the chivalric code of honor intensified the frequency and legitimacy of war. Yet war as an inescapable fact of life does not diminish the desire for peace; in fact it may intensify our human sense of its value. Because conflict was so terribly damaging to land and lives in medieval Europe, ensuring peace often meant controlling war, or at least some of the negative and destructive by-products of the seemingly interminable hostilities. Consequently, the desire for peace in the Middle Ages was intimately related to the development of the concept of the "just war."

Generally, in medieval political theory, there are two major threads that concern those writing on war and its rationale. The first, *ius ad bellum*, addresses the justification for war. In traditional theory, one may go to war if three conditions are present. First, the perpetrator must have the authority to wage war, or *auctoritas*. Second, the war leader must have an appropriate reason or goal to accomplish, or *causa*; and finally, he, his soldiers, and other combatants must have a correct interior disposition or intention, *recta intentio,* such as, for example, to do justice, rather than merely to take revenge. Traditionally, authority is limited to the emperor, because, at least hypothetically, all other rulers have recourse to him for redress of grievances. A "liberal minority," according to Jonathan Barnes, gave that authority to kings as well (1984: 771–84).

The second major thread, *ius in bello,* prescribes the conduct of war. Clearly, there is a relationship between how a war is fought and one's intentions, but ius in bello goes beyond the stipulation of attitudes of justice and fairness. Rather, it grew out of the confluence of the evolving chivalric code and the intentionalist ethics of Christianity elaborated by the *curiales* who, beginning in the eleventh century, had to reconcile their religious training with the values of the courts in which they served. Encouraged by the presence of powerful women at court, such as Eleanor of Aquitaine and Marie de Champagne, this ethic of courtliness involved not only behavior—elegance, politeness, and comportment—but also qualities of generosity, compassion, and protection of the weak. Thus the conduct of warriors was, on the one hand, to include military efficiency, loyalty, and prowess, and on the other, benevolence, charity, and safeguarding noncombatants.

It is often believed that the development of these and other medieval political ideas was the province either of clerics and Scholastics or of the aristocracy. Equally a part of the conventional understanding is the view that these rules of conduct were completely divorced both in their origins and in their application from ordinary people. Laypersons were not particularly heeded in the development of medieval political ideas in general and certainly had no influence on the conduct of war. Indeed, often the only role for the third and least important of the three orders, "those who work," was simply to pay their taxes and suffer the consequences that befell noncombatants in medieval wars. For the most part, they suffered in silence. If the burden became too great, there might be a peasant revolt, as in England under Wat Tyler, or an explosion of the urban artisanate, as in Paris under butcher Simon Caboche, but unless the ruling classes suffered the consequences, they generally ignored these injustices. While this stereotypical view was probably never entirely accurate, by the fourteenth century social, economic, and political stresses were profoundly challenging the conventions in almost every aspect of life. In particular, the evolution of lay criticism of the ruling classes is one of the most remarkable developments of the later Middle Ages. The obligation to instruct rulers had long been the province of clerics writing in the traditional genre of the mirror for princes, but in the fourteenth century poets began to take on this advisory role.

The works of two contemporaneous vernacular poets will demonstrate both the force and the courage of these voices who dared to criticize the conduct of government and to elaborate their own views of war. The first of these writers is Geoffrey Chaucer, whose "Tale of Melibee" provides a scathing critique of the normal process of deliberation by which wars were declared and then moves to instruct the prince on the appropriate use of advisory councils, concluding in the end that no war is sensible. The second voice is that of Christine de Pizan, who criticizes the blind and irresponsible behavior of the French royal family in *Lamentation on the Evils of Civil War* and then, in a contemporaneous work, *The Book of Deeds of Arms and of Chivalry*, expounds a theory of just war. Both were members of the increasingly articulate "middle class" of the late medieval period, which began to demand the laicization of politics.

The Historical Context: The Hundred Years' War

The Hundred Years' War grew out of the confluence of economic, social, and dynastic crises that were affecting both England and France between the late thirteenth and the mid-fifteenth centuries. The ostensible cause of the war was the dynastic challenge presented to the throne of France by the death of Charles IV without a direct male heir. Charles's nearest male relative was his sister Isabella's son, who at fourteen had become Edward III of England. Yet, while by English custom women could inherit the throne, by French tradition they could not. At the time of his death in 1328, Charles had named his cousin, Philip of Valois, to be regent in case his then-unborn child was male, but he stipulated that Philip would become king if the infant was a girl. The child was indeed female, and Philip was subsequently crowned king. At twenty-five, in the eleventh year of his own reign, Edward III made his claim to be king of France by virtue of his mother's birth. Philip VI responded by confiscating Aquitaine as punishment for rebellion against an overlord. Edward invaded France, touching off a century of conflict and civil war. The first stage of the war was a disaster for France. The French nobility was decimated at the battles of Crecy (1346) and Poitiers (1356), and then the French were ultimately humiliated when King John of France (r. 1350–64) was captured and carried off to England. The ensuing crisis and confusion included a peasant revolt against high taxes and the losses of war, marauding bands of soldiers terrorizing the people, and greedy nobles trying to extend their privileges. Even attempts by the Estates General to control abuses and reform taxes threatened the authority of the young regent, John's son Charles. John's release was finally negotiated in 1360 in exchange for Aquitaine and 3 million gold ecus, but complications returned John to English hands and he died in 1364, with the treaty never enacted.

The intelligent and responsible reign of his son, Charles V (r. 1364–80), allowed a brief recovery, but was followed by confusion and a struggle for power when he died in September 1380, leaving his heir, Charles VI (r. 1380–1422) not quite twelve years old. The king had named his own brother, Louis, Duke of Anjou (d. 1384), to be regent for the young king, while two of the boy's other relatives, the dukes of Burgundy and Bourbon, were to be his guardians. John, Duke of Berry, with no official role as regent or guardian, was nonetheless a significant participant in any decision making since he controlled about a third of France through his own estates. Although the young prince managed to escape the legal control of his uncles once he became an adult, he could not elude their machinations and ambition, and he was very much under the influence of his younger and more able brother, Louis, Duke of Orleans. The chaos was compounded when in 1392 the twenty-four-year-old king suffered his first attack of insanity, which afflicted him periodically for the rest of his life. The growing disability of Charles VI trapped France between the two powerful personalities of the king's younger brother, Louis, Duke of Orleans, and his uncle, Philip "the Bold," Duke of Burgundy, and after Philip's death in 1404, that of his son, John "the Fearless." The gap between the royal houses widened until on November 23, 1407, Louis of Orleans was murdered by an assassin, Raoul d'Anquentonville, who had been hired by John the Fearless. Despite John's role in the assassination, his power was so strong that the duke was later pardoned by the king. The widowed Duchess of Orleans found support and protection for her young son, Charles of Orleans, in the brutal Bernard, Count of Armagnac, who was now the leader of the opposition to Duke John of Burgundy.

Things were not much better in England, where relations between Edward III and his heir, Richard II, and the Lancastrian branch of the royal family were growing increasingly tense. The ensuing conflict would ultimately lead to the usurpation of the throne by Lancastrian Henry IV and the assassination of Richard and many of his supporters. This conflict between the York and Lancastrian factions of the royal family would also lead to civil war, not to be resolved until the end of the fifteenth century and the accession to the throne of the founder of the Tudor dynasty, Henry VII, whose success was marred by the dead left in his wake. The death of Richard II in 1400, the adventurism of Henry IV and his need for additional revenue, and the growing national spirit of the English clashed with French attempts at aggrandizement and protection of commercial interests. Moreover, the papal schism from 1378 to 1417 had left Europe without an acceptable mediator, and in fact each of the papal rivals encouraged the nation supporting him—Urban VI for the English and Clement VII for the French.

The quarrels, ambitions, greed, and self-interest exhibited by the members of the French royal family throughout this period brought the nation to civil war and impoverished it with heavy taxation. The political bankruptcy of the French nobility was further demonstrated when the Burgundians and the Armagnacs each made overtures to the English, hoping to have their help to destroy the other. The English king, Henry V (r. 1413–22) had his own agenda—to seize the throne of France—and he invaded in 1415, crushing the French army at Agincourt. Rather than rallying to defend the kingdom, the Burgundians continued to fight the Armagnacs, openly allying themselves with the English in 1420. The alliance allowed the English to impose the Treaty of Troyes on the French king, Charles VI, which made Henry V regent of France whenever the king was incapacitated by his mental illness as well as making Henry heir to the throne. This effectively disinherited the dauphin, Charles of Guyenne, third and now only living son of Charles VI. But both Henry V and Charles VI died in 1422, leaving Henry's infant son, Henry VI, nominally king of France and England.

In the meantime, the son of Charles VI had been a virtual prisoner of the Armagnacs in the south of France, without a hope of rule, until the inspiration of seventeen-year-old Joan of Arc rallied the dispirited French to win the battle of Orleans in 1429, the first French victory for many years. Soon after, he was crowned Charles VII and the French were encouraged to retake their cities. Joan's capture by the Burgundians and her subsequent trial and execution for heresy at the hands of the English in 1431 further inspired the French to continue until final victory in 1453.

This dynastic quarrel was compounded by other events. In both England and France, decades of famine and disease had reduced the population by as much as half, with tremendous psychological, social, and economic consequences. The turbulence and disintegration of the monarchies in both England and in France brought a general lawlessness, and in France in particular encouraged wandering bands of soldiers to despoil the peasantry. The Great Schism further dispirited the people and left no institution with either the moral authority or the political power to arbitrate between the warring parties. It is thus within this context of war, fragmentation, loss of moral authority, and general chaos that Geoffrey Chaucer and Christine de Pizan raised their prophetic voices.

Chaucer and "The Tale of Melibee"

Geoffrey Chaucer is considered to be the first poet of the English language and is even today considered to be its most influential. Born about 1340 in the city of London, son of a wine merchant, he was resoundingly middle class. He entered into court service as a page in 1357, serving in the military from 1359 until his capture by the French in 1360, from which he was ransomed in March of the same year. After a few years' gap in the records, he reemerges in 1367 as a member of the household of King Edward III. By 1370 he was engaged in significant diplomatic work for the king, making trips to various cities in Italy and France over a ten-year period, and in 1374 he was appointed comptroller of customs for the port of London. After Edward's death in 1377, Chaucer's diplomatic service continued, and in 1386 he was elected to Parliament. The increasing turmoil at court brought him into disfavor, however, and by the end of 1386 he had lost all of his public offices. By 1389 he was reinstated, but his career waxed and waned; he was in and out of favor and in financial difficulties until his death in 1400.

The author's professional life brought him into contact with humanistic Italian and French influences, including poets Petrarch and Deschamps, and gave him a rich appreciation of humanity. What is less often remarked upon, however, is that as a civil servant, his political experience was very broad. Chaucer is most often considered first and foremost a poet, his political experience seen as tangential to his "real" life as the creator of the rich panoply of characters in the *Canterbury Tales;* twenty-four stories told by pilgrims on the road to the renowned—and very political—tomb of Thomas Becket. Chaucer was a shrewd observer and had seen firsthand the devastation and near anarchy caused by the dynastic turmoil of the early stages of the Hundred Years' War in both England and in France.

The *Tales* themselves have been much studied, studded as they are with nuggets of social commentary and criticism hidden in the entertaining and amusing stories in verse. They have given birth to many famous characters, like the Wife of Bath and the Pardoner, and were the vehicle for significant developments in the English language. While this is not the place for an examination of the *Canterbury Tales* as a whole, it is significant that "Melibee" is one of only two stories that are put into Chaucer's own mouth, and one of only two that are written in prose.[1] For many years, scholars dismissed the tale, assuming it was the product of one of Chaucer's less mellifluous days, since it is written in the less elegant prose—indeed, in the *style clergiale* (Bornstein, 1978: 36–254) of court business, including the linguistic doubling that is still found today in legalese. It has been castigated as "tedious," "soporific," and boring. More recently the tale has been viewed with greater appreciation. Some have argued that its position within the *Tales,* just after the frankly satirical "Tale of Sir Theopas,"[2] also told by Chaucer himself, indicates that with "Melibee," too, Chaucer's intent was satirical, mocking the pompous and redundant language of official documents and didactic writing in general. One scholar argues that it is a "very subtle, stylistic parodying" of a "pretentious and undistinguished piece of bourgeois moralizing" (Johnson, 1990: 139n9). Scholars have realized that in both France and England vernacular prose was considered to be the language of serious discourse, reserved for important subjects. Diane Bornstein argued that the work profoundly affected serious vernacular writing and per-

---

1. The other is "The Parson's Tale."
2. "Theopas" mocks the chivalric ideal of knighthood in a criticism of the warrior caste and its inflated view of itself.

haps created (or transmitted) the style clergiale to English (1978: 236–54). Read, then, with a different eye, "Melibee" is rich with significance, not boring at all, and it clearly falls within the conventions of the didactic literature of the mirror for princes. In fact, some argue that it may have been composed as an independent work for either Richard II or for John of Gaunt, to whom Chaucer was connected by marriage, and then woven into the fabric of the *Tales,* which were produced after 1386. Most scholars believe that "Melibee" was among the last of the *Tales* to be written.

The main elements of "Melibee" were borrowed from a vernacular French work, *Le livre de Melibée et de Dame Prudence,* by Renaud de Louens, which was written sometime after 1336. In turn, Renaud's work is a translation of *Liber consolationis et consilii,* written in 1246 by Albert of Brescia (1193–1270). Translation is, of course, a misnomer for many medieval works, since they are often very much transformed in the process. In this case, Renaud edited about one-third out of the story and made additions to it as well. Chaucer's "translation" is fairly close to his source in its plot elements, but there is no evidence that he knew Albert's own work directly.[3]

"The Tale of Melibee" is the story of a rich young man, Melibeus, his wife, Prudence, and their daughter, Sophie. One day, while Melibeus is amusing himself at the hunt—perhaps to the neglect of his more mundane responsibilities[4]—his house and family are attacked by three of his old enemies. Sophie is dangerously wounded, having been stabbed five times and left for dead. When Melibeus returns, he begins to weep at the devastation, and his wife, Prudence, tries to comfort him. The discerning reader will no doubt immediately have noticed the significance of the characters' names and will not be surprised that while wisdom lies mortally wounded and is unable to communicate with anyone, having been stabbed in feet, hands, eyes, nose, and mouth, Prudence counsels Melibeus on the appropriate response to the violence that has been done both to his daughter and to his household. After many examples, both classical and scriptural, of virtuous behavior in the circumstances of extreme grief and stress, Prudence advises him to call together a council of ad-

---

3. For analysis of the significance of Chaucer's variations from his source, see Waterhouse and Griffiths, 1989.

4. Hunting as the preferred leisure activity of princes is a favorite topic of mirrors for princes. Whether criticized for neglecting their duties or encouraged to hunt as a legitimate pastime, princes were often warned about the dangers of spending too much time at the hunt.

visers. Following her suggestion, Melibeus gathers together a council of people. "[Some were] surgeons and physicians, old folk and young, and some were of his old enemies who seemed to have been reconciled to him. There came some of his neighbors who respected him more out of fear than of love, as it often happens. There came also a great many subtle flatterers and there were wise advocates learned in the law" (Chaucer, 1989: 254).[5] Melibeus listens to each one of this hodgepodge group of advisers as, in turn, each makes a case for action. The surgeons counsel "cure by contraries" and advise Melibeus to "cure war by vengeance" (ibid.: 255). His neighbors, envious and full of flattery, advise him to begin a war to avenge himself. One of the lawyers counsels him to shore up his own defenses while he determines what course to take, so that he is not caught off guard again. The young men advise him to "strike while the iron is hot" and to begin his counterattack while his own anger is fresh. "Warre, warre!" they cry (ibid.: 256).

Only a single voice, that of an old man, cautions Melibeus against violence, articulating an antiwar position: "Lordings, there is many a man that cries 'war, war,' that knows full little about it. War in the beginning has so great and large an entrance that every one may enter when he likes, . . . but surely, what shall come of war in the end is not so easily known" (Chaucer, 1989: 256). But the young men heckle the old man and intimidate him, so that, like Sophia, age is silenced. In an aside, the poet remarks that Melibeus had many advisers who told him one thing in public and another in private.

Since the majority of his advisers has counseled war, Melibeus is ready for battle. Then Prudence herself begins to speak. "Full debonairly and with great patience" (Chaucer, 1989: 257),[6] she demolishes each of the arguments that has been made in favor of war. In the process, she instructs him on the kinds of advisers he ought to have invited to his council and to what kinds of advice to listen. In short, Prudence instructs Melibeus in kingship, and the "Tale of Melibee" functions as a mirror for princes. Her arguments are devastating as she hammers away with quotation after quotation on the elements of good rule from authorities both as varied and as traditional as Seneca and Solomon. The cumulative effect is a powerful argument, underlined by her observation that

---

5. All translations my own.
6. Courteously, patiently, and sympathetically.

the advice a prince hears may often be directly opposed to his own true interests. Advisers who counsel haste or encourage the prince to act impetuously are not his friends. Melibeus is cautioned against listening to such rash advice on two counts: first, because he has no male heir or near relatives to avenge his death, and second, because he presents a tempting target to those around him due to his wealth. Vengeance, Prudence argues, is an inadequate reason for war, not only because "for as by right and reason, no man may take vengeance on anyone, except the judge under whose jurisdiction it falls" (ibid.: 267) but because it risks provoking a blood feud, and Melibeus's three attackers have many kinsmen. Prudence then applies the theoretical analysis prescribed, she says, by Cicero, to the question of legitimate cause for war. "Now, sire, as to the point that Cicero calls 'causes'... the wrong that you have received has certain causes, that the scholars call *oriens* and *efficans,* and *causa longinqua* and *causa propinqua,* that is, the ultimate and proximate causes. The first cause is Almighty God, who is the cause of all things. The near cause is your three enemies. The accidental cause was hate. The material cause is the five wounds of your daughter. The formal cause is the means by which they brought ladders and climbed in the windows. The final cause was in order to slay your daughter.... But to speak of the ultimate cause, as to what end shall come to them, I cannot judge" (ibid.). Because Melibee lacks comprehensive information about his particular situation and because war generates extensive uncertainty, even when one does have the right to take vengeance, Prudence convinces Melibeus to negotiate with his enemies. With his accord, Prudence "took counsel of herself, thinking about how she might bring this matter to a good conclusion and a good end. And when she saw her time, she sent for these adversaries to come to her in a private place and wisely showed them the great good to be gained from peace and the great harms and perils that are in war" (ibid.: 276). Finally, convinced by the counsels of Prudence, Melibeus and his enemies agree to arbitration, which ultimately results in the recovery of his child, his security, and his happiness. The tale concludes with his enemies begging his pardon and Melibeus forgiving them for their misdeeds.

The "Tale of Melibee" is a miniature mirror for princes, full of a nonclerical and politically experienced view of the hazards of war and the secrets of peace. It teaches the prince that no war is prudent and that wise counselors can shape the process of deliberation. It also informs him of the many pitfalls to governing wisely, and especially of the proper criteria a ruler should use in choosing his advisers. Finally, "Melibee" reminds the prince that a ruler married to prudence will have a living and functional wisdom as his offspring.

Christine de Pizan and *La lamentation sur les maux de France*

A contemporary of Geoffrey Chaucer, Christine de Pizan was engaged in a lifelong vocation as a poet of peace.[7] Considered to be the first woman of letters of France, Christine de Pizan (c. 1364–c. 1430) was born in Venice, daughter of Thomas de Pizan, medical doctor and astrologer, whose training at the prestigious University of Bologna brought him an appointment to the court of Charles V of France. In 1369 he settled his young family in Paris, which became their permanent home. Christine was encouraged in her education by both her father and her young husband, Etienne de Castel, whom she married in 1380. Christine's love of learning and her familiarity with court life brought their reward when she was suddenly left a young widow at the age of twenty-five, with three young children and a widowed mother to support. She turned to a life of letters at first for consolation, she tells us in her autobiographical works, and later put pen to paper as a source of income. She wrote in both verse and prose on topics ranging from politics and warfare to religion and philosophy for a variety of wealthy and noble patrons. Her earliest works consisted primarily of poetry on courtly themes, but between 1400 and 1420, at the height of war and civil unrest in France, she wrote ten books for the instruction and guidance of those engaged in political life, including one of the most original and influential works on just war theory. Few medieval or Renaissance political writers were as productive; no one addressed audiences so varied in social class and gender. The central theme of all of her political works is the importance of peace.

In her earliest works her message is fairly oblique, but as the polit-

---

7. After Chaucer's death in 1400, Henry IV attempted to persuade Christine to come to his court in England, while holding her teenaged son under his "protection." She distrusted the new king, since she saw him as an "usurper" to the throne of England and she believed that he was not likely to keep his promises. She sent him her books as a gift and asked that her son be returned to escort her back to England, since she was a "frail woman." Her son, Jean, came home, but she never quite got around to making the trip with him.

ical situation around her deteriorated and her own stature as a writer grew, her concern for peace became more and more explicit and direct. *La lamentation sur les maux de France,* also called *La Lamentation sur la guerre civile,* illustrates Christine de Pizan's fearlessness in confronting the French royal family for its neglect of its responsibilities. By 1410 the political chaos had intensified. The hatred between the followers of the recently assassinated younger brother of the king, the talented if calculating Duke of Orleans, and those of his archrival the young Duke of Burgundy, John the Fearless, who would himself be assassinated in 1419, had reached epic proportions. The Duke of Burgundy was custodian of the king's young heir, Louis of Guyenne, and was taking responsibility for his upbringing. The Duke of Berry, uncle of Charles VI, brother of both the late king Charles V and the late Duke Philip the Good of Burgundy, uncle of the present Duke John and granduncle of the dauphin, was allied with the Count of Armagnac, a singularly brutal man, who controlled his young son-in-law, Charles of Orleans. Christine undertook to persuade the combatants to come to their senses in *Lamentation,* which addressed the evils of civil war directly. It was apparently sent to several persons that Christine believed could influence the peace process, most notably the Duke of Berry.

Le lamentation opens with a description of the horrors afflicting France. "For Heaven's sake! For Heaven's sake! Mighty princes open your eyes.... Thus you will see cities in ruins, towns and castles destroyed, fortresses thrown to the ground! And where? In the very midst of France. The noble chivalry and youth of France, which as one body and soul used to stand ready to defend the crown and public good, now assembled in shameful ranks against each other, father against son, brother against brother, one relative against the next, their deadly swords drenching the battlefields with blood" (Christine de Pizan, 1984: 304–5). This work portrays the evils of civil war with a blunt directness that does nothing to sugarcoat or minimize the disasters befalling the French people consequent to their rulers' selfishness. As Linda Leppig has pointed out, the realism of Christine's language "stands in stark contrast to the benign terms often encountered in official documents.... Christine refuses to partake in a rhetoric designed to soften an ugly reality and belittle human suffering" (1992: 146). Christine's language is accusatory and direct, albeit posed as interrogations rather than accusations: "Oh, how can it be that the human heart ... can make man revert to the nature of a voracious and cruel beast? Where is the 'reason,' which gives him the name of 'rational animal?'" (Christine de Pizan, 1984: 304) She accuses the rulers of France of neglecting its people, their most important charge."[N]oble French princes, what wrong have those men done to you, who, like God, loved you and are reputed to honor you in every land? But it seems that you want to treat them, not as sons but as mortal enemies because the strife among you is haunting them, such as grief, war and battle" (ibid.).

In fact, Christine reproaches every member of society; not only princes, but also knights and clergy. Even noblewomen have their responsibility—indeed, culpability—in the conflict. They have neglected their roles as peacemakers, and she scolds the queen: "Oh crowned Queen of France, are you still sleeping? Who prevents you from restraining now this side of your kin and putting an end to this deadly enterprise? Don't you see that the heritage of your noble children is at stake?" (Christine de Pizan, 1984: 305-6) In the face of the inactivity of these members of the body politic, Christine appeals in her letter to the Duke of Berry himself. Her accusations, while still veiled as questions, bring her to the heart of the matter. As a senior member of the family, he is the only person with the stature to reprimand them as "a father would his children." In this part of the letter, she is no longer venting her fear and anger and frustration; rather, she attempts to persuade the prince to action by reminding him of the rewards—glory, honor, renown—that within the Ciceronian tradition are awarded to virtuous statesmen. In conclusion, the letter, dated August 23, 1410, is one of the most powerful and moving indictments of the evils of civil war ever written, and it is clearly propelled by the desire for peace. The vulnerability and helplessness that are the legacy of war for noncombatants suffuse these pages, as she cries out for political leaders to come to their senses and to recall their duties as rulers of the nation.

Christine de Pizan and *Le livre des fais d'armes et de la chevalerie*

Christine de Pizan's program as a writer was never merely to manipulate the emotions. In every one of her political treatises, she puts the conventions of didactic writing to use in order to persuade political leaders to responsible governance. Like the letter, whose conventions she manipulates in the *Lamentation, Le livre des fais d'armes et de la chevalerie* conforms to the traditions of didactic treatises, from its initial humility to its reliance on the authorities within the chosen field. The result is a technical treatise on the art of warfare commissioned by the Duke of Burgundy and intended for the edification of the dauphin. As a manual on warfare, its tone is sensible, straightforward, even entertaining. It is not preoccupied with the horrors of war; rather, it attempts to avoid them by managing war and its collateral effects. The tone of this work is very different from the *Lamentation;* there are no gushing tears or eyes turned piously upward. Yet in its first few pages, it outlines a theory of just war that is succinct, comprehensive, and original.

The first chapters address the question of when war is legitimate. The traditional criteria of *auctoritas, causa,* and *intentio* are addressed; however, in Christine's work, authority is exceptionally broadly defined. Christine allows wars to be engaged by "sovereign princes, which is to say emperors, kings, dukes, and other landed lords who are duly and rightfully heads of temporal jurisdictions. No baron, or any other person, may undertake war without the express permission and will of his sovereign lord" (Christine de Pizan, 1999: 5). While this can be read as a criticism of the Count of Armagnac, who was certainly acting outside his own territorial jurisdiction, it should also be understood as a critique of the robber bands of mercenaries that roamed the country under vagrant knights. The broad authority to wage war conceded by Christine may in fact be as much a recognition of reality as an articulation of a principle.

By contrast, just causes for war are much more restricted. Christine recognizes only three as legitimate: "There are five causes of war, only three of which are justifiable. The first lawful ground upon which wars may be undertaken or pursued is to sustain law and justice; the second is to counteract evildoers who befoul, injure and oppress the land [and the country] and the people; the third is to recover land or lordships or other things stolen or usurped for unjust cause by others who are under the jurisdiction of the prince, the country or its subjects" (Christine de Pizan, 1999: 15). Two *causae* are illegitimate but are nonetheless comprehensible consequences of the prince's illicit aggressive passions and desires for revenge. "[O]ne is for revenge for any loss or damage occurred; the other is to conquer and take over foreign lands or lordships" (ibid.: 16). The leading instigators of hostilities were of course engaged in both revenge and the desire for domination. The Orleanist/Armagnac faction wanted to avenge the assassination of the Duke of Orleans in 1407; the Burgundians wanted to control the kingdom. While Christine recognizes how common both motivations are, nonetheless, she considers them illegitimate. Both motivations, no matter how much respected by the dominant culture, are infractions of divine law. Vengeance belongs to God, she argues; thus no mortal ought to wage war to avenge wrongdoing. Covetousness is a sin; thus war to acquire the property or goods of another is illicit.

Yet Christine is no pacifist. In her view, if the prince has incurred damage from another it is appropriate for him to seek redress as a matter of justice. The logic on this point is significant. If his subjects are wronged, a king ought to fight to protect their rights. If he himself has been wronged, rather than referring him to the emperor, Christine argues that he may fight to defend his own rights, because "it is lawful for the prince to keep for himself the same right that is granted to others" (Christine de Pizan, 1999: 17). To sneak away when he has himself been wronged is to perpetrate further injustice because justice, in Christine's eyes, "requires punishment for misdeeds" (ibid.) and is in fact commanded by divine law.

Christine de Pizan articulates a third condition of just war that is not part of the traditional view. Despite proper authority and a just cause, a specific process of deliberation is necessary also. A war is just if and only if the decision to wage war is made through the correct advisory procedure. It is not enough for a king to declare war on his own, not even with the advice of seasoned warriors; he must follow the correct procedure. A council of wise advisers, including impartial foreign observers, experienced counselors and statesmen, and legal advisers, in addition presumably to the prince's regular coterie of military men, should be gathered together, a "council of wise men in his parliament or in that of his sovereign if he is a subject." After open and frank discussion, if the prince and his counselors decide that his position is just, the prince should "summon his adversary," make his case, and ask restitution. His adversary should be listened to "without willfulness or spite." If his adversary refuses to come to put forward his case, then the ensuing conflict is not vengeance but justice (Christine de Pizan, 1999: 18).

This remarkable process of deliberation resembles an international court of appeal or tribunal, in that it includes representatives of numerous affected groups as well as foreign observers. There is an emphasis on providing both accuser and accused with due process, which also allows both sides in a conflict to be heard. Only when there is a process of deliberation and mediation, and attempts to adjudicate the dispute have failed, can a war be considered just.

While no course of action is perfect, due process and mediation serve as essential precursors for any justifiable military engagement and thus are essential components for controlling the collateral effects of even a legitimate desire for revenge on an aggressor. Out of the experience of fear and civil war, Christine de Pizan has fashioned a process by which war might be averted, and which serves as an early modern exemplar or prototype for an international court of arbitration.[8]

Conclusion

These rich texts raise many questions. In the case of Chaucer's "Melibee," there are some extremely interesting gender issues. Chaucer challenges the traditional stereotypes not merely as regards the propriety of a ruler being advised by a woman—in his hands, Prudence reveals a gendered understanding of the characteristics of good rule. Ironically, perhaps, her advice to negotiate and to pacify aggressors closely resembles the marital advice given by other fourteenth- and early-fifteenth-century writers to women in abusive marriages (Collette, 1995). Prudence is central to many of Christine de Pizan's works also, most notably as the title character in her versified mirror for princes, *The Letter of Othéa, the Goddess of Prudence, to Hector, Prince of Troy*. Both poets repeatedly underline the importance of prudence wedded to kingship.

On the subject of war, there are several aspects of the work of these two poets that ought to be emphasized. First, enmeshed as they are in civil war, both poets advise their patrons to behave prudently and to listen to wise advice. Second, both give careful instruction in the arts of rule, in particular in how to choose and recognize fair and impartial counsel. Both warn about the vulnerability of rulers to flattery, self-interest, and a desire for vengeance on the part of their advisers. Both poets focus on ius ad bellam, that is, a correct determination of the right to go to war. While Chaucer's position in "Melibee" is more pacifist than that of Christine de

---

8. For discussion of the influence of this work, see Forhan, 2002; see also McLeod, 1991.

Pizan, both stress the serious and unpredictable consequences of war. In effect, they have little confidence in ius in bello, perhaps justifiably, since both witnessed conduct that was beyond the range of what was considered legally or morally acceptable, including royal assassination. On the other hand, there is something ineffably poignant about these intellectuals writing against the war, and even about the attempt to remind leaders of just war theory in general. Individually, neither Geoffrey Chaucer nor Christine de Pizan was effective at ending the war. Despite being part of a great wave of intellectuals who, confronted with national tragedy and incompetent rule, were concerned with the fate of these two nations, it was still not for many years that their voices were heard, or, indeed, laypersons were given a seat at the negotiating table. Yet both Chaucer and Christine de Pizan play a significant role in that rising tide, as catalysts for the increasing laicization and secularization of power.

It is worth emphasizing that neither poet came from the social classes that were traditionally seen as having the right to advise the king. Chaucer was middle class, although he attained knighthood in later life. His career was spent entirely in what we would call the civil service. He was not a member of the nobility, not a lawyer nor a theologian, any of which roles would have given him some official status from which to discuss just war theory. The example of Christine de Pizan is even more startling. Daughter and spouse of civil servants, and a member of the middle class as well, she was also a "foreigner" and a woman. Both authors were part of the culture of patronage and almost entirely dependent on rulers for their subsistence. Chaucer's later poverty even caused him to send a poem, "The Complaint of Chaucer to His Purse," to Henry IV in hopes of alleviating the elderly writer's financial woes. Yet both Geoffrey Chaucer and Christine de Pizan clearly felt entitled to advise princes and the ruling class in general. While both poets shared an ability to sweeten their admonitions, ironically it is the woman, the more vulnerable of the two, who is the more outspoken and critical of political leaders. In fact, her female identity undoubtedly added to the authority of her voice. Her unusual character and her fearlessness in the face of power gave an exceptional quality to her participation in this stream of protest, which ultimately was to capture the attention of political leaders. Her voice could be heard when they were deaf to others because she was "a humble creature" and "insignificant" to those of higher ranks (Christine de Pizan, 1994: 4). Finally, although other women in France had composed works that commented on political events, most notably Marie de France, Christine de Pizan wrote systematically and extensively on affairs of state, intentionally creating a clear and consistent voice with the authority and passion to speak out on political matters. She believed that she had a responsibility to the kingdom to advise its rulers. The creation of this self, her *Je, Christine*, was more than her hope for future glory and renown or even her awareness that writing was both her vocation and her destiny.

However remarkable this creation—this Renaissance "self-fashioning"—and in spite of Christine's extraordinary innovation, today she is virtually forgotten. Chaucer, too, is seldom read except by scholars, and his work is increasingly unintelligible to modern readers. Yet both have left us this important legacy: the appropriation of the authority to guide rulers, not on the basis of their social status or expertise, but as responsible "citizens" of their respective nations.

REFERENCES

Barnes, Jonathan. 1984. "Just War." In J. M. Burns, ed., *Cambridge History of Medieval Political Thought*. Cambridge: Cambridge University Press, 771–84.

Bornstein, Diane. 1978. "Chaucer's 'Tale of Melibee' as an Example of the Style Clergiale." *Chaucer Review* 12 (4): 236–54.

Chaucer, Geoffrey. 1989. *The Complete Poetry and Prose of Geoffrey Chaucer*. Ed. John H. Fisher. New York: Harcourt Brace.

Christine de Pizan. 1984. *Writings of Christine de Pizan*. Trans. C. C. Willard. New York: Persea.

———. 1994. *The Book of the Body Politic*. Trans. Kate L. Forhan. Cambridge: Cambridge University Press.

———. 1999. *Deeds of Arms and Chivalry*. Trans. S. Willard. University Park: Penn State Press.

Collette, C. 1995. "Heeding the Counsel of Prudence." *Chaucer Review* 29 (4): 416–29.

Forhan, Kate L. 2002. *The Political Theory of Christine de Pizan*. Aldershot, U.K.: Ashgate.

Johnson, Lynn Staley. 1990. "Inverse Counsel: Contexts for the 'Melibee.'" *Studies in Philology* 87 (2): 137–55.

Leppig, L. 1992. "The Political Rhetoric of Christine de Pizan." In M. Brabant, ed., *Politics, Gender, and Genre*. Boulder: Westview, 141–56.

McLeod, Glenda. 1991. *The Reception of Christine de Pizan from the Fifteenth through the Nineteenth Centuries: Visitors to the City*. Lewiston: E. Mellen.

Waterhouse, R., and G. Griffiths. 1989. "Sweete Wordes of Non-Sense: The Deconstruction of the Moral Melibee." *Chaucer Review* 23 (4): 339–61.

7

Reflections on Medieval Just War Theories

A Commentary on Part One

GERSON MORENO-RIAÑO

Paritur pax bello
        Roman proverb

A useful place to begin a discussion on the complexities of medieval just war theories is by briefly discussing two other basic ethical positions regarding the morality of armed conflict. It may be the case that medieval just war theories—both *ius ad bellum* and *ius in bello,* as well as other variants[1]—were created as possible alternatives in part to mediate between the extremes of these two basic positions, namely, political realism and pacifism. My brief opening survey is simply meant to serve as an

---

I would like to thank the academic vice president's office, Cedarville University, for facilitating this project through a 2001 Faculty Summer Research Grant. Thanks are also due to the excellent staff members of the Centennial Library, Cedarville University, for their assistance in acquiring the needed resources for this project. My thanks also go to Politica: Society for the Study of Medieval Political Thought and PRIO (International Peace Research Institute, Oslo) for facilitating the presentation and publication of this essay.

1. By other variants is meant the attempts by religious scholars, particularly Christian scholars, to justify various types of war and participation in these by religious believers. For example, some variations of just war theories focus more on the types of participation allowed for religious believers than on whether the war itself is just or whether its means are just (problems relating to ius ad bellum and ius in bello). For example, see Hoyt, 1991. Another variation that focuses more on the classical problems of the ends and means of conflict is "preventive war" as articulated in Brown, 1991.

introduction into a discussion about just war theory in the Middle Ages, using insights from the previous essays of this volume as my vehicle. My ultimate aim is to consider some ambiguities within the just war thinking of various medieval figures and to offer a critique of sundry interpretations of medieval just war theories. I hope to demonstrate that several aspects of medieval just war theories are more complex than they seem at first sight and to identify and clarify some of the essential elements on which these theories build. It is my aspiration that in doing so fruitful prospects for new research directions will be raised.

Let me add that in offering questions and comments—some of them critical—about the previous essays in this volume, I work from a sense of overall agreement with and respect for these essays. They all offer important contributions to which I hope to add by raising questions for further consideration.

The Basic Ethical Positions Regarding War

Political Realism

One of the oldest arguments justifying the morality of war, albeit not the only one, is that of political realism.[2] This, simply and schematically put, is the view that the only ethic that ought to guide and does in fact guide the conduct of a political entity—be it a city-state, empire, or modern state—is concern for that political entity's self-interest.[3] No other arguments—moral or religious—ever hold sway in the affairs of state policy but the keen calculation of how to maximize a state's "profits."[4] In a

---

2. For a good account of both realism and pacifism, see Fotion, 1990. I make use of some of Fotion's arguments in my exposition of realism and pacifism. My suggestion of "basic positions" may appear arbitrary to some since it appears to ignore other justificatory accounts such as holy war. However, holy war justifications of war can fit well within the broad parameters of realistic accounts.

3. It should be noted that various types of realism do in fact exist. The definition adopted here is most in harmony with a moral interpretation of strong realism, or the view that holds that states should be guided in their foreign affairs only by a concern for their national interest. There is a nonmoral interpretation of strong realism that argues that morality has no place at all in the behavior of states with each other (see note 4 below for further elaboration). Still, there is another account of realism that defines it as the view that morality is not *always* pertinent to the conduct of states. For an excellent exposition of these varieties of realism and other surrounding issues, see Mapel, 1996; McMahan, 1996.

4. The way in which this position is presented here is deliberately meant to distinguish it from another presentation of political realism that argues that for realists no ethical considerations or moral norms are ever taken into account in the formulation of national policy, so that all questions of policy are always prudential or practical in nature. While the practicality

sort of backhanded fashion, realism combines the traditional polar opposites of "what ought to be" and "what is." While realists reject the idealization of human life and of politics in particular, they forcefully argue that "what is" is the only "ought to be" that exists. Thus they achieve a sort of intramundane deontology by which to justify the use of violence as an instrument of politics. Furthermore, political realism in war also means that considerations of universal rights and justice along with the obligations these place on states and individuals are obsolete and may even signal moral and political turpitude.[5] Thus, political realism regards every war as just in a sort of generic sense since war is the behavior of mature states. The only justice to be attained is the realization of a state's interest with no primary concern for benevolence or the innocent. A realist ethic of war may mean that there are no boundaries to how war is conducted and that strategy, rational calculation, and "craftiness" are key virtues. Political realism views war as a natural way in which states relate to each other in the struggle for power. War is a normal condition of political life and, according to this view, may even be a fulfilling aspect of human existence.

---

of all policy questions is certainly an aspect of realism, one must not ignore the fact that the moral summum bonum of realists is the fulfillment of the national self-interest, so that it is proper to say that national self-interest—however and by whomever that is conceived—is the absolute moral principle guiding a state's decisions. Thus political realism is a moral position, albeit one with chameleonlike qualities. For a brief example of a rendition of a nonmoral view of political realism, see McMahan, 1993.

5. Consider, for example, Clausewitz's comments regarding international law and benevolence as these relate to the conduct of war: "Violence arms itself with the inventions of Art and Science in order to contend against violence. Self-imposed restrictions, almost imperceptible and hardly worth mentioning, termed usages of International Law, accompany it without essentially impairing its power. . . . Now, philanthropists may easily imagine there is a skillful method of disarming and overcoming an enemy without causing great bloodshed, and that this is the proper tendency of the Art of War. However plausible this may appear, still it is an error which must be extirpated; for in such dangerous things as War, the errors which proceed from a spirit of benevolence are the worst. . . . This is the way in which the matter must be viewed, and it is to no purpose, it is even against one's own interest, to turn away from the consideration of the real nature of the affair because the horror of its elements excites repugnance" (1968: 101–2). What is most fascinating and illustrative about these comments is how ethical realists in terms of war regard ius in bello limitations within armed conflict. Whereas just war theorists prescribe ius in bello limitations as safeguards to ensure "humane" and restrained conflict, realists hold these very limitations as evidence of, at best, political naïveté and may even consider these limitations to be fundamentally unjust. This was the same sort of argument employed by Callicles and Thrasymachus in the Platonic dialogues *Gorgias* and *Republic*, respectively. Both argued for a sort of natural justice that meant that those who were superior in physical strength and cleverness should rule and deserved a larger share of political and social goods and, so the argument followed, that morality and law were no more than conventions created by the weak to restrict the strong and the just dessert to which they were entitled.

Pacifism

While various pacifist positions exist, they all share the commonality that the "strong moral presumption against the violence and killing involved in war... cannot be overridden, that the challenge to provide a moral justification for war can never be met" (McMahan, 1993: 386). As McMahan rightly points out, pacifism is rooted in the view that there are certain acts that are inherently wrong in and of themselves without consideration of the consequences these may bring about. One such act is war. Now, the principles underlying pacifism may be religious, secular, and even prudential.[6] Principled pacifism can be rooted in a divine law forbidding violence against others or in a divine dictate commanding love and forgiveness—even to one's enemy. Secular justifications are often based on humanist grounds such as benevolence, mutual respect, and human rights or can even be based on empirical and prudential grounds.[7] Whatever the principle, as Fotion argues, pacifists "all agree that the realists are wrong in calling wars nonmoral. Wars are, instead, immoral. For the pacifists, wars are not times when ethics has no application. Rather, wars represent times when ethics can and should be applied, but is not. For them to call certain wars moral or ethical is not so much a contradiction as a tragically mistaken ethical judgment" (1990: 2).

Both pacifism and realism are difficult positions to embrace but on rather different grounds. Pacifism requires a tremendous and deep moral fortitude that is rare, especially when one's self-preservation is at stake. Pacifism may also be difficult to uphold in societies where the taking up of arms is seen as the civil if not moral duty of its members.[8] Realism,

---

6. Fotion, 1990 offers a useful exposition of various pacifist arguments. See also Fotion, 2000. It should be noted that pacifism may be rooted in some sort of moral deontology (or moral deontotheology—that is, a deontology based upon the existence of a sovereign and omnipotent God) or on secular grounds. Both approaches would agree in principle that war can never be justified while disagreeing in rationale. For a contemporary example of a moral deontotheological pacifist position, see Augsburger, 1991. For an example of a secular pacifist position, see Westling, 1984. For an example of a deontological pacifist position, see Tzu, 1987. Some may identify both deontotheological and deontological positions with other pacifist positions that are rooted in principles of love, benevolence, or mutual respect. While this may be possible, the intrinsic difference with the deontological variants is their basis for peace, namely, some universal moral order.

7. Such grounds are the inherent destructiveness of war and the presumption toward war that modern technology actually breeds. For an example of this argument, see Westling, 1984.

8. What I have in mind here is that pacifists in such a society may be subjected to the scorn that is often associated with antipatriotic or antinationalistic tendencies.

on the other hand, seems to be intuitively wrong. Its lack of moral concern for the taking of human life and, depending on the type of realism involved, its glorification of war as a necessary and even vital aspect of human life do not resonate well with our moral nature. Pacifism and realism, thus described, are ultimately difficult to embrace because they are extremes that are not in harmony with the reality of human life—our basic instinct toward self-preservation and the psychological and moral horror we experience when faced with death.

The Other Option: Just War Theories

Just war theories are realist in some sense. By this I mean that those who propose such theories have accepted the fact that wars are a basic part of human life, albeit a very dark part of human existence. And if wars do in fact exist, just war theorists at least attempt to humanize or limit these wars by imbuing morality into the considerations for (ius ad bellum) and the waging of armed political conflict (ius in bello). It is not solely the case that just war theories have arisen in an attempt to mediate between the theoretical extremes of realism and pacifism. While this may be partly correct, just war theories originated in an attempt to deal with an all-too-real and common practice of human beings. At least for some medievals, to say that no war was ever just or that morality played no role in war-making activities was either too simplistic or too sinister. War was a basic fact of medieval life, and the struggle for many of its scholars was in determining what made a war legitimate. And ultimately, this struggle to determine legitimacy was in reality a struggle to determine the nature of justice and its obligations upon social and political life. Thus, in the pages that follow, I advance and defend the claim that to grasp fully a thinker's view on what makes a war just, we must first determine that thinker's view of justice, its nature, and its logical applications. It is not merely enough to survey what a writer says about war. We must first determine what a writer says about the nature of justice.

War in Early Medieval Political Theory

John von Heyking's excellent essay in this volume (chapter 2) presents us with a tour de force in the war theories of many significant predecessors to some of the better-known medieval figures who commented on war and its justice. A twofold purpose structures the essay: a survey of just war theory in the patristic period of Christianity, with a more focused emphasis on St. Ambrose and an investigation of the classical notion of glory and its role in restraining how war is conducted. The essay rightly notes a key difference between medieval and classical just war theories, namely, that while the classical era's belief in the value of honor served, at least in theory, to limit the means of waging war, the medieval era's Christian monism limited the ends for waging war while at the same time removing the limits for how a war was conducted. The chapter then presents the reader with various attempts to justify war and some of the dynamics therein.

In the first part of von Heyking's essay we are introduced to the notion of war and play. Play here at first seems to mean some sort of structured honor game where only *fortuna* or her equivalent judges the outcome and where the agent at play is a thing of beauty and grace. What should be explored further, though, is whether this notion of play really existed among the likes of Cicero or whether it may be some sort of modern category of analysis imposed upon classical thought.[9] Upon closer inspection, part of the dilemma is that the conceptualization of play that is used in the essay—that of Huizinga—is nebulous (see Huizinga, 1950). Huizinga's notion that "play is a significant activity that transcends the immediate needs of life and imparts meaning to the action" and that "[a]ll play means something" (ibid.: 1) is ambiguous and difficult to apply in a discussion on classical and early medieval notions of war. Just what, then, is play? At best, it is some sort of meaningful activity or the meaningful element of existence imparting importance to aspects of daily life. If play is to be understood in this way, it varies little from the religious or moral element that so often served to impart meaning to the lives of the ancients. However, it is doubtful that the ancients themselves looked upon this meaning-attributing element as "play." War was a meaningful activity and discussions about its meaningfulness centered more around issues of justice, religion, honor, glory, duty, and moral obligation toward the conquered than around play.[10] Von Heyking's discussion points more to

9. I raise this objection since only one example of playful war is given in the essay, namely, Cicero's quotation of Pyrrhus (Cicero, 1991 [hereafter simply *De officiis*]: 1.38), and, as I argue below, this example may be riddled with problems.

10. I have in mind here Cicero's comments about a just war, the duty of priests in war, and

the acquisition of honor and glory by conducting oneself justly in war—certainly a meaningful activity—than to any notion of gaming or play.[11]

In support of the playful element in war, Von Heyking cites part of Cicero's quotation from Ennius's *Annales*. Here is the full passage for our consideration: "Indeed, Pyrrhus' words about the returning of the captives were splendid: 'My demand is not for gold; nor shall you give me a price. Let us each determine our lives by iron, not by gold, not by selling, but by fighting war. Let us test by our virtue whether Mistress Fortune wishes you or me to reign, or what she may bring. Hear these words too: if fortune of war spares the virtue of any, take it as certain that I shall spare them their liberty. Take them as a gift, and I give them with the will of the great gods.' (*De officiis* 1.38) That is certainly the view of a king and one worthy of the race of the Aeacidae!"[12]

This passage considered in the broader context of Cicero's conversation in *De officiis* really makes no reference at all to gaming or play in war. It refers to honorable behavior while at war with a powerful enemy. Cicero praises Pyrrhus's behavior because it exemplifies the sort of dutiful, honorable, and virtuous activity that Cicero wants his own son to model.[13]

A more interesting argument about the conduct of war that Cicero makes, and that should be further investigated, is found in *De officiis* 1.34, where he writes: "Something else that must very much be preserved in public affairs is the justice of warfare. There are two types of conflict: the one proceeds by debate, the other by force. Since the former is the proper concern of man, but the latter of beasts, one should only resort to the latter if one may not employ the former." This observation by Cicero is

---

the moral obligations of the conquerors toward the vanquished. See *De officiis* 1.34–38 and Cicero, 1995 (hereafter simply *De republica*): 3.23–25.

11. My point here is not to deny that an element of meaning resided within ancient and medieval conversations about war. Rather, it is to suggest that such conversations were understood by the ancients themselves not as centering around "playfulness."

12. As mentioned, this verse is from book VI of Ennius's poem *Annales* and tells of King Pyrrhus's virtuous deed in his war against the Romans. It is not necessarily a celebration of Regulus's manly valor, contra von Heyking. Cicero again cites the battle against Pyrrhus in *De officiis* 1.40 and 3.86.

13. Concluding his comments about Pyrrhus, Cicero writes: "Enough has been said about the duties of war" (*De officiis* 1.41). Cicero's goal has been to educate his son regarding virtuous behavior in a vital activity of Roman public life: the conduct of war. And, as Cicero reminds his son, virtuous activity is measured by honorableness, not material or personal advantages (ibid. 1.3–5). Consequently, Cicero is not tacitly acknowledging the playful element in war; rather, he is acknowledging that a former powerful enemy of Rome, even though he was waging an unprovoked war, exemplified virtue in war.

pregnant with meaning. In particular, it may serve to tame the notion of play in war since it is reminiscent of the classical notion of *spoudaios*, or *serious activity*—pursuits that aim toward the acquisition of virtue and moral excellence.[14] In the case of Cicero, settling war (a type of dispute) through debate and discussion is far superior to force and violence—the sort of activity that accompanies a playful war. If the idea of play in war is indeed a part of the classical era, then more work needs to be done regarding its existence, origin, and development. Further, the very concept of play must be more unequivocally defined so that it can be effectively applied.

From the idea of "play" von Heyking's essay then takes us to the notions of honor and glory as means by which to limit illicit behavior in war. My only comment here is that while it is correct to interpret Cicero as part of the classical tradition that focused on honor as a means to control conduct in war, it must not be forgotten that the context for Cicero's discussion about war is justice and peace, not honor.[15] Whereas in *De republica* the argument is made that "a war is never waged by the best state (*civitate optima*) except either in defense of its honor or its safety," only just is a war that is "waged for revenge or defense" or that has been "proclaimed and declared, or unless reparation has first been demanded" (*De republica* 3.23.34–35). It is not the case that Cicero is merely trying to "humanize" conflict. Rather, he is attempting to ensure that it is conducted justly and not simply by any means necessary. Furthermore,

---

14. Here I have in mind Aristotle's discussion regarding excellent or serious (*spoudaios*) activity. Aristotle writes: "Further, the happy life seems to be a life expressing virtue, which is a life involving serious actions, and not consisting in amusement. Besides, we say that things to be taken seriously are better than funny things that provide amusement, and that in each case the activity of the better part and the better person is more serious and excellent; and the activity of what is better is superior, and thereby has more the character of happiness. . . . Happiness, then, is found not in these pastimes, but in the activities expressing virtue, as we also said previously" (*Nicomachean Ethics* 1177a 1–10 [1984]).

15. In Cicero's conversations about justice, he introduces the specialized topic of warfare and argues that "wars, then, ought to be undertaken for this purpose, that we may live in peace, without injustice; and once victory has been secured, those who were not cruel or savage in warfare should be spared. . . . In my opinion, our concern should always be with a peace that will have nothing to do with treachery" (*De officiis* 1.35). Honor deals more with the means by which to wage war, or ius in bello, than with the sole purpose of fighting war, or ius ad bellum, and when discussed seems to be more of a by-product of successful conflict than necessarily the sole motivation for action. The possible exception may be wars that are fought for empire. Nevertheless, Cicero argues that even in these cases the conditions of justice must underlie the desire for glory and empire; see *De officiis* 1.38. An interpretation of Cicero's discussions of war as founded on the desire for honor and glory should be augmented with his argument for the need of *Ius* in the conduct of affairs, both public and private.

the passage in *De republica* may serve to differentiate between the wars of the ideal state (civitate optima) and the wars of real states—and when war is in the real world it is just only if it is for the purpose of reparation and curbing evil, and is waged with restraint.

I will now limit my comments to von Heyking's exposition of Ambrose's just war theory. Ambrose is introduced in the chapter as one Christian thinker who recognized the complexity of political life, especially when committed believers took an active role in public affairs. While it is argued that Ambrose recognized "to a large degree" the dynamics involved in war and morality and offers a more complete treatment of the subject, it is not certain whether Ambrose's writings offer more solutions than dilemmas. The first question that needs to be addressed is whether Ambrose *actually* composed anything resembling a theory of just war.[16] Commentators on Ambrose interpret his statements on war as an Ambrosian theory of just war, and von Heyking's essay, though in disagreement with the mainstream interpretation of Ambrose's "just war theory," also explores his passages on just war as part of an Ambrosian grand theory on the subject. This may be problematic for the simple reason that Ambrose's comments on just war appear to be nothing more than that—Christian aphorisms on the subject of war not reflective of a theoretical scheme on the subject. *De officiis ministorum* (Ambrose, 1980; hereafter *DOM*) was an ethical treatise to educate the Christian clergy and was never meant to be a scholarly and explicit treatment of the nature and complexities of war.

The education of the clergy in *DOM* centers around the notion of duty. *DOM* is the Christian counterpart to Cicero's *De officiis,* and while similar in some respects it differs in some fundamental aspects.[17] I will choose

---

16. Von Heyking makes the point that Ambrose's work *De officiis ministorum* does not "propound a thoroughgoing just war doctrine, [while] his transposition of Cicero's thought to Christian ethics distinguishes his treatment of just war from earlier Christians in important ways."

17. The similarity is more in regards to the diction and form of *DOM* than in substance. Ambrose understood that he was following the example of Cicero in writing a tract to his spiritual children. He writes: "Although some philosophers have written on this subject (i.e., duty)—Panaetius, for instance, and his son amongst the Greek, Cicero amongst the Latin, writers—I did not think it foreign to my office to write also myself. And as Cicero wrote for the instruction of his son, so I, too, write to teach you, my children. For I love you, whom I have begotten in the Gospel, no less than if you were my own true sons" (*DOM* 1.7.24).Von Heyking is correct to note Cicero's influence on Ambrose, though his comment that Ambrose "is in closer agreement with Cicero on the fundamental issues than he lets on" needs to be further explained. Part of the problem is the issue of justice and the pacifism that one finds in Am-

simply three in order to emphasize the difference. The basic tenet of Ambrose is that Christians must live for eternity. This is the fundamental impulse guiding Ambrose's treatment of duty, so that only those matters that are advantageous for the afterlife are considered (*DOM* 1.9.28–29). This being the case, discussions about war have no place among those who are living under the grace of God:

> What better pattern of righteousness is there than the divine, for the Son of God says: "Love your enemies" and again: "Pray for those who persecute and calumniate you." He so far removes from the perfect the desire for vengeance that He commands charity for those who do them harm. And since He had said in the old Scriptures: "Revenge is mine and I will repay," He says in the Gospel that we must pray for those who have done us harm, so that He who said He will have to punish will not punish them; it is His wish to pardon by your consent with which He agrees according to His promise. For, if you seek revenge, you know that the unrighteous is punished more severely by his own convictions than by the severity of his judges. (Ambrose, 1996: 48)

In *DOM*, Ambrose makes the same observation in his remarks on fortitude: "We have discussed fully enough the nature and force of what is virtuous from the standpoint of justice. Now let us discuss fortitude, which (being a loftier virtue than the rest) is divided into two parts, as it concerns matters of war and matters at home. But the thought of warlike matters seems to be foreign to the duty of our office, for we have our thoughts fixed more on the duty of the soul than on that of the body; nor is it our business to look to arms, but rather to the affairs of peace" (*DOM* 1.35.175). Ambrose's "pacifism," and here is the third key difference, is intertwined with his theistic view of justice that grounds justice in the Christian faith and mandates that grace and not harm be done to others:

> But that very thing is excluded with us which philosophers think to be the office of justice. For they say that the first expression of justice is, to hurt

---

brose's writing. On this point, see below. Furthermore, Ambrose himself argued that since this was a Christian treatment of duty, it would deal only with that which was virtuous and useful as it pertained to eternity. Consequently, his treatment would not be "superfluous" but rather quite different than that of the "philosophers." Again, Ambrose writes: "But we measure nothing at all but that which is fitting and virtuous, and that by the rule of things future rather than of things present; and we state nothing to be useful but what will help us to the blessing of eternal life; certainly not that which will help us enjoy merely the present time . . . this work of ours, therefore, is not superfluous, seeing that we and they [i.e., the philosophers] regard duty in quite different ways" (*DOM* 1.9.28–29). In these comments, Ambrose has Cicero in mind.

no one, except when driven to it by wrongs received. This is put aside by the authority of the Gospel. For the Scripture wills that the Spirit of the Son of Man should be in us, Who came to give grace, not to bring harm (ibid. 1.28.131).[18] ... The foundation of justice therefore is faith, for the hearts of the just dwell on faith, and the just man that accuses himself builds justice on faith, for his justice becomes plain when he confesses the truth. So the Lord saith through Isaiah: "Behold, I lay a stone for a foundation in Sion." This means Christ as the foundation of the Church. For Christ is the object of faith to all; but the Church is as it were the outward form of justice, she is the common right of all ... so he who denies himself is indeed a just man, is indeed worthy of Christ. For this reason Paul has made Christ to be the foundation, so that we may build upon Him the works of justice, whilst faith is the foundation (ibid. 1.29.142).

Cicero's views are fundamentally different in each of these areas. Ciceronian ethics are intensely practical in nature and lack the motivation of eternity, their primary concern being the education of the Roman (in particular his son) for matters public so as to extirpate the maladies of Roman society—in essence it is an education in achieving *honestum* in communal life.[19] Furthermore, Cicero's account of justice and its basis in *ratio* is perhaps the greatest single difference between Cicero's thought and Ambrose's ethics. For Cicero, justice is the ratio that binds communal life, and it itself can be grasped by the powers of the human mind simply because human beings partake of reason itself.[20] Such is not the case for the Christian faith of Ambrose. While Christian faith is readably available to all, it is certainly not the case that this very faith is an inherent characteristic of human beings themselves, that is, that they partake of faith in much the same way as they do of Cicero's ratio. A precondition

18. In section 138 of the same chapter, 28, Ambrose makes a comment that is applicable to wars for empire in general: "The desire to gain power also enervates the perfect strength and beauty of justice. For how can he, who attempts to bring others under his own power, come forward on behalf of others? And how can a man help the weak against the strong, when he himself aspires to great power at the cost of liberty?"
19. Cicero, *De officiis* 1.4: "For no part of life, neither public affairs nor private, neither in the forum nor at home, neither when acting on your own nor in dealings with another, can be free from duty. Everything that is honorable in a life depends upon its cultivation, and everything dishonorable upon its neglect." The honorableness of life that animates Cicero's writings is concerned with temporal life.
20. Cicero, *De officiis* 1.11: "The great difference between man and beast, however, is this: the latter adapts itself only in responding to the senses, and only to something that is present and at hand, scarcely aware of the past or future. Man, however, is a sharer in reason; this enables him to perceive consequences, to comprehend the causes of things, their precursors and their antecedents, so to speak; to compare similarities and to link and combine future with present events; and by seeing with ease the whole course of life to prepare whatever is necessary for living it."

of justice, for Cicero, is the use of human reason (possession being assumed as a given) in deciphering the universal ratio and its implications for human life. This is radically different from Ambrose, whose precondition for justice is not just the use of faith but the actual possession of faith in the revelation of God himself. Lastly, there is the question of justice and its meaning, especially with regard to war. Consider this one aspect: justice, according to Cicero, allows one to harm others if provoked by injustice.[21] Justice should circumscribe the basis of any war, and the most just war seems to be that which is provoked by the injustice of the offending party. As we have already seen, Ambrose differs markedly from this view in his claim that Christian grace obligates one to never harm others, even if they have acted unjustly.

If we accept that Ambrose did sketch a basic theory of just war, the above difference must be taken into account. And when this is done, a very complex picture appears. While von Heyking seeks to challenge the traditional interpretation of Ambrose's just war theory (e.g., Russell's argument of Christian triumphalism), Ambrose's dismissal of the classical notion of justice due to its antagonism vis-à-vis the Christian faith raises the troubling prospect as to whether Ambrose believed any war could be just that was waged by nonbelievers. Furthermore, one wonders whether Russell and others were correct after all in claiming that Ambrose's thoughts on just war were nothing more than a transposition of Roman imperialism into Christian theology.[22] The key contention on which von Heyking's argument rests is that *DOM* is really a transposition of Ciceronian ethics. But it can be suggested (see above) that *DOM* differs on vari-

---

21. Cicero, *De officiis* 1.20: "Of justice, the first office is that no man should harm another unless he has been provoked by injustice." I should note here that there are various applications of this justice principle within *De officiis* relevant for this discussion. For example, justice demands that one defend others when injustice is being done to them. Again, Cicero writes: "Of injustice there are two types: men may inflict injury; or else, when it is being inflicted upon others, they may fail to deflect it, even though they could . . . the man who does not defend someone, or obstruct the injustice when he can, is at fault just as if he had abandoned his parents or his friends or his country" (*De officiis* 1.23). There is also the question of wars for empire, which Cicero allows so long as these are fought "less bitterly." See *De officiis* 1.38.

22. See von Heyking's reference to Russell, 1975. If only Christians can be just, than only they can wage a truly just war. A case can be made that a truly just war (i.e., one waged by Christians) can be carried out that benefits the "enemy" since justice only benefits, never harms. If this is the case, Ambrose's support for wars against heretics is not problematic from an Ambrosian standpoint. One last important point would be to harmonize Christians fighting a just war with Ambrose's seeming pacifism. This can be done, in my view, since Ambrose is directing his comment to clerics and priests, whom he considers to be ministers of the spirit and not agents of the sword.

ous important issues in comparison to Cicero's *De officiis* and, further, that Ambrose himself never saw his work as a transposition of Cicero's *De officiis* but as something that, though similar in kind, was different in substance.[23] Furthermore, how can Ambrose's view of justice bringing grace, not harm (a Christian pacifist approach), be reconciled with the actual harm and perhaps even injustice that wars against heretics perpetrated?[24]

Now, even when Ambrose does take up the theme of war, his comments are sporadic at best and should not, it can be argued, be construed as aspects of a theory or of a distinctive Christian treatment of armed political conflict.[25] In most of the sections in *DOM* where war is discussed, Ambrose is speaking directly about virtue, not war. And Ambrose's treatment of virtue is not only to write about it but to offer examples of virtuous conduct. Most if not all of these examples are from the Hebrew Old Testament, and it just happens to be the case that much of the Old Testament is about war and heroic deeds in war and that most of the wars fought by the Jewish people were assumed to be just because they were initiated by Yahweh. Thus, Ambrose's use of war in *DOM* may be of minimal importance in an attempt to unearth some semblance of an Ambrosian theory of a just war, for he appears to be writing as a Christian to other Christians about what it is like to live virtuously, not about fighting wars virtuously. Thus, if we are to look for an Ambrosian theory of just war, the place may not be *DOM*.[26]

Lastly, while von Heyking and other commentators correctly identify

---

23. Von Heyking observes this same point later in his essay, although he maintains that Ambrose attempted a synthesis of Christian and Ciceronian ethics.

24. See note 18.

25. One other explicit passage in which Ambrose comments on war is found in *De Tobias* 15.51 (cited by von Heyking). The context of Ambrose's comments regards the propriety of demanding usury from others. Ambrose argues that usury may be demanded from an "enemy"—one "whom it would not be a crime to kill" since "where there is a right of war [*ius belli*], there also is the right of usury [*ius usurae*]." For examples of "enemies," Ambrose uses the Old Testament personages of "Amalech" and "the Amorite." This reference to ius belli is important though unclear in its meaning, for Ambrose does not explain its basis, what constitutes becoming an enemy, and the ultimate purpose of the conflict, although he does imply that one of the motivations for this war is simply to inflict "harm," not necessarily goodness through justice.

26. Von Heyking cites *DOM* 135.176–77, 1.27.129, 3.19.110–16, 3.8.54, as examples for just causes for war. Most of these passages, however, involve Old Testament accounts and deal with extraordinary circumstances (i.e., the chosen people of God). Some have argued that the examples in *DOM* represent Ambrose's view that wars commanded by God are indeed just and that there is such a thing as an Ambrosian theory of just war. On this point, see Morino, 1969.

the influence of Cicero upon Ambrose, one wonders how Cicero's notion of settling disputes through discourse and his tacit acceptance of war as a necessary aspect of imperial life relate to Ambrose's idea of justice bringing grace not harm and, more important, his support of war against heretics. Is it fair to say that a Christian approach to war, at least as found in Ambrose's "theory of war," shows a predisposition against discourse—and thus against being human—and a disposition toward conflict and thus toward enshrining the animalistic tendencies as somehow holy? If this is so, it is not that classical notions of glory alone, at least as exemplified by Cicero, can restrain how war is waged; it is rather that the classical notion of what it is to be a human being offered a better incentive not to fight at all. Maybe it is precisely this that some aspects of medieval just war theory lost, at least as exemplified by some Christian thinkers, namely, a fuller and richer conception of what it is to be a human being and the possibilities this encompasses for a peaceful civil life.[27]

Augustine and the Irreconcilable Problem of Justice

I have entitled this section the "irreconcilable problem of justice" because one of the most vexing questions in the medieval Christian just war tradition *is* the conceptualization of justice.[28] This problem was symptomatic of a more serious dilemma: the clash between Christianity and classical culture. Cochrane did well to remind us that the perhaps irreconcilable dilemma between classical culture and Christianity was the basis of each other's hope for *eudaimonea*—heroic man or Christ (1957). This dilemma comes into sharp focus, for example, in Tertullian's outburst "What Has Athens to Do with Jerusalem, the Academy with the Church?" And this dilemma also comes into sharp focus within the writings of Augustine of Hippo—in particular regarding his conception of justice.

Henrik Syse and Phillip Gray, in their perceptive essays in this volume (chapters 3 and 4), focus on this perennial Christian thinker, who in a way exemplifies not a very full or rich conception of what it is to be a human being (see my comments above). They investigate Augustine's treat-

---

27. I will return to this observation throughout this essay.
28. This problem is still vexing us in our modern (postmodern?) era, in which the ancient question "What is justice?" still lacks a satisfactory answer. The rise of Christianity and its dominance during the Middle Ages brought the problem into sharper focus. I use the term *vexing* because a theistic conception of justice presents various problems to modern interpreters of medieval writers—in particular Augustine—who wish to modernize their views.

ment of just war as it regards modern understandings of just war (Syse) or as it applies to political conflicts or intra-Church conflicts (Gray). In particular, Syse addresses how Augustine exemplified a "virtue ethics" approach to war over the more deontological or consequentialist modern approaches. Augustine, Syse argues, emphasized virtues and vices over steadfast rules, with this virtue-centered approach being illustrated by Augustinian arguments regarding the evil nature of war itself. Furthermore, the argument is presented that a deontological approach to just war is not Augustinian because the bishop of Hippo would have criticized the possibility of adhering to a set of rules without a person first having the needed virtuous character to obey the rules. And, lastly, a consequentialist approach to just war is problematic for Augustine since it ignores the all-too-important issues of intention and frame of mind. Gray, on the other hand, is concerned with understanding Augustine's support of "war" against the Donatists by way of the idea of *per molestias eruditio* as well as Augustine's conceptualization of just war. Gray arrives at the conclusion that in both discussions of war Augustine's logic is the same: war is a necessary moral corrective for immoral human beings both in the Church and outside it.

What I suggest below that should be further considered for both Syse's and Gray's arguments is the possibility that Augustine's ethics can be understood only within a deontological context and that even if we are to consider his approach to war character centered, it is still grounded in a basic ontology implying rules of conduct to be followed and, moreover, that his ontological presuppositions raise serious dilemmas about how to conduct a just war. Now, it would appear that to argue for an Augustinian virtue-centered approach actually serves to affirm the claim that his approach is really deontological. Any notion of virtue or excellence is rooted in an ontological order about what is truly real and good.[29] If this is not the case, then it would be very difficult to speak about virtue or excellence in human conduct. Augustine is no exception. Augustine's ontology is an ontology of love, or the *ordo amoris* found in several of his writings.[30] The whole notion of order, an ontology, to be sure, is always near in all of Augustine's writings (e.g., his notion of the order of tran-

---

29. Now, there may be questions about the sort of ontological order in question, but these are questions of clarification not necessarily undermining my claim.
30. Consider *Contra Faustum Manichaeum* 22.27; *De civitate Dei* 11.16–17 and 15.22. For some related issues, see Finnis, 1996; Russell, 1987.

quility in *De civitate Dei*), and it has serious implications for the way life is lived both privately and publicly.[31] What does Augustine mean by the ordo amoris or his ontology of love? Quite simply, it is that all of life is structured by a hierarchy of loves and a hierarchy of corresponding objects that can be loved. And this order implies a set of rules that must be followed if one is to be truly just and one's actions are to be truly virtuous. In essence, the rules dictate that just behavior entails setting one's love upon the noblest objects of the hierarchy (God and neighbor). Augustine's view, though, does not make the assumption that one becomes just or virtuous as one keeps the rules but rather that only one who best approximates justice and virtue *first* can then keep the rules.

Syse is correct that Augustine emphasizes virtue over mere rule following. However, it is important also to consider that real, complete virtue, justice, and love are a result of faith, and then and only then can persons be expected to live by the deontological dictates that the ordo amoris presupposes. Augustine makes it clear that faith in God is a precondition for loving God and our neighbors, that before one can love God and others one must first believe in God—and what is this properly ordered love for Augustine but virtue (cf. *De civitate Dei* 15.22)?[32] Thus, faith in God is a precondition to loving God, to living a just and virtuous life, and ultimately to conducting political affairs—war included—in a just fashion for, as Augustine writes, "no state is well founded and guarded except on the foundation and in the bond of faith and of firm concord" (*Epistolae* 137.17). Loving God is related first and foremost to believing in him, to placing one's faith in him. Only then can human beings be expected to be virtuous since they are then empowered to keep the rules of the ontology of love.

This being the case, several important questions suggest themselves for both Syse's and Gray's essays: If, as Augustine suggests, justice is the property of Christians alone, can a just war ever be possible that was waged by non-Christians? The answer is clearly no. This is not to say that

---

31. Augustine *De civitate Dei* 19.13: "the peace of the whole universe is the tranquility of order—and order is the arrangement of things equal and unequal in a pattern which assigns to each its proper position." Here, Augustine's entire conversation about peace centers around ontological premises of order.

32. For some exemplary comments of Augustine and the primacy of faith in regards to virtue and justice, refer to *De doctrina christiana* 1.37.41–39.43, *Enchiridion* 5, *Epistolae* 137.15, *Ioannis* 29.6, and *De ordine* 2.26–27.

all wars carried out by Christians are just. My argument simply takes into account Augustine's view that only true believers are imbued with the power to be virtuous, so that at least if a war is waged by them it has the potential to be done so in a virtuous manner. As such, an intra-Church "war" against heretics has the *potential* of perhaps being the most just war (humanly speaking) of all.[33] Second, are all wars conducted by true believers actually just wars? There are two answers to this question: no, not all wars waged by Christians are just wars; and second, one can never really ascertain whether such wars really are conducted in a just fashion. Augustine assumes that no human on earth can ever be fully just or virtuous since these are matters of progressive sanctification, with the result being completed only after death. Consequently, true believers are in the process of becoming more just and virtuous, with different believers being at different stages of this process. In regards to war, then, it can never be absolutely just, and its justice will vary depending on the degree of virtue and justice that those who wage war actually possess and enact. In practice this means that it is almost impossible to ascertain whether a war can be fully just because we do not know the sanctificatory stage in which a person finds himself. Also, a war can never be fully just because there is no true justice on earth; true justice is at the end of a long chain of development that can be reached only in the afterlife. This, then, presents some difficulties for both intra-Church wars and just wars in general.

Now, I would like to make one more observation regarding Augustine's views on just war: all wars that take place on earth are providentially just.[34] For Augustine, every instance of war is just in the sense that God in his providence has allowed them to take place. Consider the following passages where Augustine addresses part of the purpose behind the "universal catastrophe,'" or the sacking and downfall of Rome:

---

33. Augustine, to a certain extent like Tertullian, is a proponent of the irreconcilability of Christianity with classical culture and, in particular, of the irreconcilability between faith and reason and between civic justice and cosmic justice. Justice does not exist apart from faith, and to think that it does is to be arrogant. Justice and virtue, outside of religious faith, are splendid vices, so that all of civic life is robbery on a grand scale. Refer to *De civitate Dei* 19.4 for Augustine's exposition of these themes. In reference to only those wars that are conducted by Christians being just, see Augustine, *Letter 189.6*; *Letter 220*. An interesting question that arises regards what some may regard to be Augustine's pacifist tendencies as evidenced, for example, in *Letter 220* and *Letter 229*, and his comments on the importance of pursuing peace without bloodshed. On this issue see Holmes, 1999; Lenihan, 1988.

34. On this point and other related issues, see Holmes, 1999; Markus, 1983; Ramsey, 1992. Gray's conclusion regarding the moral corrective effects of war appears to accept this argument.

For God's providence constantly uses war to correct and chasten the corrupt morals of mankind, as it also uses such afflictions to train men in a righteous and laudable way of life, removing to a better state those whose life is approved, or else keeping them in this world for further service (Augustine *De civitate Dei* 1.1).... So this seems to me a major reason why the good are chastised along with the evil, when God decides to punish moral corruption with temporal calamities. Good and bad are chastised together, not because both alike live evil lives, but because both alike, though not in the same degree, love this temporal life (ibid.: 1.9).... There are however certain exceptions to the law against killing, made by the authority of God himself. There are some whose killing God orders, either by a law, or by an express command to a particular person at a particular time. In fact one who owes a duty of obedience to the giver of the command does not himself "kill" — he is an instrument, a sword in its user's hand. For this reason the commandment forbidding killing was not broken by those who have waged wars on the authority of God ... with the exception of these killings prescribed generally by a just law, or specially commanded by God himself — the source of justice — anyone who kills a human being, whether himself or anyone else, is involved in a charge of murder (ibid. 1.21). People are also amazed ... when God rebukes the human race, when he subjects it to a lashing, chastising it as a devoted father. He imposes discipline before he executes judgment; and he is not usually selective about those he will lash; for he does not want to find anyone to condemn. (Augustine, 2001: 1)

Augustine's argument is radical. Every war is just because its ultimate author is just, because its cause is just (to cause all earth dwellers to seek him), and because God is perfect and his intentions are perfect as well. Such justice, though, can be attributed only to God, never to human beings. Now, it might be objected that such a radical exposition of Augustine ignores the fact that he did articulate principles of justice upon which wars could be conducted — the "Augustinian" criteria of legitimate authority, just cause, and right intention for earthly wars.[35] However, appealing to these criteria as Augustine's answer to the issue of waging war justly ignores his skepticism about justice being realized by anyone except God. And if this is so, can there then be a virtuous war? Further, even if we are to keep these criteria as Augustine's answer to the dilemmas of war, it is only God who can completely fulfill their demands and no other.

---

35. At least as that found in *Quaestiones in Heptateuchum* 6.10. Syse is correct to point out that while many consider Augustine the originator of the just war criteria, many others before him had already composed its basic tenets. On this point, see also Nederman, 2001. Lastly, I am not even sure that Augustine agrees with these criteria or is simply telling his readers what the traditional view is. In other words, it may be the case that these criteria do not really represent Augustine's view on the subject.

Thus, while Augustine does emphasize the role of virtue and the evils of war, he does not do this at the expense of his ontological views. If there is a virtue ethics approach in his views on war, it is possible to suggest that it is firmly rooted in his ontology, an ontology that actually presupposes more rigorous demands and rules upon human beings than even that of Kant himself. It is Augustine's commitment to this ontology of love, much like Plato's commitment to the ontology of the forms, that makes Augustine's comments on war even more paradoxical and ambiguous than either Syse or Gray may admit. Why? Simply stated, it is because Augustine is wrestling with the fundamental issues of being and becoming, of the relationship between faith and reason, and of the problems of relating a world of becoming with a world that is.

Aquinas and the Presumption against Injustice

Gregory M. Reichberg's timely essay (see chapter 5 in this volume) takes up the issue of the place of Aquinas within just war theorizing, especially in regard to whether Aquinas's ethics is inherently antagonistic to war. This issue is especially important given that there are rival versions of just war theory appealing to Aquinas for support. Some, for example, argue that Aquinas's ethics carries a strong presumption against the use of force and, consequently, is more strongly in favor of peace than conflict (see Miller, 1991; National Conference of Catholic Bishops, 1983, both cited in Reichberg's essay). Others argue that for Aquinas, it is not the use of force that is condemnable but "the use of force with the wrong intention" (see Johnson, 1996: 29, as cited by Reichberg). The chapter then makes a very skillful and technical argument in support of the view that Aquinas's ethics carries a presumption against injustice, not against war.

Reichberg is correct to conclude that Aquinas is not antagonistic to war but that armed conflict has a place within the theologian's political thought. One has only to look at *De regimine principum*, where Aquinas states that for the ruler to ensure that a society lives well it is necessary that he *defend* the society and its mode of life, a defense that is certain to include armed conflict.[36] The question asked by Reichberg regarding the

---

36. Thomas Aquinas, *De regimine principum*, 15: "A king therefore, being instructed in the Divine Law, should make a special effort to ensure that the society under him lives well. This involves three things—first, he should establish the good life of the community under him;

place of Aquinas's discussion of war in the *Summa theologiae* is an important one, and the author performs an expert analysis, weeding out the textual and structural issues surrounding this thorny point.

The comments that follow will focus on issues of clarification endemic to aspects of Reichberg's argument and conclusion. While I concur with the overall conclusion that the ethics of Aquinas carries a presumption against injustice and not against war,[37] part of the argument used to reach this conclusion could prove problematic. I have here in mind Reichberg's argument that "'waging war' (bellare) is not inherently evil" but is morally neutral. More work needs to be performed in providing textual evidence for this argument lest it be criticized as an artificial fabrication. Does a "morally neutral" category for war really exist in the *Summa*? I am not sure what this category accomplishes, and its meaning is somewhat ambiguous. By "morally neutral" is it meant that war, as a linguistic concept, has no moral core? Or does it mean that war is a "morally neutral" activity in and of itself, made good or evil depending on the circumstances surrounding it? Is it no different, let us say, from eating a meal? For eating seems to be a "morally neutral" activity, becoming moral insofar as one is a glutton or an ascetic, that is to say, depending on the amounts of food one eats and for what purpose. Is this what war as a "morally neutral" term means, that the mere act of killing is just like any other activity, only becoming moral depending on the number that are killed, how they are killed, and for what purpose they are killed? This is extremely problematic, and the mode of argument the essay uses here raises some difficult questions. Further, it is not certain that Aquinas uses this "morally neutral" argument, seeing that he appears to reserve for war a very restricted and special status. If Aquinas takes care to argue that only certain types of conflict can be considered war qua war, then why would he employ a semantic argument regarding the term *war*—an argument that is ambiguous at best? Lastly, what is the importance, if any, of this semantic or theoretical argument in the actual practices of war and in the actual attempts to limit wars?

---

second, he should defend it once it is established; and third, once secured he should foster its improvement."

37. There is textual evidence for this conclusion. Consider *Summa theologiae*, II-II, qu. 40, where Aquinas defends the possibility that a just war exists insofar as it meets the criterion for justice.

For Aquinas, then, it is not that war is a morally neutral term or activity whose justice depends on circumstances. Rather, for Aquinas it is the case that there are only two sorts of wars—just and unjust—and that the argument in *quaestio* 40 of the *Secunda-secundae pars* of the *Summa* is meant to defend the view that not all wars are sinful (this seems to be the point of some of the objections considered in quaestio 40), but that there are just wars that can be waged for the purposes of peace, safety, and maybe even love of the commonwealth. Lastly, Reichberg raises a very interesting issue regarding why Aquinas's ethics carries a presumption against injustice (or, in my view, against an unjust war). The possibility is considered that this may be due to the influence of Aristotle upon Aquinas's thinking, inter alia. Perhaps it is due to a curious mixture not only of Aristotelianism but also of theological and philosophical assumptions from many other thinkers upon which Aquinas was relying.

A more serious issue that I would like to raise at this point, in light of the above, is whether Aquinas, and for that matter Augustine (depending on one's interpretation), carries a presumption in support of war itself. Most interpretations of these thinkers do not situate them as being principled defenders of violence. This is usually accomplished by arguing that Augustine and Aquinas are either absolute or qualified pacifists (i.e., presumption against war) or that they are Christian realists (i.e., presumption against injustice but not against war). However, a substantial portion of the just war tradition has always considered these two Christian figures as advocating a strong moral position against war and violence itself with a carefully devised moral argument for the legitimacy of conflict in particular circumstances. Thus, the recourse to violence advocated by Augustine and Aquinas appears to be theologically and philosophically principled. In regard to Aquinas, Reichberg argues this much when he ponders whether Aquinas's presumption against injustice may result from the influence of Aristotelianism or from some other cause. However, agreement is not complete on this point. As Hays argues: "Although the *tradition* of the first three centuries was decidedly pacifist in orientation, Christian *tradition* from the time of Constantine to the present has predominantly endorsed war, or at least justified it under certain conditions" (1996: 341).[38] I raise this issue here for the sole purpose

---

38. I am indebted to my colleague Michael Lopez for bringing this source to my attention.

of considering the thorny question of whether Christianity itself justifies violence in certain situations. If it does, it would seem to be the case that Augustine, Aquinas, and countless other Christian writers would be correct to offer theologically principled defenses of just wars and that we could look to Christian theology itself as one of the possible "causes" influencing a Thomistic or Augustinian analysis of war.

The question of the role of Christian theology and its place in war is not one that can be quickly settled here. Needless to say, much interpretative ink has been spilled on this theme. But what is important to consider is exactly where some Christian writers go to find justifications for violence. Is it the New Testament? Is it the Old Testament? Is it a combination of both? Are there other sources on which they depend? Aquinas, for example, appears to justify war on the basis of a natural conception of justice. The only New Testament passage he cites in his defense of war in the *Summa* is the infamous "beareth not the sword in vain" passage of Romans 13, where the political authority has the obligation to punish "evildoers." However, this passage is referred to only in passing, while Aquinas's argument relies heavily upon "justice" claims, the proper role for political authority (conceived in a typical Aristotelian fashion), and Augustine's treatment of the subject. Augustine, if interpreted as an advocate of "just" violence, also appears to support some wars as legitimate at least on the basis that "the natural order conducive to peace" necessitates that such conflicts take place (Augustine, 1994: 22.75). What this may tell us is that both Aquinas and Augustine base their just war theorizing on other traditions and not necessarily (or at least not only) on biblical-theological ones. Again, as Hays writes: "Only a little reflection will show that the classic just war criteria ... are ... neither derived nor derivable from the New Testament; they are formulated through a process of reasoning that draws upon natural law traditions far more heavily than upon biblical warrants" (Hays, 1996: 341). Critics may argue that in the history of war, the Church has, for the most part, sanctified armed conflict, that "for seventeen hundred years [the Church] has engaged in revenge, murder, torture, the pursuit of power, and prerogative violence, all in the name of our Lord" (Zabelka, 1980: 14). There is little doubt that this indictment is correct. Yet, it must be noted that the failure of Christian thinkers to support peace rather than war may be due in part to their reliance on other intellectual and moral traditions than the Christian one, for too often it has been the case that the Christian Church "is deeply compromised and committed to nationalism, violence, and idolatry. This indictment applies alike to liberation theologies that justify violence against aggressors and to establishment Christianity that continues . . . to [cite] just war theory and [advocate] the defense of a particular nation as though that were somehow a Christian value" (Hays, 1996: 343). Now, this is obviously only one possible interpretation among others regarding the status of war within the Christian tradition. But it is important to suggest that insofar as it is possible to raise the prospect that Christian just war theory carries with it a presumption in favor of violence, one may be able to justify such a position only on the basis of various causes that are not necessarily theological.

Other Voices in the Just War Theory Conversation

Kate Forhan's insightful essay (see chapter 6 in this volume) demonstrates how thinking about war was not an activity confined only to members of a particular social or academic status. By introducing Geoffrey Chaucer and Christine de Pizan as relevant to discussions about war, Forhan's essay serves to broaden not only the social spectrum of theorists on war but also the theoretical spectrum of considerations about war and waging war. One interesting question, not explicitly raised by Forhan due to topical constraints, is whether a separate feminist tradition on the ethics of war and peace exists. And if it does, what is the place of Christine de Pizan within that tradition?[39] Regardless of this question, Forhan's essay makes a very important contribution to broadening the perspectives that are a part of the just war tradition.

In Geoffrey Chaucer's "The Tale of Melibeus," we are introduced to the many elements, both rash and prudent, that are part of considerations regarding the waging of war. In the tale, the family of the "mighty and riche" young Melibeus is viciously attacked by his enemies. Prudence, his wife, is beaten and his daughter, Sophie, is left with five se-

---

39. This is a considerable area of debate among feminist scholars. For example, Elshtain, 1996, argues that "there is no separate feminist tradition on war and peace," maintaining that feminist treatments of war and peace can be taken into account as variants of "liberal internationalism," of which Pizan is an example (214). Others, for example, Tobias, 1996, argue that such a tradition does in fact exist—at least insofar as we consider contemporary feminist ethics in the realm of international relations theory.

vere wounds. Melibeus is counseled by Prudence to seek advice about how to respond so as to avoid rash action. Gathering a motley host of counselors, Melibeus shares his woes and seeks advice. At this point of the tale, Chaucer brilliantly illustrates that the decisions behind war are often rooted in vengeance, quick-spirited anger, and a lack of rational and moral reflection. The counselors, for the most part, all agree that the only cure for the war that has been perpetrated upon him is vengeance: "Almost in the same words the physicians answered, save that they added: 'Just as diseases are cured by their contraries, so shall men cure war by vengeance.' His neighbours, . . . his false friends, . . . and his flatterers . . . said outright, that very swiftly he should begin the war and wreak vengeance upon his foes" (Chaucer, 1915: 192–94). Admonitions to the contrary come only from a wise elder and from Prudence herself. And here, as Forhan rightly notes, Chaucer introduces his readers to an antiwar position. But upon deeper reflection it is a nuanced antiwar position, a sort of prudential pacifism not rooted in religious conviction. Chaucer's tale betrays a pacifist position that appears to be grounded in a deep skepticism and uncertainty about the outcomes of war. As both the elderly adviser and Melibeus's wife argue, no one can really judge what will happen in a war. And even if one does have the right cause to fight a war, it does not guarantee victory (ibid.: 193, 194, 214).[40] But while this pacifism appears to be rooted in a trenchant skepticism, it is ultimately grounded upon the notion of individual self-interest. This self-interested or prudential pacifism is betrayed in Prudence's comment that the advice he is receiving from some of his counselors is not in his own true interest and that he should take account of the fact that his actions risk a blood feud from which surely his attackers and their kinsmen will arise victorious and from which he stands to lose much of his wealth (ibid.: 213–14). The uncertainty that leads to Chaucer's pacifism is an uncertainty about how war affects an individual's self-interest, and since one does not know what the outcome will be and whether one's interests will be fulfilled or destroyed, it is a more prudent thing to deliberate with the enemy than to pursue armed conflict. It is extremely interesting how Chau-

---

40. Here, in essence, the wise elder alerts Melibeus that such a high and dangerous matter must be considered carefully and reflected upon with much patience and time. Chaucer seems to be telling his audience that all too often decisions of war are made thoughtlessly and too quickly, that is, in the heat of the moment. This is in fact what most of the crowd counsels Melibeus to do.

cer uses self-interest as a means to limit and even vanquish the idea of war. One usually thinks of self-interest as the root of social conflict. Here, however, self-interest is noble, perhaps even a virtue of sorts, and a very legitimate deterrent to war while at the same time a facilitator of peace and personal well-being.

Forhan's exposition of Christine de Pizan's thoughts on war is a bit more complex.[41] In her comments regarding the civil war in France, Christine de Pizan evidences a deep-seated skepticism regarding war and whether it can ever be just. But this skepticism is about a particular type of war, namely civil, and it seems to be based more on romanticism than on religious conviction or Chaucerian self-interest. Christine laments what has been lost in France due to civil war, much like Rousseau laments what has been lost in modern society due to the emergence of the arts and sciences. Her comments on civil war present the reader with a pacifist position, one that is peculiar due to the type of conflict with which she is dealing and which does not represent her complete view on issues of just war.[42]

Christine's writings on the art of warfare and on the duties of the prince do present a fuller view of her thoughts on warfare and, as Forhan points out, her special contribution to the conditions that must be met if a war is to be justified. Christine does hold that a war can be carried out justly and that war is a legitimate political activity.[43] However, she is careful to place limits on the activity itself. The first significant contribution is her exceptionally broad definition of authority in regard to waging war. She grants authority to many political actors who under mainstream medieval just war theories would have been excluded. This seems to be due more to the recognition of her own political reality than it is the articulation of an original principle. What is extremely interesting in Chris-

41. On related issues, see Forhan, 2002.
42. In particular, note her letters to the Duke of Berry and to other French nobility. See Christine de Pizan, 1984: 304-5.
43. Christine de Pizan, 1994: 1.9: "This is not the right manner of warfare, which ought to be just and without extortion." Here Christine tacitly assumes the possibility of just conflict. In this same section, Christine, explaining the duty of the prince to protect his people, writes: "Just so, the good prince is mindful of the defense and care of his country and people, even though it is impossible in person. In every place he has responsibility, he will always provide himself with very good assistance, in deeds of knighthood and for other things; that is, the brave leaders whom he knows are good and loyal and who love him, such as constables, marshals, admirals, and others, to whom he gives responsibility for furnishing other good soldiers, well-taught and experienced in war."

tine's thought is her condition that before a war can be deemed just, a body of advisers must meet to deliberate, along with the prince, to see if his position is just and, ultimately, this process of deliberation must include the adversary as well. This argument is found not only in Christine's *Le livre des fais d'armes et de la chevalerie* but also in *The Book of the Body Politic*, where Christine argues: "But to pass from examples of great rigor [in regard to the application of justice], let us discuss how the good prince keeps justice and what is necessary for him to do so. First, and principally, to do this he ought to be provided with wise and prudent men and good councillors, who love his soul and honor and the good of the country more than their own benefit" (1994: 1.19). This process of deliberation in Christine's theory suggests several fruitful areas for consideration. First, why the need for deliberation? Is it because she distrusts political power? Or is it because she distrusts human nature and self-interest? Could it be that Christine is thinking here about comparative claims of justice? Is it, perhaps, that too often human beings are blinded by their own self-interest so that—reminiscent of Hobbes—they tend to magnify the faults of others while observing their own faults only at a distance? Furthermore, what was the impact of the French civil war upon Christine's theory of war in general? I raise this issue here since Christine's interesting comments about deliberation and the other conditions for a just war betray what appears to be a presumption against war. Moreover, what, if any, is the influence of the classical tradition upon Christine's thought, especially from the likes of Cicero (and we should also consider Cicero's influence upon Chaucer)? I raise this question because it is Cicero who argues that it is more proper for human beings to settle disputes through deliberation than through force and conflict. And it is Chaucer who makes use of Cicero in "The Tale of Melibeus," with Christine making use of classical notions such as prudence and appealing to the importance of deliberation to settle conflicts, while simultaneously filling *The Book of the Body Politic* with a multitude of examples from the classic Roman tradition.[44]

What is also interesting is that both poets have deep reservations about war, but their reservations are not based directly on their religious

---

44. The impact of the ancients in general can be seen in other of Christine's works. For example, in *The Book of the City of Ladies* three goddesses, Rectitude, Reason, and Justice, establish an ideal city.

convictions. While both "The Tale of Melibeus" and *The Book of the Body Politic* have various references to God and to biblical passages, the antiwar reservations expressed in these works seem to be based upon the meaning and richness of *humanitas,* which is endangered during war, and upon a deep-seated noble ignorance or humility that always advices prudence rather than harsh action. If this is correct, we should investigate this matter further. Why would two literary figures choose to base their views about war on nonreligious grounds and come to conclusions that do not enshrine war but rather propose serious limitations on its practice—limitations that almost make war impossible? Is this further evidence that perhaps Christian just war theory often shows a presumption toward war based on its poor conception of humanitas? Lastly, it would be worthwhile to consider in this vein whether Chaucer's and Christine's thoughts about war are an improvement over or even superior to Augustine's or Aquinas' just war theorizing. As I have presented Augustine, he seems to be deeply skeptical about the possibilities of there being a just war simply because we do not know if the actors are acting in a just fashion and because true justice is not of this world. But in spite of this skepticism, Augustine never considers the possibility of deliberation but presses ahead with restricting the conditions of conflict. Both Chaucer and Christine de Pizan are also skeptical about war but rather than merely restricting the conditions for conflict, they both adopt principles of deliberation meant to avoid war altogether. Why is this the case? Is it that these poets knew something that Augustine did not? Did they think more deeply about war than Augustine? What would have prompted them to introduce such a novel concept into just war theorizing? Again, is it that the devaluation of humanitas that Augustine and many other Christians accepted in the early Middle Ages led them to accept the evil of war more readily as simply an inevitable part of human life?

There are no easy answers. But what is certain is that Chaucer and Christine offer a counterposition to many of the medieval Christian expositions of just war theories, one that is quite appealing not only for its possible results but also due to its basis in general principles that encourage the humanity of human beings. Thus, at still another point, we find again a possible clash between Christianity and medieval remnants of classical culture.

REFERENCES

Ambrose. 1980. *De officiis ministorum*. In Henry Wace and Philip Schaff, eds., *The Nicene and Post-Nicene Fathers of the Church*, 2nd ser., vol. 10. Grand Rapids, Mich.: William B. Eerdmans, 23–90.
———. 1933. *De Tobias*. Ed. Lois Miles Zucker. Washington, D.C.: The Catholic University of America Press.
Aristotle. 1984. *Nicomachean Ethics*. Chicago: University of Chicago Press.
Augsburger, Myron S. 1991. "Christian Pacifism." In Robert G. Clouse, ed., *War: Four Christian Views*. Downers Grove, Ill.: Intervarsity, 79–97.
Augustine. 1994. *Contra Faustum Manichaeum*. In Philip Schaff, ed., *Nicene and Post-Nicene Fathers*, 1st ser., vol. 4. Peabody, Mass.: Hendrickson, 155–346.
———. 2001. *The Sacking of the City of Rome*. In E. Margaret Atkins and Robert J. Dodaro, eds., *Augustine: Political Writings*. Cambridge: Cambridge University Press, 205–13.
Brown, Harold O. J. 1991. "The Crusade or Preventive War." In Robert G. Clouse, ed., *War: Four Christian Views*. Downers Grove, Ill.: Intervarsity, 151–67.
Chaucer, Geoffrey. 1915. "The Tale of Melibeus." In John Urban Nicolson, ed., *Canterbury Tales*. Garden City, N.Y.: International Collectors Library, 189–236.
Christine de Pizan. 1984. *Writings of Christine de Pizan*. Ed. Charity Cannon Willard. New York: Persea.
———. 1994. *The Book of the Body Politic*. Cambridge: Cambridge University Press.
Cicero. 1991. *De officiis*. Cambridge: Cambridge University Press.
———. 1995. *De republica*. Cambridge: Cambridge University Press.
Clausewitz, Karl von. 1968. *On War*. New York: Penguin.
Cochrane, Charles N. 1957. *Christianity and Classical Culture*. Oxford: Oxford University Press.
Elshtain, Jean B. 1996. "Is There a Feminist Tradition on War and Peace?" In Terry Nardin, ed., *The Ethics of War and Peace: Religious and Secular Perspectives*. Princeton: Princeton University Press, 214–27.
Finnis, John. 1996. "The Ethics of War and Peace in the Catholic Natural Law Tradition." In Terry Nardin, ed., *The Ethics of War and Peace: Religious and Secular Perspectives*. Princeton: Princeton University Press, 15–39.
Forhan, Kate L. 2002. *The Political Theory of Christine de Pizan*. Burlington, Vt.: Ashgate.
Fotion, Nick. 1990. *Military Ethics*. Stanford, Calif.: Hoover Institution Press.
———. 2000. "Reactions to War: Pacifism, Realism, and Just War Theory." In Andrew Valls, ed., *Ethics in International Affairs*. Lanham: Rowman and Littlefield, 15–32.
Hays, Richard B. 1996. *The Moral Vision of the New Testament*. New York: Harper Collins.
Holmes, Robert L. 1999. "St. Augustine and the Just War Theory." In Gareth B. Matthews, ed., *The Augustinian Tradition*. Berkeley: University of California Press, 323–44.
Hoyt, Herman A. 1991. "Biblical Nonresistance." In Robert G. Clouse, ed., *War: Four Christian Views*. Downers Grove, Ill.: Intervarsity, 27–57.
Huizinga, Johan. 1950. *Homo Ludens: A Study of the Play-Element in Culture*. Boston: Beacon.
Johnson, James T. 1996. "The Broken Tradition." *National Interest* 45 (Fall 1996): 27–36.
Lenihan, David A. 1988. "Augustine and the Just War." *Augustinian Studies* 19:37–70.
Mapel, David R. 1996. "Realism and the Ethics of War and Peace." In Terry Nardin, ed., *The Ethics of War and Peace: Religious and Secular Perspectives*. Princeton: Princeton University Press, 54–77.
Markus, Robert Austin. 1983. "Saint Augustine's Views on the 'Just War.'" In William J. Sheils, ed., *The Church and War*. London: Basil Blackwell, 1–13.
McMahan, Jeff. 1993. "War and Peace." In Peter Singer, ed., *A Companion to Ethics*. Oxford: Blackwell, 384–95.
———. 1996. "Realism, Morality, and War." In Terry Nardin, ed., *The Ethics of War and Peace: Religious and Secular Perspectives*. Princeton: Princeton University Press, 78–92.
Miller, Richard B. 1991. *Interpretations of Conflict: Ethics, Pacifism, and the Just-War Tradition*. Chicago: University of Chicago Press.

Morino, Claudio. 1969. *Church and State in the Teaching of St. Ambrose*. Washington, D.C.: The Catholic University of America Press.

National Conference of Catholic Bishops. 1983. *The Challenge of Peace: God's Promise and Our Response*. Washington, D.C.: United States Catholic Conference.

Nederman, Cary J. 2001. "War, Peace, and Republican Virtue: Patriotism and the Neglected Legacy of Cicero." In Norma Thompson, ed., *Instilling Ethics*. Boston: Rowman and Littlefield, 17–30.

Ramsey, Paul. 1992. "The Just War according to St. Augustine." In Jean Bethke Elshtain, ed., *Just War Theory*. New York: New York University Press, 8–22.

Russell, Frederick H. 1975. *The Just War in the Middle Ages*. Cambridge: Cambridge University Press.

———. 1987. "Love and Hate in Medieval Warfare: The Contribution of St. Augustine." *Nottingham Medieval Studies* 31:108–24.

Tobias, Sarah. 1996. "Toward a Feminist Ethic of War and Peace." In Terry Nardin, ed., *The Ethics of War and Peace: Religious and Secular Perspectives*. Princeton: Princeton University Press, 228–44.

Tzu, Lao. 1987. "Tao Te Ching." In Wade Baskin, ed., *Classics in Chinese Philosophy*. New York: Philosophical Library, 53–87.

Westling, Arthur H. 1984. "How Much Damage Can Modern War Create?" In Frank Barnaby, ed., *Future War: Armed Conflict in the Next Decade*. London: Michael Joseph, 114–24.

Zabelka, George. 1980. "I Was Told It Was Necessary." *Sojourners* 9 (8): 14.

PART TWO

Contemporary Problems of War, Nationalism, and Ethics

THE TERRORIST ATTACKS *of September 11, 2001, have given rise to much speculation about their implications for the ethics of war. Surely, the political map as well as the rhetoric about armed force seem to have undergone a radical transformation since the day when the Twin Towers fell and the Pentagon was attacked. The long-term implications of 9/11 are, however, much harder to measure. In this respect, we would do well to remember the words of former Chinese premier Zhou Enlai who, when asked about the impact of the French Revolution, answered, "It is too soon to say."*

Indeed, it is still too soon to determine whether 9/11 marks a paradigm shift in our view of war, or whether it is merely another event that continues the twentieth-century trend toward civilians being directly targeted in war, amply demonstrated by the Second World War and continued in numerous internal conflicts since then, with Rwanda in 1994 as the apex so far.

One thing, though, is certain: Several of the problems that were most eagerly discussed in the immediate post–cold war era, while currently eclipsed by events in the war on terror, are still with us, having manifestly not been solved. Among these are the fate of noncombatants at a time when warfare puts an increasingly heavy burden on civilians. The pressure on civilians is further increased by the fact that most wars today take place within rather than between states, and in such settings the demarcation line between combatants and noncombatants is often extremely difficult to draw.

Another important issue is the fate of the environment in war. In an age when the human impact (illness, starvation, etc.) of war-caused environmental destruction is so significant, and the ability of weapons and warfare to cause such destruction is so far-reaching, protection of the environment surely needs to be addressed as an important part of the ethics of war.

Armed humanitarian intervention remains another divisive yet crucial issue. Grave abuses continue to be perpetuated against people who have no reasonable chance of defending themselves, as for instance today in the Sudan. Simultaneously, the globalized news media bring ever more of the world's suffering to our doorsteps and television screens, creating strong moral pressure to act. But who should act, when, and how? And is there a danger that by undertaking armed humanitarian action, even with a United Nations mandate, we will do more harm than good?

The U.S.-led invasion of Iraq in 2003 provoked a heated controversy on the ethical merits of preventive defense, a debate that is still very much with us. The grave risks posed by weapons of mass destruction have lent credence in some quarters to the justifiability of preemptive action, especially when such action is directed against "rogue states." When joined to the related notion of "regime change," this discourse on preemption has raised pressing issues that must be met by any contemporary normative treatment of the ius ad bellum (right and wrong resort to armed force). The roles and responsibilities of the nation-state vis-à-vis regional organizations and what is often called the "international community" is another topic that will only grow in complexity as calls for sovereignty and independence increase alongside economic globalization and interdependence. Understanding the underlying problems of nationalism and identity is thus crucial for any serious ethical approach to war.

War crime trials reveal yet another face of modern war: the increasing ability and willingness of many actors, state and nonstate, to bring to justice those who have committed the worst war crimes. In denouncing the actions of genocidal rulers, unscrupulous military commanders, and their respective subordinates, the public comes to expect real and swift judicial action rather than merely pious resolutions, and thus the need for well-functioning and respected law courts becomes an integral part of present-day war ethics.

Finally, we come to the responsibilities of bystanders—those who do not command or fight the wars but who contribute to them nonetheless, through political support, intellectual ideas, or merely inaction. If it is true that the causes of war are complex, and that the causal chains in a globalized world are manifold and intersecting, we cannot analyze the actions merely of a narrow band of political and military leaders; we must also look to other actors who make substantial contributions, yet who all too often escape our moral judgment.

These are the topics addressed in the second part of this book. They all build on the conviction, explored in the first part, that normative perspectives on war are crucially important, and that it is actually possible—albeit difficult—to formulate guidelines for minimizing the destructiveness of war.

While the essays in this volume do not directly address issues associated with 9/11 or the war on terror—with the exception of Janssen's chapter 14, which indeed deals with its aftermath—we believe, in part for that very reason, that they provide original and topical insights on problems that will, alas, lose none of their urgency in the years to come.

8

Maintaining the Protection of Noncombatants

JAMES TURNER JOHNSON

All warfare imposes a burden of harm on noncombatants. This burden may be relatively light, as when the citizens of a nation engaged in a faraway war fought by mercenaries are taxed to support that war. The weight is heavier when the soldiers are drawn from the same population that is at war, whether by volunteering or by a draft. And of course it is heaviest of all on people caught up in the swirl of war, whose lives and livelihoods are disrupted, whose property may be damaged, destroyed, or taken away, and who may have no say in their ultimate fate, as their nation's boundaries are changed or even obliterated by the outcome of the war. These burdens increase as the magnitude of war itself increases. Modern warfare has often been criticized because of its scale: the numbers of people drawn into its armies, the destructive power of its weapons, its global reach.

Still, these burdens are of a different kind from those imposed by warfare in which either or both belligerent parties consciously make no distinction between noncombatants and combatants or, worse yet, in which one or both belligerents target noncombatants directly as a method of war. Either sort of warfare tends to place a disproportionately heavy load on noncombatants, for a variety of reasons: military personnel may be better sheltered from armed attack, while noncombatants are more exposed and vulnerable; military personnel may have preferred access to good food and medical care; military personnel are able to fight back, a fact that may deter attacks on them while redirecting attacking force to the softer targets represented by noncombatants. When no distinction is made between enemy combatants and enemy noncombatants, the noncombatants suffer disproportionately. When noncombatants are chosen as preferred targets, this burden of suffering becomes heaviest of all.

In these comments I make two assumptions that are of fundamental moral importance and are central to the argument of this chapter. The first is that it is right and morally necessary to distinguish between noncombatants and combatants in a society at war. This would perhaps seem obvious to many people; yet it has often been challenged theoretically by people who argue that this distinction is meaningless in modern wars and, directly to the point of the present essay, it is often denied both in theory and in practice in contemporary armed conflicts, especially those involving ethnic or religious differences or the like. The second assumption from which I am proceeding is that it is right and morally necessary to distinguish direct, intended harm toward noncombatants from indirect, unintended harm. This is the concept usually called the "rule of double effect" in moral discussions. In the following sections I examine both of these assumptions—and the challenges to them—in some detail, and I depend on them throughout the discussion below.

The chapter is divided into five major parts: the first analyzing the general problem of warfare on noncombatants in moral terms; the second looking at the historical development of the idea of noncombatant protection as an element of just war tradition; the third summarizing this idea as it has taken shape in positive international law; the fourth examining the problem of warfare on noncombatants in three contemporary armed conflicts, those in Rwanda-Zaire, the former Yugoslavia, and the Iraq war of 2003; and a concluding section of moral reflections. The overall framework for my analysis throughout is the moral tradition of just war, of which Michael Walzer's *Just and Unjust Wars* (1977) provides a widely known contemporary expression. More broadly, this tradition is significant because it constitutes the major effort of Western culture to define when use of military force is morally justified and what are the moral limits to the employment of justified force. Historically, this tradition, through the work of such theorists as Vitoria and Grotius, lies at the basis of the law of war in international law; it is also reflected in codes of military behavior and other forms as well as in specifically moral discussion. (See further Johnson, 1975, 1981; Ramsey, 1968; Walzer, 1977.)

Defining Noncombatant Protection Morally

The Moral Basis of the Combatant-Noncombatant Distinction

In moral terms, in war it is the enemy's engagement in activity that aims to do me harm that gives me the right to do harm to him. That is, it is actions, not hostile sympathies or simple membership in a group with which one's own is in conflict, that justify the use of force: force is justified as response to threat or use of force. Of course, much more needs to be said that qualifies and restricts this right, and just war tradition as a whole defines such qualifications and restrictions. In the present context, though, it is important to observe that the distinction between combatants and noncombatants follows directly from the above rationale: in the most basic terms, this is the distinction between those members of the enemy society or party who are engaged in such activity and those who are not. We may examine this concept more closely by considering three lines of challenge to the combatant-noncombatant distinction found in contemporary discussion.

First, some critics argue that in modern societies the degree of integration between civilian and military functions is so tight that whatever the theoretical difference, no practical distinction can be made between the two. The employee of the electric power company, it is observed, serves civilian and military users alike. So does the operator for the telephone company. So does the worker on the factory line that cans fruits and vegetables. All these, and others in other tasks all across the society, are argued to be implicitly contributing to the military effort of a country at war. By extension, so are those people who support them physically and emotionally, such as members of their families.

This line of argument has a certain plausibility, but it goes too far in its claims. In its effort to draw military and nonmilitary activities as close together as possible, it overlooks or collapses all possibility of distinctions having to do with degree of cooperation in specifically military activities. Yet not only is it in fact possible to make such distinctions, they are morally meaningful. There really is a difference between, for example, a worker in a munitions factory and one engaged in processing food that is distributed alike to the civilian population and members of the military forces. While there may be some cases of ambiguity, these do not justify a general decision that warfare today must be indiscriminate. As Paul

Ramsey once observed, in thinking about how to wage modern war morally, the distinction between combatants and noncombatants does not have to be clear on a person-by-person basis: "We do not need to know *who* or *where* the noncombatants are," only "*that* there are noncombatants—even 'only small children and the helpless, sick and aged'—in order to know the basic moral difference between limited and total war" (1968: 157; emphasis in original).

Another line of attack goes still further in denying the idea of a distinction between noncombatants and combatants. This argument is that among one's enemies, all—regardless of age, relative health or helplessness, or degree of involvement in political decision making or military activity—may be assumed to support the war, and thus all may be rightly targeted. This kind of argument identifies the entire enemy society or party, and not just its armed forces or its responsible political leadership, as the foe. While it takes different forms, perhaps the most virulent is the identification of all members of another ethnic or linguistic group, tribe, or religion as equally the enemy. When to this is added the identification of one's own cause with ultimate right and the contrary cause as ultimately wrong, then the members of the enemy group have lost all rights to fair treatment and even to life itself. The problem with this position is that it loses sight of what it is in war that confers the right on one person to do harm to another: the threat of harm that this person represents. Contrary beliefs, different ethnicities or languages or citizenship do not in themselves constitute such a threat.

A third line of challenge to the idea of a noncombatant-combatant distinction makes reference to the alleged inherent destructiveness and indiscriminate character of modern weaponry and thus of modern warfare as such. This argument has most flourished as a means of attack on nuclear weapons and on war itself in the age of such weapons. On this position, though the weapons of war have become so destructive that they are inherently indiscriminate, in order to fight wars, belligerents have to make use of them. Thus modern wars *necessarily* can make no distinction between noncombatants and combatants.

There are three sorts of problems with this argument. First, it overgeneralizes: not all contemporary weapons are so grossly destructive that they can be called indiscriminate; rather, some are exceedingly accurate and of relatively low yield, while others are hand weapons of the same sort that have been used in wars for centuries. The second problem is that this conception makes war into a kind of technological determinism in which human decisions have no role—for not all uses of grossly destructive weapons are indiscriminate, and not all uses of less destructive ones are discriminate; the difference is how belligerents choose to use them. The third problem is that it entirely misses the point of the indiscriminateness found in contemporary armed conflicts, in which the warfare waged against noncombatants makes use of knives, clubs, and hand guns, which are not inherently indiscriminate.

Despite its problems, this line of argument does raise an important point: some means of war are in fact *mala in se,* evil in themselves—that is, their use is morally justified under no circumstances whatsoever. Their use constitutes, prima facie, a violation of the moral limits that should be observed in war, and such use may be a war crime. A considerable international consensus outlaws weapons of mass destruction for this reason. Yet it is morally important to keep in mind that mass destruction does not require such weaponry but can be achieved by quite ordinary arms, such as knives, clubs, and handguns, or by deprivation of food, water, and shelter—methods widely exemplified in contemporary conflicts. Again, the central moral problem is how the available weapons of war are employed against the enemy, and because of this it is fundamental to distinguish noncombatants from combatants.

All these arguments have positive and negative versions; that is, at one end of the spectrum of debate over morality and war they are used to argue for a kind of warfare in which protection of noncombatants has no place, and at the other end they are used to argue that war itself has become so awful that it must be abolished. Taken together, these produce an argument from false alternatives: if there is to be war, it must be total war; if total war is to be avoided, then war as an institution must be abolished. There is, however, a third alternative: that the conduct of war can be subjected to moral limits. Distinguishing between noncombatants and combatants is a basic and necessary step in this direction.

Direct vs. Indirect, Intended vs. Unintended Harm

The second fundamental assumption I make in discussing the moral protection due noncombatants is between direct, intended harm to persons deserving such protection and harm that comes to them indirectly and unintentionally in the way of war. There are two qualifiers here, and both are important. The ideal would be an attack on a legitimate military target with a weapon able to be aimed accurately at it and of destructive power no greater than needed to destroy the intended target. It is possible, even in such a tightly construed case, that some harm to noncombatants might result from the attack. More realistically, since in war the ideal possibility is normally not the rule, a direct attack on a legitimate target by a weapon not mala in se and with the intention to destroy only that target will often produce collateral harm to noncombatants. Tragic though such harm may be, this is a different kind of case from one in which there is a direct attack on noncombatants (for example, if refugees are rounded up and shot) or when the intention includes the harming or killing of noncombatants (as when a conscious choice is made for a particular target because significant numbers of noncombatants live in the immediate vicinity). The difference between the former kind of case and these two latter kinds is explained by what moralists call the rule of double effect.

Michael Walzer provides an inclusive statement of this rule in terms of four conditions:

1. The act is good in itself or at least indifferent, which means, for our purposes, that it is a legitimate act of war.
2. The direct effect is morally acceptable—the destruction of military supplies, for example, or the killing of enemy soldiers.
3. The intention of the actor is good, that is, he aims only at the acceptable effect; the evil effect is not one of his ends, nor is it a means to his ends.
4. The good effect is sufficiently good to compensate for allowing the evil effect. (1977: 153)

A major issue is how to measure the actor's intention. This may, in the first instance, be addressed by determining what orders were given, what targets were specified, and so on. The existence of orders to target noncombatants directly is clear evidence that harm suffered by them as a result was not indirect and unintended but direct and intended. But lacking such evidence, whether right intention is present can also be judged by considering whether the actual action is plausibly consistent with a good intention on the part of the agent. Thus after further consideration, Walzer tightens the requirement as to intention, phrasing it in terms of a required "double intention" both not to do evil and to seek actively to minimize any evil done:

3. The intention of the actor is good, that is, he aims narrowly at the acceptable effect; the evil effect is not one of his ends, nor is it a means to his ends, and, aware of the evil involved, he seeks to minimize it, accepting costs to himself. (1977: 155)[1]

What is important here is not only the specifying of a "double intention" but the recognition that intention may be judged by the form of the act. Walzer (1977: 157) gives as an example of the two ways of construing double effect (one without "double intention" and one with it) bombing attacks carried out by the Free French air force against targets in occupied France during World War II. The targets of these attacks were German military operations, but "inevitably too, they killed Frenchmen who simply happened to live in the vicinity" of the targeted sites. By the traditional version of the requirement of right intention in the rule of double effect, these deaths were tragic but not immoral. But Walzer notes that the raids posed "a cruel dilemma for the pilots," who decided to reduce the risk to French civilians by accepting more risk for themselves, flying lower so that they could aim their bombs with more precision at the desired targets. He notes also that partisan raids might have had the desired effect with even less risk of collateral harm to noncombatants, but with considerably more risk to the partisans. In the end, he observes, "There is obviously room for military judgment" in weighing "the importance of the target against the importance of their soldiers' lives." That is, the moral obligation runs both ways, toward the combatants as well as toward the noncombatants. But, Walzer believes, the noncombatants have a special claim not to be harmed by military actions, and combatants should be willing to take a measure of risk to themselves in order to honor this claim.

It is crucial to note that in this example, the original high-altitude bombing was not directed at noncombatant lives or property or intend-

---

1. Paul Ramsey, in defining the rule of double effect, takes account of its origin in the observation of Thomas Aquinas that "[n]othing hinders one act from having two effects, only one of which is intended, while the other is beside the intention" (*Summa theologiae* IIa-IIae, q. 64, a. 7). A morally good act does not become blameworthy if it has unintended collateral bad effects. See Ramsey, 1961: 39–45.

ed to cause noncombatant harm. It would satisfy most understandings of the double effect requirement, including that given in Walzer's original statement of the rule and that embedded in international law on war. Carrying out such bombing would be neither morally forbidden, on these standard interpretations, or a crime of war. Walzer's qualification builds on what is already a significantly high standard of respect for the difference between combatants and noncombatants and has the effect of seeking further to ensure the safety of noncombatants. It functions like a rabbinical rule that sets a "fence around the Torah" that keeps one from violating a more fundamental law.

Were the noncombatants part (or all) of the target, the matter would be entirely different in moral terms. Paul Ramsey, for example, draws attention to the wrongness of intentional decisions to "enlarge the target" to include noncombatants in strategic bombing and other kinds of military actions (1961: 61–63). Walzer himself discusses two cases from World War II that illustrate the direct, intentional targeting of noncombatants, reaching different judgments on them. The first is the 1942 British decision to bomb German cities, with the aiming points "the built-up areas, not . . . the dockyards or aircraft factories," for the explicit purpose of "the destruction of civilian morale" (1977: 256). In this case there was an explicit decision to target German noncombatants directly and intentionally as a means of war. Walzer admits this decision (and the bombing) violated the fundamental rule regarding harm to noncombatants, but in this special case, he argues, this was justified by the presence of a "supreme emergency," the realistic and "ultimate" threat of a Nazi conquest of Britain (ibid.: 251–63). His second example is the atomic bombing of Hiroshima, which was a case not of choosing a noncombatant target in preference to a military one but of choosing to "enlarge the target" to include both. Walzer argues that this decision (and the subsequent bombing) was not justified, since the evil averted by it was neither imminent nor ultimate in character (unlike the threat of the Nazi conquest of Britain in 1942) (ibid.: 263–68).

The Moral Obligation to Noncombatants during Armed Conflict

While these examples from Walzer and Ramsey, as well as much other moral analysis, deal with the question of collateral harm done to noncombatants by strategic bombing, the point of the assumptions to which

I am drawing attention, and of the rule of double effect as a way of interpreting the meaning of the second assumption, is not limited to such cases alone. Rather, the point is that not all the harm done in warfare, especially not all the killing that occurs during war, is morally the same. There are two real differences that matter morally: first, between harm done to noncombatants and harm done to combatants, and second, between direct, intentional harm to noncombatants and that which indirectly and unintentionally accompanies justifiable acts of war.

What is morally wrong about the practice of much contemporary warfare is that it denies these assumptions in one or another way, either treating the above differences as meaningless, as when all members of a particular ethnic group or religion are defined as equally the enemy and equally targets for armed force, or the even worse case of deliberate attacks on noncombatants as a way of defeating the enemy.

Where do these ways of thinking come from, and why are they morally binding? In the following two sections of this paper I answer this question in two different ways, looking first at the deep roots of just war thinking in the Middle Ages and the early modern period, and then examining the development of positive international law on war as it has taken shape over the last century and a quarter.

Noncombatant Protection in Historical Just War Tradition

Understanding how the just war rationale for noncombatant protection developed historically is important for two main reasons. First, this tradition provides the context out of which the international law on war developed; in fundamental ways, this law carries and continues to develop just war tradition. Second, this tradition focuses core moral concerns of Western culture regarding noncombatancy during conflict, concerns that remain at the center of contemporary moral attitudes, arguments, and judgments.

The Coming Together and Development of the Just War Idea

Just war tradition first coalesced, drawing on various sources, in the period from the twelfth to the fifteenth centuries. It included a specifically Christian religious tradition built especially on the thought of Augustine and expressed in both canonical and theological efforts to restrain war. A second distinct source was chivalric tradition, with roots in older ideals of warriorhood. A third source, influential in different ways at different times, was Roman law—more specifically, Roman ideas of *ius naturale* and *ius gentium*. And not least important among the major sources that interacted and combined to form just war tradition was the developing experience and customs of political order (what later can be called statecraft) and of the use of force in the service of such order. In short, it is incomplete to think of just war tradition as a product of specifically Christian religious values or of specifically moral reflection. These were certainly involved, but they were only parts of a considerably broader flow of ideas and practices, and the result reflected this larger whole. The merging of ideas from different sources can be seen clearly, for example, in the canonists of the late twelfth and early thirteenth centuries, whose interpretation of their theological inheritance was deeply shaped by reference to Roman law, and in late medieval writers like Honoré Bonet and Christine de Pizan, who blended the code of chivalry and customary practices together with religion and secular legal concerns.[2]

The purpose of the developing just war idea was twofold, expressed in the distinction between the *ius ad bellum* (the part of the tradition dealing with the decision to use military force) and the *ius in bello* (that part of the tradition that had to do with what might morally be done in the process of fighting a justified war). Harm to noncombatants was addressed in both connections, but in different ways. The ius ad bellum was at first the particular concern of Church theorists, who sought to restrict recourse to armed force to the highest political authorities acting to serve the aims of just political order. Thomas Aquinas's statement of the fundamental requirements for a just war was both typical for its time and a major influence on later thought. "In order for a war to be just," he wrote, "three things are necessary": sovereign political authority, a just cause, and a right intention (1912–22: IIa-IIae, q. 40, a. 1). Sovereign authority exists, argued Thomas, for the service of the common good, and it is this purpose that gives the sovereign the right to authorize force, both against internal disturbers of the public peace and against external aggressors. This reasoning implies a clear distinction between those against whom

---

2. The above summarizes a history of development I have treated in more detail elsewhere; see Johnson, 1975: 26–80, 1981: 121–71, both for more on this history and for more detailed treatment of the content of the tradition discussed below.

force may be used (evildoers; Thomas referred here to Romans 13:4) and those whom force seeks to protect (the innocent and those oppressed by the evildoers; Thomas cited Psalms 81:4). There can be no just use of force against the latter. This is reinforced in the discussion of just cause, which Thomas defined in terms of what has since been called "vindicative justice," that is, a justice that seeks to vindicate those harmed by injustice by punishing the evildoers and restoring any persons or property seized unjustly. But the purposes of just force also require a right intention in the use of force, which Thomas defined by directly quoting Augustine: just wars "are waged not for motives of aggrandizement, or cruelty, but with the object of securing peace, of punishing evil-doers, and of uplifting the good" (Thomas Aquinas, 1912-22, II/II, q.40, a. 1).

Though the theoretical content of the ius ad bellum was chiefly developed by canon lawyers and theologians, it had to do centrally with a theory of political life, as illustrated by the above text from Thomas Aquinas. Indeed, his three core requisites for just resort to arms—sovereign authority, just cause, and right intention—correlated directly with the purposes of political life as conceived in normative medieval political theory—order, justice, and peace. In this conception there was not a great deal of room for personal freedom of the sort favored by contemporary democratic political thought, but there was equally no room for the use of armed force to coerce and oppress ordinary members of society, whether the society in question was one's own or that of an enemy on whom one was forced to make war to set right some wrongdoing. Warriors making just war were to fight only the guilty and those persons who took arms to support the guilty. This conception of justified war left no space for what has come to be termed counterpopulation warfare or for the practice of warfare directed against noncombatants.

Alongside this overarching conception of the purposes and limits of justified use of arms, the developing ius in bello defined noncombatant status and the obligations of warriors to noncombatants in more specific ways. On the side of churchly thought, the fundamental position was established in the various actions collectively known as the "Peace of God" movement.[3] This movement provides the earliest formal statement of non-

---

3. The Peace of God movement, which originated in the south of France in the late tenth century and subsequently spread to other regions, was an effort to protect persons associated with the Church, peasants, and townspeople, as well as their property, from brigandage, van-

combatant status, its definition by customary peaceful occupation within the social order, the obligation of soldiers not to prey on such people or their property, and the obligation of the temporal authorities to protect them, by use of force of arms if necessary. Subsequent churchly thought held to these fundamentals, though it added emphasis to the effort to protect Church persons and property and tended to multiply the specific occupations of people protected. The rationale was a simple reference to justice: such persons are people of peace, and they therefore do not deserve to have war made on them. (See further Johnson, 1981: 127–28.)

All this was fixed in canon law by the thirteenth century. Subsequent development of the idea of noncombatancy and the duties of warriors toward noncombatants took place principally within the framework of the chivalric code. While it overlapped and reinforced the Church's canons, this development had a closer connection to the actual behavior of individual knights and the empirical practice of warfare. It also differed from the Church's approach in other important ways. First, chivalric tradition recast the definition of noncombatancy as determined by occupation into a distinction between knights, who were socialized into the code of chivalric conduct in war, and all other members of society. Presumptively, knights were to fight only other knights, because only members of the knightly class should be in arms. If nonknights appeared under arms (as in popular revolts or as part of mixed armies on the battlefield), they could be attacked; otherwise warriors should leave them alone. Second, the chivalric position grew out of values indigenous to chivalry, particularly courtesy, prowess under arms, loyalty, and individual honor. These values implied an expanded conception of noncombatancy in which personal inability to bear arms figured importantly. Hence chivalric lists of types of persons against whom knights should not use arms and whom knights should seek to protect typically included women, children, the aged, the maimed or infirm, and the mentally deficient—all groups of people that had not been explicitly named in the canonical listings. (See further Johnson, 1981: 135–41.)

---

dalism, bullying, and thievery by individual soldiers and armed bands, often out-of-work mercenaries. The Church's weapons of choice in this effort were excommunication and penance directed at offenders. Since the problem addressed was fundamentally one of public order, the royal authorities in the regions affected used their own military power in parallel with the sanctions of the Church to punish offenders and bring them into line. See further Contamine, 1984: 443–46.

By the time of Honoré Bonet's *L'arbre des battailes* in the latter part of the fourteenth century, the canonical and chivalric conceptions of noncombatancy and of how noncombatants should be treated had coalesced. Moreover, Bonet makes clearer the underlying requirement: only people who actually take part in war are to be treated as combatants; others, regardless of status, are noncombatants (1901: 237–39).

Running through these developments was a realistic thread; this was, after all, a period when armies on the march had to live off the land and when sieges against fortified places, often also housing considerable communities of noncombatants, were a frequent feature of war. While the Church sought to establish a zone of immunity to protect its own people and property, the effect where nonecclesiastical noncombatants were concerned, on both the canonical and chivalric conceptions, was to rule out wanton pillage and other depredations but to accept use of noncombatant property required by the necessities of war. Similarly, harm suffered by noncombatants during sieges was not regarded as a violation of the protection due them. But these exceptions were self-limiting; no ruler or army had any real interest in leaving total devastation behind them, because the ruler might come to rule over the same people and properties at the end of a war, and the army, if defeated, might have to return the way it had come and would need to turn to these people and their properties for support.

The Settled Conception of Noncombatant Protection

The fundamentals of normative Western thought on noncombatancy were thus in place by the end of the Middle Ages. The ius ad bellum provided a general context: armed force may be employed justly only when it serves the common goods of human society—social order, justice, and peace. From the ius in bello came three provisions: a definition of noncombatancy by customary peaceful employment, ability to bear arms, and a formal distinction between soldiers and civilians deriving from that between the knightly class and nonknights; a general prohibition on direct, intended use of armed force against persons so defined and their property; and an obligation for soldiers to protect noncombatants and their goods.

Such was the conception of justice in war inherited by early modern theorists like Vitoria and Grotius and embodied consensually in the practice of war. Though the limits thus defined were challenged from time to time—indeed, sometimes completely rejected, as in some of the religious warfare of the Reformation era—they were time and again reasserted, along with attempts to strengthen them. Indeed, Grotius's own work, coming after some of the worst violence against noncombatants of the Thirty Years' War, exemplifies this, as he gave new emphasis, breadth, and depth to the importance of protecting noncombatants in warfare.

The development of positive legal efforts to regulate warfare, beginning with Francis Lieber's Code (U.S. Army General Orders No. 100 of 1863) during the American Civil War (Friedman, 1972: 1:158–86) and the contemporaneous first Geneva Convention of 1864 (the Red Cross Convention; Friedman, 1972: 1:187–91) built on the conceptual basis and cultural consensus established much earlier, by the end of the Middle Ages. Indeed, positive law should be understood as one of the streams that has continued to carry just war tradition into the twentieth century, alongside military codes of conduct and rules of engagement and philosophical and theological moral reflection. The law of war and moral thought on the conduct of war are thus directly related, and they build on the same assumptions about the nature of war as an element of the quest for political order, justice, and peace. Yet the method and language of the law of war are different from those found in moral reflection, and moreover, in the contemporary context international law on war provides a unique universal vehicle for stating, accepting, and enforcing the limits that also follow from moral reflection.

The Development of Noncombatant Protection in Positive International Law

Protection of noncombatants in international law is defined today in that portion of international humanitarian law now called the law of armed conflicts and formerly called the law of war.[4] (Broader protections follow from international human rights law, and it is increasingly customary to refer to the law of armed conflicts and human rights law together as international humanitarian law.) The shift from "law of war" to "law of armed conflicts" is more than simply one of nomenclature; sub-

---

4. Useful compilations of the law of war/law of armed conflicts in English include Friedman, 1972; Roberts and Guelff, 1989; Schindler and Toman, 1973.

stantively, it signifies the effort of the international community to extend to all armed conflicts, whether domestic or between states, whether formally declared wars or not, the same rules for conduct earlier imposed on states formally at war with each other. Other important elements in the new conception include broader responsibility for the international community to enforce the rules for right conduct in armed conflict and a shift toward understanding violations of these rules as crimes of war for which individuals may be prosecuted. Our present focus is on the idea of protection of noncombatants in positive international law. I will discuss three themes that are particularly important for providing such protection: the definition of noncombatancy itself; the pervasiveness of concern for noncombatant protection in agreements and declarations of various sorts that do not have such protection as their principal focus, including especially efforts to regulate the means of war; and the nature of the rationale for providing such protection and avoiding direct harm to noncombatants.

The Definition of Noncombatancy

First, as to the definition of noncombatancy, while positive international law does not employ the term *noncombatant*, it provides a broad definition of persons who are to be protected from direct, intended harm in armed conflict because of their noncombatant status. In the Geneva Conventions of 1864 and 1906, the focus was on combatants (another term not used there) who have been rendered incapable of serving in that capacity by wounds or illness. In the 1907 Hague Convention IV Respecting the Laws and Customs of War on Land, the Geneva protections are acknowledged (article 21) and the definition of persons due protection is broadened by an extensive discussion of obligations toward prisoners of war (articles 4–20), limits on means of war (articles 22–23), restrictions on bombardment and pillage (articles 24–28), and treatment of the inhabitants of territory under military occupation (articles 42–56). Again the term *noncombatant* is nowhere used in the Hague Convention, but its various provisions define an extensive and detailed list of persons to be protected in various ways: persons who were formerly combatants but have lost their ability to function as such because of illness, wounds, or being made prisoners; inhabitants of undefended towns, villages, dwellings, or other buildings; the inhabitants of defended places, who must be warned and allowed to leave before an attack is launched; property dedicated to various public uses, including churches, hospitals, schools, and historic monuments; and, after an occupation is in place, all inhabitants unless they rise in arms or engage in spying.

This listing has been improved on in detail but not in breadth by subsequent developments, including the 1949 Geneva Conventions, the 1977 Geneva Protocols, the 1978 Red Cross Fundamental Rules, and other statements and agreements aiming to limit or prohibit indiscriminate means of war. Post–World War II positive international law has, though, extended the protection due to noncombatants thus defined in several ways: by expanding the scope of the law to include armed conflicts between states that are not legally wars (common article 2 of the 1949 Geneva Conventions) and noninternational armed conflicts (1977 Geneva Protocol II); by providing various new measures for monitoring and enforcing the rules for conduct in armed conflict (e.g., 1949 Geneva Convention IV, articles 1, 3, and 11); by redefining the liability for violation of the laws so as to make individuals, not simply states, responsible; and by a trend toward regarding the law, as applied to individuals, on the model of criminal law (both these latter developments are best exemplified in the war crimes trials that followed World War II and those currently under way for the conflicts in Rwanda and the former Yugoslavia).

There are three important points to be observed in the approach to the definition of noncombatancy taken by positive international law. First, not civilian or military status as such but whether the person in question is functioning as a combatant is the deciding factor, whatever the reason for this. Second, no theoretical definition of noncombatancy is provided or even attempted; rather, classes of persons are simply listed as deserving certain considerations and protection from the belligerent parties. Third, the restrictions and protections laid out, as well as the classes of people to whom they apply, are represented as generally accepted in the laws and customs of war—that is, they are not innovations in the practice of war or conceptions of restraint derived from another sphere (e.g., moral philosophy or religion), but internal to what war is itself about.

The Broad Scope of Noncombatant Protection

The second major theme in the development of positive international law on noncombatant protection is the pervasiveness of concern for such protection in agreements of various sorts, not only those that focus on the treatment of noncombatants.

The Geneva Conventions and Protocols, the Hague Convention just discussed, and some other elements of the international law of armed conflicts treat noncombatant protection directly; yet this concern is also a theme found in instruments whose main focus is other issues, such as the limitation of certain means of war (e.g., bombardment and pillage, already mentioned) and weapons of war (restrictions or prohibitions aimed at chemical, biological, and nuclear weapons and at conventional weapons with indiscriminate effects), the prevention of genocide, and the protection of cultural property.

The bearing of the concept of genocide on the phenomenon of warfare against noncombatants deserves a particular look. Warfare on noncombatants is constituted by the direct, intentional targeting of noncombatants in an armed conflict. Not all such targeting is genocidal, but genocide occupies a unique place in contemporary moral consciousness as an extreme form of reprehensible conduct. It differs from other forms of warfare against noncombatants by having been given its own legal definition, laid out in the Convention on Genocide ratified by the General Assembly of the United Nations in December 1948:

[G]enocide means any of the following acts committed with intent to destroy, in whole or in part, a national, ethnical, racial or religious group, as such.
a. Killing members of the group;
b. Causing serious bodily or mental harm to members of the group;
c. Deliberately inflicting on the group conditions of life calculated to bring about its physical destruction in whole or in part;
d. Imposing measures intended to prevent births within the group;
e. Forcibly transferring children of the group to another group. (United Nations Convention on the Prevention and Punishment of the Crime of Genocide, cited in Kuper, 1981: 19)

That is, for genocide formally to exist, three distinct conditions must be satisfied: there must be a pattern of one or more of the specific kinds of acts named; there must be an "intent to destroy ... as such"; and the target must be "a national, ethnical, racial or religious group." This definition is both broader and narrower than that of warfare against noncombatants during an armed conflict. The range of acts forbidden means that genocide may take place even when no armed conflict is under way between the perpetrators and the victims, as exemplified by the Nazi Holocaust. At the same time, the direct, intentional targeting of noncombatants during an armed conflict may not be genocidal, if this is not intended to destroy them "as such" or if they are targeted because of their political preferences, their economic status, their education, or for some other reason rather than their identity as members of a "national, ethnical, racial or religious group." Thus, for example, though the term *genocide* has sometimes been applied to one of the worst examples of warfare against noncombatants in recent history, the massacre perpetrated by the Khmer Rouge in Cambodia, this did not match the legal definition of genocide given in the Genocide Convention, since the victims were not targeted as members of one of the types of groups named there. (See further Kuper, 1981: 155.)

Other recent cases raise the same issues in their own distinctive ways. The best approach, in my view, is to regard genocide as simply one of the forms that may be taken by warfare against noncombatants, a practice evil in itself whether or not it includes genocidal practices. This is the approach taken in the statutes establishing the only two war crimes tribunals brought into being under international auspices since World War II, those for the former Yugoslavia and Rwanda, where genocide is laid alongside other violations of international law these two tribunals are given competence to prosecute. The statute for the Yugoslavia tribunal defines it as for the prosecution of "persons responsible for serious violations of international humanitarian law committed in the territory of the former Yugoslavia since 1991," following with four particulars: "grave breaches of the Geneva Conventions of 1949," "violations of the laws or customs of war," "genocide," and "crimes against humanity" (United Nations, 1993: annex, opening paragraph, and articles 1–4). The language of the statute for the Rwanda tribunal differs only slightly. The introductory paragraph of this statute defines it as for the purpose of prosecuting "Persons Responsible for Genocide and Other Serious Violations of International Humanitarian Law" committed in Rwanda and by Rwandan citizens in neighboring states during 1994, following this with three particulars: "genocide," "crimes against humanity," and "violations of Article 3 common to the Geneva Conventions and of Additional Protocol II"—this last a more specific reference to the sections of the cited conventions and protocols having to do with the protection of victims of war (United Nations, 1994: annex, opening paragraph, and articles 1–4). The various legal categories identified in the statutes of these two contemporary war crimes tribunals all attempt, each in its own way, to provide protection to people who should never become the targets of war. As G. Scott Davis comments, to attack such people is "murderous" (1996: 19). In the context of armed conflict the concept of genocide gives legal specificity to one form of warfare against noncombatants; other elements of international law address other forms of such warfare. Collectively these provide purchase for the prosecution and punishment of persons who violate the laws in question. Yet the more fundamental moral issue is that, both within and outside the reach of law, it is quite simply wrong to make noncombatants direct and intentional targets in an armed conflict. It is their status as noncombatants that endows them with this moral immunity. That they may be targeted because they are members of one or another "national, ethnical, racial or religious group" tells us something about the motivations of those who disregard that immunity, but it adds nothing to the nature of the immunity that is being disregarded.

Within the context of armed conflict, efforts to regulate the means of war are important for their bearing not only on combatants but on the protection of noncombatants. These efforts have had two major thrusts: toward ruling out the use of certain types of weapons, even if directed against combatant targets, because of their disproportionately destructive or indiscriminate effect (e.g., the 1925 Geneva Protocol for the Prohibition of the Use in War of Asphyxiating, Poisonous or Other Gases, and of Bacteriological Methods of Warfare; the 1981 United Nations Convention and Protocols on the Use of Certain Conventional Weapons Which May Be Deemed to Be Excessively Injurious or to Have Indiscriminate Effects) and toward ruling out certain uses of types of weapons otherwise acceptable in armed conflict (e.g., 1907 Hague Convention IX: Concerning Bombardment by Naval Forces in Time of War; the 1923 Hague Rules of Aerial Warfare). The first kind of effort differentiates between weapons whose effect can be reasonably limited to combatants and those whose effects are so destructive as to go beyond the bounds of allowable collateral damage, indiscriminate because their effects cannot be limited to combatants, and so durable that they continue to affect people in the area of use long after the conflict has ended, when everyone is by definition a noncombatant. Weapons of mass destruction fit these descriptions in every regard, but there is increasing awareness that many weapons based on conventional explosives (e.g., cluster bomblets, land mines) also have one or more of these undesired effects. Even when the weapon itself is not inherently wrong to employ, some uses of it may be; this is the point of the second type of control aimed at the means of war: efforts to rule out certain kinds of targets (undefended towns or individual dwellings, schools, churches, hospitals, and so on), which clearly follow from the reference of such places to noncombatant life.

The Obligation to Honor the Protection Due Noncombatants

These first two themes in international law bearing on noncombatant protection have to do with the nature of noncombatancy and the broad presence of noncombatant protection in the laws of armed conflict. They are important for establishing the extent to which protection for noncombatants has been established by international agreement. The third theme I wish to highlight is the nature of the rationale underlying such protection: more specifically, where the obligation to honor such protection comes from and on whom it is binding.

Two importantly different kinds of answers have been given to these questions over the history of the development of positive international law on warfare. One form of answer is quite minimalist: the obligation comes from the agreement of the signatory parties to be so obliged (or the observance of the obligations by nonsignatories during a conflict), and the obligation is binding on them. This form of answer makes no claim as to the source of the obligation; each party chooses to be obliged for its own reasons, and it is the choice, not the reasons behind it, that is important. Thus, for example, the 1949 Geneva Conventions begin with common article 1, a statement of agreement as to what is provided and the obligations undertaken: "The High Contracting Parties undertake to respect and to ensure respect for the present Convention in all circumstances." A second form of answer to the source and binding force of the rules on noncombatant protection takes an opposite tack, explicitly grounding the obligations enumerated and accepted by the contracting parties in a preexistent, pervasive, and independent moral consensus. The language of the preamble to 1907 Hague Convention IV well exemplifies this approach: "Until a more complete code of the laws of war has been issued, the high contracting Parties deem it expedient to declare that, in cases not included in the Regulations adopted by them, the inhabitants and the belligerents remain under the protection and the rule of *the principles of the law of nations, as they result from the usages established among civilized peoples, from the laws of humanity, and the dictates of the public conscience*" (1907 Hague Convention IV, cited in Roberts and Guelff, 1989: 70; emphasis added).

That is, the first of these approaches exemplifies a strictly positivist understanding of the nature, extent, and binding power of the obligations agreed to, while the second locates the specific rules laid down and the specific obligations undertaken by the contracting parties within a larger consensual frame, reflecting and embodying moral perceptions that provide a more fundamental description of the distinction between noncombatants and combatants and how the latter should behave toward the former in armed conflict. To point out the relation of international law on armed conflicts to just war tradition is a more specific way of stating this latter approach to understanding the reasons for noncombatant protection; yet in practice the positivist approach may provide a more useful tool in the form of a record of formal agreements to honor such protection.

Precisely the breakdown of the moral consensus on noncombatant protection and a widespread rejection of the legal restraints on direct, intentional harm to noncombatants is the problem characteristic of much contemporary armed conflict. In the following section I look more closely at some forms this problem has taken.

War on Noncombatants: Selected Problems from Recent Conflicts

While examples of intentional, direct targeting of noncombatants can be found in warfare from any period, such targeting has been characteristic of much recent armed conflict, and it has been particularly so in the form armed conflicts have taken since the end of the cold war. As a century has ended in which impressive steps have been taken in defining legal protections for noncombatants during war, a pressing problem for the new century is how to ensure the actual protection from harm of noncombatants caught in the midst of such struggles.

Distinctive Features of Contemporary Armed Conflict

Contemporary armed conflicts have not, in the first place, been formally constituted wars between sovereign states but conflicts of other sorts, often within the borders of existing states. In some contemporary conflicts (e.g., Rwanda), the struggle may be over dominance and rule within the state, while in other cases (e.g., Croatia, Bosnia) it may be over the secession of an element of an existing state in order to form a new one. In either case the government (or governments, in the case of conflicts over secession) of the state in question may be one of the parties to the fighting but may not be sufficiently powerful to ensure protection of noncombatant citizens, or it may itself be a source of attacks directed against noncombatants.

A second feature of contemporary armed conflicts is that special importance has typically attached to particular differences of identity between the parties fighting each other. These differences may or may not correspond to the categories of membership in "national, ethnical, racial or religious groups" specified in the Genocide Convention, but they function in much the same way, providing a basis for ascribing guilt by association to all persons whose identity marks them as enemies, regardless of whether they have any active involvement in the fighting.

A third characteristic typical of such conflicts is that they have been intensely territorial, becoming defined, by one or both parties, as zero-sum games in which the entire enemy group must not only be defeated militarily and/or dominated politically but killed or otherwise removed from one's own territory.

A fourth characteristic of such conflict, different in kind from the first three, is that the actual fighters may include a variety of kinds of individuals, armed groups, and paramilitary forces as well as soldiers theoretically subject to military discipline. It is through military discipline that states at war impose restraint on the conduct of their armed forces and can responsibly seek to enforce behavior in accord with the laws of armed conflict and of humanity. While a disciplined military force may of course be used as an instrument of warfare against enemy noncombatants, a special problem of contemporary armed conflict is that many of the persons under arms take part in the fighting for private reasons—for example, because of old feuds or to pursue criminal activities—and may operate essentially as they please in the areas through which they move. A further sort of problem is posed when paramilitary police are employed as part of a fighting force in a civil conflict, since many societies give more license to such forces in dealing with members of the general population than international law gives to military forces in dealing with noncombatants.

When the combatant-noncombatant distinction is ignored and, more pointedly, when a noncombatant population is itself directly and intentionally targeted as a method of waging war, not only does the burden of the war shift decisively to them, but the means of war more broadly shift toward being uncontrolled, as enemy soldiers engage in murder, rape, torture, pillage, and wanton destruction with the aim of creating terror among those persons who know they may be the next victims. In the worst cases, when such warfare aims not only at dominating the enemy population but removing them entirely as a competitor, warfare against noncombatants may escalate to mass killings and even genocide.

All these characteristics have been present in different degrees throughout the range of recent armed conflict. In the following discussion I examine warfare against noncombatants as exemplified in three recent conflicts, those in Rwanda-Zaire, the former Yugoslavia, and the Iraq war of 2003, which provide important and highly visible examples of deliberate attacks on noncombatants as a means of waging war. I will focus on specific forms of assaults on noncombatants in each of these conflicts: in the case of Rwanda-Zaire, instigation of genocide and war against refugees; in the case of the former Yugoslavia, war against population centers; in the case of the Iraq war, the endangerment of noncombatants as a means to gain military advantage.

Genocide and Ethnic Cleansing: Every One of "the Other" as Worthy of Death

A justification for attacking noncombatants often found in contemporary warfare is that all the members of the opposing group are equally enemies because of some common identity factor—religion, ethnicity, language, practice of intermarriage and cultural toleration or blending—that marks them as different from the group identity held by the attackers. From the standpoint of moral tradition and international law this is not so much a counterargument as a denial of the fundamental perspective of both morality and war: that combatancy and noncombatancy are determined by function, not membership in a group. This perspective holds that common moral rules apply even in war; the rejection consists in the claim that war is necessarily total. The rationale for distinguishing noncombatants from combatants and for treating them differently was succinctly stated by Emmerich de Vattel, the eighteenth-century philosopher, diplomat, and jurist, who spoke both out of the just war tradition he had inherited and for the positive international law whose development he influenced: "Women, children, the sick and aged, are in the number of enemies. And there are rights with regard to them as belonging to the nation with which one is at war, and the rights and pretensions between nation and nation affect the body of the society, together with all its members. But these are enemies who make no resistance, and consequently give us no right to treat their persons ill, or use any violence against them, much less to take away their lives" (Vattel, 1740: section 145).

The same understanding, set in the context of practical directions for the treatment of a hostile population, is found in an example from the American Civil War. While not a case of ethnic difference, this was clearly one of deep cultural difference, and the basic issue was the same: may all the enemy be treated as worthy of harm? In 1863 General Henry W. Halleck, then general in chief of the Union army, wrote on this matter to General Rosecrans, commander of a Union force stationed in Middle Tennessee. Much of the letter is given to distinguishing at some length among three classes of people in the civilian population of the occupied area. The first class named, persons loyal to the Union, Halleck treated very briefly: Rosecrans should protect them, avoid requisitioning supplies from them, and pay them if requisitions were necessary. Halleck treated the other two classes in much greater detail. All three classes, he stipulated, were noncombatants: they did not bear arms or otherwise participate in the war. Yet the second and third belonged to the enemy population. The difference between them, Halleck pointed out, was not level of sympathy for the Confederate cause or loyalty to it; such sympathy was to be assumed for members of both classes. The distinction that mattered was their actions, not their attitudes. The second class consisted of those who, "so long as they commit no hostile act and confine themselves to their private avocations, are not to be molested by the military forces, nor is their property to be seized, except as a military necessity." The third class, "[t]hose who are openly and avowedly hostile to the occupying army" and showed this by actions along a spectrum from refusing the obligations laid on them by the occupying army to actively aiding their own forces in ways up to and including violence, might be punished for lack of compliance, confined as prisoners of war, or expelled as "combatant enemies." In the worst cases, they might be treated as spies. But the important point was that it was their actions, not their sympathies, that subjected them to such treatment (Halleck to Rosecrans, Sunday, March 15, 1863; Huntington Library Index Number LI 176).

This was, of course, a civil war, and much recent warfare has been civil war. But what a difference there is between Halleck's distinctions, reflecting both the moral tradition and the trajectory of development of the law of war, and the direct, intentional targeting of whole populations of persons as enemies in recent internecine warfare.

Writing of the Serb forces' practice of ethnic cleansing in the war in Bosnia, Michael Sells notes, "In each army occupied by the Serb military, killing camps and killing centers were established, and individual massacres were carried out.... In such places the killing went on for weeks. Thus the famous Visegrad Drina Bridge ... was used for nightly killing 'sport festivals' by Serb soldiers who would torture their victims, throw them off the bridge, and try to see if they could shoot them as they tumbled down into the Drina River" (quoted in Davis, 1996: 26).

The aim was not simply to kill and terrorize persons designated by their non-Serb identity as enemies, but to attack the very bases of these persons' culture. In Banja Luca and Bijeljina, Sells observes, "[t]he first victims were intellectual and cultural leaders.... The object of such 'eliticide' was to destroy the cultural memory" (ibid.). The same aim motivated three other examples catalogued by Sells: the destruction by an army under General Mladic of the Oriental Institute in Sarajevo, which housed "the largest collection of Islamic and Jewish manuscripts in South Eastern Europe"; the burning of the National Museum; and the systematic destruction of all the mosques in the formerly Muslim-majority city of Zvornik, after which the Serb commander responsible declared, "There were never any mosques in Zvornik" (ibid., 25).

In the genocidal massacres in Rwanda in 1994 the Hutu leadership systematically identified not only persons of the Tutsi tribal group but also Hutus who had intermarried with Tutsis as well as their children. Common institutions, such as the Catholic Church, were not destroyed, but Hutu Catholic clergy and even nuns supported and sometimes took direct part in the killing of non-Hutus.

Once noncombatancy has been so fundamentally violated, as in these examples, it is hard or even impossible to keep the same disregard for the protection of noncombatants from infecting the other side as well. This pattern appeared in both Bosnia and Rwanda. In the latter it took the specific form of the targeting of Hutu refugees who had fled Rwanda in the face of the advance of a Tutsi force that ended the massacres and established a new government. As the Tutsi force advanced, approximately a million Hutus crossed over into neighboring regions of Zaire. This number included both noncombatant refugees and former militiamen who had taken part in the massacres of non-Hutu Rwandans, who now sought to shelter themselves among the noncombatant refugees. The latter began to launch cross-border raids back into Rwanda in 1996. In October of that year elements of the new Tutsi-dominated Rwandan army entered Zaire in response; this force was quickly augmented by Zairian Tutsis and by members of the Zairian rebel army led by Laurent Kabila.

Since the Hutu militiamen continued to shelter themselves within the refugee population, efforts to strike at the former inevitably gave harm to the latter. Yet outside observers, including U.N. and NGO personnel involved in relief efforts, did not regard this as direct warfare against the refugees, and the fact that the Rwandan force repatriated significant numbers of the refugees into Rwanda argues that the refugees were themselves not being targeted at this time. As the conflict continued, though, the Hutu fighters began to move about to avoid the Rwandan army forces, and as they moved, they took large numbers of refugees with them, using the refugees both for support and as shields. Discrimination between the fighters and the refugees, always difficult under the circumstances, eroded, and at some point the refugees themselves began to be targeted. As the war wore on toward an end, these attacks escalated, with the worst reported atrocities after the rebel victory in Zaire and the establishment of the Kabila government. Reports from the war suggest that the shift to direct targeting of the refugees was a deliberate policy choice, not by the Tutsi forces or the Rwandan government but by officials in Kabila's army, who wanted to "remove the Hutus from the border with Rwanda and crush the radical Hutu movement by killing as many Hutu refugees as possible" (*Washington Post National Weekly Edition*, June 16,

1977: 16). Clearly, though, the decision by the Hutu fighters to endanger the refugees by sheltering among them was a contributing factor in the breakdown of the protection due the refugees as noncombatants.

Endangering Noncombatants as a War-Fighting Policy

As the example of the Hutu fighters shows, not all endangerment to noncombatants originates with enemy forces; it may be a conscious element in a policy of war fighting aimed at gaining military advantage over a stronger enemy. Even more clearly than with the Hutu fighters, this was the case with some Iraqi paramilitary fighters, who used such endangerment as a tactic to oppose American and British troops in the war of March 2003. Consider the following news stories:

> The *Star-Ledger* (Newark, N.J.), March 24, 2003: 1: "By ambush and faked surrender, Iraqi forces killed, wounded, and captured Americans— and some of them, alive and dead, were exhibited on Iraqi television."
>
> The *New York Times,* March 24, 2003: B6: "Coalition officials ... reported that Iraqi forces had fought out of uniform, had flown false flags of surrender and then attacked, and had massed civilians to shield themselves from attack."

These excerpts from newspaper stories chronicle the first instances in what turned out to be a continuing practice by members of the Fedayeen Saddam and other paramilitary groups to gain military advantage by trading on the coalition forces' commitment to maintain the protection of noncombatants. In one instance, reported in the first story cited above, Iraqi combatants feigned surrender, then took up hidden weapons and fired on the approaching Americans. In other instances, Iraqi combatants disguised themselves as civilians and then, when they were close to American soldiers, took out weapons and fired on them. In Basra, defending Iraqi fedayeen drove civilians out before them as human shields so as to attack the British soldiers seeking to take that city, and on another occasion the fedayeen fired on a large group of civilians, including women and children, who were crossing a bridge to take refuge with the British soldiers.

It is important to stress that these various actions are all related in moral and legal terms. A noncombatant is anyone who does not take direct part in military activities or give direct support to such activities. Not only civilians (and indeed, not all civilians) are noncombatants, but soldiers who have surrendered have moved from combatant to noncombatant status. Thus, to take the case of the Iraqi fighters who feigned surrender, when noncombatants pretend to surrender in order to gain military advantage, this undermines the protection due to others who are genuinely surrendering. When combatants pretend to be noncombatant civilians to gain military advantage, it undermines the effort to maintain noncombatant protection for civilians, for civilians as a class may become suspect. Though the commitment may remain to keep from harming such persons, carrying this through in practice inevitably becomes more difficult, and mistakes may be made that were less likely before. The incidents at Basra were of still another sort, though they share a common theme with these. Intentionally using civilians as shields turns them into persons operating in direct support of the military effort of those who are using them in this way. Since the traditional moral and legal understanding of combatancy and noncombatancy hinges on whether the people in question function as combatants or in direct support of a military operation, people being used involuntarily as human shields are, functionally speaking, not noncombatants any more and may be fired upon. While there remains an obligation to try to avoid harming them when they are obviously being coerced, doing so in practice may be difficult or impossible. This is the basis for using them as shields in the first place: not only to gain physical protection by having the noncombatants in front, but to gain a propaganda victory when the British killed the human shields and also to demoralize the British soldiers by forcing them to act contrary to their training, their rules of engagement, and their own moral sense.

It is sometimes argued that in warfare between a militarily superior force and a militarily weaker one (a form of asymmetric warfare), the latter has the right to use whatever means it can, including such means as these. This argument is simply wrong. There is no moral justification for endangering noncombatants in this way, and legally it constitutes a crime of war. Moreover, its effects, real enough in the case of the particular conflict in which it occurs, may be even more far-reaching, eroding the protection of noncombatants in other similar conflicts or indeed in all conflicts.

Siege Warfare and the Intentional Destruction of Towns and Cities

Let me turn again to the warfare in the former Yugoslavia for one last contemporary example of warfare against noncombatants: the case of direct attacks on noncombatants in the sieges of Sarajevo and other Bosnian cities, with a brief look at the related case of the intentional destruction of Albanian Kosovar cities as a way of attacking their inhabitants.

Siege warfare raises particular and pressing moral problems, but it is largely ignored in recent writing on the ethics of war. Among contemporary theorists, Michael Walzer (1977: ch. 10) is the only major contributor to the ethical analysis of war to directly treat the subject of sieges. Many of the concerns arising from strategic air bombing arise also in sieges, and it is possible to extrapolate moral reasoning from the one to the other; yet there are also moral questions specific to sieges, and these deserve to be examined directly. Military theory, like moral analysis, has largely ignored siege warfare or treated it only indirectly. International law, as noted above, has sought to prevent certain kinds of military actions that might be employed in sieges, notably bombardment of undefended places and damage to cultural property. But, as in moral thought, the focus of concern has not been sieges as such, and the provisions set in place do not address the full range of moral problems raised by siege warfare.

What is morally critical in siege warfare, as in other forms of war, is the degree to which noncombatants in the besieged place are themselves directly and intentionally targeted by the besiegers. Siege warfare is not inherently war on noncombatants. Walzer makes this point early in his discussion of sieges, employing two examples from Jewish history. The first, Josephus's account of the Roman siege of Jerusalem in A.D. 72, tells of horrific suffering and death in a sealed-off city deprived of food. Josephus comments, "[T]hat is what [a siege] is meant to be like," and explains what he means: "The death of the ordinary inhabitants of the city is expected to force the hand of the civilian or military leadership. The goal is surrender; the means is not the defeat of the enemy army, but the fearful spectacle of the civilian dead" (Walzer, 1977: 161). This is a depiction of siege warfare as direct, intentional warfare on noncombatants. But Walzer does not give Josephus the last word. Rather, he turns to a normative counterexample, the Talmudic law of sieges as summarized by Maimonides in the twelfth century: "When siege is laid to a city for the purpose of capture, it may not be surrounded on all four sides, but only on three, in order to give an opportunity for escape to those who would flee to save their lives" (ibid.: 168). This is a quite different understanding of a siege, one in which the besiegers intentionally seek to allow noncombatants the opportunity to avoid harm from attacks on the city's defenses. Though this may increase the risk to the besieging army (since the same opening allows for supply and reinforcement, if any is available), it is in line with the requirements of double effect reasoning applied to noncombatant protection. Nor is increased risk a foregone conclusion: it is also possible that the defending force may use the same route to withdraw, giving the objective to the besiegers at less cost to themselves.

In any case, this conception of the proper conduct of siege warfare is strikingly different from that of Josephus, in which causing the suffering and death of noncombatants is itself the means of conducting the siege. The Talmudic model, by contrast, seeks deliberately to protect noncombatants from such suffering and death during the course of a siege. Those who remain may be harmed by the besiegers' efforts to take the city, but this harm should not be aimed at them directly and should not be intentional on the part of the besiegers. Those noncombatants who do not leave the besieged place are simply in the way of legitimate acts of war.

But this is not the entire story, as Walzer's discussion also recognizes. Noncombatants who remain in the city, where they are in the way of harm, may be there for various reasons, and these reasons are morally important. The purest case for moral analysis using the double effect rule is that of noncombatants who freely decide to remain, perhaps because this is, after all, where they live. These remain noncombatants, and they may not be targeted directly and intentionally, though it is not morally wrong if they are harmed indirectly and unintentionally by military actions of the besiegers. But there are other reasons why civilians may be present. If the civilians in the besieged place participate materially in its defense, whether voluntarily or involuntarily (for example, by digging a ditch or building a wall to assist the defense), they lose their noncombatant status while they are at this work, but not when they are going about their regular lives at home or in their civilian work or in civilian shelters. A further possibility is that inhabitants of the besieged place have been prevented from leaving by the defending force, which has forced them to remain to use them as shields or as labor or as a source of supply for the soldiers (a case similar to that of the Hutu refugees discussed above); in this case the defending force bears a measure of the blame for harm to the noncombatants, but the attackers still have an obligation, both in morality and in the law of war, to avoid targeting them directly and intentionally. Finally, there is the possibility that the noncombatants cannot realistically leave the besieged place. This may be because the besiegers have closed the circle around the place and drive back everyone who tries to leave (the possibility that most closely matches what Josephus took to be the normative way of carrying on a siege), or else they have so devastated the surrounding countryside that would-be refugees know they could not survive if they left. Related to this last possibility is another one not mentioned by Walzer: that the noncombatant population remaining in the besieged place has been enlarged by refugees driven in by the attacks of the besiegers and unable to leave for the same reason. In trapping the inhabitants and driving in refugees, the besiegers bear the entire responsibility for harm to these noncombatants, since they could choose to provide a way to leave for those who wish to do so.

Siege warfare, then, is not inherently warfare against noncombatants, but it becomes so in any one of three cases. The first is when the besiegers encircle the besieged place and prevent noncombatants from leaving as a way to weaken and ultimately defeat the defenders by causing harm to the noncombatants present. This targets the defenders through the noncombatants, effectively reversing the logic of double effect reasoning. Second, a siege is also warfare against noncombatants when the besiegers adopt disproportionately destructive means that utterly devastate the city with the aim of causing the defenders to yield the place in order to save it from such devastation. This second case exemplifies what international lawyer Tom Farer calls the "master principle" of "no Carthaginian peace," that is, no destruction that strikes at the basis of noncombatant life after the conflict is over, when all are noncombatants (1971: 16, 53). The moral reasoning here recognizes that protection due noncombatants in war includes not only their persons but the circumstances on which noncombatant life depends. Direct, intentional devastation of that which is necessary for noncombatant life is itself a form of warfare against noncombatants, a violation of the moral principle of discrimination on which noncombatant immunity is based. If siege warfare proceeds by means of such devastation, it is warfare against noncombatants. The third case is that in which the noncombatants in the besieged place are directly targeted, as when their homes, schools, hospitals, or other public places are intentionally bombarded or when individual noncombatants going about their daily lives are subjected to sniper fire. The sieges of the Bosnian cities provide examples of all three of these forms of warfare against noncombatants.

The case of the siege of Sarajevo, the longest-running case of siege warfare in the Bosnian conflict, allows a close look at the practice of war against noncombatants during a siege in progress. In this siege noncombatants were routinely fired on to keep them from leaving the city or bringing in supplies; apartment blocks, schools, religious buildings, hospitals, and market places were shelled, often at times chosen for maximum presence of members of the population. A random reading of Zlatko Dizdarevic's *Sarajevo: A War Journal* (1994) provides a day-by-day sampler of ways in which the conduct of the siege directly targeted the city's noncombatant population: snipers taking shots at "everything that moves" (104); the gradual improvement of conditions so that "now only a few children get killed every day" (108); the point at which the snipers began using silencers and dum-dum bullets (119); the shelling of the building housing his newspaper (122); the mortar shelling of a downtown Sarajevo street between major streetcar stops, killing six people and wounding twenty (130); the hanging of a huge banner from a downtown Sarajevo hotel in order to blind snipers who otherwise would shoot at anyone walking on the street below (131); shelling for no other purpose than "to obliterate what has already been destroyed" (138); the intentional cutting off of electricity and water, then firing on the besieged inhabitants as they try to restore the supply or get water from the limited sources left (144–46).

All these examples have to do with the harming of noncombatants, but more to the point, they exemplify the direct, intentional targeting of noncombatants in their own right. Some efforts seem more calculated than others: shooting at "everything that moves" is indiscriminate and thus bad enough, but other kinds of actions by the besiegers clearly aimed specifically at causing civilian harm. One of these is the shelling of a busy downtown street between tram stops in a city in which the streetcar system served the noncombatant population, not the defending forces. Another is the deliberate restriction of water supplies so that people would have to seek water from the remaining sources, where they were targeted by snipers or mortar fire.

Thinking more closely about this last kind of case, it is important to observe that cutting off water and power supplies during sieges is as old as the practice of sieges, and that such actions are allowed, in traditional moral reasoning, by the rule of double effect. Properly such actions aim at the defenders, even though everyone inside the besieged place is equally harmed by the action. But restricting water, leaving it available only in exposed places, and then firing on noncombatants seeking it is a very different matter. The firing is a plain violation of their noncombatant status, arguing that the original action against the water supply was part of an effort directly and intentionally to target the noncombatants in the city. The whole train of action thus represents a direct and intentional attack on noncombatants, the opposite of the protection they are due.

The sieges and assaults on the eastern Bosnian cities of Gorazde, Zepa, and Srebrenica in mid-1995 show a similar pattern of targeting noncombatants and add a dimension of ethnic cleansing after these cities fell. The United Nations had attempted to render these three cities off limits to attack by designating them as "safe havens" and placing small numbers of blue-helmeted peacekeepers in posts around them. But before their "safe haven" designation the three cities, as lonely enclaves controlled by Bosnian government forces within a Serb-controlled countryside, had become refugee centers for noncombatants who had intentionally and directly been driven out of their homes by "ethnic cleansing" in the smaller towns and rural areas surrounding the cities. The presence of the pro-government forces gave the Serb forces their rationale for attacking the cities, though it was more an excuse than a serious reason, since the government forces were not even strong enough to defend the cities, let alone pose a military threat outside them. Rather, the sieges and attacks on the three cities appear as steps in the larger campaign of ethnic cleansing aimed at the Bosnian Muslim population as a whole.

The offensives against the three eastern cities followed patterns set earlier: an increase in artillery fire, aimed not at the defenders but at the center of the city, where the noncombatants were concentrated; then an infantry attack and takeover. Afterward, in the cases of Srebrenica and Zepa, males ten years of age and older were separated and made prisoners, while the women and other children were forcibly driven out as refugees. The men and boys, we now know, were killed and buried in mass graves, while the women told stories of rape and mistreatment at the hands of the victors. Red Cross figures list 6,456 persons missing from Srebrenica after it was captured, mostly men and boys; in all, 23,000 persons were expelled from this city alone (Honig and Both, 1977: xviii, 65).

While a siege, no matter how indiscriminately carried out, ultimately aims at the control of the besieged place by the besiegers for their purposes, a sharper form of war against population centers aims at the complete destruction of such places or at rendering them utterly uninhabitable. In such cases there is no question of possible double effect; the direct, intended target is the population of the places attacked, and the purpose is to kill the inhabitants or drive them out and make it impossible for them to return. Such means have been employed for the end of "ethnic cleansing" in all stages of the armed conflicts following the breakup of Yugoslavia, and they are exemplified by Dizdarevic's reference to shelling "to obliterate what has already been destroyed"; more recently, both in the months leading up to and during the NATO bombing of Yugoslavia in 1999, the complete destruction of population centers was a preferred means of war employed by Yugoslav Serb forces against the ethnic Albanian population of Kosovo. The following account from the *New York Times* (September 28 1998: A3) describes this practice in action:

> In the Drenica area, more than two dozen villages have been virtually destroyed in the last week, Western monitors say. That adds to the tally of more than 200 villages described by European Union monitors as moderately or severely damaged since ... late July.
>
> Between 10,000 and 15,000 people have been pushed out of their homes in the last week, adding to the estimated 250,000 who were already refugees. ...
>
> [T]here was evidence that once the residents ran away, the houses were torched.

As painful as the creation of refugees is, the laws and customs of war—and the moral rule of double effect—do not totally forbid actions to this end; yet turning noncombatants out of their homes and communities as refugees may be done only as a secondary, not directly intended effect of action against a justified military target. To carry on a war through directly seeking to create refugees and/or kill members of the enemy's civilian population is another matter entirely: this is warfare against noncombatants, pure and simple. While the sieges of the Bosnian cities discussed above involve elements of such warfare, this was the main character of the conflict in Kosovo. In prima facie terms, it rises to the level of the legal definition of genocide: the people targeted were chosen because they were Albanians, members of a specific national and religious group; the methods involved three of the kinds of actions forbidden in the Genocide Convention—killing, causing serious bodily or mental harm, and deliberately inflicting conditions of life calculated to bring about the group's destruction in whole or in part. As in the case of the Rwandan killings discussed above, though, even without a formal designation of this form of warfare as genocide, direct attacks aimed at destroying population centers so as to kill or drive out their inhabitants violate fundamental moral obligations to persons in an area of conflict who, whatever their sympathies, are simply attempting to live their daily lives in as normal a manner as possible. Such attacks are no less than a form of direct, intentional warfare against noncombatants.[5]

Reflections

The increase in the magnitude, deliberateness, and variety of harm to noncombatants in present-day armed conflicts poses a special irony, since this same century witnessed impressive developments in international law designed to protect noncombatants, as well as intense and sustained moral argument on behalf of such protection. Though I have focused on Western moral tradition in this chapter, concern to distinguish noncombatants from combatants and to protect them from harm during armed conflict is by no means unique to the West but is recognized in the major moral traditions of other world cultures as well (see, for example, Kelsay, 1990). Nor is the rejection of such warfare limited to elites: media accounts and public consciousness react strongly to violence directed against noncombatants. The problem is not that the need for such protection is poorly realized or is not widely accepted or that the protections due noncombatants are ill defined; indeed, the irony is that exactly the opposite is the case.

---

5. It might be argued—and it sometimes has been—that the Serb military's destruction of ethnic Albanian homes and villages was simply the application of a strategy often found in wars against guerilla insurgencies, like that of the Kosovo Liberation Army (KLA)—namely, the drying up of the water (the sympathetic population) in which the fish (the insurgents) swim. This strategy is deeply problematical in itself, both morally and in terms of international law, since it directly targets people who are not themselves directly engaged in the insurgency, whatever their sympathies may be. The ferocity of the destruction directed against ethnic Albanian homes and villages—for example, deliberate shelling of villages and razing of houses with the result that their entire population was driven into the wilderness with hardly any provisions or protection against the weather—argues further that the effort was intended not simply to remove support from the guerilla forces but to harm ethnic Albanian noncombatants themselves. In moral terms, the Serb military's actions against ethnic Albanians in Kosovo were both indiscriminate and disproportionate.

At the same time, though, as noted toward the beginning of this essay, arguments persist that the noncombatant-combatant distinction is meaningless in modern warfare, or meaningless in wars over ideology, ethnicity, or religion, or cannot be made a standard for the actual conduct of war because of the great destructive power of modern weapons. If it were only war criminals who made these arguments, they would be of little account; yet in fact they are common among well-meaning, highly moral people who see them as supporting their principled opposition to all war. Modern war, these argue, cannot be conducted so as to honor moral distinctions and restraints; therefore, war as such must be abolished. Such an argument does not explain why it is presumably possible to abolish war entirely yet impossible to restrain it within moral limits. Whatever the long-term prospect, in the present day war has not disappeared, and it does not seem likely to do so in the foreseeable future. This poses an immediate moral obligation: so long as there continue to be armed conflicts, there remains an urgent need to hold fast to the moral and legal restraints defining noncombatant status and seeking to protect noncombatants during such conflict. In reflecting on this need I want to return to the various arguments against special status and protection for noncombatants identified at the beginning of this chapter in order to consider further the case *against* those arguments.

As to whether it is meaningful anymore to distinguish noncombatants from combatants during warfare, it is well to recall Paul Ramsey's extensive and careful efforts to explain the moral distinction between the two (e.g., 1968: 153–56). The need for care in making this distinction reflects the fact that noncombatants are often mixed with combatants in the way of war, but the moral obligations and permissions toward them differ radically. The line distinguishing noncombatants from combatants may move about from time to time, and there have always been ambiguous cases: particular exceptions may need to be made in any general list of who qualifies as a noncombatant. Moreover, careful attention needs to be paid to uses of the terms "civilian" and "noncombatant" (or "soldier" and "combatant"). They are not, at bottom, interchangeable. The moral issue is the functional role of combatancy or noncombatancy. That functional role of civilians in war has differed, not only over history but from culture to culture and even, within a culture, from one armed force to another, depending on its structure; it will continue to change according to context. To admit such variations is not to say that the concept of noncombatancy is meaningless or irrelevant today, but that it needs to be understood and applied with care and precision in every war in any age, both by combatants and by others—for example, the media and moral analysts—who comment on particular wars. The point of the distinction, after all, is to require active moral effort to identify *who* are noncombatants so as to spare them from direct, intentional harm. When the effort is made for exactly the opposite reason—to identify noncombatants as "soft targets" who can be attacked with impunity as a means of injuring the enemy's ability to fight—then this utterly reverses the moral purpose behind the combatant-noncombatant distinction. In the examples from the conflicts in Rwanda-Zaire and the former Yugoslavia, there is evidence not only of a disregard of noncombatant status and protection but of an effort that is just the reverse of what it should be: to target noncombatants directly and intentionally *as noncombatants.*

As to whether the weapons of modern war make it inherently incapable of noncombatant-combatant discrimination, in the contemporary cases of warfare against noncombatants I have described here, what is noteworthy is precisely that such weapons have *not* been involved. In these conflicts the weapons used—from sticks to knives to automatic rifles to artillery fire—became indiscriminate in their effects only because the persons using them or their commanders made the conscious choice to use them in this way. That choice and the resulting action are immoral in any and every war in any and every time, past, present, or future. Of course weapons of mass destruction are rightly rejected as mala in se; this is because their inherent purpose is to target noncombatants. But even clubs, knives, and bullets become weapons of mass destruction when they are used intentionally and directly to kill masses of people. The point of insisting on a distinction between noncombatants and combatants is exactly to avoid this.

I have already treated another justification for attacks against noncombatants often offered in contemporary warfare, and especially in cases of "ethnic cleansing" and genocide: all the members of the opposing group are equally enemies because of ideology, religious belief, ethnicity, or some other cultural factor, so that the noncombatant-combatant distinction does not matter in conflict with them. From the standpoint of moral tradition and international law on war, this is not so much a counterargument as a denial of the fundamental perspective of both morality and law. This perspective holds that common moral rules apply even in war; the rejection consists in the claim that war is necessarily total. In moral terms the argument that allows warfare to be intentionally directed against ethnically or religiously different noncombatants in such conflicts as those in the former Yugoslavia and Rwanda-Zaire is simply wrong. Only what persons *do* makes them morally liable to have armed force used against them, not what they *believe* religiously or who they *are* ethnically or culturally.

Why should parties to a conflict observe the protection of noncombatants, if their goal is to win? Posing the question this way assumes in advance that winning requires total war. But the moral tradition of just war and the law of armed conflict reject this assumption. They do so not simply as expressions of abstract ideals with no connection to the real demands of warfare or political action; rather, both the moral tradition and the law reflect a rich and varied historical experience of war and of statecraft, and in the case of the law, the rules laid down also express formal agreements by states working out of their own interests and values. Fundamentally, the limits set on the conduct of war by morality and the law of war aim at ensuring that warfare does not destroy everything that is worth living for in peacetime, or make it hard or impossible to return to peace after the end of armed conflict. "[W]e go to war that we may have peace," and not simply for the sake of war, wrote Augustine. He continued with this counsel for the conduct of war: "Be peaceful, therefore, in warring, so that you may vanquish those whom you war against, and bring them to the prosperity of peace" (Augustine, *Letter clxxxix, To Boniface*, cited in Thomas Aquinas, 1912–22: IIa-IIae, q. 40, a. 1). The underlying point, seen clearly by Augustine, is that the way a war is fought determines whether peace can be created once again and, if so, what kind of a peace it can be. Unjust conduct in war works against the achievement of a just peace—that is, a genuine peace. Bringing a conflict to a close in which the parties are able to reach reconciliation and cooperate in rebuilding their society or societies depends importantly on how they fought each other during the armed phase of their dispute.

Thus both because it is inherently wrong to make war on noncombatants and because of the goal of peace and stability in domestic and international affairs, it is vitally important to maintain the restraints on the

Protection of Noncombatants 189

conduct of war found in moral tradition and in international law on war. Doing so affects everyone, and so does failure to do so.

REFERENCES

Bonet, Honoré. 1901. *The Buke of the Law of Armys or Buke of Battalis*. London: William Blackwood and Sons.
Contamine, Philippe. 1984. *War in the Middle Ages*. Oxford: Basil Blackwell.
Davis, G. Scott, ed. 1996. *Religion and Justice in the War over Bosnia*. New York and London: Routledge.
Dizdarevic, Zlatko. 1994. *Sarajevo: A War Journal*. New York: Henry Holt.
Farer, Tom J. 1971. *The Laws of War 25 Years After Nuremberg*. International Conciliation, no. 583. New York: Carnegie Endowment for International Peace.
Friedman, Leon, ed. 1972. *The Law of War: A Documentary History*. 2 vols. New York: Random House.
Honig, Jan Willem, and Norbert Both. 1997. *Srebrenica: Record of a War Crime*. New York: Penguin.
Johnson, James Turner. 1975. *Ideology, Reason, and the Limitation of War*. Princeton and London: Princeton University Press.
―――. 1981. *Just War Tradition and the Restraint of War*. Princeton and Guildford: Princeton University Press.
Kelsay, John. 1990. "Islam and the Distinction between Combatants and Noncombatants." In James Turner Johnson and John Kelsay, eds., *Cross, Crescent, and Sword: The Justification and Limitation of War in Western and Islamic Tradition*. New York, Westport, Conn., and London: Greenwood, 197–220.
Kuper, Leo. 1981. *Genocide: Its Political Use in the Twentieth Century*. New Haven and London: Yale University Press.
Ramsey, Paul. 1961. *War and the Christian Conscience*. Durham: Duke University Press.
―――. 1968. *The Just War: Force and Political Responsibility*. New York: Charles Scribner's Sons.
Roberts, Adam, and Richard Guelff, eds. 1989. *Documents on the Laws of War*. 2nd ed. Oxford: Clarendon.
Schindler, Dietrich, and Jiri Toman, eds. 1973. *The Laws of Armed Conflicts: A Collection of Conventions, Resolutions, and Other Documents*. Leiden: A. W. Sijthoff; Geneva: Henry Dunant Institute.
Thomas Aquinas. 1912–22. *Summa theologiae*. 3 vols. London: R. and T. Washbourne; New York: Benziger Brothers.
United Nations. 1993. *Report of the Secretary-General Pursuant to Paragraph 2 of Security Council Resolution 808 (1993), Including the Statute of the Tribunal*. U.N. doc. S/25704 and add. 1.
―――. 1994. *Security Council Resolution on the Establishment of the International Tribunal for Rwanda, Including the Statute of the Tribunal*. U.N. doc. S/RES/935.
Vattel, Emmerich de. 1740. *The Law of Nations; or, Principles of the Law of Nature*. London: n.p.
Walzer, Michael. 1977. *Just and Unjust Wars: A Moral Argument, with Historical Illustrations*. New York: Basic.

9

Protecting the Natural Environment in Wartime
Ethical Considerations from the Just War Tradition

GREGORY M. REICHBERG AND HENRIK SYSE

Ethics, War, and Nature

What protection does the natural environment merit in wartime? It was in the aftermath of the Vietnam War of 1961–75 that this question came into focus. Wars have always brought destruction in their wake; and the twentieth century was by no means the first to show concern for the effects of armed conflict on our natural surroundings. However, the Vietnam War does "stand out in modern history as one in which intentional anti-environmental actions were a major component of the strategy and tactics of one of the adversaries, one in which such actions were systematically carried out for many years and over large areas" (Westing, 1976: 1). Concern over these and similar practices—such as the Iraqi attacks on oil installations during the Gulf War of 1990–91, when hundreds of wells were deliberately set aflame—has fueled debate over the moral and legal implications of environmental despoliation in war. Should military acts that cause widespread harm to the environment be counted among the grave breaches of the laws of armed conflict? And why should the environment deserve this special protection? Is it because vital human interests depend upon it—or because of its own inherent worth?

Normative considerations about the status of the natural environment in wartime are not readily translated into absolute prohibitions. As concerns natural, nonhuman entities, the laws of armed conflict have no direct analogue to the statutes that unequivocally condemn the intentional killing of noncombatants, sexual violence, or the use of torture. The environmental interdictions that do exist are invariably couched in the language of military necessity and proportionality.

Since legal and moral discussions of war are now so closely intertwined, we begin with a representative sampling (by no means a complete list) of some legal instruments that seek to safeguard the environment in wartime.[1] This will bring into greater relief some key points in the ethical analysis that follows.

Article 2, paragraph 4 of Protocol III annexed to the U.N. Convention on Certain Conventional Weapons (1980) declares that "it is prohibited to make forests or other kinds of plant cover the object of attack by incendiary weapons except when such natural elements are used to cover, conceal or camouflage combatants or other military objectives, or are themselves military objectives." Similarly, article 35.3 of the 1997 Protocol I Additional to the Geneva Conventions of 1949 prohibits attacks on the natural environment by reference to the *extent*, not the *kind* of destruction wrought: "It is prohibited to employ methods or means of warfare which are intended, or may be expected, to cause widespread, long-term and severe damage to the natural environment." It is, however, possible to read this last proscription as implying an outright condemnation of environmental destruction *when it reaches a certain level*. This is the interpretation proposed in the U.S. Army's *Operational Law Handbook:* "GP [Geneva Protocol] I does not employ the traditional balancing of military necessity against the quantum of expected destruction. Instead, it establishes this level as an absolute ceiling of permissible destruction" (Judge Advocate General's School, U.S. Army, 1997: 5–18). Still, even on this interpretation, no special category of natural entity is excluded from attack per se. By contrast, the provisions of the 1976 ENMOD (Environmental Modification Techniques) Convention would seem to offer an instance in which international law identifies certain kinds of natural phenomena as deserving of special protection in wartime, since articles 1 and 2 expressly forbid the hostile use—under any circumstances whatsoev-

---

1. For more detailed treatment of the environmental aspects of laws of war, see the essays in part 2 of Austin and Brunch, 2000.

er—of "environmental modification techniques" such as "any technique for changing—through the deliberate manipulation of natural processes—the dynamics, composition or structure of the earth, including its biota, lithosphere, hydrosphere and atmosphere, or of outer space" (Green, 1993: 149). In point of fact, however, this convention "deals essentially, not with *damage to the environment,* but with *the use of forces of the environment as weapons*" (Roberts, 2000: 58; emphasis added). Hence it bears little direct applicability to the issue now under consideration: protection *of* the environment in wartime. The 1959 Antarctic treaty is perhaps the international provision that comes closest to bestowing a special immunity on nature. It prohibits military activities and nuclear tests in the region, "partly motivated by the desire to preserve the fragile ecology of the Antarctic" (ibid.: 71).

Even if the laws of war could be shown to contain an implicit moral teaching on the environment, this would still not suffice for elaborating an ethical theory about the proper treatment of the natural environment in war. *Ethics* is broader in scope and more explanatory than *law.* Moreover, positive laws are enacted under circumstances that can entail silence regarding important moral truths, hence St. Thomas Aquinas's observation that "human law does not forbid all bad acts ... as neither does it prescribe all acts of virtue" (1981 [hereafter simply *Summa theologiae*]: Ia-IIae, q. 96, a. 3, ad 1). This is especially true of international law, which issues from a consensus forged among nation-states with divergent moral traditions. And this in turn means that ethical reflection about war cannot be reduced to tidy generalizations from the relevant international legislation.[2]

In examining the moral aspects of environmental destruction in war, our concern in this chapter is with harm to the natural world that occurs as a result (whether intentional or collateral) of military conflict. Thus we will not be dealing with the question of whether environmental security can stand as a legitimate rationale for waging war—as when a party initiates conflict to protect or gain control of valued resources (land, clean air and water, etc.).[3] Categories from the just war tradition form

---

2. International lawyers are in large measure divided on the question of whether the current international statutes provide adequate legal protection for the natural environment in times of war (cf. Falk, 1984; Goldblat, 1991; Austin and Brunch, 2000, part 2).

3. Nor will we take up the related question of whether an increased scarcity of natural

Protecting the Natural Environment 193

our point of departure, as we wish to show how the resources of this tradition can provide a basis for a properly ethical discourse on war and the environment. Thereby we hope not only to contribute to the debate on the environment and war, but equally to highlight some neglected aspects of the just war tradition and its philosophical background.

For our present purpose, the just war approach to international conflict can be viewed as a middle way that avoids the drawbacks of both pacifism and realpolitik, each of which denies the applicability of morality to acts of war. On the other hand, the philosophical background of the just war tradition explains why nature is valuable, without going so far as to ascribe inherent rights to nonhuman entities. Also avoiding the other extreme, it does not view nature as something merely to be shaped or disregarded at human whim. The idea of just war belongs to a tradition that sees humankind as the steward or custodian of nature, not its despotic master. This complements other approaches to ecology and war, such as the Gandhian approach summed up by Weber (1999: esp. 350–56).

In the next two sections we look into the background of the just war tradition of moral reflection to see how it can help us to navigate between the positions just mentioned. We are seeking not to tie these concepts exclusively to one specific philosophy or theology but rather to show how the rich soil from which the just war tradition has grown includes elements relevant to the contemporary debate on the environmental consequences of war. In this connection, a reading of St. Thomas Aquinas (c. 1225–74) should prove instructive.

We then go on to show how the principles and criteria elucidated by the just war tradition may be usefully applied not only to the wartime relation of persons to each other but also to the relation of human agents to the environment.

At the outset, some challenges to our overall approach should be

---

resources will likely lead to a higher incidence of armed conflict. For two contrasting accounts of the relationship between environment, scarce resources, and conflict, see Gleditsch, 1998, and Homer-Dixon, 1999. This literature, however, is chiefly empirical and descriptive in scope; it does not take up the normative question of whether environmental interests can morally justify a resort to armed force. A related debate revolves around the question as to whether and to what extent there is such a thing as long-lasting damage to the environment. A good summary of the debate between "pessimists" (neo-Malthusians for the most part, who emphasize the long-term implications of environmental degradation) and "optimists" (who normally ground their optimism in the growth of technology and human inventiveness) can be found in Gleditsch, 1998: 381–84.

briefly discussed. It might, for instance, be objected that recourse to the teaching of a thirteenth-century friar-theologian will inevitably entangle its proponents in a Eurocentric anachronism ill suited to the complexities of our contemporary, pluralistic world. Can Thomas Aquinas be at all relevant when what we are dealing with are the concrete problems of current military politics? Can this medieval framework be used in a world that is, in culture and in religion, more heterogeneous than anything Aquinas had to deal with? Should it not be the aim of moral and legal philosophy to devise a groundwork that does *not* have any ties to or explicit links with a particular worldview?

We hold that this medieval perspective yields some notable advantages over the modern philosophical outlooks that usually inform present-day discussions on ethics in international relations. Developed before the age of the sovereign nation-states, the medieval approach to the morality of war offers valuable resources for articulating the idea of *an international common good* (see George, 1998), an idea very much in keeping with the contemporary trend toward globalization. At the same time, the medieval Scholastic philosophers of the Christian West were *not* unacquainted with the phenomenon of ethnic and cultural diversity. Aquinas, for instance, was an avid reader of works by Islamic and Jewish authors, for whom he often expressed a profound respect and indebtedness. With those thinkers he shared a philosophical language that was open to the religious dimension of human life, without being tied to specific religious dogmas.[4] Thus, unlike most post-Enlightenment approaches, the medieval discourse on ethics did not exclude religious viewpoints from the theater of intercultural dialogue and debate. In a world where many, not least in the Islamic world, express deep skepticism and resentment toward a Western, secularized discourse that sets aside all reference to religious mores and beliefs, the medieval tradition may have much to teach us today. Thus, the medieval framework that gave rise to the just war tradition was not as parochial as is sometimes suggested. It can rather be characterized as basically global and open—in theory, if not in political practice.

Our main reason for turning to the just war tradition is not to secure a comprehensive worldview that would fully encompass war as well as the

---

4. This points to what is often referred to as the teaching of *natural law*, a teaching about a common moral law for mankind. This teaching has exercised much influence on modern rights discourse; see Sigmund, 1971.

environment. Our main aim is rather to articulate a philosophical *vocabulary* that can help us reflect meaningfully on how the two are interconnected. Much of the contemporary debate on the morality of warfare—apropos humanitarian intervention, for instance—is hampered by the enormous complexity of the issues involved. A unified vocabulary, based on crosscultural moral concerns and perspectives, is urgently needed. This is where we believe the just war approach can prove beneficial.

Second, in interstate peace negotiations, it is important that the parties to the settlement find a way of justifying it *within their own cultural context*. If international legal statutes protecting the environment come across as totally estranged from particular customs and beliefs, there is little chance that they will win widespread acceptance. The challenge, then, is to discern how *different* perspectives and foundations can yield *common* agreements that will contribute to less conflict and more peace. Here, international human rights provide an interesting example. It can plausibly be argued that human rights can be grounded in different ways—for example, by Kantian moral philosophy, by utilitarianism, or by the Christian, Jewish, and Islamic religious traditions. To reach common conclusions it is not always necessary that everyone share the same premises. Rawls has developed this into the idea of an "overlapping consensus" (1993: lecture 4). In his view different comprehensive doctrines can sustain and support, albeit on different philosophical and/or religious grounds, a common political conception of justice (and, we should add, peace).[5] This is highly relevant for our discussion. Even if one discards the way of viewing humanity and nature outlined here, one may nonetheless accept it as *one* way of grounding a moral view of the environment and warfare. This may, in turn, challenge adherents of other philosophical and/or religious traditions to reconsider *their* theoretical foundations and find ways of using them constructively as contributors to an "overlapping consensus."

Finding a Middle Ground between Pacifism and Realpolitik

The just war tradition maintains that right human living sometimes requires the taking up of arms in order that wrongful violence, especial-

---

5. For a discussion of overlapping consensus (that predates Rawls's more famous treatment) from the standpoint of a religiously inspired philosophy, see Maritain, 1961.

ly as perpetrated by states, may be forcibly resisted. Violence of this sort is held to involve harms of such magnitude that those who oppose it are *justified* in using force in ways that, under ordinary circumstances (i.e., peacetime), would be condemned as reprehensible. This being the case, the aim of just war thinking is to assist statesmen and citizens in understanding what is a morally apt use of force. Its value resides not so much in offering hard-and-fast rules that must be applied in each and every situation but rather "in its capacity to set the right terms for rational debate on public policies bearing on the problem of war" (Murray, 1988: 269). The famous three criteria elaborated by Aquinas (*Summa theologiae*, IIa-IIae, q. 40, a. 1)—legitimate authority, just cause, right intention—are best thought of as the fundamental questions that a people (particularly its leaders) should ask when entertaining the prospect of armed conflict.

Attempts such as this to link the use of force with morality have traditionally encountered stiff resistance from both pacifists and political realists. Appealing to the principle "The end never justifies the means," pacifists maintain that the employment of armed force is in fact incompatible with its purported goal: the establishment of just and humane relations among independent states. Basing their arguments on the exigencies of love or benevolence, the unique value of human life, or the inviolability of human rights, principled pacifists contend that it is inherently wrongful to commit warlike deeds, whatever the circumstances. Other pacifists, however, base their opposition to warfare not on high-minded religious, philosophical, or ethical principles, but instead simply on a perception of the dangers attendant upon modern, technological warfare. These qualified pacifists suggest "that modern wars are immoral where older wars were not necessarily so" (Fotion, 1990: 3),[6] because in our time sophisticated weapons systems, and the military-industrial complex which produces and maintains them, stand as a constant encouragement to violence, a violence that, once unleashed, will quickly result in a pattern of widespread destruction nearly impossible to halt. Accordingly, no justification can be given for maintaining such weapons systems, and even less so for using them.

Against the pacifists, realists allege that there is little sense in stigmatizing any engagement in warfare as inherently immoral, for the good

---

6. Fotion summarizes the various arguments (pacifist and realist) against the morality of war and offers a useful point-by-point discussion and rebuttal.

reason that war is neither moral nor immoral. It is simply *non*moral: it takes us outside the realm in which moral judgments can have any real bearing.[7]

Two reasons are generally given in support of this position. Some realists, referring to the doctrine of *raison d'état*, maintain that the defining goal of political action, especially with regard to the conduct of foreign affairs, is to promote national self-interest. Consequently, although statesmen are bound to observe the dictates of morality when they act as private individuals, when they act on behalf of the state they have an obligation to do whatever is necessary to preserve the state's security. Altruism, the supreme virtue in the realm of interpersonal relations, becomes a vice when taken as an ideal for statecraft.

Appealing to the principle "Ought implies can," other realists assert that choosing between right and wrong, altogether feasible and praiseworthy during peacetime, is well-nigh impossible in times of war. "Under conditions of war," it is argued, "all of us, soldier and civilian alike, lose all sense of control over our behavior. We inevitably become more like beasts than humans, at least insofar as the enemy is concerned" (Fotion, 1990: 11). In such situations, it becomes "quite out of the question to expect people to behave ethically" (ibid.: 12). After all, we can reasonably hold people accountable only to standards that they have some realistic chance of attaining. The quick-response features of modern weaponry augments this accountability problem, since the utilization of such weapons leaves little or no time to engage in the kind of clear-headed deliberation necessary for moral action. That means, to the realist, that we need to face up to the unhappy truth about war: it plunges us into a nonmoral universe where anything goes. Statesmen should not delude themselves by entertaining fictive moral principles that ordinary human beings will be unable to follow in times of war. In this vein, Clausewitz famously wrote in *Vom Kriege* that "war is such a dangerous business that the mistakes which come from kindness are the very worst," for which reason he concluded that "to introduce the principle of moderation into the theory of war itself would always lead to logical absurdity" (quoted in Reichberg, Syse, and Begby, 2006: 555).

Interestingly, then, pacifists and realists reach quite parallel conclu-

---

7. We are reminded of General Sherman's dictum: "War is cruelty, and you cannot refine it"; or famously, "War is hell" (quoted in Christopher, 1994: 3).

sions: whereas pacifists say that "because war is full of injustice, we must avoid it" at all costs, "realists reply that because those in war can act neither justly nor unjustly, we must avoid ethics" (Fotion, 1990: 12). Thus neither can find any meaningful way "to fit the use of military force into the objective order of justice" (Murray, 1988: 268).

The response of the just war tradition to these objections is two-pronged: First, the tradition urges us not to conflate the moral exigencies of institutional action (especially as concerns the nation-state) with the morality of personal and familial life. "The obligatory public purposes of society and the state impose on these institutions a special set of obligations which . . . are not coextensive with the wider and higher range of obligations that rest upon the human person" (Murray, 1988: 268). From this point of view, "the effort to bring the organized action of politics and the practical art of statecraft directly under control of the . . . values that govern personal and familial life is inherently fallacious" (ibid.). Thus, when the tradition identifies legitimate authority as a necessary criterion for the just employment of public force, it thereby testifies to the special conditions that attach to morality in this sphere. In this connection it leans away from pacifism in the direction of realism. Yet, against political realism, it maintains that national interest includes goods that are moral in kind, goods like the rule of law and civic amity (national and international) — and, we should add, a diverse and healthy environment — that should not be sacrificed for the sake of physical security. For to sacrifice them would be tantamount to abandoning goods that are essential to the very well-being of the state, to the common good as integrally conceived. For this reason the very notion of national interest, well understood, requires that we draw a distinction between force and violence — the former being "the measure of power necessary and sufficient to uphold the valid purposes both of law and politics"; the latter being whatever exceeds it, thereby destroying "the order both of law and of politics" (ibid.: 288).

Finally, to the argument that warfare renders us virtually incapable of exercising free choice ("inability realism," as Fotion calls it [1990: 10]), proponents of the just war tradition concede that the passions unleashed by war are among the most recalcitrant to reason. Yet from this concession they draw a far different conclusion than that of their realist counterparts. It is the efficacy of education, and not mere resignation to human weakness, that ought to inform the formulation of public policy in this domain. Instituting a sound military education—one that comprises theoretical reflection on the ethics of war as well as practical programs for disciplining the emotions—can do much to reinforce the field commander's capacity for reasonable choice when under duress, provided, of course, that the education in question is systematically begun during peacetime. Only then will there be sufficient time to inculcate a moral readiness for war.

Moral Grounds for Respecting Nature

We have now tried to show how the just war tradition can discuss the morality of war by placing itself between pacifism on the one hand and hard-nosed realism, or realpolitik, on the other. What, then, about the environmental aspects? Can an *ethics* properly speaking be developed for the environment? We hope to show that the just war tradition—set in its broader intellectual context—can again be of service.

Is our natural environment simply raw material to be manipulated at will for the satisfaction of human beings? Or does the environment bear an intrinsic value that can (and should) be defined entirely apart from human interests? The "raw material" view was part and parcel of the scientific outlook that arose in the early modern period among thinkers like Descartes and Bacon. Today many confound this approach to nature with the one recommended by the Judeo-Christian tradition ("go out and subdue the earth").[8] Both views have been reproached for an anthropocentrism that neglects nature's inner worth. We are accordingly urged to abandon the stance of homo-chauvinism in favor of ecological egalitarianism, animal rights, and/or the moral primacy of the entire biospheric community.[9]

---

8. A typical example of such an interpretation of Judeo-Christian thought may be found in a recent treatment of Thomas Aquinas that states that according to him, "humans and other animals can treat plants *as they please*, and humans can use lower animals *as they desire*" (Armstrong and Botzler, 1993: 278; emphasis added). As we will try to show, this point misses essential aspects of the Christian tradition as expressed by, for example, Aquinas. On the different values accorded to nature in the scientific outlook of early modernity, on the one hand, and the Judeo-Christian tradition, on the other, see Lewis, 1947: 88.

9. For a succinct and nuanced presentation of the main approaches to environmental ethics today, see Elliot, 1991. A selection of some of the most important articles on this topic may be found in O'Neill, Turner, and Bateman, 2001.

An argument can be made that this represents a case of false dilemma: either embrace the autonomous value of the ecosystem or endorse a purely anthropocentric, utilitarian conception of nature. However, neither of these two alternatives adequately captures the understanding of nature that served as a point of reference to the medieval thinkers who elaborated the just war doctrine. Thomas Aquinas, in particular, sought to bridge the two points of view that are sometimes set in opposition within contemporary ethical discussions of the environment: the inherent goodness of natural objects, on the one hand, and the privileged status of humankind, on the other. Whether his synthesis provides a fully adequate metaphysical basis for an environmental ethic is not our express concern here. Rather, we advert to Aquinas's teaching because we find him struggling with a difficulty that is still very much with us today; in so doing he brought to this problem a set of useful distinctions. Moreover, in its formulation and much of its conceptual content the just war tradition is indebted to Aquinas and his followers; looking at Aquinas's wider philosophical view of nature and the place of human beings in it is therefore highly relevant in our context, both from a systematic and historical point of view.

Aquinas makes note of the fact that natural objects can be put to a wide variety of *uses* by humankind: for sustenance and shelter, technological development, scientific investigation, as well as aesthetic pleasure and contemplative wisdom.[10] In these ways natural entities enter into the fabric of *justice* that binds human beings together: we aid or harm each other by giving and taking, protecting and destroying, caring for and neglecting the things that live and lie around us in the world of nature. The value that we place on natural things will consequently condition our behavior in wartime: enemies attack not only the life and limb of the other but also the natural items that the other, for one reason or another, holds dear.

In war, natural objects enter the sphere of moral concern from several human-centered points of view: they provide support for war-making activities; they serve as targets of attack (e.g., defoliation to deny cover to the enemy); and they may even supply a motivation for going to war, as when wars are fought over the possession of valuable natural resources. Although natural entities thus occupy only a mediate role in war—war by

---

10. For a careful study of Aquinas's views regarding nature (and humankind's place in it), see Blanchette, 1992. This work supplies numerous references to the primary sources.

definition is always waged by human beings against human beings—it is nevertheless plausible to ask whether the damage wrought on the natural environment in wartime ought, in some circumstances at least, to be avoided *out of concern for the environment itself.* This problem is but a corollary to the much broader (and more basic) theoretical question of whether natural objects can have any moral standing in their own right.

It is true that important strands in Aquinas's teaching seem to militate against conferring moral standing to the nonhuman entities of the natural world. On his account, neither justice nor charity can fittingly extend to individual plants or animals (or a fortiori to inanimate things such as stones). Absent free choice, nonrational beings are unable to enter into relationships of justice. Hence nothing will be due to them by force of right, since they lack the dominion over self that is the prerequisite for ownership. Nor can animals and plants be inserted within the circle of charity. A communion founded on goods perceived by reason, charity can fittingly be directed only to creatures possessed of rationality (*Summa theologiae*, II-IIae, q. 25, a. 3). On this basis, Aquinas's account appears to offer little or no rationale for protecting natural objects independently of human interests. Killing an ox, to use his example, can never count as murder; it may, however, amount to theft if the ox is the property of another person.[11] In this respect his argumentation could be read as a philosophical justification for the human-centered orientation of (nearly all of) the international statutes currently offering protection to the environment in times of armed conflict.

Significantly, however, Aquinas's conception of human interests opens up the possibility of an environmental ethic based on something more than a purely instrumentalist conception of nature. There is, he suggests, an order among human interests: placing natural things at the service of human want (for food, shelter, and the like), or using them to further man's technological prowess, was to his mind subordinate in the hierarchy of values to the activity of *contemplation*. To recognize the "truth" of things, to behold their inner nature and to appreciate their beauty, constitutes an inherently better employment of the human mind than knowledge sought for the for the sake of some practical end.[12] Paradoxically,

---

11. This example may be found in *Summa theologiae*, IIa-IIae, q. 64, a. 1, ad 3.
12. On the superiority of theoretical over practical knowledge, see *Summa theologiae*, Ia-IIae, q. 3, a. 5.

then, the highest use to which we can put natural things is to delight in their truth; this is a use that does not use things up, but leaves them just as they are.

Moreover, if we reason from Aquinas's presuppositions, the privileged status of humankind within the natural order has an ecological ethic implicitly built into it. Among all the other entities in the physical universe, we alone have cognitive powers that are not restricted to a particular ecological niche. The mind of the human being is, in his view, open to the totality of what is (Blanchette, 1992: 268–82).[13] Our ability to thematize the whole of the universe can, like all other human powers, be put to a good or a bad moral use. And by this power we are rendered stewards of the whole. In this connection Aquinas leads us to two points that are relevant to the elaboration of a just war environmental ethic.

In the first place, the stewardship in question, premised as it is on humankind's special affinity with nature taken as a whole, is not the prerogative of any one individual or people; it belongs to the entire species. And because in fact a great multitude of individuals (and peoples) are called to exercise this stewardship, a moral obligation dictates that it be carried out with an eye to the common good of all. On this basis, Aquinas concludes, somewhat radically, that taking from another's private property in time of urgent need does not count as an act of theft (presuming that the other from whom one takes is not in dire straits himself); this would not be so if our collective ownership of the world's material goods did not take precedence over their appropriation by discrete individuals (*Summa theologiae* IIa-IIae, q. 66, a. 7).

Second, this stewardship of material creation, if it is to be a *just* stewardship and not a despotism, must respect and safeguard the essential diversity of natural things. Against some ancient and medieval philosophers who saw diversity as a mode of imperfection resulting from the action of an evil principle or from chance, Aquinas argued on theological grounds that God, the maker of the universe, directly intended there to be a broad range of different kinds of beings in the world. Of all the wholes encountered in nature, Aquinas concludes that none is more perfect than the totality of nature itself, for it is here that we encounter the widest possible degree of diversity. Any destruction of essential parts of

---

13. The affirmation that the human mind extends to all things is not at all equivalent to saying that we can even come close to having an exhaustive knowledge of this totality.

nature would thereby detract from the integrity of the whole, a whole in which humankind is itself nested as a part. Similarly, taking up this diversitarian outlook on explicitly philosophical grounds, Aquinas argues that the widest possible variety of species is necessary for the overall perfection of the universe. From this we may deduce the existence of a moral obligation to protect this variety whenever we exercise our stewardship over nature.[14]

Aquinas differentiates between two sorts of diversity: *formal* and *material*, the first consisting in *difference of species*, the second denoting *multiplicity within a species*. It is the former that most pertains to that which Aquinas calls "the perfection of the universe" (Blanchette, 1992: 140–41). In other words, it is the species itself, and not each individual within it, that constitutes the primary locus of value in the natural world.

Responsible human agents will accordingly in their dealings with natural entities; they will take great care to promote the viability and diversity of species. The individuals within each species warrant protection not so much for themselves but rather for the preservation of their respective kinds. Individual human beings stand, however, as an exception to this rule. Possessed of dominion over self and having a special affinity with the whole of nature, each of us merits protection for our own sake, not just for the good of our species (Blanchette, 1992: 146–47). To restrict this privileged status to human beings is not, however, equivalent to withholding moral consideration from all other members of the natural world. We have just seen that the common good of the universe depends on the integrity of its parts, a good of which we too are members. Hence our self-respect and well-being (material and spiritual) demand that we treat nature as partner and friend.

To sum up, the just war tradition has developed within a perspective where humankind is seen as a steward or custodian of nature, not its self-serving ruler. This stewardship thereby promotes not only human needs and interests but ecological diversity in the whole of nature as well.

Our point here is not to claim that this philosophical (and partly theological) underpinning offered by Aquinas constitutes the only possible way to apply just war principles to the environment. We have merely suggested a framework within which to articulate humankind's obliga-

---

14. See Blanchette, 1992: 118–48, for an exposition of Aquinas's texts on the theme of diversity.

tions toward nature, a framework in which the diversity of nature is duly respected—and a framework within which the just war tradition actually developed. This we have done without appealing to ethical evaluations that would stand wholly apart from anthropocentric interests; but neither has it been denied that natural beings, apart from humans, have an *inherent value*, such that human beings have an obligation to protect them. Thus we have sought to show that this medieval framework strikes a plausible middle ground between problematic and contested positions in what are often very heated discussions about the environment and how to protect it. We believe that this framework may usefully be borne in mind in the following discussion on war and the environment.

Applying the Just War Criteria

In a way it is misleading to refer to the just war approach as a "theory." It should more correctly be regarded as a "framework" or a "tradition of thought," since it comes to us from a multitude of writers over a considerable span of time.[15] This diversity notwithstanding, several attempts have been made to develop a unified theory of the just use of armed force. These attempts have mainly centered around the formulation of moral *criteria* for engagement in war: competent authority, just cause, right intention, discrimination and proportionality, and so on. Not often, however, have these criteria been brought to bear on the question of environmental destruction in war. We believe that they can serve as a useful tool for organizing moral reflection on this theme.

Environmental destruction in war is sometimes *deliberate;* other times it arises as a *side effect*. When a platoon commander orders the bombing of a military installation, the ensuing devastation is said to be intentional. By contrast, if in this attack a nearby forest is coincidentally burned down, it is deemed a side effect of that military operation. If the commander knew (or reasonably could have known) that this would happen, but in no way desired this outcome, we say it arose as an unintended yet foreseeable consequence of his military decision. From an ethical standpoint both forms of destruction—intentional and collateral—are subject to moral evaluation. The first we will discuss primarily by reference to the crite-

---

15. See the editors' preface to Reichberg, Syse, and Begby, 2006.

ria of right intention, just cause, and legitimate authority; the second primarily by reference to the criteria of discrimination and proportionality.

The criteria elaborated by the just war tradition do not constitute isolated, self-enclosed standards. It would in most cases be wholly invalid to argue, for example, that one's cause is so meritorious that it overrides the claims of discrimination or proportionality. The basic insight of just war reasoning is that these criteria constitute a unified whole. No one criterion is freestanding. The right application of each requires that due consideration be given to the others.

In what follows, we consider some of the ways in which the just war criteria can inform our decision making about the impact of war on the environment.[16]

Right Intention

This criterion signifies that war should be waged neither for domination or revenge but solely for the reestablishment of a just concord between peoples. Those who make the decision to engage in military action must seriously consider what they hope to achieve afterward, once victory is achieved. Winning is never sufficient unto itself. From an ethical point of view, the restoration of civic amity and peace is the only legitimate goal of waging war. This criterion makes note of the fact that an agent may indeed have a legitimate cause: repelling an unjust attacker—but nevertheless act from a wrongful intention. Victims of unjust aggression can swiftly become aggressors themselves. How many defenders have sought to dominate their enemy in turn instead of striving to achieve conditions that will bring about an equitable peace?[17]

Medieval theorists of the just war observed that the *intention of peace* was not a moral requirement for political leaders alone; it should also

---

16. Just war criteria are often divided into *ius ad bellum* and *ius in bello* criteria: that is, criteria for the justness of *going to* war and criteria for justice *in* war respectively. However, the ius ad bellum criteria have clear relevance for conduct in war, and the separate elaboration of ius in bello criteria is a relatively late development in the just war tradition. For the purposes of this chapter, it is not necessary to distinguish clearly between them. As will be clear, we apply the criteria mostly in their in bello sense, even those that are normally designated ad bellum criteria.

17. Boyle aptly notes that "without the condition of right intention, the connection between one's action and the reason that justifies it remains contingent, and this allows for the possibility that just cause could be a pretext or excuse for bellicose action aimed at some further goal beyond that which one's justifying reason supports, or at some completely independent goal that can be pursued using the justifying reason as a rationalization only" (1996: 45).

shape the actions of the military personnel who plan and take part in the fighting. In other words, right intention should govern both the decision to resort to armed force (ius ad bellum) and conduct in the war itself (ius in bello).[18] Two reasons can be adduced for this. *First*, if participation in war is to have an ethical basis, it is necessary that effective coordination be maintained between the political aim (to oppose grave injustice, to achieve a fair and lasting peace) and whatever means are used to achieve that aim. Absent such coordination, engagement in war will likely foster injustice and enmity instead. Right intention is relevant in a *second* manner, insofar as it ought to inform the inward disposition (*affectus*) of those engaged in the war effort. Hatred of the enemy and desire for sheer revenge were deemed wholly impermissible, even in times of war.[19] Commanders should take care not to compromise the moral integrity of those under their charge by encouraging sentiments and deeds incompatible with the precepts of justice and brotherly love. The distinction between righteous anger (force at the service of justice) and lust for revenge (a hate-inspired cruelty) should be maintained at all costs.[20]

People value the natural environment for a variety of reasons: its utility, its beauty, and even (for some) its sacredness. Thus, in wartime it can be tempting to attack features of the environment (farmland, nature preserves, sites of religious significance) precisely in order to destroy what that the opponent holds dear. *Right intention* absolutely rules out acts of this sort. To practice scorched-earth tactics solely to inflict pain on the enemy is wholly incompatible with the just war ethic. This incompatibility obtains even if no human beings are killed, injured, or otherwise endangered in the attacks. Destroying environmental goods that the oppos-

18. These two aspects are joined in the medieval just war teaching of Alexander of Hales (c. 1185–1245), who termed the former *iustus affectus* and the latter *debita intentio* (see Reichberg, Syse, and Begby, 2006: 156–59).

19. On this score Aquinas draws a distinction between just and unjust vengeance. The first looks to the neighbor's wrongful *action*, which, if gravely damaging to the peace, may rightly warrant a response of forcible opposition. The second looks to the neighbor's *person*, with the intent simply to make him suffer (*Summa theologiae* IIa-IIae, q. 108, a. 1; cf. also the treatment of Alexander of Hales in Reichberg, Syse, and Begby, 2006: 156–59).

20. It should be noted that this moral condemnation of revenge need not apply in all cases to *retaliation*. Reprisals can function as a deterrent; hence they may be justified under certain circumstances, provided of course that the actions undertaken in retaliation are themselves morally (and legally) permissible. Significantly, the 1977 Protocol I Additional to the Geneva Conventions of 1949 expressly forbids attacks in the form of (1) reprisals against "the natural environment" (article 55.2), (2) reprisals against "certain agricultural areas" (article 54.4), and (3) reprisals using "certain dangerous forces" (article 56.4). For a general discussion of the ethics of reprisals, see Walzer, 1977: 207–22.

ing party values—to break down its morale or simply to vent hatred—is ethically reprehensible. This point is reflected in the international laws of war that condemn wanton violence.[21]

Furthermore, where vital natural resources have been seized or destroyed wantonly, the likelihood of reaching just settlement when the war has ended will be greatly reduced. The perception that one's means of subsistence (and items of cultural significance) have been deliberately destroyed by others seeking to gain a dominant political or military position will further fuel the cycle of violence and bad intentions.

Just Cause

This criterion is most often invoked by political leaders *prior to* the outbreak of hostilities as their rationale for going to war (ius ad bellum). Since war is prima facie an evil, participation in it requires moral and legal *justification*. Thus, according to the moral logic of "just cause," war making will be deemed rightful or just solely when it arises as a response to grave wrongdoing committed by the other side.

In a more limited sense, however, "just cause" enters into the evaluation of particular acts committed within the context of an armed conflict already under way (ius in bello). It states that the destruction of civilian property is allowable only when it serves a determinate military purpose. If "civilian property" is construed to include features of the natural environment—not only farmland and livestock but also lakes, forests, fauna, and other entities within the public commons—then at the very least this criterion will exclude all forms of wanton violence. It also would proscribe all attacks on the natural environment that aim at demoralizing the civilian population: to deter civilians from giving food and other supplies to soldiers, to provoke terror (thus persuading civilians to vacate their homes and land), or to prompt civilians to withdraw their political support for the war.

---

21. "The only legitimate object which States should endeavor to accomplish during war is to weaken the military forces of the enemy" (1968 St. Petersburg Declaration, in Reisman and Antoniou, 1994: 35). Wanton destruction is expressly declared unlawful in article 147 of the 1949 Geneva Convention IV, wherein it is confirmed that grave breaches of the convention include "extensive destruction and appropriation of property, not justified by military necessity and carried out wantonly." Roberts remarks that "such prohibited destruction would include much that has serious environmental effects. The fact that this prohibition is contained in a treaty that has virtually universal acceptance by states, and is indisputably in force in international wars, adds to its significance" (2000: 56–57).

Taken on its own, without reference to the other criteria, just cause (understood in its in bello sense as another name for "military necessity")[22] allows for a variety of deliberate actions involving environmental destruction, inter alia:[23]

- Flushing-out tactics: destruction of forested or otherwise vegetated areas in order to force enemy soldiers from their hiding places, and to reveal military posts, camps, or installations.
- Protection tactics: destruction of forested or otherwise vegetated areas in order to protect one's own soldiers from ambush.
- Scorched earth: the wholesale destruction of civilian infrastructure in occupied territory (which has sometimes been countenanced by international law under exceptional circumstances of great urgency), including mines and farmland, when carried out with the intent to deprive the opposing force of material essential to the war effort.[24]

To reach an ethical determination on whether such tactics would be justified in particular cases, it is imperative not to limit one's deliberation to just cause (i.e., military necessity) alone. Sound moral judgment must take into account the exigencies stipulated by the other criteria; otherwise reference to just cause would amount to nothing more than a code of expediency.

---

22. Among the first explicitly to draw a link between just cause and military necessity was the philosopher Christian Wolff, who wrote in *The Law of Nations Treated According to a Scientific Method* (1749): "[t]hat is licit in war, for one who is waging a just war, without which he cannot acquire his right (*ius suum*) from the other party; that is not allowable which does not help to attain this end" (§781); thus, by extension, "so much is allowable in a just war against the person of an enemy as is sufficient to ward from us and our property the force used by him" (§791) (cited in Reichberg, Syse, and Begby, 2006: 473).

23. For an alternative list of kinds of environmental destruction in war, see Dahl, 1992: 113–15.

24. Thus the German general responsible for the scorched-earth policy in northern Norway during World War II was acquitted of war crimes "on the basis that [this] destruction was necessary due to [the] general's (mistaken) belief that Russians were pursuing his forces" (case cited by Schmitt, 1997: 66n300). More recently, however, international law has moved in the direction of outlawing such practices. Thus article 54 (2) of the 1977 Protocol I Additional to the Geneva Conventions of 1949 states: "It is prohibited to attack, destroy, remove or render useless objects indispensable to the survival of the civilian population, such as foodstuffs, agricultural areas for the production of foodstuffs, crops, livestock, drinking water installations and supplies and irrigation works, for the specific purpose of denying them for their sustenance value to the civilian population or to the adverse Party, whatever the motive, whether in order to starve out civilians, to cause them to move away, or for any other motive" (cited in Green, 1993: 136).

Competent Authority

This criterion reinforces the point that war is no private matter, and that not simply anyone within the halls of power is competent to engage the nation on a course of armed conflict. It also implies that rules governing the decision-making *procedure* are in themselves important when such grave decisions as declaring war are to be made: one must go through the lawful (and publicly stipulated) channels when making such a weighty decision (see Syse and Ingierd, 2005).

Many wartime actions have consequences that extend well beyond the persons who happen to be directly harmed. This lends ammunition to an argument long favored by pacifists: the actions that soldiers and officers are called on to perform are so grave that no person has the legitimate or competent authority to command them.

Although we do not adopt a pacifist stance in this essay, we still deem it pertinent to ask: Who has the competent authority to destroy natural resources? On the one hand, the authority over specific areas and resources has been (and is still being) elaborately fixed by the international law of land and sea, and from there it has made its way into the laws of armed conflict. But on a more philosophical level we may ask: Do military and political leaders have the authority to destroy features of the natural environment? In one way, this can be termed a naïve question. If these commanders have the authority, given military necessity, to inflict harm on human beings, why should they not be allowed, given the same necessity, to target the environment?

However, a vital question is indeed at stake in connection with legitimate (or "competent") authority and the natural environment. Seen in the context of the philosophical perspective delineated above, human beings are best viewed as participants in the natural world rather than as masters over it. Moreover, we have a very limited understanding of the complexity of nature, a point that has been much stressed in the environmentalist literature. But which leaders—political or military—have the competent authority to command actions that will do grave harm to the natural environment? The use of nuclear weapons would be a case in point.[25]

---

25. Concern over the environmental impact of nuclear testing appears to have been one of the motivations behind the 1963 and 1996 test ban treaties. Despite the well-documented threat that nuclear bombs and projectiles pose to the natural environment, there are at pres-

This line of reasoning leads us to suggest that some decisions involving environmental destruction should never be taken solely by commanders in the field. Times arise when such decisions should rather be referred to a higher authority and given the closest possible scrutiny at that level. This would apply to situations where it must be decided whether to engage in military maneuvers in areas where natural items of great value (such as scarce ground water, fragile ecosystems, or endangered species) would likely be harmed. Registries of sensitive areas are highly useful in this connection.[26] This would allow for more environmentally sensitive targeting decisions. While military manuals and laws of armed conflict already specify some of the actions that ought to be avoided in war because of their effects on our natural surroundings,[27] the added dimension of competent authority could do more to differentiate and sharpen both the statutes and the legal decisions concerning the environment and war by saying more explicitly on what level—military and political—such decisions ought to be taken.

Discrimination

This criterion signifies that attacks should target only the military capability of the enemy. It is never permissible intentionally to kill or maim noncombatants on the other side, even when to do so would be highly expedient—say, to break down the enemy's morale. Deliberate destruction of the environmental setting upon which civilians depend for the satisfaction of their basic needs is itself a violation of their noncombatant status. For similar reasons, noncombatants should be shielded, so far as is possible, from the harmful side effects of military action. Thus, in waging war, we should seek to minimize the losses for those not involved in the war action.[28] Environmental degradation caused by biological, chem-

---

ent few international statutes governing the actual military use—as opposed to the deployment and testing—of these weapons (cf. Roberts, 2000: 78–79). A related threat to the natural environment are the many "weapons that happen to contain hazardous substances [e.g., depleted uranium in munitions], as distinct from weapons which use the harmful quantities of such substances for their effect" (ibid.: 82). As yet there has been scant international legislation regulating weapons with hazardous components.

26. The compilation of an authoritative worldwide list was recommended at the 1991 Munich conference on war and the environment (cf. Schmitt, 1997: 24).

27. See Roberts, 2000 and Schmitt, 1997 for a discussion of some military manuals (apropos of the interpretation of Protocol I Additional to the Geneva Conventions).

28. Walzer, 1977: 151, states this as a positive duty incumbent upon soldiers: "For we draw a circle of rights around civilians, and soldiers are supposed to accept (some) risks in order to save civilian lives. It is not a question of going out of their way or of being good Samaritans. They are the ones who endanger civilian lives in the first place, and even if they do this in the

ical, or nuclear weapons has an indiscriminate effect on human beings as well as the environment. Putting such weapons to use would likely constitute an egregious violation of the criterion of discrimination.

One way of framing this principle in connection with the environment is by way of an argument from *property*. The destruction of the environment that often occurs in war can indeed be said to be based on a skewed view of property rights. According to the just war tradition—closely tied to the tradition of natural law, which later came to have such an influence on international law—all property is originally common.[29] Only because it is practical and good for people to have private property can one say that this is "mine," "ours," or "yours." Thus, the destruction of, say, farmland, rain forests, or oil resources constitutes not only a violation of the property rights of those who live in or own that area now; it is also a way of destroying property that in a sense is common to all of humankind, including future generations.[30] This is *not* a view that entails a rejection of private property as such or proposes a radically communist view of property.[31] It simply points to the immorality of spoiling land that can be of good use to other human beings, present *or future*. This entails a moral prohibition against large-scale devastation of territory, even within one's own national jurisdiction. This view of property is especially pertinent to counterinsurgency campaigns carried out in the context of civil wars. Antiguerrilla campaigns have often made use of land mines, defoliants, and other measures, which "have contributed to severe famine and to rendering the land unusable" (Roberts, 2000: 75). Few interna-

---

course of legitimate military operation, they must still *make some positive effort to restrict the range of damage they do*" (emphasis added). Walzer's point is applicable not just to civilian lives but also to the natural environment, at least insofar as civilians depend upon it to meet their basic needs.

29. See our discussion above on the medieval view of property and stewardship.

30. Several international declarations (for instance, the 1899 and 1907 Hague Regulations and the Geneva Conventions of 1949) place restrictions on the destruction or seizure of property in enemy territory. Thus, article 147 of Geneva Convention IV declares that grave breaches of the convention include "extensive destruction and appropriation of property, not justified by military necessity and carried out unlawfully and wantonly" (Green, 1993: 287). It is not altogether clear whether these restrictions extend to public environmental goods such as common land, wilderness tracts, the atmosphere, water resources, and the like. Roberts remarks that "[a]ssuming that 'property' can be interpreted in a broad manner, the cited provisions [Hague and Geneva] may constitute the strongest ground for asserting the illegality of a great deal of wanton environmental destruction in war" (2000: 57). He adds that this is a "typical case in which protection of the environment, even where it is not mentioned in existing law, may nonetheless be a logical implication of that law"(ibid.: 53).

31. It may, however, be said to conflict with hard-line individualist (libertarian) theories of property rights, such as the one advanced by Nozick, 1974.

tional rules of restraint are binding in situations of internal armed conflict—all the more reason to emphasize the applicability of the relevant in bello moral requirements.[32]

Proportionality

This criterion signifies that the destructive impact of particular military operations must be proportional to the intended benefits. Causing great harm—including significant collateral damage—for the sake of a strategic goal of minor importance is unethical. Proportionality is notoriously difficult to handle since it seems to call for comparisons between incomparable things. Can the occupation of a certain amount of land be judged as proportional to a certain number of casualties? How substantial must a war gain be if we are to justify, say, the destruction of a thousand hectares of farmland? Such a question defies answering in the abstract (Cassese, 1986: 272). Interrelating the criteria of proportionality and discrimination can, however, help to shed light on the more general problem. If we hold, as was intimated above, that natural resources are in some way "owned by" or "due to" those who depend on them for their survival (and whose lives are enriched by the natural environment in a manifold of other ways), and that this includes future generations, then the destruction of such resources will often stand in disproportion to the contemplated war gains. In any event, calculations of the seriousness of environmental destruction should always take into account how the destruction will indiscriminately affect noncombatants both now and in the future.

Large-scale intrusions into complex ecosystems may have effects that are extremely difficult to estimate in advance. Yet to condemn intrusions of this sort, it is unnecessary to argue for or against "animal rights" or for or against a "land ethic," to mention only two examples. The premises needed are the more pedestrian ones that (1) humans are part of nature and depend on it; (2) humans have the capacity morally and legally to consider and judge their own actions; and (3) some actions, not least in war, have far-reaching consequences, in time and space, on the environment. This last point is especially true of harm done to the natural environment. When man-made structures are damaged, they can be rebuilt. "The impact of environmental damage," in contrast, "will often play out through

---

32. See Roberts, 2000: 75–77, for a discussion of environmental law of war statutes within the context of civil war.

many iterations; an effect on one species influences many, a phenomenon which in turn repeats itself at each higher level" (Schmitt, 1997: 96). In addition, such damage can be irreversible, as when species are eradicated or when means of warfare are used that have mutagenic effects.

A number of significant problems still come up, of course. Some will say that a version of the "precautionary principle" must be employed here; that is, that there should be little room for any risk taking whatsoever as concerns the environment. Thus it is sometimes argued that even if there is a relatively small chance that important natural entities may be destroyed, this should carry decisive weight. However, such a reasoning involves a complicated kind of weighing and measuring that it is difficult to conceptualize here—let alone for field commanders to apply in the heat of battle.

The point is that the just war tradition urges us to *combine* the criteria of proportionality and discrimination. Viewed in this way, destruction with severe and/or long-term consequences may in some cases (albeit not in all) be deemed both *proportionally* wrong in connection with the projected military gains (not least since they most likely outlast the military campaign) and *indiscriminate*, since they threaten to eliminate vital natural resources upon which civilian life depends.[33] In addition, such destruction may be condemnable insofar as it irreparably destabilizes ecosystems for which humans can rightly be seen to be a sort of custodian.

Double Effect

The preceding discussion of proportionality and discrimination has taken us into the realm of what the Scholastic philosophers termed the principle of "double effect." Double effect holds that actions deliberately carried out can (and usually do) have two series of effects—one good, the other bad—and that there can be moral justification for allowing the bad effects to come about only under condition that they are not themselves chosen. Solely the good effects can legitimately be taken as the object of direct intention; the bad effects are morally acceptable only when they have the character of unavoidable and unintended side effects.[34]

---

33. Such terminology as *long-term, widespread,* and *severe* is admittedly difficult to apply to the natural environment, as evidenced by the controversies surrounding the usage of these terms by Protocol I and ENMOD (cf. Schmitt, 1997; Roberts, 2000).

34. For a general treatment of double effect, see Reichberg and Syse, 2004. This principle

This coincides, in other words, with the aforementioned distinction between intentional and side effect damage. It is not difficult to construct examples where this line of thought comes into play. Indeed, wartime examples have been among the most prominent in the discussion of this rule—as, for instance, cases in which the killing of noncombatants will be a foreseen side effect of one's actions, but not the intended end or means to the end. Far from being an insignificant accompaniment to war, side effect damage can sometimes dwarf in intensity (and extent) the destruction that is deliberately caused.

Doubtless, the rule of double effect can be abused so as to be made irrelevant. If "military necessity" is adduced as the decisive factor, one could then say that *all* other concerns must be set aside. Thus, if an enemy platoon can be stopped by the spreading of biological or chemical weapons over a large area of land, on grounds of military necessity some would say that this course of action is "justified." After all, the intention was to stop the soldiers; it was merely a foreseen, but not intended, side effect that civilians would suffer greatly and that the environment in the area would be severely damaged. The principle is, however, not meant to encourage such arguments. The double effect principle can legitimately be used to *justify* certain courses of action. But in and of itself the rule cannot be used as an *excuse,* since it does not say that the unintended side effects are not imputable to the agent. Rather, he or she knowingly and willingly accepts them (Boyle, 1980: 529–30; Finnis, 1991). The *measure* in which one is morally responsible for them will certainly differ, depending on (inter alia) the agent's degree of foresight. Some side effects cannot possibly be foreseen, while in other cases an agent can be faulted for having neglected matters that *ought to* have been investigated. In the latter case, the agent remains morally responsible for the said effect.

Most important, unintended, yet foreseen, effects can and should be made part of the moral judgment of an action and its actor. Hence the rule of double effect cannot validly function as a blanket excuse for all harmful side effects whatsoever. Moreover, pleading ignorance of these consequences offers little excuse: political and military leaders have a

---

is often traced back to Thomas Aquinas's classic formulation in *Summa theologiae* IIa-IIae, q. 64, a. 7, although it should be read in conjunction with the distinction between direct and indirect volition, as presented in *Summa theologiae* Ia-IIae, q. 6, a. 3 and q. 77, a. 7. For a collection of contemporary philosophical essays on double effect, see Woodward, 2001.

moral (and often legal) responsibility to investigate the likely side effects of the actions they enjoin.

Furthermore, the rule of double effect cannot legitimately be cited to justify the use of evil means to achieve a good end. Means are items deliberately chosen for the sake of some end; as such they are as *consciously* intended as the end itself (Finnis, 1991).

In short, it is only where the intention is meritorious—in just war parlance that signifies that it must contribute to the aim of a just peace—and where the evil side effects are indeed just that, *side* effects that arise as an *unavoidable* concomitant to the action, that this rule is applicable.[35] In these cases, the rule does not say that the agent is not accountable for the collateral destruction, but simply that this destruction may be justified considering the context of the action.[36] These side effects, then, must not be reasons for acting but rather conditions *in spite of which* one acts, which would be avoided were it possible to achieve the objective otherwise (Boyle, 1980: 535). They must clearly be brought into the deliberation over the act in question, and they must conform to the principles of proportionality and discrimination.

Proportionality is certainly crucial here. The end aimed at must be serious enough to justify the evil side effect produced. The criterion of "last resort" comes into play as well, since it must be clear that one's (justifiable) aim could not reasonably be achieved without the undesirable side effect; likewise, it must be clear that the war effort would be hampered without the execution of precisely this action.

The skeptic might ask: Does the rule of double effect make it more, rather than less, likely that environmentally damaging warfare will be condoned? If the rule is to conform to the just war framework, the answer should be no. The point is that most of our acts in this world have *several* effects, which are often interrelated in complicated ways. Some of these effects have no part in what we intend to bring about. And some of them will be bad. In applying the rule of double effect, we are called

---

35. See the analysis of double effect in Walzer, 1977: 157–58. His discussion of the Vemork Raid in occupied Norway during World War II—which caused (foreseen) harm to civilians but was deemed overridingly important due to the possibility that the Germans were using heavy water produced at Vemork to manufacture nuclear weapons—offers a useful illustration of this principle.

36. Donagan misunderstands exactly this point when he says that the doctrine underlying the theory of double effect is that "what lies outside the scope of a man's intention in action does not belong to his action, and so is not subject to moral judgement" (1977: 164).

on to investigate diligently what these effects are likely to be, take them into consideration as part of the description of our action, and then in the final instance weigh them against the state of affairs we intend to bring about. This is not about ends justifying means but rather about some unintended effects being justified because the intended effect of an action is so important to our overall end: peace.

Conclusion

The aim of this chapter has been to indicate how ethics can and should play a part in judging the environmental consequences of war. To that end, we have shown how criteria from the just war tradition—right intention, just cause, and competent authority, together with proportionality and discrimination—provide invaluable guidance. We have situated this discussion within the larger framework of the just war tradition and its philosophical roots in the medieval period. In so doing, we have sought to extend this tradition by bringing it to bear on contemporary discussions about environmental outrages in war. This discussion has led us to the conclusion that the ethical vocabulary as well as the philosophical framework of the just war tradition have much to contribute to a strengthened consciousness about and possibly also an improved legal protection of the natural environment in wartime.

REFERENCES

Armstrong, Susan J., and Richard G. Botzler, eds. 1993. *Environmental Ethics: Divergence and Convergence*. New York: McGraw-Hill.
Austin, Jay E., and Carl E. Brunch. 2000. *The Environmental Consequences of War: Legal, Economic, and Scientific Perspectives*. Cambridge: Cambridge University Press.
Blanchette, Oliva. 1992. *The Perfection of the Universe According to Aquinas*. University Park: Pennsylvania State University Press.
Boyle, Joseph. 1980. "Toward Understanding the Principle of Double Effect." *Ethics* 90:527–38.
———. 1996. "Just War Thinking in Catholic Natural Law." In Terry Nardin, ed., *The Ethics of War and Peace: Secular and Religious Perspectives*. Princeton: Princeton University Press, 40–53.
Cassese, Antonio. 1986. *International Law in a Divided World*. Oxford: Clarendon.
Christopher, Paul. 1994. *The Ethics of War and Peace*. Englewood Cliffs, N.J.: Prentice Hall.
Dahl, Arne Willy. 1992. "Environmental Destruction in War." *Disarmament* 15 113–27.
Donagan, Alan. 1977. *The Theory of Morality*. Chicago: University of Chicago Press.
Elliot, Robert. 1991. "Environmental Ethics." In Peter Singer, ed., *A Companion to Ethics*. Oxford and Cambridge, Mass.: Blackwell Reference, 284–93.
Falk, Richard A. 1984. "Environmental Disruption by Military Means and International Law."

In Arthur Westing, ed., *Environmental Warfare: A Technical, Legal, and Policy Appraisal.* London: Taylor and Francis, 33–51.
Finnis, John. 1991. "Intention and Side-effects." In R. G. Frey and Christopher W. Morris, eds., *Liability and Responsibility.* Cambridge: Cambridge University Press, 32–64.
Fotion, Nicholas. 1990. *Military Ethics.* Stanford, Calif.: Hoover Institution Press.
George, Robert. 1998. "Natural Law and International Order." In David R. Mapel and Terry Nardin, eds., *International Society: Diverse Ethical Perspectives.* Princeton: Princeton University Press, 54–69.
Gleditsch, Nils Petter. 1998. "Armed Conflict and the Environment: A Critique of the Literature." *Journal of Peace Research* 35:581–400.
Goldblat, Jozef. 1991. "Legal Protection of the Environment against the Effects of Military Activities." *Bulletin of Peace Proposals* 22:399–406.
Green, Leslie C. 1993. *The Contemporary Law of Armed Conflict.* Manchester and New York: Manchester University Press.
Homer-Dixon, Thomas F. 1999. *Environment, Scarcity, and Violence.* Princeton: Princeton University Press.
Judge Advocate General's School, U.S. Army. 1997. *Operational Law Handbook.* 1st rev. ed., JA 422.
Lewis, C. S. 1947. *The Abolition of Man.* New York: Macmillan.
Maritain, Jacques. 1961. "Truth and Human Fellowship." In *On the Use of Philosophy.* Princeton: Princeton University Press, 16–43.
Murray, John Courtney. 1988. *We Hold These Truths.* Kansas City, Mo.: Sheed and Ward.
Nozick, Robert. 1974. *Anarchy, State, and Utopia.* Oxford: Blackwell.
O'Neill, John, R. Kerry Turner, and Ian J. Bateman. 2001. *Environmental Ethics and Philosophy.* Cheltenham, U.K.: Edward Elgar.
Rawls, John. 1993. *Political Liberalism.* New York: Columbia University Press.
Reichberg, Gregory, and Henrik Syse. 2004. "The Idea of Double Effect—In War and Business." In Lene Bomann-Larsen and Oddny Wiggen, eds., *Responsibility in World Business: Managing Harmful Side-Effects of Corporate Activity.* Tokyo: United Nations University Press, 17–38.
Reichberg, Gregory M., Henrik Syse, and Endre Begby, eds. 2006. *The Ethics of War: Classic and Contemporary Readings.* Oxford: Blackwell.
Reisman, W. Michael, and Chris T. Antoniou. 1994. *The Laws of War.* New York: Random House.
Roberts, Adam. 1998. "Implementation of the Laws of War in Late 20th-Century Conflicts: Part I." *Security Dialogue* 29:137–50.
———. 2000. "The Law of War and Environmental Damage." In Jay E. Austin and Carl E. Brunch, eds., *The Environmental Consequences of War: Legal, Economic, and Scientific Perspectives.* Cambridge: Cambridge University Press, 47–86.
Schmitt, Michael N. 1997. "Green War: An Assessment of the Environmental Law of International Armed Conflict." *Yale Journal of International Law* 22:1–109.
Sigmund, Paul. 1971. *Natural Law in Political Thought.* Lanham: University Press of America.
Syse, Henrik, and Helene Ingierd. 2005. "What Constitutes a Legitimate Authority?" *Journal of Social Alternatives* 24:11–16.
Thomas Aquinas. 1981. *Summa theologicae.* 5 vols. Trans. Fathers of the English Dominican Province. Westminster, Md.: Christian Classics.
Walzer, Michael. 1977. *Just and Unjust Wars: A Moral Argument, with Historical Illustrations.* New York: Basic.
Weber, Thomas. 1999. "Gandhi, Deep Ecology, Peace Research, and Buddhist Economics." *Journal of Peace Research* 36:349–61.
Westing, Arthur. 1976. *Ecological Consequences of the Second Indochina War.* Stockholm: Almqvist and Wiksell.
Woodward, P. A., ed. 2001. *The Doctrine of Double Effect: Philosophers Debate a Controversial Moral Principle.* Notre Dame: University of Notre Dame Press.

10

U.N.-Authorized Interventions
A Slippery Slope of Forcible Interference?

ANNE JULIE SEMB

The philosophical tradition of just war has concentrated on two questions. First, what, if any, are the legitimate reasons for engaging in war (*ius ad bellum*)? Second, what is it justifiable to do, against whom, when fighting a war (*ius in bello*)? The topic of this chapter, which is the changed scope of the principle of nonintervention, is rooted in the tradition of ius ad bellum. Whereas nonintervention was, for much of the twentieth century and going further back to the Peace of Westphalia in 1648, honored as the most appropriate principle for the regulation of interstate relations, a number of specific concerns were referred to as justifications for interventions in the 1990s.[1] The principle of nonintervention was challenged not only with reference to human rights but also with reference to considerations concerning de facto statehood as well as democratic governance. This suggests that the scope of the principle of nonintervention in the internal affairs of sovereign states went through important modifications in the aftermath of the end of the cold war. The scope for justified resort to force in particular circumstances expanded accordingly.

The backdrop of my essay is my interest in the principle of noninter-

---

1. In this essay the concept of *intervention* will be narrowly defined. Intervention will be understood to mean the conscious use of military force for the purpose of compelling another government to act or refrain from acting in a certain manner.

vention and the large-scale changes with regard to interventions that took place within the Security Council over the last decade. The dramatic events of September 11, 2001, in the United States no doubt affected foreign policy—as well as scholarly agendas—but in no way resolved the question of the proper scope of the principle of nonintervention in the internal affairs of sovereign states and the entire issue of the range of legitimate exceptions to the general rule of nonuse of force between states. In my opinion, this is a testimony to the continued relevance of the question posed.

This chapter has a twofold aim. First, I present the criteria for justified interventions that developed during the 1990s. Second, I discuss whether this softening of the principle of nonintervention implies that the U.N. embarked on a slippery slope of forcible interference. One reason for resisting a softening of the principle of nonintervention is that once one allows for interventions for some normatively defensible purposes, it may prove difficult to establish barriers against a *further* softening of this principle. This may eventually have intolerable consequences. The U.N. Security Council practice of authorizing interventions suggests that states may lose their claim to protection under the principle of nonintervention if (1) the state engages in systematic human rights violations, (2) it is incapable of protecting human rights due to the breakdown of state authority, or (3) the government in power is unlawfully constituted. When these conditions have been present, the Security Council has considered the situation a "threat to the peace" and authorized enforcement measures under chapter VII.

I will start by examining the foundation and scope of the traditional principle of nonintervention. Then I will describe the ways in which a number of U.N.-authorized interventions in the 1990s deviate from that principle. Thereafter I will discuss the dangers of the so-called slippery slope. The slippery slope argument is frequently invoked when a practice is changed so as to allow something rather than nothing. In this connection, I will argue that the conception of "threat to the peace" expanded considerably in the 1990s. I will, in light of this, discuss the danger that wider interpretations of this conception further softens the principle of nonintervention. Then I will discuss a further danger: that ideas of what constitutes a "threat to the peace" will be subject to other interpretations. It would seem that a wide range of situations can be termed such a threat. It would seem, then, that it is difficult to establish stopping points along the slippery slope by suggesting substantial criteria for when force may legitimately be used.

This, however, does not necessarily mean that it is impossible to get off the slippery slope once on it. The relevant actors' perceptions of what can be achieved by the use of armed force, weighed against the likely costs of military operations, are likely to serve as restraints against a limitless softening of the principle of nonintervention. Furthermore, the composition of the Security Council and the decision-making procedure of that body seem to make the slope of interventions considerably less slippery. It may be argued, however, that once there has been an attitudinal change with regard to interventions, and U.N.-authorized interventions have become widely accepted, there is the danger that interventions that are *not* authorized by the U.N. will be accepted as well. As long as decisions concerning the use of force are subject to the strict voting procedures in the Security Council, however, the slope of U.N.-authorized interventions is not as slippery as it may seem.

The Traditional Doctrine of Nonintervention

The U.N. Charter does not contain an explicit and specific rule of nonintervention. It does contain article 2(4), which prohibits the "threat or use of force against the territorial integrity or political independence of any state." It needs to be stressed that the U.N. Charter does not prohibit the use of force per se. It makes a fundamental distinction between offensive and defensive resort to force, and the prohibition refers only to the former. According to article 51, states do have a right to self-defense, both individually and collectively.

Stating that the use of force for offensive purposes is illegal, the U.N. Charter joins other twentieth-century legal documents such as the Covenant of the League of Nations from 1919 and the Kellogg-Briand Pact of 1928 in attributing legality to the use of military force if and only if it is employed in an act of self-defense.

The only article in the U.N. Charter that deals explicitly with interventions is article 2(7): "Nothing in the present Charter shall authorize the United Nations to intervene in matters which are essentially within the domestic jurisdiction of any state or shall require the Members to submit such matters to settlement under the present Charter; but this principle shall not prejudice the application of enforcement measures under Chapter VII." This article does not, however, concern the relations between individual states. It applies only to the U.N. itself and is designed to regulate the relations between the U.N. and its constituent member states. The crux of the article is an emphasis on domestic jurisdiction, that is, the right of sovereign states to control their own internal affairs. Thus, internal affairs in U.N. member states have not been deemed to be within the organization's competence. This prohibition is, however, qualified by the reference to chapter VII. According to article 39, the Security Council has the powers to authorize enforcement measures under articles 41 or 42, provided the situation is one that constitutes a "threat to peace, breach of the peace, or act of aggression."

Although the U.N. Charter, strictly speaking, lacks an explicit principle of nonintervention that applies to the behavior of states toward each other, the U.N. General Assembly has on several occasions adopted a negative attitude to interventions. The *Declaration on the Inadmissibility of Intervention in the Domestic Affairs of States and the Protection of Their Independence and Sovereignty* (GA Resolution 2131 (XX), 1965) and the *Declaration on Principles of International Law concerning Friendly Relations and Co-operation among States in Accordance with the Charter of the United Nations* (GA Resolution 2625 (XXV), 1970) state the prohibition in an unambiguous way. According to the latter: "No state or group of states has the right to intervene, directly or indirectly, for any reason whatever, in the internal affairs of any other state. Consequently, armed intervention and all other forms of interference or attempted threats against the personality of the state or against its political, economic and cultural elements are in violation of international law." These resolutions reaffirm the principles of sovereignty and nonintervention in what amounts to an unqualified general principle of nonintervention.

What, then, has been the traditional requirement for a state to achieve sovereign status and thus to enjoy protection under the principle of nonintervention? Adopting the phrase of Alan James (1986), I shall take that feature to be a state's *constitutional independence*. According to this understanding, a state is sovereign by virtue of meeting a requirement of a legal nature: It is an independent entity in terms of its own constitution. Nonintervention has traditionally been regarded as a logical sequel to sovereignty in the sense of constitutional independence. This position is neatly summarized by R. J. Vincent: "If sovereignty, then non-intervention" (1986: 113). The principle has protected the rights of all sovereign states to determine their own political, social, economic, and cultural systems without interference.

It is clear, then, that international law has adopted a restrictive view on the issue of intervention; it is founded on a presumption against interventions. This view is reflected in what Michael Walzer terms "the legalist paradigm" (1977: 58–63). The core of this paradigm is that the international society consists of independent states that have the rights of territorial integrity and political independence. Actual use of force or threat of force against these independent states constitutes aggression, and nothing but aggression justifies wars. To be sure, Walzer's defense of the principle of nonintervention is far from unconditional, and he has stated in a later work that he is "more willing to call for military intervention" (2004: xiii) now than he was at the time when his seminal book *Just and Unjust Wars* was first published. It goes beyond the scope of the present essay to engage in a detailed presentation and review of Walzer's philosophical defense of the legalist paradigm and his corresponding conditional defense of the principle of nonintervention. Still, I believe that Walzer's claim that the purpose of a theory of aggression is to "limit the occasions for war" (1977: 62) is a useful reminder of the broader philosophical and political context of the discussions regarding when the presumption against intervention may legitimately be overridden.

Challenges to the Principle of Nonintervention

The above description of the traditional principle of nonintervention does not seem to capture its present status and scope. Interventions authorized by the U.N. in the 1990s suggest that the principle has gone through important changes and that it is no longer the case that states have a right not to be intervened in solely by virtue of their constitutional independence. It seems that states have to pass a test that is considerably more severe in order to enjoy protection under the principle of nonintervention.

What, then, is the current scope of the principle of nonintervention? The practice of international interventions since the one in the northern part of Iraq in April 1991 suggests that the scope has been significantly decreased. The principle of nonintervention has faced three different challenges: (1) the challenge from the requirements of universal human rights, (2) the challenge from the requirement of de facto statehood, and (3) the challenge from the requirement of democratic government.

The Challenge from Human Rights

The principle of nonintervention, as traditionally understood, has in practice provided a shelter from external efforts at terminating gross and systematic violations of universal human rights. This is demonstrated by the extreme case where "the sovereign territorial state claims, as an integral part of its sovereignty, the right to commit genocide, or engage in genocidal massacres, against peoples under its rule" (Kuper, 1981: 161). Such a "right" is, to be sure, not stated in any document, but the implication of the traditional principle of nonintervention is that states have not lost their claim to protection under the principle, even if human rights violations have assumed genocidal proportions. Certainly, this is not to suggest that human rights have never been a proper issue for interstate relations. And the U.N. Charter contains several provisions that deal with human rights. Suffice it here to mention article 1(3), which says that the purpose of the U.N. is to "achieve international co-operation in solving international problems of an economic, social, cultural, or humanitarian character, and in promoting and encouraging respect for human rights and for fundamental freedoms for all without distinction as to race, sex, language, or religion." The Universal Declaration of Human Rights of 1948 as well as the two International Covenants of Human Rights from 1966 confirm the universal character of human rights. What is important, however, is that the U.N. has traditionally let the prerogatives of state sovereignty take precedence over those of human rights when the two have come into conflict. This is to say that the requirements of human rights have been subordinated to the principle of nonintervention. This is clearly demonstrated by the U.N.'s reaction to Vietnam's intervention in Cambodia in 1978, which toppled Pol Pot's genocidal regime. The regime installed by Vietnam, whose human rights violations were far less massive than those of Pol Pot, was not recognized as legitimate. Representatives of the overthrown genocidal regime continued to occupy Cambodia's chair in the U.N. General Assembly until the Paris Peace Agreement in October 1991, from June 1982 as part of the Coalition Government of Democratic Kampuchea (CGDK).

It would seem, however, that the order of priority between the prerogatives of state sovereignty and the requirements of human rights has since been reversed. The single most important event that triggered the post–cold war debate on the legitimate scope of the principle of nonintervention was the Iraqi suppression of the Kurdish revolt in the northern part of Iraq in the aftermath of the Gulf War in 1991.[2] The Kurds' situation triggered a debate on the interpretation of article 2(7) in connection with attempts to design appropriate U.N. responses to "crimes against humanity." The French foreign minister Roland Dumas said that the plight of the Kurds ought to spur the U.N. to discuss the principle of nonintervention: "I believe that the Kurdish crisis could act as a detonator.... When new crimes exist, why should not rules of law be planned to respond to these crimes?" (*International Herald Tribune*, April 5, 1991). The Security Council however, avoided the politically explosive question of redefining the content of article 2(7) by stressing the cross-border implications of the humanitarian crisis as justification for intervention.

On April 5, 1991, the Security Council passed Resolution 688, which "condemns the repression of the Iraqi civilian population in many parts of Iraq, including most recently in the Kurdish populated areas, the consequences of which threaten international peace and security in the region." The resolution was followed by Operation Provide Comfort. French, British, and U.S. forces were deployed to create "safe havens" for the Kurdish refugees.

There has been some dispute about the legal status of this intervention. Resolution 688 stops short of invoking chapter VII, and it does not contain the expression "to use all necessary means."[3] James Mayall warns that "it would be imprudent in practice, and wrong in theory, to generalize from the international obligations towards the Kurds in favour of an international enforcement mechanism for human rights wherever they

---

2. The debate is not a new one. For proposals to assert the legal right to humanitarian intervention, see, e.g., Franck and Rodley, 1973; Lillich, 1973, 1974; Brownlie, 1974; Kuper, 1984. Also, within the field of moral philosophy, the status of the principle of nonintervention relative to contending values such as human rights has been hotly contested; see, e.g., Walzer, 1977, 1985; Luban, 1985.

3. China had made it clear that it would have vetoed the resolution if it had been more intrusive (Damrosch, 1993:104).

U.N.-Authorized Interventions   225

are abused" (1991: 428). Still, international lawyers have argued that the action on behalf of the Kurds was a watershed (Chopra and Weiss, 1992: 110). And subsequent events were to show that the intervention in northern Iraq could not be conceived of as an isolated incident.

The Challenge from De Facto Statehood

According to the traditional principle of nonintervention, the right not to be intervened in has been a corollary of a state's constitutional independence rather than its effectiveness. It has been suggested that there exist two radically different foundations of sovereignty in interstate relations (Jackson, 1990). The first is made up of the empirical attributes that developed through the process of state formation in Europe and in some other parts of the world, such as Japan, Thailand, and Ethiopia. The second is the result of the process of unconditional decolonization, which made sovereignty an externally granted right rather than a reflection of an internal reality. According to this view, states survive either by virtue of their will and capacity to remain sovereign or by virtue of the externally granted right to territorial integrity and political independence—that is, by virtue of the principle of nonintervention.

The U.N.'s involvement in Somalia, however, suggests that it is no longer the case that "quasi-states" automatically enjoy protection under the principle of nonintervention.[4] The Security Council's involvement in Somalia started as a response to a request from Somalia's representative to the U.N. The Security Council took several steps, the most important of which was the launch of a traditional peacekeeping operation in Somalia (UNOSOM), which had humanitarian aid as its main concern. Faced with the eventual breakdown of state power, the UNOSOM forces proved unable to carry out their task. The international relief efforts were subject to robberies, and relief workers were attacked. The humanitarian crisis that followed was immense.

In a letter of November 29, 1992, U.N. secretary-general Boutros Boutros-Ghali addressed the situation in Somalia: "At present no government exists in Somalia that could request and allow [the] use of force. It would therefore be necessary for the Security Council to make a deter-

---

4. The term *quasi-states* is borrowed from Jackson, 1990, and denotes states whose empirical qualities are shaky.

mination under Article 39 of the Charter that a threat to the peace exists, as a result of the repercussions of the Somali conflict on the entire region, and to decide what measures should be taken to maintain international peace and security" (quoted in Roberts, 1993: 440).

On December 3, 1992, the Security Council unanimously adopted Resolution 794. The resolution expresses grave concern for the humanitarian situation in Somalia and declares that the Security Council determines "that the magnitude of the human tragedy caused by the conflict in Somalia, further exacerbated by the obstacles being created to the distribution of humanitarian assistance, constitutes a threat to international peace and security." The council further "[acts] under Chapter VII of the Charter of the United Nations [and] authorizes the Secretary General and Member States co-operating to implement the offer referred to in paragraph 8 above to use all necessary means to establish as soon as possible a secure environment for humanitarian relief operations in Somalia."[5] A few days later the U.S.-led United Task Force (UNITAF) began Operation Restore Hope.

This intervention may be seen as a response to the immense humanitarian crisis that was generated by the breakdown of state power in Somalia. There is no doubt that Somalia was without an effective government with territorial control at the time of the U.N. authorization of Operation Restore Hope. Internal conditions in Somalia were closer to anarchy than to empirical statehood. In that sense, Operation Restore Hope in Somalia was an intervention in a stateless society.[6] No government existed that could secure human rights—or, indeed, consent or object to the operation.

But traditionally, the right not to be intervened in has been independent of a state's empirical attributes. If it had been the case that the principle should apply only to those states that fulfill the requirements for empirical statehood, a lot of states would be devoid of protection from the principle. And if it is the case that practice suggests that the principle

---

5. Paragraph 8 reads in part: "Welcomes the offer by a Member State described in the Secretary General's letter to the Council of 29 November 1992 (S/24868) concerning the establishment of an operation to create such a secure environment . . ." (the member state referred to is the United States).

6. Some authors, like Donnelly (1993) and Roberts (1993), seem to be reluctant to employ the term *intervention* when the target is a stateless society. As the defining feature of sovereignty is of a legal nature, I see no reason why the term should not be used in situations like the one in Somalia.

of nonintervention is based on empirical rather than juridical statehood, the scope of the principle is further reduced and the scope of possible justified interventions further enlarged. And, as will be shown in the next section, the scope of possible justified interventions became further widened, as the Security Council adopted an even wider understanding of what situations constitute a threat to the peace in the case of Haiti.

The Challenge from Requirements for Democratic Rule

The unconditional principle of nonintervention implies a distinction between the existence of a sovereign state and hence the application of the principle of nonintervention, on the one hand, and the question of who exercises sovereign power on behalf of whom, on the other. This distinction is vital. It suggests that the state's international legitimacy is not derived from the state's domestic legitimacy.

Prior to the case discussed here, Haiti, there were two notable exceptions to this general rule. On two occasions, considerations about a particular government's domestic legitimacy have played a very important role in determining the standing of these states among other states. The Security Council has twice acted under chapter VII to impose mandatory economic sanctions on states due to denial of internal self-determination (McCoubrey and White, 1992). The mandatory economic sanctions against Southern Rhodesia between 1966 and 1979 and against South Africa between 1977 and 1990 were, however, imposed on these states due to the policy of apartheid and subordination of the black majority to the white minority. Consequently, these sanctions had implications only for racially segregated states. Furthermore, these enforcement measures were imposed under article 41 rather than 42, and thus did not involve the use of military force.

This is not to say that international law is devoid of references to the domestic legitimacy of states, and it has been suggested that there is an emerging right to democracy in international law (Franck, 1992). The implication of this is that we can no longer conceive of a particular state's system of governance to be part only of that state's internal affairs. In Franck's words, "This newly emerging 'law'—which requires democracy to validate governance—is not merely the law of a particular state that, like the United States under its Constitution, has imposed such a precondition on national governance. It is also becoming a requirement of international law, applicable to all and implemented through global standards, with the help of regional and international organisations" (ibid.: 47).

The question whether a particular government is democratic or not is thus not to be conceived of as being only part of the "internal affairs" of a state. The crucial point for the present purposes, however, is that traditionally states have not lost their claim to protection under the principle of nonintervention even if they have clearly failed to meet the standards of democracy. The right to protection from forcible intervention has applied to democratic and nondemocratic states alike. As will be shown, the Haitian case demonstrates that this is no longer the case.

The election in Haiti on December 16, 1990 was monitored by both the OAS and the U.N. The civilian Jean-Bertrand Aristide received 67 percent of the votes and was inaugurated in February 1991. About eight months later, he was ousted from office in a military coup. The coup was widely condemned, and the new government was recognized by neither the OAS nor the U.N. General Assembly. The Security Council termed the situation a threat to the peace in Security Council Resolution 841 of June 16, 1993, and economic sanctions were imposed on Haiti under this resolution. The sanctions were made more extensive under Resolution 873 of October 13, 1993, and Resolution 917 of May 6, 1994. These sanctions did not, however, lead to the resignation of the nondemocratic government.

On July 31, 1994, after three years of unsuccessfully trying to restore democracy through economic sanctions, the U.N. Security Council adopted Resolution 940. In this resolution, the situation in Haiti is termed a "threat to peace and security in the region." The resolution further condemns the "illegal de facto regime." It says that the Security Council "[acts] under Chapter VII of the United Nations Charter [and] authorizes member-states to . . . form a multinational force under unified command and control and, in this framework, to use all necessary means to facilitate the departure from Haiti of the military leadership [and] the prompt return of the legitimately elected President and the restoration of the legitimate authorities of the Government of Haiti."

The resolution, which was sponsored by the United States, Canada, Argentina, and France, was passed by twelve votes to none, with Brazil and China abstaining. The resolution says that a U.N. peacekeeping force may be deployed at some unspecified date, when the Security Council judges the conditions to be appropriate. U.S. troops entered Haiti on September 19, 1994. However, on September 18 an agreement had been reached between a mission led by former U.S. president Jimmy Carter and the military junta. The junta thus formally consented to the military operation launched the next day, and this operation consequently cannot be viewed as an intervention in the strict sense of the term. The major effect of the agreement was that the U.S. troops did not meet armed resistance when they entered Haiti. The crucial point for the present purposes, however, is that Security Council Resolution 940 did in fact authorize the use of force for the purpose of compelling the junta to resign, which implies a further softening of the principle of nonintervention.

Resolution 940 questions the validity of the *sub modo* way of conferring rights on states. When principles of international law have conferred rights on states, they have done so sub modo. This is to say that international law has conferred rights on states subject to the rule that "the actor on behalf of the State, and the agency to which other States are to look for the observation of the obligations of the State and which is entitled to activate its rights, is the government of the State" (Crawford, 1988: 55). According to the resolution, de facto governments are not automatically entitled to activate the state's rights. This is also the case when what is at stake is the right not to be intervened in. Rather than regarding de facto governments as holders of the state's rights, sovereignty is here considered to be vested directly in the people. If the government has not been granted the right to rule by the people but rules contrary to the will of the population, should the state that it leads be granted a right not to be intervened in? Security Council Resolution 940 goes a very long way toward answering this question in the negative. If the government in power does not represent the popular will but rather suppresses it, then a military intervention that could bring an end to this suppression can, in principle, be justified.

This opens up the possibility of using force in order to overthrow an illegitimate regime. This confirms the third major challenge to the principle of nonintervention and constitutes a further reduction of the scope of the principle.

How Slippery Is the Slope of U.N.-Authorized Interventions?

As has been shown, the Security Council in the 1990s undoubtedly expanded the conception of threats to the peace and thus widened the scope for justified resort to force. Cosmopolitan philosophers have long argued in favor of narrowing the scope of the principle of nonintervention. The trend has been to allow human rights concerns to take precedence over state sovereignty in situations where the two cannot easily be reconciled. The focus of this section will, however, be on one particular kind of argument *against* intervention that is sometimes invoked when discussing what actions are morally acceptable, namely the slippery slope argument. This argument is typically used when a practice is changed so as to allow for *something* rather than *nothing,* and so seems highly relevant when discussing the changes that pertain to the practice of U.N.-authorized interventions.

The structure of the slippery slope argument is the following: (1) if we allow A, then B will necessarily or very likely follow; (2) B is morally unacceptable; therefore (3) we must not allow A (van der Burg, 1991: 42). The argument proposes that there is a contrast between "a tolerable solution to a *problem now before us* and an intolerable result with respect to some currently hypothetical but potentially real *future state of affairs*" (Schauer, 1985: 365). The problem now confronting us and the proposed solution to this problem (the A in the outline above) may be termed the "instant case," whereas the state of affairs that we fear and want to avoid (the B in the outline above) may be termed the "danger case."[7]

Haas (1993) has invoked an argument against U.N.-authorized interventions that resembles a slippery slope argument. He adopts a very wide concept of intervention that includes actions ranging from retaliatory economic sanctions and economic conditionality to military intervention. Moreover, the slippery slope that Haas warns against is the "likely progression of steps that begin with humanitarian intervention and end with enforcement measures under Chapter VII of the Charter" (65). Still, the argument is not posed as a general warning against any kind of involvement. Haas instead wants to "save the UN's legitimacy for situations that

---

7. I borrow the terms *instant case* and *danger case* from Schauer, 1985: 365.

can be improved by multilateral action by preventing the organization's sliding down the slippery slope illustrated by the cases of Somalia, Bosnia and Cambodia" (ibid.). The argument then becomes a warning against ineffective U.N. involvement, be it forcible or not. This is indeed a sound warning, but hardly a slippery slope argument against U.N. involvement.

As the Security Council has embarked on a process of reducing the scope of the principle of nonintervention by admitting domestic injustice in states as a reason for authorizing the use of force, it may be very difficult or even impossible to prevent a further softening of the principle of nonintervention. Ultimately, this may drastically widen the scope of U.N.-authorized resort to force in interstate relations. What seem to be acceptable or even desirable solutions to immediate problems of large-scale human rights violations, humanitarian crises, and nondemocratic regimes may turn out to have unavoidable and intolerable consequences at some later stage. This, at least, is the charge of the slippery slope argument.

When specifying the mechanisms that may make the slope slippery, a distinction can be made between two versions of the general argument: (1) the logical or conceptual version and (2) the empirical or psychological version (van der Burg, 1991: 43). The two versions differ in their mechanisms, as will become apparent below. I shall consider both forms of the argument, starting with the logical or conceptual version.

The Conceptual or Logical Slippery Slope Argument (the "Line-Drawing Argument")

The conceptual or logical version of the slippery slope argument holds that once the Security Council has allowed A, there is a high probability that it will end up allowing B as well, as one cannot make a distinction between A and B. The use of the term *logical* in relation to the realm of human actions is certainly disputable and thus warrants a brief comment. It is founded on the assumption that when an intervention in situation A is justified on a moral basis, this creates pressures for intervening in situation B as well, when situation A and B seem indistinguishable. What I have in mind, then, is the pressure to intervene in situation B that may arise from, for example, public accusations of "selective humanitarianism" or public allegations that governments apply double standards.[8] Does the logical slippery slope argument produce a valid case against the softening of the principle of nonintervention?

The Challenge from Human Rights

As has been shown, the U.N. has expanded the conditions that must be met before the principle of nonintervention applies. The first challenge to the principle of nonintervention is human rights. One version of the logical slippery slope argument says that situation A is indistinguishable from situation B. Taken as an argument against allowing interventions for the purpose of terminating human rights violations, it may be stated as follows: When it is established that violations of human rights may constitute a threat to the peace, thus warranting an intervention, there is a large number of situations that also qualify for external intervention. When an intervention is justified on the basis of the need for terminating gross and systematic violations of human rights (situation A), this will create pressures for intervening in a wide range of situations in which human rights are being violated (situation B). This is all the more true since the intervention may be considered a precedent and thus itself be a reason for future interventions. The result is that the principle of nonintervention is further softened, and the range of possible interventions is further enlarged.

I shall term a situation in which an intervention would be justified an "intervention situation" and a situation in which it would not a "nonintervention situation." There have been numerous attempts at specifying criteria for when an intervention should be carried out in the case of gross violations of human rights. Lillich (1974: 248) includes the *immediacy* and the *extent* of the human rights violations among the criteria by which one can judge the legitimacy of a humanitarian intervention. Walzer has suggested that an intervention is in principle justified when it is a response to actions that "shock the moral conscience of mankind" (1977: 107). Criteria such as these are, however, imprecise. It is not clear whether the gravity of the situation refers to the number of people killed, that the killings and other atrocities take place solely or mainly among one subgroup of the population, or that the atrocities have continued over a considerable period of time. None of these suggestions leave

---

8. I borrow the term *selective humanitarianism* from Brown, 2003.

us with any clear-cut criteria for when the situation is grave enough to justify an intervention. Criteria such as these suggest that interventions should be triggered only in extreme situations, and that cases of "ordinary repression" do not qualify for such actions. They are, however, not very helpful in specifying a line of demarcation between an intervention situation and a nonintervention situation.

To be sure, it is not difficult to make a distinction between a situation in which several thousand people are threatened with extinction and one in which a handful of individuals have their human rights violated. The version of the logical slippery slope argument that says that situation A is indistinguishable from situation B carries little force when applied to human rights violations. This version of the argument is, however, not the only one to be considered. The problem in the present context is rather that there is a continuum between the former and the latter situation. And there is a second version of the slippery slope argument that deals with situations of this kind. This second version may be termed the *(n – 1) argument*.[9] In the context of interventions the argument may be stated approximately like this: Even though it is possible to make a distinction between a situation in which, say, one hundred thousand people have their human rights systematically violated (situation A) and a situation in which one thousand people suffer the same fate (situation B), the distinction between A and B breaks down, because any cutoff point along the continuum between A and B will necessarily be arbitrary. Therefore, if the Security Council authorizes interventions to terminate gross and systematic human rights violations, there is a high probability that it will authorize interventions to terminate less severe situations as well. This means that the scope of interventions is close to limitlessly enlarged.

It has been suggested that one solution to the problem of the gray zone between A and B is to draw a sharp line between cases that are allowed and cases that are not (Williams, 1985: 133).[10] In the context of interventions, the idea is that while the (n – 1) argument produces a valid case against the possibility of establishing a *reasonable* line of demarcation between an intervention situation and a nonintervention situation, this does not mean that we cannot establish *some* such line. Let us, for the

---

9. This is Williams's (1985) interpretation of the logical slippery slope argument.
10. One example of this from the field of medical ethics is the Norwegian abortion law, in which it is specified how far into a pregnancy an abortion is still allowable.

sake of the argument, say that a line can be drawn between an intervention situation and a nonintervention situation at fifty thousand victims of human rights abuse. This line is, admittedly, arbitrary in the sense that the line is drawn between two situations that do not seem to be relevantly different. And the point is not that it is easy or even possible to come up with some convincing arguments for the choice of *this* line. It is, nevertheless, a line, and the point about the slippery slope argument, in its logical form, is that it is impossible to draw such a line. This, it would seem, is not the case.

Is the proposed solution to the problem convincing? I believe there is one major drawback to it. If the drawing of a sharp line between cases that are allowed and cases that are not shall prevent us from sliding down the slope, the line must be based on facts that are easy to establish beyond doubt. In actual conflict situations, the range of human rights violations will be extremely difficult to confirm. What is a logical possibility in the case of, for example, abortion, then, seems to fail in the case of intervention to protect human rights.

It would seem, therefore, that attempts at specifying what situations are of such a character as to justify an intervention have not come to grips with the problem of indeterminacy. Human rights violations are a matter of degree rather than of kind. Once it is established that violations of human rights may justify forcible interventions, it seems hard to establish logical barriers against a further softening of the principle of nonintervention.[11] The logical slippery slope argument, applied to the challenge of human rights, therefore certainly carries force.

The Challenge from De Facto Statehood

The second challenge to the principle of nonintervention, using the logical slippery slope argument, is the challenge from de facto statehood. "De jure statehood" was first developed as an analytical tool employed to explain why states devoid of most, if not all, of the traditional features of sovereignty were still able to sustain themselves as members of the interstate society.

---

11. The conditions for sliding down the slope of interventions include, however, more than just the existence of possible cases. In addition, one has to identify specific actors with motives for undertaking the slide. Furthermore, the procedure by which the decision to intervene is made must be one that makes it fairly easy to turn motives into actual decisions. I will return to these questions.

The African continent has its share of weak or even failed states. However, the empirical qualities of many old states are also shaky, and the dissolution of Yugoslavia and the USSR paved the way for a number of new states that have no tradition of sovereignty on the international scene. This means that it is more inaccurate than ever to put the distinction between "empirical" and "juridical" statehood on a par with the so-called North-South distinction. At the same time, it has become apparent that effectiveness is not easily stated in terms of either-or.

What does the initial softening of the principle of nonintervention imply for the prospect of other so-called quasi-states? It is worth noticing that Resolution 794 is very weak on references to cross-border implications of the situation in Somalia at the time. It is rather the domestic situation that is deemed to constitute the threat to the peace. And a logical slippery slope argument against allowing interventions in a stateless society may thus be stated in the following way: Once the Security Council determined that the situation in Somalia constituted a threat to the peace and thus justified the use of force, there is clearly a large number of other quasi-states that qualify for intervention as well. When an intervention is justified on the basis of the absence of de facto statehood, this will create pressures for intervening in other states whose empirical qualities are also shaky. The result is that the range of possible interventions is further enlarged.

At first glance, it would seem that the challenge from de facto sovereignty raises the same kind of problems as the challenge from human rights. If effectiveness essentially remains a matter of more-or-less rather than either-or, and if the Security Council has determined that lack of effectiveness constitutes a threat to the peace, it may be very difficult to make a distinction between the existence of an ordinary "quasi-state" and situations that would justify a U.N.-authorized intervention. And if this is so, the logical slippery slope argument applies to the challenge from de facto statehood as well as to the challenge from human rights.

I believe, however, that it is possible to establish a barrier against such a softening of the principle of nonintervention: Even if the empirical qualities of many states are shaky, cases of total breakdown in state authority are rare, albeit a problem of greater magnitude today than at the time when Resolution 794 was adopted. The logical slippery slope argument, applied to the challenge of de facto statehood, consequently does not seem to produce a valid objection against extending the concept of threats to the peace to cover cases of breakdown in state authority. In this instance, it is logically possible to establish barriers against a further softening of the principle.

The Challenge from Requirements for Democratic Rule

Perhaps the most noticeable challenge to the principle of nonintervention is the third one: the challenge from democratic governance. As will be remembered from the previous discussion, many authors argue that there is an emerging international right to democracy but stress that violations of this right should be internationally rather than unilaterally enforced. According to such a view, the right to democracy is moving toward the status of *ius cogens,* which means that states cannot contract themselves out of the obligation to obtain popular consent. The normative case for interventions in nondemocratic regimes is then clear: Sovereignty is vested in the people, and if the government in power does not represent the people but rather suppresses the popular will, an intervention that could bring an end to this oppression is justified.[12]

A slippery slope argument against interventions in nondemocratic regimes could then be stated as follows: Once it is established that a regime that rules contrary to the will of the people may constitute a threat to the peace and warrants an intervention, there is a large number of states that also qualify for intervention. When an intervention is justified on the basis of the existence of an illegitimate regime, this creates pressures for intervening in other states that are not governed democratically. The relevant slippery slope argument is that situation A (the situation in Haiti prior to the passing of Resolution 940) is indistinguishable from situation B (the situation in other nondemocratic states). And if undemocratic states are no longer accorded protection under the principle of nonintervention, the result is that the scope of the principle is further narrowed.

The soundness of the argument hinges on the premise that the Haitian situation did not differ from the situation in other nondemocratic states. I believe, however, that the situation was in fact relevantly different. The democratically elected president, who had been elected in

---

12. But see Walzer, 1977 for the argument that undemocratic and illiberal regimes may be the expression of the shared beliefs of the population, and that this implies a presumption for nonintervention in the case of nondemocratic regimes.

accordance with national laws, had been ousted from office in a coup d'état. The ensuing intervention was meant to come to the support of a domestic democratic choice. It is perfectly possible to term this situation a threat to the peace without implying anything about the international standing of states in which the people have not yet had the opportunity to express their political preferences in free elections. That is, it is possible to make a distinction between the situation in Haiti and the situation in other undemocratic states. The logical slippery slope argument, applied to the challenge of democratic government, does not seem to produce a valid objection regarding the softening of the principle of nonintervention.

The Danger of Expanding the List of Special Concerns

Before turning to the empirical slippery slope argument, I want to address the question of whether the three challenges I have dealt with so far are the only putatively good reasons for U.N.-authorized interventions. The term "threat to the peace" may certainly be subject to *wider* interpretations than has hitherto been the case, but the term may also be subject to *other* interpretations. In other words, once the Security Council has accepted that some special concerns may justify U.N.-authorized interventions, it may be hard to reject that other special concerns may also justify such interventions.

To date, the Security Council has defined gross violations of human rights, lack of effective government, and the existence of an "illegitimate de facto regime" as threats to the peace and authorized intervention on those bases. It would seem that the "'threats" concept has been stretched to cover a wide range of situations, interstate and intrastate alike. And once the concept has been stretched in these three directions, it is likely that it can be stretched in even more directions. A number of other situations could easily be included on the list of good reasons for deviating from the principle of nonintervention. This implies a second way in which it may be logically difficult to prevent a further softening of the principle of nonintervention.

The Security Council on several occasions prior to the U.S.-led invasion of Iraq in March 2003 passed resolutions declaring that the proliferation of weapons of mass destructions constituted a threat to the peace but did not authorize the use of force. Severe environmental degradation and violence against ethnic minorities may no doubt also be understood as threats to the peace, thus possibly outweighing the principle of nonintervention in particular situations. To be sure, this should not in any way be understood as an attempt at providing a complete list of situations and events that could be understood as threats to the peace and justify a U.N.-authorized intervention. The point is only to show that once the concept of threat to the peace has been stretched to the extent it already has, it can easily be made to encompass an even broader range of situations and events. And if so, the scope of the principle of nonintervention may be further reduced and the scope of resort to force further enlarged.

To summarize: The logical slippery slope argument seems to be valid in the case of the challenge from human rights. Once it is determined that massive violations of human rights constitute a threat to the peace, it may be difficult to establish barriers against a further softening of the principle of nonintervention. The situation looks different when the slippery slope argument is applied to the challenge from de facto statehood and democratic governance, however. In the latter two cases, it seems to be perfectly possible to establish distinctions between the instant case and the danger case, which could prevent a further softening of the principle of nonintervention. In these cases, then, the logical slippery slope argument does not seem to present a valid reason to avoid taking the first step, that is, to avoid letting the prerogatives of de facto statehood and democratic government take precedence over the principle of nonintervention. But once the Security Council has embarked on a process of letting the principle of nonintervention be outweighed by competing concerns, it seems logically difficult to establish barriers against extending the concept of threats to the peace to an even wider range of situations. This means that there are numerous potential cases of U.N.-authorized interventions.

The Empirical Slippery Slope Argument

Thus far I have dealt with logical versions of the slippery slope argument. Now I turn to the empirical version of this argument, which may also be termed the "falling dominoes argument."[13] Focus is then shifted

---

13. I borrow this expression from Feinberg, 1985.

U.N.-Authorized Interventions 239

from the logical impossibility, or at least difficulty, of establishing barriers against what is taken to be an undesirable outcome to the psychological and political processes that may ultimately lead to the danger case. Both versions of the slippery slope argument share the same concern — the fear that the principle of nonintervention may eventually be seriously undermined and the scope of U.N.-authorized use of force in interstate affairs excessively broad. They differ, however, when it comes to specifying the mechanisms that are supposed to make the slope slippery. The empirical slippery slope argument says that once we have accepted the instant case, we will sooner or later end up accepting the danger case as well. The initial softening of the principle of nonintervention is politically dangerous, as it will diminish respect for state sovereignty and cause changes in attitudes toward interventions. This may be used by parties that have an interest in a further softening of the principle of nonintervention, which may eventually lead to the danger case.

The question of whether the members of the Security Council have changed their attitudes toward interventions is not one that can be answered with an unqualified yes or no. It seems likely that the phenomenon of interventions came to be viewed more positively as a result of the intervention in northern Iraq in April 1991. As former U.N. secretary-general Javier Perez de Cuellar noticed in the aftermath of this intervention: "We are clearly witnessing what is probably an irresistible shift in public attitudes toward the belief that the defense of the oppressed in the name of morality should prevail over frontiers and legal documents" (quoted from Weiss and Campbell, 1991: 455). And the mere fact that the council authorized a number of interventions after 1991 is a testimony to the gradual acceptance of the view that interventions may legitimately be used to achieve political objectives. This view is shared by Nicholas Wheeler, who argues that "[t]he key normative change in the 1990s was that the Security Council, under pressure from Western governments — who were themselves responding to the demands of public opinion at home — increasingly interpreted its responsibility under Chapter VII as including the enforcement of global humanitarian norms" (2002: 289).

It would be wrong, however, to jump to the conclusion that this implies that the members of the council are prone to move further down the slope of interventions. The council's reluctance to intervene has at times been striking. I will argue that both perceptions of the likelihood of success and considerations of costs (in a broad sense) have served as restraints, if not as actual stopping points, along the slope of U.N.-authorized interventions. It would seem that the dominoes are simply not lined up in order. This means that the fall of those that have already fallen does not automatically imply the fall of others. In addition, the procedure by which decisions concerning chapter VII operations are taken is such as to make it difficult to convert one or a few actors' motives for further softening the principle of nonintervention into actual decisions to this effect. This procedure then represents an additional restraint against a further softening of the principle of nonintervention.

Perceptions of Probability of Success

The intervention in northern Iraq in April 1991 led some to declare that we had finally reached the historical turning point at which humanitarian concerns would trump the prerogatives of state sovereignty (Chopra and Weiss, 1992). The situation in Iraq at the time of this intervention was, however, unique. Iraq had just been defeated in the Gulf War, and the allied forces met little, if any, resistance during the operation.

Operation Restore Hope in Somalia proved a far more credible test of the conditions for enforcement operations. The goal of the operation, as defined in Resolution 794, was to "establish a secure environment for humanitarian relief operations in Somalia as soon as possible," which indicates that the operation was to have purely humanitarian objectives. This goal was not sufficiently specific, however, and the concrete steps that were taken to realize that objective, such as disarmament of some of the warring factions, soon came to be looked upon as political acts. Consequently, the intervening forces were soon to be charged with pursuing political as well as humanitarian objectives. The relationship between the UNITAF forces and the Somali population became more and more tense. Eventually, the forces came to be perceived as a party to the conflict and were treated accordingly.[14]

One lesson that was learned from the intervention in Somalia was that enforcement operations involve rules of engagement that differ fundamentally from traditional peacekeeping operations. Probably the single most important condition for a successful operation is having at one's dis-

---

14. UNOSOM II succeeded the UNITAF operation in May 1993.

posal—and being willing to use—the necessary means to realize the objectives of the operation. This, however, raises the crucial question of the relationship between the means of intervention and the aims pursued. When an intervention is planned as a limited action, what aims can it realistically achieve? Human suffering does not have a single source, and there is every reason to ask oneself which of the sources of human suffering can be removed by way of a U.N.-authorized intervention. The easiest case, that is, the case with the highest prospect of success, is probably a situation where the source of human suffering is a tyrannical regime, devoid of popular support. Once the regime is removed, the problem is solved, at least on paper. The situation is quite different when the suffering has other sources: "[W]hat if . . . the inhumanity [is] locally and widely rooted, a matter of political culture, social structures, historical memories, ethnic fear, resentment, and hatred? Or what if the trouble follows from state failure, the collapse of any effective government?" (Walzer, 1995: 36). I will not engage in a detailed evaluation of the suitability of different measures that may be taken in such circumstances. Many situations, however, quite clearly call for measures that are far more intrusive than is an intervention. The main point for the present purposes is that the actors' considerations of what can be achieved by more limited operations may serve as an important restraint against a further softening of the principle of nonintervention. Even if the attitudes toward interventions have changed, there has been a growing awareness of the limits to such operations as well, not least within the U.N. system.

Considerations of Costs

The immense difficulties that the U.N. faced in Somalia no doubt made the members of the Security Council reluctant to engage in similar operations. This probably explains the lack of reaction to the tragedy that unfolded in Rwanda shortly afterward. It is far more likely that the failure to intervene in Rwanda was due to unwillingness on the part of the U.N. member states to carry the financial as well as human costs of an operation, as well as skepticism that a military operation could be successful, than that the U.N.'s failure to act was motivated by concerns about state sovereignty.[15] The humanitarian situation in Somalia did improve during

---

15. See, e.g., Wheeler, 2002: 208–41, for a discussion of the international society's reactions to the genocide in Rwanda.

Operation Provide Comfort, but the operation was definitely costly—in the political, human, and financial senses.

Of particular importance here is the unwillingness to put soldiers at risk in military operations with a largely humanitarian objective. The U.S. casualties in Somalia were, in fact, moderate. The reactions nonetheless show that human costs of this magnitude are hard to accept. This means, then, that the actors' considerations of what could be achieved by force, weighed against the likely costs of such operations, may be seen as important restraints against a further softening of the principle of nonintervention.[16]

Procedural Restraints

To what extent does the procedure by which decisions concerning authorization of use of force are taken represent a further restraint, if not a stopping point, along the slope of the softening of the principle of non intervention? Article 27(3) requires a positive vote by nine members, including all the permanent members, for a resolution concerning chapter VII to be adopted. It has been accepted, however, that an abstention by one or more of the permanent members does not invalidate the resolution. This procedure is restrictive in the sense that a decision will be blocked if there is serious disagreement and conflict of interest between the permanent members of the council. And even if there is no such disagreement among the permanent members, a minority consisting of seven nonpermanent members can block decisions that would further undermine the principle of nonintervention. It would seem, then, that the voting procedures in the Security Council represent a fairly high barrier against an indefinite softening of the principle of nonintervention.[17]

It may be argued, however, that once there has been an attitudinal change and U.N.-authorized interventions have become widely accepted, there is the danger that interventions that are *not* authorized by the U.N. Security Council will be accepted as well, if the reason the Security Council does not authorize the use of force is that one or several of

---

16. To be sure, the unwillingness to put soldiers at risk may also affect the choice of military strategy in particular interventions, as was quite clearly the case in Kosovo. Such choices have widespread implications for many of the questions raised under the heading of ius in bello.

17. The composition of the Security Council and the decision-making procedures are, however, no guarantee against *arbitrariness*—quite the contrary.

the permanent members block a decision. It is worth noticing that what is conceived as the "danger case" has changed in this last statement. Whereas focus so far has been on the danger that the scope of U.N.-authorized interventions will eventually become excessively broad, the fear in the present argument is that the initial softening of the principle of nonintervention by the U.N. will ultimately lead to the acceptance of *unauthorized* interventions against states that have not committed external aggression—exactly the kind of actions that are prohibited in article 2(4) in the U.N. Charter. The concern, then, is that the initial softening of the principle of nonintervention gradually and eventually may erode the ban on offensive use of force.

It would seem that the strongest barrier one has against such a development is the insistence that an intervention, in order to be legitimate, must be U.N.-authorized and thus be subject to rather restrictive procedural constraints. This leaves us with a serious dilemma, however. One reason for being skeptical toward nonauthorized interventions is that the acceptance of such interventions would deprive us of the possibility of condemning on procedural grounds unauthorized military interventions by other states or regional bodies such as NATO at some later stage, when these states or bodies deem the situation appropriate. But if one adheres to the view that interventions are defensible if and only if they are authorized by the U.N., one would have to accept nonaction in the sense of nonintervention in situations where human suffering is widespread, while conflicts of interest block decisions in the Security Council. The NATO action against Yugoslavia in the spring of 1999, the so-called War over Kosovo, represents, of course, a fairly recent reminder of the potential conflict between the need for obtaining U.N. authorization and the perceived need to act in the face of human suffering.

Conclusion

The relationship between justifications and interests is, to be sure, complex. In practice, this means that specific interventions may be triggered by causes other than concern for human rights, effective statehood, and democratic governance. These interest-based concerns will also affect the question whether a particular slope is slippery or not. Still, I have chosen to stick to the explicit justifications for interventions. Precisely because these justifications are explicit and open, I believe they are the most important factors for considering the question of whether the U.N. is on a slippery slope of forcible interference.

In the 1990s, the Security Council quite clearly expanded the conditions that must be met before the principle of nonintervention applies. Does this imply that the U.N. embarked upon a slippery slope of forcible interference? The discussion has shown that this danger is not overwhelming. In two of the three cases discussed, it is not logically difficult to establish barriers against a further widening of the scope of justified resort to force. And even if the attitudes toward intervention have no doubt become more positive, perceptions of the probability for success and considerations about different types of costs clearly inhibit a limitless softening of the principle of nonintervention. This means that the actors who have the authority to further widen the scope of U.N.-authorized interventions are not particularly inclined to do so. Last but not least, the voting procedure in the Security Council represents a rather strong restraint against such a softening. This seems to me to be a good reason for adhering to the view that an intervention, in order to be normatively defensible, must be authorized by the U.N.. This is so even if this leaves us with a serious dilemma in cases where resolutions in the Security Council are vetoed.

It would seem, then, that the slope of U.N.-authorized interventions is not particularly slippery. This reduces the risks of starting on it in the first place. The lesson to be learned, thus, is that we should not fear a dramatic increase in interstate use of force, as long as the interventions are authorized by the U.N. On the other hand, the twin principles of state sovereignty and nonintervention no longer prevent the U.N. from taking forcible action in some extreme situations where human dignity is threatened on a massive scale. I believe this is a change to be welcomed.

REFERENCES

Brown, Chris. 2003. "Selective Humanitarianism: In Defense of Inconsistency." In Deen K. Chatterjee and Don E. Scheid, eds., *Ethics and Foreign Intervention*. Cambridge: Cambridge University Press, 31–50.
Brownlie, Ian. 1974. "Humanitarian Intervention." In John Norton Moore, ed., *Law and Civil War in the Modern World*. Baltimore and London: Johns Hopkins University Press, 218–28.
Chopra, Jarat, and Thomas G. Weiss. 1992. "Sovereignty Is No Longer Sacrosanct: Codifying Humanitarian Intervention." *Ethics and International Affairs* 6:95–117.

Crawford, James. 1988. "The Rights of Peoples: 'Peoples' or 'Governments'?" In James Crawford, ed., *The Rights of Peoples*. Oxford: Clarendon, 55–67.
Damrosch, Lori Fisler. 1993. "Changing Conceptions of Intervention in International Law." In Laura W. Reed and Carl Kaysen, eds., *Emerging Norms of Justified Intervention*. Cambridge, Mass.: American Academy of Arts and Sciences, 91–110.
Donnelly, Jack. 1993. "Human Rights, Humanitarian Crisis, and Humanitarian Intervention." *International Journal* 48 (4): 607–40.
Feinberg, Joel. 1985. *Offense to Others: The Moral Limits of the Criminal Law*. Oxford: Oxford University Press.
Franck, Thomas M. 1992. "The Emerging Right to Democratic Governance." *American Journal of International Law* 86:46–91.
Franck, Thomas M., and Nigel S. Rodley. 1973. "After Bangladesh: The Law of Humanitarian Intervention by Military Force." *American Journal of International Law* 67:275–305.
Haas, Ernst. 1993. "Beware the Slippery Slope: Notes toward the Definition of Justifiable Intervention." In Laura W. Reed and Carl Kaysen, eds., *Emerging Norms of Justified Intervention*. Cambridge, Mass.: American Academy of Arts and Sciences, 63–87.
Jackson, Robert H. 1990. *Quasi-States: Sovereignty, International Relations, and the Third World*. Cambridge: Cambridge University Press.
James, Alan. 1986. *Sovereign Statehood: The Basis of International Society*. London: Allen and Unwin.
Kuper, Leo. 1981. *Genocide: Its Political Use in the Twentieth Century*. New Haven and London: Yale University Press.
———. 1984. *International Action against Genocide*. Rev. ed. Report 53. London: Minority Rights Group.
Lillich, Richard B. 1973. *Humanitarian Intervention and the United Nations*. Charlottesville: University Press of Virginia.
———. 1974. "Humanitarian Intervention: A Reply to Ian Brownlie and a Plea for Constructive Alternatives." In John Norton Moore, ed., *Law and Civil War in the Modern World*. Baltimore and London: Johns Hopkins University Press, 229–51.
Luban, David. 1985. "Just Wars and Human Rights." In Charles R. Beitz et al., eds., *International Ethics: A Philosophy and Public Affairs Reader*. Princeton: Princeton University Press, 195–215.
Mayall, James. 1991. "Non-Intervention, Self-Determination and the New World Order." *International Affairs* 67 (3): 421–29.
McCoubrey, Hilaire, and Nigel D. White. 1992. *International Law and Armed Conflict*. Aldershot, U.K.: Dartmouth.
Roberts, Adam. 1993. "Humanitarian War: Military Intervention and Human Rights." *International Affairs* 69 (3): 429–49.
Schauer, Frederic. 1985. "Slippery Slopes." *Harvard Law Review* 99:361–83.
van der Burg, Wibren. 1991. "The Slippery-Slope Argument." *Ethics* 102 (1): 42–65.
Vincent, R. John. 1986. *Human Rights and International Relations*. Cambridge: Cambridge University Press.
Walzer, Michael. 1977. *Just and Unjust Wars: A Moral Argument, with Historical Illustrations*. New York: Basic.
———. 1985. "The Moral Standing of States: A Response to Four Critics." In Charles R. Beitz et al., eds., *International Ethics: A Philosophy and Public Affairs Reader*. Princeton: Princeton University Press, 217–35.
———. 1995. "The Politics of Rescue." *Dissent* (Winter): 35–41.
———. 2004. *Arguing about War*. New Haven and London: Yale University Press.
Weiss, Thomas G., and Kurt M. Campbell. 1991. "Military Humanism." *Survival* 33 (5): 451–65.
Wheeler, Nicholas J. 2002. *Saving Strangers: Humanitarian Intervention in International Society*. Oxford: Oxford University Press.
Williams, Bernard. 1985. "Which Slopes Are Slippery?" In Michael Lockwood, ed., *Moral Dilemmas in Modern Medicine*. Oxford: Oxford University Press, 126–37.

11

Ethical Uncertainties of Nationalism

DAN SMITH

The nature of nationalist movements and how to address them became key issues of world politics with the end of the cold war in the three-year period 1989 to 1991, and have remained so through the 1990s and into the new century. They are important issues both for social science theory and for practical politics. Among the variety of themes encompassed by the term *nationalism,* one that continues to require discussion is the ethical dimension. The language of nationalism is a language of rights and duties, which is an ethical discourse, yet it is often used to justify and encourage gut-wrenching violence and cruelty. It is a language of freedom and liberty that is all too often associated with intolerance and repression. It is no surprise that nationalism brings forth a range of ambivalent responses among concerned observers of international politics.

The rights and wrongs of nationalist movements became intensely relevant in the discussion about humanitarian intervention in armed conflicts in the second half of the 1990s. "Humanitarian intervention" became a central concept in peace and security issues in the same way that deterrence had been during the cold war. Since September 11, 2001, and the destruction of the World Trade Center and attack on the Pentagon by al-Qaeda, there has been a change of focus in the security agenda. The post-9/11 agenda has highlighted a so-called war on terror and the perception of imminent threat from what have been called "rogue states" (ones that egregiously defy international security norms) armed with weapons of mass destruction. In the Bush administration in the United States, these issues were taken as justification for a preemptive strategy against what were seen to be direct threats to national security and interest. Because some proponents of military intervention in Afghanistan and Iraq used the term *humanitarian intervention* for both actions, the term itself has lost legitimacy and persuasive power.

Yet the core problems of humanitarian catastrophes within sovereign states and how to deal with them have not become any the less important. In the first years of the twenty-first century, Afghanistan and Iraq are both cases in point, as are the Democratic Republic of Congo and Sudan, among others. Forcible humanitarian intervention is only one of a range of means used in response to such catastrophes. Moreover, one part of a more sensible and sensitive approach to the problem of attacks on civilian targets by nonstate armed groups would be to explore the root causes of such actions. In some cases such an enquiry will indicate the need to take a position on the rights and wrongs of demands made by nationalist movements. Thus, the humanitarian intervention debate and the ethical issues connected to nationalism remain central and related concerns.

This link, however, has not been reflected in the discussion of the issues. The literature of the 1990s on armed conflicts and humanitarian disasters showed a relatively swift adjustment in the international relations (IR) discipline to the challenge of new concepts. For some time, however, it lacked explicit and systematic attention to ethical problems (Fixdal and Smith, 1998), although the deficiency was somewhat remedied by the high-level report *The Responsibility to Protect* (ICISS Report, 2001). It was therefore hardly surprising that the literature also lacked close attention to ethical issues raised by nationalism.

However, the importance of including an ethical inquiry into nationalism in the discussion on humanitarian intervention did not arise as a matter of abstract theoretical necessity. In principle, it is not merely possible but easy to discuss interventionism in a way that ignores the rights and wrongs of the contending parties in an armed conflict. The focus of attention could fall instead on the suffering of ordinary people or on concepts such as regional security. But while this is straightforward in logic, it is difficult in practice; put differently, it is easy to avoid addressing the rights and wrongs of the parties when discussing intervention as a general concept, but it is next to impossible when discussing specific cases.

The term *humanitarian* cannot disguise the unavoidably political nature of large-scale interventions, especially those using armed force (Smith, 1997). Once states that are not party to the conflict get involved, and especially when major powers contemplate intervention, it is not possible to avoid considerations of interest and of which side the intervening powers favor. The larger the resources that are committed to the intervention, and the more forcible the intervention is, the more important these considerations become. Both considerations lead intervening states toward supporting one party to some degree. State interest stresses the importance of working with a local actor so as to avoid an open-ended commitment to policing the conflict area, and mobilizing support for the intervention policy will be easier if that local actor's cause can be presented as a just cause. These arguments are equally germane whether the main factor driving intervention is to mitigate a humanitarian disaster, to avoid the threat of regional instability and international terrorism, or a combination of both.

Thus, a political logic that is hard to escape means that forcible intervention is likely to lead to taking sides. This is not necessarily undesirable. Some critics of the United Nations in Bosnia-Hercegovina from 1992 to 1995 asserted that the U.N. failed by trying to be impartial; they argued that impartiality was a trap, that the U.N. should favor justice and, consequently, that it should take sides (Betts, 1994; Rieff, 1994; Weiss, 1994). If it is both likely and right that intervention in a complex conflict means at least to act strongly against one party, if not to act wholly for the other, then it is important to have a capacity for reasoned analysis of where right and wrong lie in the conflict. In the case of a conflict involving contending nationalist claims, this means a capacity to address the specific ethical issues thrown up by nationalism, at the core of which lies the question of whether there is a moral right to national self-determination.

There are difficulties in such an analysis, and it is at first sight improbable that those difficulties can be relieved by developing a general ethical theory of nationalism. On the one hand there is the complexity of many of the cases, which involve intensely felt claims on more than one side that are backed by disputed and sometimes heavily mythologized historical accounts. At a more general level, part of the problem for theory is that the general term *nationalism* covers a multifaceted phenomenon. As is outlined below, nationalism is many things. The quest for a single explanatory theory of them all is arguably a misleading and misconceived enterprise (Smith and Østerud, 1995). It may be equally unproductive to look for a single ethical theory of nationalism.

A further difficulty in ethical assessment arises from the cosmopolitanism of most anglophone scholarship on nationalism, which results in an inbuilt hostility to this subject of study. Gellner (1983) and Hobsbawm (1990) make no effort to disguise their antipathy toward nationalism and nationalists. Greenfeld (1992), who has a more neutral tone, and Anderson (1991) and Smith (1983, 1986), who are more sympathetic, are equally cosmopolitan in their underlying assumptions. The point here is not to argue against normative cosmopolitanism, not least because it has made possible some outstanding scholarship on nationalism, but to register that when it is assumed rather than argued, the result is to imply that no worthwhile ethical debate is possible about nationalism.

Buchanan (1991), Miller (1995), and Tamir (1993) have argued for a liberal version of nationalism. Yet their stance remains heavily cosmopolitan, tolerant toward nationalism and supportive of its claims as long as it appears in its most benign guise. If nationalism were like this, what would the fuss be about? Tamir's version of nationalism even severs the connection between nation and state (150; see also Lichtenberg, 1997: 159), which most writers and most nationalists place at the heart of the doctrine and enterprise of nationalism. This liberal revision of the nationalist script is attractive in many ways. It shows how nationalist political doctrines could be rational and ethical, pluralistic and inclusive. However, it does not meet the need for an ethical discourse on nationalism as it is in all its variety, nor does it go far along the road to determining whether there is a moral right to national self-determination.

Amid the variety of nationalist movements and the situations in which they operate, George identifies two principles that are common to all nationalist doctrines (1996: 13). The first is the claim of a right to national self-determination, and the second is the exclusive legitimacy of nation as the basis of state and government.

This chapter's central question is whether there is a moral right to national self-determination, meaning national independence.[1] The principle that the nation is the sole basis of legitimacy for a state and government

---

1. The right to self-determination was included in the Universal Declaration of Human Rights. When all other related statements about sovereignty were taken into account, this did not amount to a right to secession, though it was used as the basis for the legal right of colonies to gain independence. If the right of self-determination does not necessarily mean the right

and the claim that there is a moral right to national self-determination are mutually supportive propositions. If it is not possible to sustain the claim that there is a moral right to national self-determination, the attendant principle of the nation's exclusive legitimacy for statehood will also fall. The argument that follows therefore gives priority to discussing the claimed right to national self-determination. In doing so, it focuses on two problems. The first is the question of who is the self in the claimed right of national self-determination. The second is the process by which the right is fulfilled and the doctrine of nationalism is implemented.

The chapter combines moral philosophy and social science. After this introduction, the next section draws on widely used social science definitions of nation and nationalism to set out the subject that is addressed in the normative argument that follows. Thereafter, the essay shifts into philosophical vein. The section entitled "Community and Partiality" argues that a characteristic mode of ethical philosophizing on nationalism, consisting of recourse to arguments about partiality, is not an adequate basis on which to discuss the ethics of nationalism. This is because of the need to make two parallel distinctions: between nationalism and nation and between an individual's right to belong to a community and the rights of that community. The section entitled "Rights and Conditions" explores two ways in which the right to self-determination has been proposed, showing that in neither case is a moral right established, though a pragmatic argument can be made that sometimes independence or secession is beneficial. The section entitled "The Right to Power" argues that the moral right to self-determination cannot be sustained, both because the "self" in question is arbitrary and because the process by which a nation is constructed means that "right" is untenable under both Kantian and consequentialist ethical perspectives. The concluding section connects this to the moral ambiguity of nationalism as a doctrine.

Definitions

Connor has described the need to define the term *nation* as "[s]urely the most tediously repetitive chore facing the writer on nationalism"

---

of secession, the implication is that self-determination could be achieved in other ways than through asserting independent statehood. Given various other declarations and undertakings since the Universal Declaration, the distinction between different forms of self-determination was less clear at the start of the twenty-first century than it was in the early years of the U.N.

(1992: 48). It can also make tedious reading. With that warning, it is nonetheless necessary to indicate the basis in social science of the subject of the argument here. The key point is that in contemporary scholarship on nation and nationalism, the most widely accepted definitions of nation are pragmatic. This should have an impact on any attempt to make a case that there is a moral right to national self-determination. This section does no more than summarize the mainstream social science conclusions on nation and nationalism. The argument that follows will time and again circle back to their underlying pragmatism.

Seton-Watson summed up the difficulty of finding a fully applicable definition thus: "All I can find to say is that a nation exists when a significant number of people in a community consider themselves to form a nation, or behave as if they formed one" (1977: 5). The more famous formulation by Anderson (1991: 6) that a nation is "an imagined political community—and imagined as both inherently limited and sovereign," pays footnoted homage to Seton-Watson's prior version. Smith put his definition in more formal and sociological terms: "The nation is a large, vertically integrated and territorially mobile group featuring common citizenship rights and collective sentiment together with one (or more) common characteristic(s) which differentiate its members from those of similar groups with whom they stand in relations of alliance and conflict" (1983: 175).

Two related elements of the arguments of these writers are worth further comment: their definitions are pragmatic, and the processes of nation making that they report are arbitrary. This point bears emphasizing. There are significant differences of emphasis between these writers. The most important differences concern origins or foundations of the nation and the process by which nations are made. Despite such differences, these writers are united by their conclusion that the nation is constructed rather than given, and that it is a relatively recent development rather than ancient. The mainstream position in anglophone scholarship on nations is that there is no natural basis for a nation. This finding is in diametric and irreconcilable opposition to the claims of most nationalists.[2]

---

2. One of the commonest arguments against the idea that nations are constructed arbitrarily is that they grow out of communities that are united by language. Graham gives the examples of Germany and Italy (1997: 3), yet different German dialects were mutually unintelligible at the time of unification, and in Italy at the time of unification Italian was the first language of 2 percent of the population (Hobsbawm, 1990: 54). On the other side of the coin, Serbian, Croatian, and Bosniak nationalisms have arisen against each other in the area of for-

From nation, we move to nationalism. Gellner (1983: 1) characterizes nationalism as "primarily a political principle, which holds that the political and the national unit should be congruent." Smith (1983: 171) offers a more embracing definition of nationalism as "an ideological movement, for the attainment and maintenance of self-government on behalf of a group, some of whose members perceive it to constitute an actual or potential 'nation' like others." What both these definitions and the work of Hobsbawm (1990; see also Hobsbawm and Ranger, 1983) all emphasize is that the role of nationalism is to create nations. Hroch, using a rather different terminology, formalizes this into a process moving through historical stages from cultural assertion to national movement, out of which the new nations of nineteenth-century Europe were created (1985). It is nationalism, in short, that carries out the act of imagination highlighted by Anderson. Thus, nations do not create nationalism; rather, nationalism creates nations. The nation is not merely constructed; it is politically constructed.

One of the challenges in studying nationalism is to keep sight of all its facets. It is an ideology that nation and state should be territorially congruent (Gellner, 1983), and it is a movement bearing that ideology. It is also a complex intellectual and emotional reaction to a range of large-scale socioeconomic and political stimuli (Plamenatz, 1976), including modernity (Smith, 1983), colonialism (Anderson, 1991; Seton-Watson, 1977), and the collapse of state socialism (Smith & Østerud, 1995). Though political to the core, nationalism has much in common with religion and kinship (Anderson, 1991: 5). It has been the key to successful economic development (Nairn, 1993) and could therefore be characterized as the transformation of an economic development strategy into a principle worth dying for (Smith, 1994). This perspective takes some of the weight of the discussion off the depiction of nationalism as an urge or a primordial instinct. It makes it possible to see nationalism as a rational choice in certain circumstances (Breton et al., 1995).

---

mer Yugoslavia despite their access to a common language. And since all Scots speak English and very few Irish speak Gaelic, it would be hard to explain Scottish and Irish nationalism by reference to language difference. And so on. There are, in short, many examples that debunk the importance of language as the basis of nation. Smith surveys the empirical record and concludes that a national language is neither a necessary nor a sufficient condition for nationhood (1983: 180–85). This is not to say that language is an unimportant issue in defining difference and community. Rather, it means that language is not a strong candidate for explaining why nations are formed, though it is often relevant in describing how.

At the risk of overformalizing the argument that follows this excursion into definitions, the reason for grasping the multiplex nature of nationalism and retaining a clear view of the doctrinal element is in part formal. If the emphasis were to fall on sentiment as the defining element of nationalism, ethical assessment would necessarily focus on the actions and behavior of, for example, national movements and politicians. However, the argument about whether there is a moral right to self-determination is not affected either way by the actions of movements and politicians. Saintlike behavior will not create a right that does not otherwise exist and, where such a right does exist, morally abysmal behavior will only abuse the right, not erase it.

Community and Partiality

Hurka asserts that the moral questions about nationalism arise because of its character as a form of partiality (1997: 139). The problem of partiality is a common starting point for philosophers to tackle the ethical issues raised by nationalism (McKim and McMahan, 1997; Miller, 1995; Caney, George, and Jones, 1996; Walzer, 1994: 63–83). Here the question is whether, in order to act ethically, we should treat all people as equals, or may we rightly favor some over others, and is nation an acceptable basis for such partiality?

The criticism of this approach comes in a moment. It is worth beginning by stressing the importance of the partiality question. First, in whatever ways one nationalist ideology differs from another, the identification with nation that it demands is a common thread, and this element of nationalism is about belonging to a community and being loyal to it and to its other members. It is, therefore, inevitably about partiality. Second, partiality itself is of profound importance in theorizing politics, society, and morality. Nagel has gone so far as to argue that the unsatisfactory nature of "all political and social arrangements so far devised" is traceable to the failure to solve the problem "of reconciling the standpoint of the collectivity with the standpoint of the individual" (1991: 3). This dichotomy, he argues, is not primarily between each individual and society, but rather within each individual.

It would weigh this chapter down too much to get into the much bigger question of the sources of fellow feeling. Nagel has himself explored some way into the question, arguing that its sources are "forms of thought and action which it may not be in our power to renounce" (1970: 144). The relevant point for us, however, is not the source of partiality but its pertinence.

For Nagel, the point, to précis a carefully phrased argument, is that political theory has to pay attention to the coexistence within each of us of the individualistic and the empathetic. And in addressing the relationship between those two tendencies within each of us, Nagel further argues, political theory has to acknowledge both the breadth and the limits of empathy (1991). It should be noted that this is an argument about political theory as a whole, not simply about theories of nationalism. However, in that nationalism is an ideology about the nation, and the nation as it has famously been defined is an imagined community (Anderson, 1991), then partiality is at the heart of the matter.

Applying the partiality argument is therefore appealing, but it is also an error. It leads us astray if we try to use it to argue about nationalism. For it takes us not to nationalism but to nation. The same is true about Miller's (1995) invocation of ethical particularism. This deliberate narrowing of partiality in order to stress the duties owed to fellow nationals, while downplaying duties owed to other fellow humans, is inevitably controversial, though it does seem to reflect the way many people feel. Regardless of one's views about it, however, a defense of the idea of special obligations to fellow nationals is not the same thing as a defense of nationalism.

It is in fact a strange thing to attempt to discuss the ethics of nationalism by discussing nation, but the reason for this error is not hard to fathom. It comes from acceptance that what nationalism is about is love of nation. The main normative questions that derive from that starting point concern whether it is right and reasonable to love one's nation and, depending on the answer, what then follows for ethics. That nationalism includes love of nation is not to be doubted; that it can be reduced to love of nation is a different matter. Notwithstanding Anderson's emphasis on nationalism as a sense of identification with others (1991: 5), nationalism is first and foremost a doctrine and, second, a movement that is the bearer of that doctrine. The goal of the doctrine is mobilization of people in order to form a state that represents the nation. That is the meaning of the formula of territorial congruence between the political unit and the nation. An evaluation of the moral quality of nationalism and an assessment of the case that there is a moral right to national self-determination both have to keep their eyes on the ball marked nationalism. Losing focus and gazing on the nation instead is missing the point.

There remain Nagel's argument, which places partiality at the center of our thinking about political systems, and the arguments of writers such as Miller, Tamir, and others, which place a national community at the core of our sense of partiality. The case made here that the partiality argument is not adequate as a basis for a moral evaluation of nationalism should by no means be confused with a case not made here, that partiality is unimportant.

An extended process of social and political transformation in Europe beginning in the sixteenth century affected everything from the constitution of states to the content of philosophy. It included the changes through which subjects became citizens and identified with the national state. It involved partiality for a community that stretched further than the people and the geographical locations of which individuals had direct knowledge. Today there are arguments that the time is right for a further transformation, toward a cosmopolitan identification (Archibugi, Held, and Köhler, 1998; Midgley, 1999). The contemporary momentum toward cosmopolitanism can be understood as part of the globalization of communications, economics, and politics. It has two major forms of expression. One is in the language and ever more intrusive practice of international human rights law. While human rights activists and advocates routinely treat universal human rights as self-evident and pregiven, this is no more true of legal norms than of nations; international human rights, like nations, are constructed (Donnelly, 1999: 79; Brown, 1999: 104, 120). That does not mean they are unimportant or untrue, only that they are the result of a complex interplay of social and political practice and philosophy. The other major expression of moral cosmopolitanism today is humanitarian, the outpouring of emotion and money for the victims of tragedies in faraway countries about which the television appeal's viewers knew nothing and cared less until the tragedy broke.

However, an entirely universal partiality, what one might call impartial partiality, seems to be out of reach for most people. As Ignatieff argues, on the one hand the idea of trusting "only those of your own blood" is intuitively obvious (1994: 6); on the other hand "cosmopolitanism is the privilege of those who can take a secure nation-state for granted" (ibid.: 8). So for most people, most of the time, the circle of partiality is smaller than universal. How much smaller is, if not entirely arbitrary, nonetheless as much a matter of social construction as both nations and human rights.

There is, in principle, no reason to make a moral objection to people having a smaller circle of partiality, and in practice there are many reasons to accept and approve it. There are inevitable limits to empathy and partiality; Nagel explored them in an essay memorably entitled "What Is It Like to Be a Bat?" (1979). If there are limits, and they coincide with the bounds of community involving common traditions, religion, language, and other aspects of a way of life (food, dress, music, architecture, etc.), it would be specious to object to a community of empathy simply because it is less than universal. Better a degree of empathy than no empathy. Indeed, since empathy is a desirable ethical trait, it is not complex to make a moral case for such a sense of community, and therefore a moral case for the existence of community. It is likewise straightforward to go beyond that moral case into an assertion of the individual right to live in a community in dignified contact with its own traditions, language, religion, and other aspects of its way of life. Indeed, the right to a community is important and provides an appropriate forum within which to feel, express, and act on partiality. And it is not impossible or even difficult to combine that forum and that sense of community with others both smaller (family or neighborhood, for example) and larger (in response to a humanitarian appeal).

Thus, the point of the arguments in this section has not been to deny the importance of partiality or reject the right to community. It has been to deny that they form an adequate basis on which to assess whether there is a moral right to national self-determination and to evaluate the moral quality of nationalism.

This highlights an important distinction in the arguments about rights which is often glossed over. It needs to be made explicit now because it shapes much of the argument that follows. The distinction can be expressed as follows: the right of individuals to belong to a community is analytically different from the putative rights of that community to which the individuals have a right to belong. In this section we have discussed the rights of individuals; in the next, the rights of communities.

Rights and Conditions

The predominant conclusion in contemporary research on nation and nationalism is that the nation is not given but constructed, and that it is constructed by nationalism. The nation cannot be taken for granted. In view of that, a problem lurks at the core of the concept of national self-determination: the problem of what the self is. In the case of a putative right to self-determination, who or what is the right bearer? According to Anderson it is an imagined community. According to Seton-Watson it is a group of people who behave like a nation. The issue is whether a group of people who have collectively achieved by an act of creative imagination a common bond among them have the right to self-determination in the name of the product of that creative imagination.

Buchanan's arguments are noteworthy as a systematic discussion of the conditions under which that right applies and what it adds up to. His conclusions (1991: 152–53) can be summarized as asserting a right to secession if the following conditions exist:

1. The existing state refuses to cease injustice against the group seeking secession;
2. The existing state violates group rights as well as individual rights;
3. There is a need to protect group culture, which is only valid if
   a. the group's culture is "really threatened";
   b. anything less than secession (e.g., federalism, group rights) will not work;
   c. the culture "meets minimum standards of moral decency";
   d. the group's aim in seceding is not an illiberal state that violates basic individual rights or smaller ethnic groups' rights; and
   e. no other party has a valid claim to the territory in question;
4. There is a need to provide for physical survival of the group's members against third party attack.

It is worth noting how circumscribed is this case for a right to secession as the expression of national self-determination. It begins with the would-be national group being under persistent attack from the existing state, which refuses to stop, to the extent of not just attacking individual and group rights but threatening the very survival of the group's way of life. Even then, secession cannot be supported merely because it is the solution the would-be national group prefers; it has to be the only possible solution, and there must be no other valid claim on the territory that the group occupies. And still the would-be national group has to satisfy a number of liberal conditions, guaranteeing to behave considerably better than the state whose grip it is fleeing.

These conditions are demanding but not impossible. Though they do not resolve the dilemma of who is the self in self-determination, and though the "group" and its "culture" are necessarily taken as given, Buchanan's criteria help clarify the issues in, for example, an argument about a case such as Kosovo. However, these criteria do not add up to an argument for nationalism nor make the case for a moral right to self-determination.

Buchanan does not make an argument that the political unit should be congruent with the national unit, which is what Gellner identifies as the core nationalist demand (1983: 1). Indeed, because secession could have serious negative consequences, Buchanan accepts that it is often right as well as necessary for the political and national unit not to be congruent. Like Tamir (1993: 150), Buchanan is no supporter of those whom McMahan (1997: 108) calls "universal nationalists," who believe that all people have the right to belong to a nation that enjoys self-determination. No more can the arguments of Buchanan or Tamir be called in aid of those whom McMahan (ibid.) calls "radical particularists," who are nationalists who don't give a damn about anybody else's nation or the rights of any group but their own. Buchanan's arguments do not establish a case for a right to self-determination and could easily be called in aid of an argument that there is no such right. In this sense, the approach of Buchanan and Tamir is a shortcut past the question of whether there is a moral right to national self-determination.

Buchanan's argument summarized above in favor of a conditional right of secession is based on what may be called negative rights, that is, the rights of groups not to be ill treated. Walzer argues for a positive right to self-determination, using a formulation of just such a negative right as his starting point. He argues that "the right of a nation or people not to be invaded derives from the common life its members have made on this piece of land" (1977: 55). However, his argument for the right of self-determination is more demanding than simply making "a common life." Drawing on John Stuart Mill, Walzer (ibid.: 88) argues that self-determination is the right of a people to fight, labor, and struggle for their freedom and independence, and that the principle of nonintervention means that outside powers will neither help nor hinder them.

In these arguments, Walzer brings in the national principle where it is unnecessary, then, like Buchanan, makes it extremely difficult to fulfill. In the first place, it is hard to see why a right not to be invaded derives from a common life on a particular piece of land. The right not to be invaded is more fundamentally the right not to have one's life taken, threatened, or at the very least disrupted by military or other violent action. This is a basic human right. A hermit has that right regardless of his refusal to talk to anybody else and has no moral need to make a common life with others in order to earn that right. In the second place, this argument for the right to self-determination is hinged on the idea that it is "the right of a people 'to become free by their own efforts'" if they can" (Walzer, 1977: 88, citing Mill, 1873). It is not clear what is, could, should, or might be entailed by the phrase "their own efforts," but the history of nations is full of war and bloodshed. Thus, this argument for a right to self-determination appears to demand that the people in question must first be willing to walk through blood, if necessary. One might identify this principle in the Kosovo Liberation Army's (KLA) willingness to fight in 1998 and 1999, for that willingness was arguably the key factor in gaining the support of the NATO member states for freeing Kosovo from Serbian control. Without the KLA's willingness to fight, it is unlikely that NATO would have launched a war against Yugoslavia over Kosovo. With this argument, Walzer submerges morality in favor of power, and thus brings us to the core of the matter.

The Right to Power

Hugh Seton-Watson's definition of a nation is that it is a group that behaves as if it were a nation (1977: 5). It would have been even more apposite if he had added the subclause "if they can get away with it," for this would have emphasized that whether the group is able to act like a nation depends in the end on a question of power. As we have seen, Walzer absorbs the issue of power into his proposition of a right to self-determination. These arguments, like Buchanan's (1991) cited above, seem to be based as much on political insight as on moral argument. From Buchanan's argument, one can conclude that there are times when secession may be a good idea, but that is not at all the same as saying that secession is a right. The fact is, like it or not, that unless a group makes trouble, which it may do only because it is in trouble, its putative right to form a nation with a state of its own is unlikely to be realizable.

Power has a logic to it. Those who get it wanted it, and will continue to want it, and will therefore try to keep it. When "a significant number of people in a community . . . behave as if they formed" a nation (Seton-Watson, 1977: 5), they may have to fight for their proclaimed right against a group that previously got away with it. This is what Walzer has called "the persistent failure of new nation-states to meet the minimal moral test: to recognize in the nation-that-comes-next the rights vindicated by their own independence" (1994: 79). The first formulation by Kant of the categorical imperative of moral behavior is that an action is ethical if it can be expressed in a maxim that can be universally applicable (1991: 67). The "minimal moral test" that Walzer sees new nation-states failing is the test of that formulation of the categorical imperative. What the new nation has gained it does not grant to others.

It may be argued that this failure is not inherent to the nationalist enterprise, merely contingent upon particular circumstances. Anticolonial movements offered each other mutual support and recognition. However, when their own interests and claims are threatened, nationalist leaders are no more inclined than any other kind of state leaders to permit secessionist claims close to home. This has been repeatedly illustrated in the refusals of larger-nation nationalists to recognize the competing claims of smaller-nation nationalists within their own territory. These instances have been especially visible when large multinational empires and federations have broken up. Examples include the Habsburg and Ottoman empires, the USSR and former Yugoslavia, the British empire in South Asia and Africa, and the Dutch empire in Southeast Asia, where conflict between nationalists still reverberates with chilling violence. The general rule is that nationalist movements acknowledge the rights of other nationalist movements only if the latter are at a safe distance. For the larger nation, refusal to recognize the claims closer to home is supported by the core claim of the territorial congruence between national and political units.

This being so, from a Kantian standpoint, with its concern for individual rights and dignity within a cosmopolitan perspective, the idea of a moral right to national self-determination must fall. The actions it sanctions cannot be expressed in a maxim that can be universalized. The best that could be offered is that groups in trouble and making trouble may be pragmatically granted nationhood in the hope that this will bring peace. It is, however, not only a Kantian standpoint that is relevant here; analyzing the issues from a consequentialist perspective is equally fruitful.

It is because fulfilling the claimed right to self-determination involves walking through blood—or at least taking the risk that this will be necessary—that the same right will be granted to others only pragmatically and only if they too are willing to walk through blood. The self-determination that has been achieved not in fact by moral right but through the painful exercise of power is too precious a possession to carve a bit off and give away. Nations are ultimately defined by power and, when necessary, they are created and defended by force. Thus, if international law and practice were to acknowledge a right to self-determination for all groups that proclaim themselves to be nations, there would be a high risk of great cost to peace and security. The issue here is not what is right or wrong in Kantian terms but what the effects are of opting for a particular policy. As with risks in many contexts, it is hard to specify the risks to people's welfare that arise from a general moral right to national self-determination. In general terms, it is a risk of war, bloodshed, and ethnic cleansing, but it is not clear whether the risk is necessarily worse for one group than another. It may be the larger or the smaller, the older or the newer nation that suffers the greatest harm. It is not even clear that, if lack of national self-determination is regarded as an injustice, it is the perpetrators of injustice who would risk the most harm if a general principle of self-determination were to be granted. Bitter experience shows that granting the principle risks making victims out of its intended beneficiaries.

In other words, Kantian and consequentialist arguments appear to be in harmony on this question. In a Kantian perspective, the right of nationhood cannot be granted because the ensuing maxim cannot be universalized. For consequentialism, the costs to general welfare of granting a general moral principle of national self-determination are too high.

If the nation were created by nature, these objections to the idea of a moral right to self-determination would have to be placed alongside the demands of nature, and the resulting dilemma would have to be resolved. But nations are not created by nature. The nation is the creation of the group, which is in actuality represented by a smaller group made up of nationalists, who claim a moral right for their creation, which they are highly unlikely to grant to another group's creation. The representatives and leaders of the nation are, in different cases, elected or self-appointed, democrats or autocrats. The "self" in national self-determination is a product of politics and, except from the standpoint of the representatives, leaders, and supporters of the "self," it is impossible to understand why they should be granted rights that cannot be universalised and that have dangerous consequences.

This is what is important about the distinction between the right of individuals to belong to a community and the rights of the community to which the individuals belong, which was stated above. There is no moral reason to attack the right to belong to a community and every reason to defend it, unless in some other way it diminishes welfare and other moral goods. This is the normal way in which minority rights are defended. However, there is no reason to link those rights to the project of national self-determination. My right to be part of my identity group does not necessarily mean that my group has the right to any particular political arrangement in any particular geographical area. Likewise, denying that the community has such a right is not the same as denying the individual's right to belong to that community. And the individual has that right even if the community's leaders make misleading and arbitrary claims about the community's rights.

Moral Ambiguity

There is, then, no reason to accept that there is a moral right to national self-determination. The self in question is too arbitrary and the process by which it is realized cannot be universalized, nor can a right of national self-determination be granted as a general principle except at unacceptable risk of high cost to important moral goods. All the arguments that affect the issue of whether there is a moral right to national self-determination are relevant when assessing the related claim that the nation is the exclusive basis of legitimacy for state and government. While one could imagine arguing that there is a moral right to national self-determination, but also other bases of legitimacy for government, it is impossible to sustain the argument of the nation's exclusive legitimacy for state and government if there is no moral right to national self-determination. The moral foundations of nationalism are, therefore, rather weak.

Nationalism's failure against the first formulation of the Kantian categorical imperative has already been discussed. The second[3] (full) formulation is that people should not be treated as means to an end but valued as ends in themselves (Kant, 1991: 95). Nationalist movements are all too often guilty of also breaching this second formulation. What makes it particularly distasteful is that, in order to achieve the greater goal, the movement will often sacrifice significant numbers of the people of the nation for which it claims to speak. At the same time it must be granted that nationalism has often been the bearer of ideals of freedom and liberation and has not always ended by selling those ideals short. Nationalist movements have often been justified in their arguments against powerful, centralized states and empires oppressing national minorities. The breaking up of larger units into smaller does not have a uniform record for either good or bad. In short, the moral quality of nationalism cannot be pinned down for one single denunciation or celebration.

This could be interpreted as being a product of the multiplex nature of the phenomenon, noted at the outset. We could retreat from the evidently impossible task of assessing the moral quality of nationalism as either, on balance, good or bad, by arguing that some nationalisms are good, some bad. Nairn has offered an eloquent argument against this viewpoint. He argues that "the huge family of nationalisms cannot be divided into the black cats and the white cats, with a few half-breeds in between. The whole family is spotted, without exception" (1977: 348). More formally but equally metaphorically, he also states that, "all nationalism is both healthy and morbid. Both progress and regress are inscribed in its genetic code from the start. This is a structural fact about it. And it is a fact to which there are no exceptions: in this sense it is an exact (not a rhetorical) statement about nationalism to say that it is by nature ambivalent" (ibid.: 347–48).

---

3. The first formulation of the categorical imperative is formulated twice, so different readers of Kant can decide for themselves whether the means-not-ends formulation is the second or the third.

For Nairn, this moral ambiguity stems from the propensity of nationalist movements to fabricate imaginary pasts and to invent national traditions (Hobsbawm and Ranger, 1983) in order to gain the courage with which to face the future. From a different perspective, a similar conclusion can be drawn out of a consideration of nationalism's shared ideological origins with irrationalism; Berlin's exploration of the work of Johann Georg Hamann, mentor of the original German nationalist philosopher, Johann Gottfried Herder, is instructive in this respect (1994). Hamann, Berlin shows, dealt both in lofty ethics with a heavy dose of spirituality and in base prejudice. He combined both levels into rigorously argued intolerance of whatever and whoever diverged from his own norms and preferences. It could be said that Hamann, as an ideological forerunner of nationalism, himself displayed both the morbid and the healthy tendencies Nairn diagnosed two centuries later. For the discussion in this chapter, the same conclusion is possible by focusing more tightly on the questions of peace and conflict, the claim of a right that is not granted to others, and the arbitrary basis of the whole enterprise of nationalism.

Nationalism is a discourse of freedom that contains within itself the seeds of repression. It is a discourse that emphasizes the right to self-expression and to an identity that contains within itself the tendency toward intolerance of nonconforming expression and other identities. Even in liberal forms of nationalism, this darker side is and must be present. In the end the ethical problem with nationalism lies at its heart, in the project of forming a state. It is there that the potential for generosity and liberation is all too likely to break down. It is because of that project that the national group is likely to fail to grant to others what it claims for itself. Community is always a good, but not the national project.

REFERENCES

Anderson, Benedict. 1991. *Imagined Communities*. Rev. ed. London: Verso.
Archibugi, Daniel, David Held, and Martin Köhler, eds. 1998. *Re-imagining Political Community*. Oxford: Polity.
Berlin, Isaiah. 1994. *The Magus of the North: J. G. Hamann and the Origins of Modern Irrationalism*. London: Fontana.
Betts, Richard K. 1994. "The Delusion of Impartial Intervention." *Foreign Affairs* 73 (6): 20–33.
Breton, Albert, Gianluigi Galeotti, Pierre Salmon, and Ronald Wintrobe, eds. 1995. *Nationalism and Rationality*. Cambridge: Cambridge University Press.
Brown, Chris. 1999. "Universal Human Rights: A Critique." In Tim Dunne and Nicholas J. Wheeler, eds., *Human Rights in Global Politics*. Cambridge: Cambridge University Press, 103–27.

Buchanan, Allen. 1991. *Secession: The Morality of Political Divorce from Fort Sumter to Lithuania and Quebec.* Boulder, Colo.: Westview.
Caney, Simon, David George, and Peter Jones, eds. 1996. *National Rights, International Obligations.* Boulder, Colo.: Westview.
Connor, Walker. 1992. "The Nation and Its Myth." In Anthony D. Smith, ed., *Ethnicity and Nationalism.* Leiden: E. J. Brill, 48–57.
Donnelly, Jack. 1999. "Social Construction of International Human Rights." In Tim Dunne and Nicholas J. Wheeler, eds., *Human Rights in Global Politics.* Cambridge: Cambridge University Press, 71–102.
Fixdal, Mona, and Dan Smith. 1998. "Humanitarian Intervention and Just War'" *Mershon International Studies Review* 48 (supplement 2): 283–312.
Gellner, Ernest. 1983. *Nations and Nationalism.* Oxford: Blackwell.
George, David. 1996. "National Identity and Self-Determination." In Simon Caney, David George, and Peter Jones, eds., *National Rights, International Obligations.* Boulder, Colo.: Westview, 13–33.
Graham, Gordon. 1997. *Ethics and International Relations.* Oxford: Blackwell.
Greenfeld, Liah. 1992. *Nationalism: Five Roads to Modernity.* Cambridge: Harvard University Press.
Hobsbawm, Eric. 1990. *Nations and Nationalism since 1780.* Cambridge: Cambridge University Press.
Hobsbawm, Eric, and Terence Ranger, eds. 1983. *The Invention of Tradition.* Cambridge: Cambridge University Press.
Hroch, Miroslav. 1985. *Social Preconditions of National Revival in Europe.* Cambridge: Cambridge University Press.
Hurka, Thomas. 1997. "The Justification of National Partiality." In Robert McKim and Jeff McMahan, eds., *The Morality of Nationalism.* Oxford: Oxford University Press, 139–57.
ICISS Report. 2001. *The Responsibility to Protect: Report of the International Commission on Intervention and State Sovereignty.* Ottawa: International Development Research Centre.
Ignatieff, Michael. 1994. *Blood and Belonging.* London: Vintage.
Kant, Immanuel. 1991. *The Moral Law: Groundwork of the Metaphysic of Morals.* Trans. Herbert J. Paton (1948). London: Routledge.
Lichtenberg, Judith. 1997. "Nationalism: For and (Mainly) Against." In Robert McKim and Jeff McMahan, eds., *The Morality of Nationalism.* Oxford: Oxford University Press, 158–75.
McKim, Robert, and Jeff McMahan, eds. 1997. *The Morality of Nationalism.* New York: Oxford University Press.
McMahan, Jeff. 1997. "The Limits of National Partiality." In Robert McKim and Jeff McMahan, eds., *The Morality of Nationalism.* Oxford: Oxford University Press, 107–38.
Midgley, Mary. 1999. "Towards an Ethic of Global Responsibility." In Tim Dunne and Nicholas J. Wheeler, eds., *Human Rights in Global Politics.* Cambridge: Cambridge University Press.
Mill, John Stuart. 1873. *Dissertations and Discussions.* New York: Holt.
Miller, David. 1995. *On Nationality.* Oxford: Oxford University Press.
Nagel, Thomas. 1970. *The Possibility of Altruism.* Princeton: Princeton University Press.
———. 1979. *Mortal Questions.* Cambridge: Cambridge University Press.
———. 1991. *Equality and Partiality.* New York: Oxford University Press.
Nairn, Tom. 1977. *The Break-up of Britain.* London: NLB.
———. 1993. "Demonising Nationalism." *London Review of Books,* February 25.
Plamenatz, John. 1976. "Two Types of Nationalism." In Eugene Kamenka, ed., *Nationalism: The Nature and Evolution of an Idea.* London: Edward Arnold, 23–36.
Rieff, David. 1994. "Accomplice to Genocide." *War Report,* no. 28 (September): 35–40.
Seton-Watson, Hugh. 1977. *Nations and States.* London: Methuen.
Smith, Anthony D. 1983. *Theories of Nationalism.* 2nd ed. London: Duckworth.
———. 1986. *The Ethnic Origins of Nations.* Oxford: Blackwell.
Smith, Dan. 1994. "Nationalism and Peace: Theoretical Notes for Research and Political Agendas." *Innovation* 7 (3): 219–36.

———. 1997. "Interventionist Dilemmas and Justice." In Anthony McDermott, ed., *Humanitarian Force*. Oslo: International Peace Research Institute, 13–39.

Smith, Dan, and Øyvind Østerud. 1995. *Nation-State, Nationalism, and Political Identity*. Oslo: Advanced Research on the Europeanisation of the Nation-State, University of Oslo.

Tamir, Yael. 1993. *Liberal Nationalism*. Princeton: Princeton University Press.

Walzer, Michael. 1977. *Just and Unjust Wars: A Moral Argument, with Historical Illustrations*. New York: Basic.

———. 1994. *Thick and Thin: Moral Argument at Home and Abroad*. Notre Dame: University of Notre Dame Press.

Weiss, Thomas G. 1994. "UN Responses in the Former Yugoslavia: Moral and Operational Choices." *Ethics & International Affairs* 8:1–22.

12

The Sort of Nationalism and Patriotism That Europe Needs

ANDREAS FOLLESDAL

What should be the common basis of a European identity? Should all citizens of the European Union share, and be made to share, certain values, memories, or beliefs—and if so, which and why?

Politicians and scholars have addressed these questions of European identity for more than thirty years, since the European Community 1973 Declaration on European Identity. Recent political events have increased public attention to the topic, most notably two apparently unrelated and different forms of integration failure. Multicultural integration has left much to be desired, most visibly in cases of Muslim immigrants and their children. And the recent "Constitutional Treaty for Europe" failed to get sufficient public support in the French and Dutch referendums. In response to the latter challenge, but clearly relevant to both of them, president of the European Commission José Manuel Barroso called for Europe-wide debates on the future of Europe, in the recognition that "it is simply wrong to think that a single market can be sustained without social cohesion, a political vision and the solidarity that flows from the feeling of belonging to a common project" (Barroso, 2005). There can be little doubt that the debates about the European Union—its shape, fu-

---

This chapter is a revision of Follesdal, 2000, which was partially funded by TSER grant SOE2-CT97-3056—EURCIT. The author is grateful for this support.

ture, and social preconditions—offer instructive contributions to a broad range of normative discussions about nation-states, their legitimacy, and how to avoid armed conflicts within and between them.

One of the most pressing issues within international ethics today is the question of national sovereignty and the attendant conundrums of nationalism. These concerns are of special pertinence and importance to Europeans given the history of civil wars and wars between nation-states on the European continent. Indeed, one central aim of the "founding fathers" of the European Union was no doubt to keep unrest between nation-states in check. If Europeans could build and maintain trust and stability with the aid of fair and common institutions, Europe might not become again the violent battleground that it was too often in the twentieth century. The twofold challenge of integration that the European Union faces today requires even further extensive and mutual trust, on topics that include both the ends and means of integration. Where does Europe end? Should Turkey be included? Should the EU develop a further common security policy, so that European soldiers may be required to give up their lives for the sake of European rather than national interests? How can officials motivate public support for common institutions that impose burdens on some for the sake of other Europeans? Citizens and politicians must also be able to trust one another across state borders, trust that others will do their share in the common practices of the EU. The shift from unanimity to majority rule for many common decisions requires even further trust, as do rules of "mutual recognition" of other member states' production standards.

Calls for a European identity often seem to be in response to such problems of borders and trust. Yet a shared and unique European-wide national identity need not be part of the solution to these challenges, or so I shall argue. I shall defend this view concerning the role and contents of a European identity with regard to redistributive arrangements in particular, against the backdrop of British political philosopher David Miller's arguments about the need for nationality. These concerns seem to be central to both of the two challenges of European integration mentioned in the beginning.

Miller provides a thought-provoking defense of nationality as the "cement of society." The national community "embodies a real continuity between generations; and performs a moralising role, by holding up before us the virtues of our ancestors and encouraging us to live up to them. . . . people are held together not merely by physical necessity, but by a dense web of customs, practices, implicit understandings, and so forth. . . . in a national community a case can be made out for unconditional obligations to other members that arise simply by virtue of the fact that one has been born and raised in that particular community" (1995: 36, 41, 42). Miller's arguments for the need for national identity challenge the prospects of legitimate European institutions. His conclusions are dire for proponents of an ever-closer Union since he is pessimistic about the prospects of European-wide nationalism of the appropriate sort. I shall question Miller's pessimism since first, his defense of nationalism is unconvincing. Second, his pessimism is premature, if relevant at all. Alternative grounds for supporting common institutions are available and may be within reach for the European Union.

After a presentation and elaboration of Miller's argument, I will consider its problems. We may agree with Miller's claim that trust among citizens is important. But it remains an open question whether nationalism is the only source of trust—whether it indeed is such a source at all—and whether what Miller proposes is nationalism at all. Next I consider Miller's reasons for rejecting alternative bases for trust drawn from "universalist" theories. I then defend liberal contractualism against such objections, in support of the role of constitutional patriotism (Habermas, 1992) or a public theory of justice (Rawls, 1971a, 1993). These alternatives withstand Miller's criticisms, or so I argue. Thus Miller's pessimistic prognosis for a fair Europe is premature.

By way of introduction, I first consider the main motivation that fuels Miller's contribution. He argues for nationalism as a source of trust required for redistributive welfare regimes.

Dire Prospects for European Welfare Regimes?

Is a fair Europe likely? Pessimism about where the European Union is heading is not new, particularly among the defenders of redistributive arrangements. Some critics have noted that efforts at limiting or compensating for the perceived injustices of the market have failed as a result of the decision procedures of the European Union. Coordination problems among member states render it difficult to maintain the domestic safety nets, yet prevent the emergence of a European-wide alternative. Such coordination traps may be resolved by joint action, but the political prospects are dim (Scharpf, 1988, 1999).

Others note that democratic arrangements at the European level are missing. Thus we have little reason to hope for a democratically enacted pan-European welfare regime to supplement the domestic efforts. Democratic institutions have yet to be developed and, importantly, there is no European "public sphere" of media for deliberation. In the absence of opportunities for taking others' weal and woe into consideration through public discussion and scrutiny, majority rule runs the risk of tyranny (Grimm, 1995).

These pessimists are prepared to accept that institutions and media might change, and that these institutional features and lack of deliberative arenas may be transient. Thus, careful reform over the long haul cannot be ruled out. David Miller, on the other hand, provides a more fundamental argument against European redistributive policies, on the basis of thought-provoking claims about the role of nationalism and its permanent absence in the European Union (Miller, 1993, 1995). Over the years, David Miller has provided sustained and often sound arguments concerning equality and community, so his present warnings should give us pause.

Any acceptable normative political theory, in Miller's view, must justify redistribution beyond self-interest. Such a theory must support two considered judgments. Individuals unable to provide for themselves must be protected and provided for, and there are special obligations holding between compatriots: "obligations that we owe to one another—obligations of the sort that are manifested in social security schemes and public provision for citizens' needs" (Miller, 1995: 178). These commitments to solidarity make Miller wary of theories that regard community membership as a "cultural supermarket," since they fail "to address the question what holds a society together, and what is the source of the obligations that we owe to one another" (ibid.). Miller holds that arguments of "reciprocity" based on self-interest are insufficient. Instead, he has sought to rehabilitate the notion of nationalism, in some disrepute in recent political philosophy. Shared nationality provides the answer to the question of who has responsibility for those unable to provide for themselves. It is only "because we have prior obligations of nationality that include obligations to provide for needs that arise in this way that the practice of citizenship properly includes redistributive elements of the kind that we commonly find in contemporary states" (ibid.: 72). His version of nationalism provides one justification for redistribution, and no other accounts appear to fit the tasks he identifies: "Nationality has to be credited with much that is valuable in our political life, especially . . . those social-democratic institutions that in European states have served to counteract the economic polarisation and social fragmentation that a market economy tends to produce" (ibid.: 81). Global markets threaten this solidarity. Duties toward the vulnerable may corrode due to the "polarising effects of the global market" (ibid.: 187). When domestic national identities dissolve, political elites will not be stopped from dismantling the institutions that protect the vulnerable.

For the purposes of this chapter, let us accept such solidarity norms of redistributive obligations and hence lay aside libertarian conceptions of justice such as those of David Gauthier (1986, 1990). The issue to be addressed is Miller's defense of the nation-state as the largest circle of such solidarity. Miller holds that his account—and apparently no other—will allow "that redistributive elements can be built in which go beyond what the rational self-interest of each participant would dictate" (1995: 75). I shall suggest that Miller dismisses such alternative theories prematurely.

Miller seeks to argue for nationalism on the basis of trust, and this renders him pessimistic about the prospects of redistributive arrangements in Europe. Yet his argument seems flawed. I shall suggest that the need for redistributive arrangements based on trust need not draw on nationalism of the kind Miller suggests. In consequence, the prospects of redistributive arrangements in Europe need not be as bleak as Miller suggests. The quest for Europe-wide trust is important, but a European national identity of the sort Miller supports may not be required.

Nationalism to Maintain Trust and Stability

One reason Miller's argument is of obvious interest for the study of international relations and the future of the European Union is his explicit concern for stability. General compliance with existing policies and institutions is a paramount condition for a political order worthy of the name. One—of several—mechanisms for securing the requisite expectations of reciprocal compliance builds on shared values. Miller's main argument for nationalism provides a thought-provoking exposition of this argument: "[A] viable political community requires mutual trust, trust depends on communal ties, and nationality is uniquely appropriate here as a form of common identity" (Miller, 1994: 143). This argument from stability seems to proceed in four steps.

1. Compliance with redistributive arrangements typical of welfare state regimes requires trust. The state is more stable if based on a national community, since compliance with costly policies requires trust. The population must believe that need-based provisions will in fact be distributed fairly according to need (Miller, 1994: 142). The reasons trust is important for welfare arrangements appear to stem from problems of partial compliance: the suspicion either that the contributors or the beneficiaries of redistribution are failing to do their part, to the detriment of others. The participants in redistributive welfare arrangements will want to know that others contribute when they contribute themselves. Partial compliance may make already costly burdens excessively costly for those who do their share. Even the suspicion of such partial compliance can wreak havoc with cooperative arrangements. This is because the motives for compliance are often complex.

Three different motivational setups may be distinguished. First, people may comply *unconditionally*—regardless of whether others do their share. For this segment of the population, the expected behavior of others is irrelevant. People may instead have a preference for not doing their part, even when others cooperate—but they prefer general compliance to general defection. This second kind of motivation—the *free rider*—gives rise to dilemmas. Each of the participants may prefer all others to comply without themselves complying. The result may be the end of collective action. A collective solution to this conundrum is coercive compliance, sanctioning unilateral defection for the sake of general cooperation. In our setting, sanctions can ensure that citizens of Europe contribute to redistributive schemes benefiting nonnationals or punish those Europeans who seek benefits beyond their due entitlements. The third preference setup is known as an "assurance game": each prefers general compliance, and prefers to comply, if all (or most) others comply—but each prefers to defect if all others defect (Sen, 1967). "I am prepared to do my part, but only if I am convinced that others will do theirs."

2. Trust is important to remove problems of partial compliance. Trust in the behavior of others can serve to reduce the problems generated by the suspicion that others are free riders and by conditional compliers. Such trust can be secured by sanctions, which shift individuals' preferences, so that even free riders will prefer to comply if the risk of being caught is high enough. Since sanctions provide more reliable expectations about the compliance of others, they offer an additional reason why *conditional compliers* should indeed comply. But for a community of conditional compliers, information alone may suffice for trust. Sanctions are necessary, then, when individuals do not know whether others are conditional compliers or free riders. However, sanctions are a less than perfect mechanism for ensuring compliance. Sanctions can be costly and cumbersome, and suspicion of others' low risk defection can threaten complex cooperative ventures such as redistribution.

Thus, unconditional or conditional compliers are to be preferred over free riders. When all participants are known to prefer such compliance, suspicion of defection is reduced—and hence the defection by conditional compliers is reduced (Ostrom, 1991).This makes for more stable redistributive practices. Trust that others are conditional or unconditional compliers with redistributive arrangements, rather than free riders, is necessary for general compliance and hence stability.

3. Nationality provides the common identity appropriate for redistributive arrangements. Miller then claims that communal ties and common identity, in the sense of shared interests, are central for ensuring the requisite trust. Clearly, individuals who prefer conditional or unconditional compliance, and who are known to have these preferences, will secure stable redistribution better than individuals who are free riders. Thus, a shared, public commitment to such arrangements seems beneficial to redistribution.

Miller regards nationality as a particular collective source of personal identity: "These five elements together—a community (1) constituted by shared belief and mutual commitment, (2) extended in history, (3) active in character, (4) connected to a particular territory, and (5) marked off from other communities by its distinct public culture—serve to distinguish nationality from other collective sources of personal identity" (1995: 27). The need for shared beliefs and mutual commitment is presumably due to the role of nationality in removing problems of partial compliance through trust.

4. Nationalism provides the unique common identity appropriate for redistributive arrangements. Miller then appears to hold that nationalism provides the uniquely appropriate common identity for redistributive arrangements. It is not clear how this premise follows, except as an argument by exclusion—that there are no alternative accounts left, once libertarianism is rejected. The consequences for the European Union are clear: European integration among citizens of different nations, and of different religions, threatens and cannot create the appropriate forms of such nationalism.

Miller's Argument Considered

What are we to make of Miller's argument for nationality from trust? Let us agree with Miller's observation that trust plays an important role for stability, and that correct stable expectations about the behavior of others is important for maintaining redistributive arrangements. However, it is not clear that Miller's conception of *nationality* is required to solve the problems of partial compliance.

1. What must participants be committed to? In light of the sketch offered about why trust is needed, it is not clear that those maintaining a practice need to share a broad or fundamental set of beliefs or commitments—beyond a commitment to upholding the redistributive arrangements. An important, and unresolved, issue is thus what shared values and "shared public culture" Miller can have in mind—and whether this is reasonably called "nationality." For the issue of redistributive arrangements in the European Union, the relevant questions are parallel: What shared values and culture are needed to sustain such solidarity in Europe?

Three alternatives may be indicated. First, there may be agreement on complying only with certain principles of action. Thus, famously, Jacques Maritain argued for human rights as constituting a very thin overlapping consensus: "It is not reasonably possible to hope for more than the convergence in practice in the enumeration of articles jointly agreed. The reconciling of theories and a philosophic synthesis in the true sense are only conceivable after an immense amount of investigation and elucidation of fundamentals, requiring a high degree of insight, a new systematisation and authoritative correction of a number of errors and confusions of thought" (1949: 11–12). However, it is not clear that mere agreement on certain principles or practices suffices. Rules of practices must be interpreted, revised, and applied; and suspicion of defection will flourish unless the reasons others have for complying are visible for others.

Second, a "thick" set of values, if shared by all, can have a substantive content confirming the redistributive practices as expressing the proper responsibility of each member of society for one another. This approach faces the challenge of value pluralism. How can these institutions and such comprehensive values be imposed on all members of a society, even when citizens disagree about the good life? This is one fundamental challenge facing Miller's view insofar as it is taken to support "nationalism." Furthermore, of course, only some such substantive values will endorse redistribution. Miller must thus provide some criteria for determining which beliefs, commitments, and cultures are within the acceptable range for legitimate nationalism—domestically and in the European Union.

A third strategy requires agreement on certain practices, and on their immediate justification, sufficient to ensure shared interpretation, application, and stable compliance, all the while seeking to avoid controversial metaphysical assumptions or contested views about the proper ends of humans. I take John Rawls, Jürgen Habermas, and other liberal theorists to contribute to such projects. Indeed, Rawls underscores the concern for stability and claims that "the problem of political liberalism is: How is it possible that there may exist over time a stable and just society of free and equal citizens profoundly divided by reasonable though incompatible religious, philosophical, and moral doctrines?" (1993: xviii) It would seem possible for Miller to pursue the third strategy. However, he hesitates about the alleged "neutrality" imposed by such views. This brings us to the second issue pertaining to Miller's position.

2. *What common political culture must be shared?* An important issue concerns the content of the "common political culture." Miller regards this as "a set of understandings about the nature of a political community, its principles and institutions, its social norms, and so forth, [as opposed to] . . . a private culture is all those beliefs, ideas, tastes, and preferences that may be unique to an individual, or more likely shared within a family, a social stratum, an ethnic group, or what has been called a 'lifestyle enclave'" (1995: 158, referring to Bellah et al., 1985). However, Miller's

account fails to explain in a convincing way what is—and should be—part of the political culture. The problem is partly one of contested demarcations. This can be illustrated by his own view that Scots, the Welsh, and the Northern Irish are not separate nations. Britain should not be thought of as "a multinational state in which common political institutions hold together communities with separate identities" (ibid.: 173), but rather as one nation. This surely raises the issue of what are necessary or sufficient elements of a common political culture.

The distinction between private and public culture becomes even more important insofar as Miller wants to distinguish his nationalist position from liberalism. He notes that his nationalists, "though perhaps favouring neutrality on some cultural questions, are committed to non-neutrality where the national culture itself is at stake. In other words, where some cultural feature—a landscape, a musical tradition, a language—has become a component part of national identity, it is justifiable to discriminate in its favour if the need arises" (1995: 195). Moreover, it is unclear why Miller requires a "thick" political culture in order to maintain trust in shared institutions—beyond that suggested by liberal theorists.

3. Why political and territorial aspirations? If trust and a narrow political culture are required, we are led to wonder why Miller insists that the nation must have political and territorial aspirations. Here he departs from other defenders of moderate nationalism, such as Yael Tamir (1993). Miller claims that "it is an essential part of having the [national] identity that you should permanently occupy that place.... A nation ... must have a homeland" (1995: 24). This "helps to explain why a national community must be (in aspiration if not yet in fact) a political community" (ibid.). However, making this into a defining criterion of nationality does not explain why general compliance with institutions requires such aims.

It is not clear that considerations of trust support the restriction to groups with political and territorial claims. To be sure, he notes that traditional sovereignty may not always be needed, but still the nation itself must decide on what to claim and what counts as constitutive of their culture:

The guiding ideal here is that of a people reproducing their national identity and settling matters that are collectively important to them through democratic deliberation. To achieve that, they need a political unit with au-

Nationalism and Patriotism for Europe 277

thority of the relevant scope, but what that scope must be will depend on the particular identity of the group in question, and on the aims and goals that they are attempting to pursue. . . . It is therefore going to be difficult to set apriori limits to the proper scope of sovereignty from this perspective. Moreover, we cannot tell in advance which particular features of a society's way of life will come to assume importance as markers of national identity. . . . In this area [i.e., national currency], a collective belief that something is essential to national identity comes very close to making it so. Once you combine the principle of national self-determination with the proposition that what counts for the purposes of national identity is what the nation in question takes to be essential to that identity, it follows that nothing in principle lies beyond the scope of sovereignty (1995: 100–101).

One reason for insisting that nations must have political autonomy is to protect the common culture, which in turn is regarded as a condition "for a person's having an identity and being able to make choices in the first place" (Miller, 1994: 154). This defense seems unsatisfactory. It would support legal immunity not only for groups we intuitively may grant are nations but also for a wide variety of groups that share values and seek to pursue them. At the same time, this defense stops far short of justifying sovereign statehood. What seems to be required is systematic argument, in sector after sector, on the basis of a variety of interests, about what sorts of legal powers a group needs to secure the legitimate elements of its common culture. Thus this argument might support the claims of any set of individuals to enjoy whatever powers they need to ensure the flourishing of their own "culture." The result would be a much broader range of social groups enjoying a broad variety of legal powers and immunities than what is traditionally meant by "sovereign nation-states." In response, Miller might pursue two further reasons for the concern with political and territorial claims, relating to trust.

This definition of nationality may make sense when shared territory is a good indicator of shared values or interests. This territorial focus also identifies one set of comprehensive and mutually exclusive cultures, avoiding the myriad of conflicting claims that would otherwise arise for individuals with multiple loyalties and "identities."

However, neither of these two is decisive in today's world. First, in states with freedom of religion and speech, territorial borders do not identify a population with a broad range of shared values and a common, dominant identity. Political borders may delineate the reach of common institutions and sanctioning mechanisms, but these cannot uncontroversially be used in the pursuit of common values. Nor, I have suggested, are shared thick values needed. Second, the territorial focus removes conflicts only if contested territorial claims can be adjudicated. However, this is notoriously not the case in the present world order. Furthermore, even though undisputed borders may eliminate conflicting claims, other solutions are also available—for instance, a distribution of authorities in a federal or consociational arrangement according to private-public distinctions, or social functions, or by appeals to subsidiarity. Miller is right to point out that such arrangements often entail less redistribution across subunits (1995: 84–85), but this fact does not entail that less redistribution is wrong. The force of this observation depends on whether we agree with Miller that redistributive claims are completely independent of the extent of mutual interdependence in collaborative arrangements.

To conclude, it is not clear that Miller's defense of nationality on the basis of the need for trust succeeds. What *is* justified vis-à-vis the need for trust is a shared set of practices with some public, common value platform, but this requires neither a "thick" public political culture nor a set of individuals who have political or territorial aspirations. This modest shared normative platform would seem a poor explication of the term "nationality."

Miller's Objections to Universalist Theories of Justice

Miller raises several concerns against "ethical universalist" normative theories, apparently including those associated with Habermas and Rawls.[1] He holds that the personal commitments such theories focus on are not sufficient for the tasks performed by nationality. In the European context this is relevant, as Habermas for one has stressed the need for a shared political culture focused on the constitution or its equivalent. Such a constitutional patriotism must suffice (Habermas, 1992, 1997). Miller disagrees: "the national identities that support common citizenship must be thicker than 'constitutional patriotism' implies. If we are attempting to

---

1. He also appears to hold that these theories aspire to offer deductions of all principles and rules from abstract premises, and he challenges the plausibility of this strategy (Miller, 1997: 71). I share his misgivings about such projects but fail to find evidence that this is a correct description of the theories offered by Habermas or Rawls.

reform national identity so that it becomes accessible to all citizens, we do this not by discarding everything except constitutional principles, but by adapting the inherited culture to make room for minority communities" (1995: 189). Miller offers two reasons why these identities must be "thick," summarized by his claim that "[s]ubscribing to them [the constitutional principles] marks you out as a liberal rather than a fascist or an anarchist, but it does not provide the kind of political identity that nationality provides" (ibid.: 162).

1. Universalist principles fail to provide the political identity offered by nationality. Talk of citizenship should not replace nationality. To get a grasp of Miller's argument, it is worth quoting in full. Citizenship cannot solely be

> understood in terms of subscription to a set of political principles: tolerance, respect for law, belief in the procedures of parliamentary democracy, and so forth. These principles should undoubtedly feature centrally in any story about what it means to be British today, and . . . it would be very helpful to have them formally inscribed in a constitutional document. It does not, however, seem that these principles, which after all are the common currency of liberal democracies everywhere, can by themselves bear the load that would otherwise be carried by a national identity. . . . a national identity helps to locate us in the world; it must tell us who we are, where we have come from, what we have done. It must then involve an essentially historical understanding in which the present generation are seen as heirs to a tradition which they then pass on to their successors (1995: 175).

It seems correct that a set of such principles provides little in the way of identifying the proper role of a people in the world, or the appropriate story of its past. However, two comments are indicated. It remains to be seen whether these theories *only* allow shared principles of this general form — we turn to this later. Moreover, and against Miller's claim, it is unclear why there must be a "thick" and shared set of values and practices that should serve as the justification for political power — within a nation-state or in the European Union. As discussed above, the arguments from trust do not support the need for a shared "thick" platform.

2. Constitutional principles do not mark unique features of the nation. The principles Miller lists would be similar and shared among citizens of many or most legitimate states. This creates a problem for theories focusing on such principles, or so Miller argues. Nothing distinguishes one nation from others, in this view. For Miller this is a flaw. He holds that "a national identity requires that the people who share it should have something in common, a set of characteristics that in the past was often referred to as a 'national character,' but which I prefer to describe as a common public culture" (1995: 25). Elsewhere Miller writes: "National divisions must be conceived as natural ones; they must correspond to what are taken to be real differences between peoples" (1994: 140). As discussed above, the reasons for nationality based on trust do not require that the shared values are unique to the participants: The point is to ensure general compliance among themselves, not to set them apart or exclude anyone else.

Against this, Miller might respond that the problem remains because these principles do not bind individuals to the practices and people of just their own state, rather than to any other state. Thus, universalist theories seem unable to account for "political obligations"—the special ties that hold between individuals and their state. I consider this worry next.

Liberal Contractualism

For these purposes, the normative tradition of "liberal contractualism" includes writers such as Brian Barry (1995), John Rawls (1971a, 1993), and T. M. Scanlon (1982, 1998)—as well as several elements of Jürgen Habermas's contributions (1992, 1996). The aim here is to sketch some elements consistent with these approaches in order to indicate how liberal contractualism avoids the problems identified by David Miller.

Liberal contractualism addresses the conditions under which citizens have reason to accept institutions and cultures as normatively legitimate and binding on their conduct. The set of social institutions as a whole should secure the relevant interests of all affected parties to an acceptable degree. Institutions are legitimate in this sense only if they satisfy principles that can be justified by arguments in the form of a social contract of a particular kind. The principles of legitimacy to which we should hold institutions are those that the persons affected would unanimously consent to under conditions that secure and recognize their status as appropriately free and equal. Through this process one aims at institutions that contribute to a fair distribution, enjoy social acceptance and, hence, contribute to the avoidance of social unrest and conflict. That this is an approach of great relevance and interest to basic peace and conflict research should thus be quite clear.

Note that, unlike the contractualist tradition of Thomas Hobbes and David Gauthier, liberal contractualism does not seek to justify morality from a premise of self-centered individuals. Rather, it assumes that individuals generally have an interest in being "able to justify one's actions to others on grounds they could not reasonably reject" (Scanlon, 1982: 116). They "desire to act in accordance with principles that could not reasonably be rejected by people seeking an agreement with others under conditions free from morally irrelevant bargaining advantages and disadvantages" (Barry, 1989: 8). This commitment to give reasons is an expression of our belief in and respect for the reasonableness of others (Macedo, 1990). The aim of liberal contractualism is thus not to justify morality but rather to bring this commitment to justice to bear on our rules and practices—be they domestic or European.

The Limited Significance of Consent

One contribution of liberal contractualism is to delineate some limits to the morally binding rules and practices we find ourselves surrounded by, regardless of actual consent. Every individual's interests must be secured and furthered by the social institutions as a whole (Dworkin, 1978). This commitment is honed by the notion of possible consent, allowing us to bring the vague ideals of equal dignity to bear on pressing questions of legitimacy and institutional design.

Our moral obligation to obey the law of the land is justified in part by the claim that this particular social order could hypothetically have been the subject of consent among all affected parties. But this does not entail that such hypothetical consent *creates* the moral obligation or duty in the same way as free and adequately informed consent binds those who so consent. Instead, liberal contractualism serves to delineate what limits apply to these duties that hold regardless of actual consent, including what Rawls's theory of justice as fairness calls the natural duty of justice, "to support and to comply with just institutions that exist and apply to us" (Rawls, 1971a: 115; cf. Klosko, 1994).

Thus, liberal contractualism does not entail that individuals are bound only by obligations voluntarily taken on. The existing legitimate institutions are not binding on us because we actually consent or participate in a daily tacit plebiscite (Renan, 1992). To be sure, we usually act according to the practices we find ourselves part of (Walzer, 1977: 54), but we do not have, and have never had, a real freedom with regard to the social institutions. Indeed, ordinarily we cannot choose to reject them, and not even the act of voting expresses a morally binding tacit consent to be governed. Nevertheless, we have many duties that we have not explicitly or tacitly consented to. Actual, tacit, or hypothetical consent is not the source of a moral obligation to comply. The idea of possible consent in the contractualist tradition does not provide the *source* of moral duty, but it is an expression of one important condition for such duties. Obedience is required only when power is distributed fairly. Appeals to consent thus serve to legitimize authority, although consent is still not held to generate the moral authority of institutions (Murphy, 1994).

Mode of Arguments: Consistency vs. Deduction, Underdetermination

Of some relevance to the issues at hand, we should note that the contractualist approach leads us to search for principles against which no reasonable objections can be made. Principles are presented for such assessment, and the process of checking whether objections can be made yields a set of permissible principles. There are two important features to note. There is no sense in which such principles of justice, or particular institutions, are *deduced* or *generated* by the process of checking whether equal respect is secured. The procedure checks for consistency and does not offer a deductive path. Moreover, the process can in principle allow several alternative principles. Thus, the set of principles may be underdetermined, in the sense that alternative principles may all be unobjectionable. Furthermore, the same set of principles for legitimacy may allow a variety of sets of institutional arrangements, each of which satisfies the distributive requirements of liberal contractualism. The moral unity provided by such a theory is not one, therefore, of deduction, but of an analysis of institutions that show they are consistent with, and can be regarded as an expression of, a view of individuals as enjoying equal respect.

In light of these comments, it should be clear that this tradition might allow for *different* just institutional arrangements; the procedure should thus not be expected to generate blueprints of institutional design. And instantiations of just institutions may be different, yet possibly equally just—for instance, within different European states.

The Interest in Culture

Contractualist theories are said to deny the intrinsic value of community and ignore the "embedded" nature of human beings.[2] Instead, society is exclusively regarded as instrumental for benefiting the interests of "atomistic" individuals. However, we may agree from a liberal contractualist standpoint with Taylor's conception of the self as embedded, and with MacIntyre's claim that our duties can be determined only by reflecting on the roles we are born into, which expand and constrain our choices (Taylor, 1985; MacIntyre, 1981: 216).

Liberal contractualism recognizes that the basic societal structure shapes our expectations and aspirations in fundamental and inescapable ways. Social institutions have a pervasive impact on the development and satisfaction of our interests by framing our expectations. We are concerned with the legitimacy of social institutions precisely because they exercise a strong influence on us, or our life plans and our expectations (Rawls, 1978). With changes in values, norms, institutions, history, and language, new options for life choices appear, while others disappear. Members have an interest in revising their plans as options and consequences change. Liberal contractualism can thus accommodate the communitarian concern for constitutive attachments and commitments found within the traditions and roles we take part in, and not chosen by the individual. The satisfaction of legitimate expectations is an important interest, and stable social institutions are crucial for making and pursuing life plans. We thus have good reason to maintain social institutions, insofar as it is only under fairly stable institutions that expectations can be created and met (Follesdal, 1996).

Challenge 1: The Significance of Particular Practices

The relationship between principles of justice and participation in particular institutional practices must be made clearer in order to determine how the "sense of justice" expresses itself among compatriots. Recall that a sense of justice in Rawls's terms does not mean only a commitment to two very general principles of justice or to abstract constitutional

---

2. For different sorts of criticisms and defenses on other grounds, see Buchanan, 1989; Caney, 1992; Cohen, 1986; Gutmann, 1985; Mulhall, 1994; Mulhall and Swift, 1996.

principles. Rather, the sense of justice is "an effective desire to comply with the existing rules and to give one another that to which they are entitled" (Rawls, 1971a: 312). Thus acting on a sense of justice entails interacting in our day-to-day lives with other individuals in accordance with the legitimate expectations they have about our behavior, honoring their trust in our responses.

Miller, as well as some communitarians, holds that the fact that we inhabit certain roles and are members of certain communities provides us with a *sufficient* justification for acting in a certain way. Thus the fact that an institution is *ours* is taken to be morally relevant when justifying the institutions and our compliance with its rules. The contractualist perspective, on the other hand, is criticized for leaving little if any justificatory role to the common life of an existing community, appealing *instead* to abstract principles.

But this objection misunderstands the raison d'être of principles of justice. These principles help to explain the standards that a set of institutions *should* satisfy. For this task, it is irrelevant whether I or we live under those institutions. It does not matter for this topic, "from the moral point of view," that *this* is the society that has shaped me into who I am. But of course, *within* any set of institutions, individuals justify their actions by appeal to the rules of the set of institutions in place (Rawls, 1971b). So one's culture may well spell out the content of these special duties that are said to bind us, but these rules and practices do not give a *complete* justification of the duties, since we must then offer a justification of the existing culture as well. And for this purpose it does not matter that *this* particular set of institutions has shaped me into who I am.

Liberal contractualism thus grants a justificatory role to existing practices one is part of (cf. Tamir, 1993: 134). To illustrate where this account differs from Miller's, note that he holds that "the relevant question to ask, if some question arises about what I owe to my compatriots, is not just how I feel about them at present, but what flows from my (normally unchosen) membership of a constitutive community" (1997: 74). Similarly, Stuart Hampshire says that institutions are sometimes justified "historically" by showing that "they have become an essential element in the subject's way of life" (1983: 5), *instead of* by reference to a general principle of justice.

In comparison, liberal contractualism offers an account of justification that accepts such a sociological or historical account as a part of, *but only one part of,* a full justification of the institution. The justification of my duty to abide by the rules of a specific social institution must consist of (1) an argument that it is just (i.e., part of a just set of institutions), (2) an argument that this institution is operative in my society, and (3) an argument that its rules apply to me. The fact that other institutions existing elsewhere might be somewhat more just does not by itself generate a duty on my part to abide by them, because the second and third steps are missing.

Thus, a complete justification of an existing and just set of institutions must refer to our shared history, even on the contractualist view. When we justify compliance with the existing institutions (or sanction noncompliance with them, as the case may be) we must do two things: (1) show that they satisfy (or alternatively violate) the relevant principles of justice; and (2) show that this particular set of institutions, and not another one, does in fact exist in our society: these rules, and not another set of rules, are publicly known and generally complied with. Thus a thoroughgoing justification of our institutions *over* other just ones must refer in part to our shared history, the general acceptance of these rules, and so on. In this view, then, we may agree with Miller about granting *some* normative importance to "the historical identity of the community, the links that bind present-day politics to decisions made and actions performed in the past" (1995: 163). I thus submit that, in contrast to the theories criticized by Miller, liberal contractualism can accommodate and justify special duties and the value of community, based on an ideal of the individual as deeply embedded in social relations.

Challenge 2: Whence Special Duties?

We often have special duties toward particular others, both our family and compatriots. Miller stresses special duties, holding that they are incompatible with universalistic theories. Again, on this issue liberal contractualism agrees with Miller—but offers a better justification of special duties.

To be sure, special duties such as patriotism are not provided or generated by contractualism, but they are permitted, duly pruned, as compatible with principles of justice. Thus, John Rawls appeals to the natural duty of justice "to support and to comply with just institutions that exist and apply to us" (1971a: 115). For instance, citizens have special patriotic duties to their own country *insofar as* the nation-state, including the office of citizenship, first *is a just set of institutions,* and second *applies to the citizens*. Special duties, then, are ultimately supported by an "impersonal" theory of justice: The special duties an institution imposes are morally binding insofar as the institution is permissible, that is, part of a society that satisfies contractualist principles of justice.

Conclusion

A stable and just peaceful order among states requires converging expectations about mutual compliance with practices and institutions. The pervasive influence of nationalism has traditionally been regarded as a major hindrance to stability in this sense. David Miller's arguments in defense of nationality are therefore a striking contribution, particularly since he defends national identity for reasons of trust. I have argued that Miller's argument yields flawed conclusions on the basis of sound premises. He points to an important insight concerning the need for trust in ensuring stable institutions and practices. However, this basis does not offer support for nationalism of the kind he sketches. Moreover, other accounts, including liberal contractualism, appear to be equally appropriate solutions to the problem he identifies. Miller's substantive concerns appear to be compatible with liberal contractualism as I have sketched it here. Liberal contractualism may also avoid some of the problems of the "universalist" theories Miller is concerned with—including the need to acknowledge the value of culture and shared practices in the right way.

Miller's dire expectations for Europe are too hasty, particularly given his claim that even national identities can be molded. Historically, allegiances have proven fluid, as has been the case in Ireland. And he holds it important to "purge the national identity of elements that are repugnant to a particular minority group" (1994: 156): "If we wish to be a self-determining nation, and if we share our territory with people who are like us in respects A, B and C but unlike us in respect D, it would be perverse to insist on D as a condition of membership. In real cases groups may choose the perverse option; but where a common national identity already exists, it can always potentially at least be extended to embrace all those who inhabit a geographical area" (ibid.: 143). Nevertheless, Miller would warn against a deliberate political strategy for fostering a European nation: "A national identity depends upon a *pre-reflective* sense that one belongs within a certain historic group, and it would be absurd to propose to the subjects of state X that, because things would go better for them if they adopt a shared national identity, they should therefore conjure one up" (1995: 143; emphasis added).

We can agree with Miller that the development of a European nation in his sense would be a bad idea. Nevertheless, we might look more favorably on Habermas's suggestion that "our task is less to reassure ourselves of our common origins in the European Middle Ages than to develop a new political self-confidence commensurate with the role of Europe in the world of the twenty-first century" (1992: 12). We might conclude, then, that Miller's pessimism about the prospects of redistributive arrangements in the European Union is unwarranted as of yet. This is not to say that time may not prove him right, for instance, due to the coordination problems discussed by Fritz Scharpf (1988, 1998).

The defeat of the Constitutional Treaty in two popular referenda suggests at the very least that the "Constitution for Europe" was too much, too early. And the political conflicts wrought by poorly integrated Muslim communities in Europe question the extent and strength of redistributive commitments even within member state borders. But the grounds Miller offers for long-term pessimism are insufficient. Instead, we may be well advised to heed Barroso's (2005) call to debate the values promoted by the common project that is the European Union. A European national identity may be beyond reach, but European patriotism may suffice.

REFERENCES

Barroso, José Manuel. 2005. "Building an Open Europe in Times of Change." Speech /05/546, at European Ideas Network, Lisbon, September 22. http://europa.eu.int/rapid/pressReleasesAction.do?reference=SPEECH/05/546&format=HTML&aged=0&language=en&guiLanguage=en
Barry, Brian. 1989. *Theories of Justice: A Treatise on Social Justice*. Vol. 1. Berkeley: University of California Press.
———. 1995. *Justice as Impartiality*. Oxford: Oxford University Press.
Bellah, Richard, et al. 1985. *Habits of the Heart: Individualism and Commitment in American Life*. Berkeley: University of California Press.
Buchanan, Allen E. 1989. "Assessing the Communitarian Critique of Liberalism." *Ethics* 99 (4): 852–82.

Caney, Simon. 1992. "Liberalism and Communitarianism: A Misconceived Debate." *Political Studies* 40:273–89.
Cohen, Joshua. 1986. Review of Walzer's *Spheres of Justice*. *Journal of Philosophy* 83:457–68.
Dworkin, Ronald. 1978. "Liberalism." In Stuart Hampshire, ed., *Public and Private Morality*. Cambridge: Cambridge University Press, 113–43.
Fishkin, James. 1986. "Theories of Justice and International Relations: The Limits of Liberal Theory." In Anthony Ellis, ed., *Ethics and International Relations*. Manchester: Manchester University Press, 1–11.
Follesdal, Andreas. 1996. "Minority Rights: A Liberal Contractualist Case." In Juha Raikka, ed., *Do We Need Minority Rights? Conceptual Issues*. The Hague/London/Boston: Kluwer Academic Publisher/Kluwer Law International, 59–83.
———. 2000. "The Future Soul of Europe: Nationalism or Just Patriotism?" *Journal of Peace Research* 37 (4): 503–18.
Fried, Charles. 1978. *Right and Wrong*. Cambridge: Harvard University Press.
Gauthier, David. 1986. *Morals by Agreement*. Oxford: Clarendon.
———. 1990. *Moral Dealing: Contract, Ethics, and Reason*. Ithaca: Cornell University Press.
Grimm, Dieter. 1995. "Does Europe Need a Constitution?" *European Law Journal* 1 (3): 282–302.
Gutmann, Amy. 1985. "Communitarian Critics of Liberalism." *Philosophy and Public Affairs* 14 (3): 308–22.
Habermas, Jürgen. 1992. "Citizenship and National Identity: Some Reflections on the Future of Europe." *Praxis International* 12 (1): 1–19.
———. 1996. *Between Facts and Norms*. Trans. William Rehg. Cambridge: MIT Press. Originally published as *Faktizität und Geltung* (1992).
———. 1997. "The European Nation-State: On the Past and Future of Sovereignty and Citizenship." In *The Inclusion of the Other: Studies in Political Theory*. Cambridge: MIT Press, 106–27.
Hampshire, Stuart. 1983. *Morality and Conflict*. Cambridge: Harvard University Press.
Klosko, George. 1994. "Political Obligation and the Natural Duties of Justice." *Philosophy and Public Affairs* 23 (3): 251–70.
Macedo, Stephen. 1990. *Liberal Virtues: Citizenship, Virtue, and Community in Liberal Constitutionalism*. Oxford: Clarendon.
MacIntyre, Alasdair. 1981. *After Virtue: A Study in Moral Theory*. Notre Dame: Notre Dame University Press.
Maritain, Jacques. 1949. *Human Rights: Comments and Interpretation*. London: Allan Wingate.
Miller, David. 1993. "In Defense of Nationality." *Journal of Applied Philosophy* 10 (1): 3–16.
———. 1994 "The Nation-State: A Modest Defence." In Chris Brown, ed., *Political Restructuring in Europe: Ethical Perspectives*. London: Routledge, 137–62.
———. 1995. *On Nationality*. Oxford: Oxford University Press.
———. 1997. "Nationality: Some Replies." *Journal of Applied Philosophy* 14 (1): 69–82.
Mulhall, Stephen. 1994. "Liberalism, Morality, and Rationality: MacIntyre, Rawls, and Cavell." In John Horton and Susan Mendus, eds., *After MacIntyre: Critical Perspectives on the Work of Alasdair MacIntyre*. Cambridge: Polity, 205–24.
Mulhall, Stephen, and Adam Swift. 1996. *Liberals and Communitarians*. Rev. ed. Oxford: Blackwell.
Murphy, Mark C. 1994. "Acceptance of Authority and the Duty to Comply with Just Institutions: A Comment on Waldron." *Philosophy and Public Affairs* 23 (3): 271–77.
O'Neill, Onora. 1975. *Acting on Principle: As Essay on Kantian Ethics*. New York: Columbia University Press.
Ostrom, Elinor. 1991. *Governing the Commons*. Cambridge: Cambridge University Press.
Rawls, John. 1971a. *A Theory of Justice*. Cambridge: Harvard University Press.
———. 1971b. "Two Concepts of Rules." In Samuel Gorowitz, ed., *Utilitarianism: John Stuart Mill, with Critical Essays*. Indianapolis, Ind.: Bobbs-Merrill, 175–94. Reprinted from *Philosophical Review* 64 (1955): 3–32.

———. 1978. "The Basic Structure ss Subject." In Alvin I. Goldman and Jaegwon Kim, eds., *Values and Morals: Essays in Honor of William Frankena, Charles Stevenson, and Richard B. Brandt.* Dordrecht: D. Reidel, 47–71.
———. 1993. *Political Liberalism.* New York: Columbia University Press.
Renan, Ernest. 1992. *Qu'est-ce qu'une nation?* Paris: Presses Pocket.
Scanlon, Thomas M. 1982. "Contractualism and Utilitarianism." In Amartya K. Sen and Bernard Williams, eds., *Utilitarianism and Beyond.* Cambridge: Cambridge University Press, 103–28.
———. 1998. *What We Owe to Each Other.* Cambridge: Harvard University Press.
Scharpf, Fritz W. 1988. "The Joint Decision Trap: Lessons from German Federalism and European Integration." *Public Administration* 66 (3): 239–78.
———. 1999. *Governing in Europe: Effective and Democratic?* Oxford: Oxford University Press.
Sen, Amartya K. 1967. "Isolation, Assurance, and the Social Rate of Discount." *Quarterly Journal of Economics* 81:112–24.
Tamir, Yael. 1993. *Liberal Nationalism.* Princeton: Princeton University Press.
Taylor, Charles. 1985. "The Nature and Scope of Distributive Justice." In *Philosophical Papers.* Cambridge: Cambridge University Press, 289–317.
Walzer, Michael. 1977. *Just and Unjust Wars: A Moral Argument, with Historical Illustrations.* New York: Basic.

13

Defining and Delivering Justice

The Work of the Ad Hoc International Criminal Tribunals

JAMES MEERNIK

> *It is one of the greatest objects of human wisdom to mitigate those evils which we are unable to remove.*
>
> Edmund Burke

Paradoxically, the twentieth century witnessed both the bloodiest and most horrific carnage in the history of humankind and the first global attempts to hold those responsible for the violence accountable. From these unjust wars came a dawning sense that a just peace was necessary to prevent their recurrence and right the scales of injustice. But whereas in the past the victors would apportion blame to other states to redress wrongs and balance the scales of power, now their leaders came to realize that neither governments as abstract entities nor the "people" in whose name they committed such atrocities should be held directly responsible. Rather, the politicians who chose to commit the crimes, the bureaucratic henchmen who facilitated their commission, and the soldiers or the concentration camp guards who brutally executed the orders would be held liable. At the Nuremberg and Tokyo tribunals that dispensed justice to the top officials in Germany and Japan after World War II, the international community displayed a heretofore unseen willingness to punish those who violated international humanitarian law

(Bass, 2000). But if the post–World War II tribunals and the subsequent ratification of international agreements on human rights, genocide, and other humanitarian issues seemed to presage a new willingness to prevent such crimes and punish individuals who acted contrary to international norms, unfortunately it took a great deal more violence before the world actually used international law to right massive wrongs.

The civil wars in the former Yugoslavia in 1991–99 and the 1994 Rwandan genocide provided the impetus for the creation of the first international criminal tribunals since World War II. The United Nations Security Council acted under its chapter VII powers to take measures to "maintain or restore international peace and security," to establish the International Criminal Tribunal for the former Yugoslavia in 1993 (ICTY) and the International Criminal Tribunal for Rwanda in 1994 (ICTR). Many viewed the tribunals as a poor substitute for an end to the conflicts in the former Yugoslavia and Rwanda, especially given their slow starts, inadequate financing, and the failure by the major powers to arrest the more notorious war criminals. But if at first their actions failed to meet expectations, the tribunals' mandates promised a great deal. The ICTY and ICTR are supposed to contribute to peace and reconciliation, redress violations of international humanitarian law, and deter future incidents. Peace, reconciliation, and deterrence may all be realized someday in these conflict-torn nations, and the tribunals will have done much to contribute to this effort. The tribunals can, through force of example, demonstrate to the peoples of the former Yugoslavia and Rwanda that the criminal masterminds will be punished and that they need not take justice into their own hands. They can set an example for other would-be tyrants that the world will ultimately not tolerate genocide and crimes against humanity.

Yet, it is really the aim of "doing justice" that is the hub and the heart around which peace, reconciliation, and deterrence will evolve and mature. After all, we are often told, "If you want peace, work for justice" (Paul VI, 1972). Everyone wants justice, for no one favors injustice, but its meaning turns on where one sits in the Trial Chambers. Justice for the victim in the witness chair; justice for the accused in the dock; and justice for those who sit in the public gallery looking in will be based on different experiences and will demand different outcomes. I will argue that the ICTY and the ICTR were established and have been organized to achieve both redress, sometimes conceived of as retribution, and procedural fairness. Justice for the victims requires and justice for the international community desires an accounting for the violations of humanitarian law. These immoral and illegal acts are to be publicized and punished to acknowledge the victims' suffering and restore the moral equilibrium in their communities. Truth telling and retribution are also needed to proclaim the international community's intolerance for violations of its laws, especially in light of the previous reluctance to stop them. Victims seek punishment as redress for the impunity that *their* tormentors once enjoyed, while the international community seeks to demonstrate that the present and future war criminals will not enjoy impunity.

Nonetheless, the international community, through its agents the tribunals, cannot simply pass judgment. As Robert Jackson, the chief U.S. prosecutor at the Nuremberg Tribunal once said, "The world yields no respect to courts that are merely organized to convict" (Ellis, 1997: 520). Well aware of the charges of "victors' justice" that were leveled against the World War II tribunals, and even against the ICTY and ICTR, the United Nations and the tribunals themselves have sought to grant to the accused the best possible protections for their rights recognized in the world today. Anything less, it is feared, will provide ammunition to those who question the fairness of the tribunals, and may taint the judgment of history on their work. But I will argue that fairness and justice for the accused, while critical to the tribunals' operations and reputation, have sometimes been superseded because of the overriding demand to provide justice for the victims.

My purpose is thus to evaluate the work to date of the ICTY and ICTR toward achieving justice as redress for the victims primarily and the international community secondarily, and justice as procedural fairness for the accused. (I do not analyze the work of the International Criminal Court since, at the time of writing, it had issued no decisions.) More specifically, I analyze how the interests of victims, the accused, and the international community have influenced the manner in which the tribunals have sought to realize these goals. There is certainly an enormous and growing record of the tribunals' decisions, verdicts, and sentences that has not yet received systematic analysis. Indeed, with the exception of many legal analyses, there have been few studies of the work of the tribunals by social scientists, perhaps because many dismiss the tribunals for the same reasons diplomats and human rights groups questioned their efficacy when they were first created. Are the tribunals superfluous to international relations and its study? Do they have an independent meaning and existence outside the balance of power that would justify serious scholarly analysis? Are the tribunals unimportant if their creation was the result of a failure to take stronger action to address violations of international humanitarian law? In fact, I would argue that precisely because the international community was persuaded by moral and legal interests, not compelled by geopolitics, to create these institutions, the tribunals' decisions have valid meaning as an expression of the international community's judgment. To that extent their pronouncements carry substantial political and moral weight, we will learn much about the meaning of justice today.

Background

The International Criminal Tribunal for the former Yugoslavia was created in May of 1993 by the United Nations Security Council. Acting on the recommendation of a Commission of Experts, which had investigated the claims of violations of international humanitarian laws in Croatia and Bosnia, the Security Council established the ICTY under its chapter VII powers to keep the peace. After the 1994 genocide and the civil war in Rwanda were over, a special rapporteur to the United Nations Commission on Human Rights, as well as an independent Commission of Experts, found evidence that the atrocities were planned and systematic (Carroll, 2000: 170). Once again, the Security Council determined that the Rwandan situation constituted a threat to international peace and security and so authorized the creation of the International War Crimes Tribunal for Rwanda in November of 1994.

The ICTY is headquartered in The Hague, Netherlands. The ICTY's mandate provides it with the power to try cases involving: (1) grave breaches of the Geneva Conventions regarding the treatment of soldiers and civilians in wartime,[1] (2) genocide,[2] (3) crimes against human-

---

1. According to the Statute of the International Tribunal for Yugoslavia, article 2, grave breaches include "willful killing, torture, causing great suffering and serious injury, extensive destruction of property, not justified by military necessity, compelling prisoners of war and civilians to serve in enemy forces, depriving a POW or civilian the right to a fair trial, unlawful deportation, and taking civilians as hostages" (www.un.org/icty/).
2. According to article 4 of the ICTY Charter, "Genocide means any of the following acts

ity,[3] and (4) violations of the laws and customs of war.[4] The tribunal is charged with investigating all such violations that have occurred in the wars in the former Yugoslavia since 1991, including the most recent action in Kosovo. The ICTR is located in Arusha, Tanzania, and is authorized to prosecute persons accused of genocide, crimes against humanity, and violations of article 3 common to the Geneva Conventions (on war crimes) and of Additional Protocol II,[5] which occurred in Rwanda in 1994. Each tribunal is divided into a Registry, Prosecutor's Office, and Trial Chambers. The Registry performs administrative duties for the tribunal, such as language translation, witness protection, and provision of defense counsel. There are three Trial Chambers, which consist of three-judge panels that hear cases. The United Nations now also provides for a number of temporary, or *ad litem*, judges who will help the tribunals with the backlog of cases. The U.N. General Assembly elects the judges to four-year terms from a list submitted by the Security Council. Seven

---

committed with intent to destroy, in whole or in part, a national, ethnical, racial or religious group, as such: (a) killing members of the group; (b) causing serious bodily or mental harm to members of the group; (c) deliberately inflicting on the group conditions of life calculated to bring about its physical destruction in whole or in part; (d) imposing measures intended to prevent births within the group; (e) forcibly transferring children of the group to another group.

The following acts shall be punishable: (a) genocide; (b) conspiracy to commit genocide; (c) direct and public incitement to commit genocide; (d) attempt to commit genocide; (e) complicity in genocide." (www.un.org/icty/)

3. Crimes against humanity are defined as "murder, extermination, enslavement, deportation, imprisonment, torture, rape, persecutions on political, racial and religious grounds and other inhumane acts" (Statute of the International Tribunal for Yugoslavia, article 5, www.un.org/icty/). The ICTY mandate empowers it to prosecute those responsible for such crimes "when committed in armed conflict, whether international or internal in character and directed against any civilian population" (www.un.org/icty/).

4. In the case of the ICTY, such violations include, but are not limited to, "employment of poisonous weapons or other weapons calculated to cause unnecessary suffering; wanton destruction of cities, towns and villages, or devastation not justified by military necessity; attack, or bombardment, by whatever means, of undefended towns, villages, dwellings, or buildings; seizure of, destruction or willful damage done to institutions dedicated to religion, charity and education, the arts and sciences, historic monuments and works of art and science; plunder of public or private property" (Statute of the International Tribunal for Yugoslavia, article 3, www.un.org/icty/).

5. The language in the ICTR statute on crimes against humanity and genocide is largely identical to the ICTY's. Regarding article 3 violations, the ICTR statute reads: "Article 3 violations shall include, but shall not be limited to: a) Violence to life, health and physical or mental well-being of persons, in particular murder as well as cruel treatment such as torture, mutilation or any form of corporal punishment; b) Collective punishments; c) Taking of hostages; d) Acts of terrorism; e) Outrages upon personal dignity, in particular humiliating and degrading treatment, rape, enforced prostitution and any form of indecent assault; f) Pillage; g) The passing of sentences and the carrying out of executions without previous judgment pronounced by a regularly constituted court, affording all the judicial guarantees which are recognised as indispensable by civilised peoples; h) Threats to commit any of the foregoing acts."

judges sit on one Appeals Chamber that hears appeals from both tribunals. The tribunals have developed and continually revised their "Rules of Procedure and Evidence," which are derived from both common law and civil law criminal systems (http://www.un.org/icty/basic/rpe/IT32_rev21con.htm).

There is now a chief prosecutor for each of the tribunals. The prosecutors investigate allegations of war crimes and other violations of international law brought to their offices by staff, victims, the media, human rights organizations, and other sources. If the prosecutor decides there is a sufficient basis to establish the guilt of the accused, he or she delivers an indictment to the Trial Chambers, where a judge determines if the prosecutor has established a prima facie case. If the judge confirms the indictment, it is either made public or, sometimes, kept sealed to facilitate capture of the suspect. The decision regarding who to indict, when, and for what alleged crimes is to be the responsibility of the prosecutor, who is not supposed to "seek or receive instructions from any Government or from any other source" (http://www.un.org/icty/basic/statut/stat2000.htm#16). Once the accused has been taken into custody, he or she is entitled to legal counsel, which may be paid for by the tribunal if the defendant cannot afford to do so, and to all reasonable claims for assistance in developing his or her case. The Trial Chambers decide by majority vote questions of guilt and punishment. Guilt must be proved beyond a reasonable doubt, and verdicts can be appealed. The most severe punishment the tribunals are authorized to enforce is life in prison. Those found guilty serve their prison sentences in states that contract with the tribunals. The tribunals have primacy over national courts and can request that they refer cases.

The Tribunals' Mandates

The origins and outcomes of the wars in the former Yugoslavia and Rwanda may differ in some respects, but the aims the United Nations conceived for the two tribunals run parallel. They are each charged with promoting peace and reconciliation, deterring the commission of future war crimes, and furthering justice. Before assessing the quality and quantity of justice meted out by the ICTY and ICTR, we should briefly consider these other responsibilities. Peace, reconciliation, and deterrence are vital and farsighted aims. They promise much to the victims and the devastated societies that felt abandoned by previous inaction. For those outside the war zones, the tribunals represent an embodiment of hopes for the future. And with the passage of time we will be able to tell if these institutions are providing a beacon of light that people and nations can move toward to end the cycles of violence. For now, however, we must be cautious when evaluating the tribunals' role in peace and deterrence in light of developments in the former Yugoslavia, Rwanda, and the myriad of other nations around the world where war crimes and massive violations of human rights are taking placing. Their justice can encourage, not compel, people to abide by standards of decency.

The aim of furthering peace and reconciliation is an integral element of each tribunal's mission. By apportioning blame and punishment the tribunals can alleviate the need victims may feel to seek revenge against their tormentors today and their tormentors' ethnic brethren tomorrow. The very creation of the tribunals does send a signal to victims that their suffering has been recognized, which is often a critical first step in furthering reconciliation. Akhavan writes, "the international community's policy of using the ICTY as an instrument to eliminate indicted leaders has contributed to post conflict peace building by creating incentives for political parties to behave in a more conciliatory manner," and that the ICTR "has palpably improved the post conflict situation by impeding resurrection of the former government and enhancing the political attraction of criminal justice as an alternative to Hutu violence" (2001: 16, 26).

But as the extent of the tribunals' control over the behavior of victims and perpetrators is limited, so too is their responsibility for peace and reconciliation. Obviously the ICTY and ICTR cannot provide the security and the political solutions that are required to address the root causes of these conflicts and prevent their recurrence. They cannot change peoples' hearts and minds. For the tribunals to succeed in making their contribution to peace and reconciliation within the former Yugoslavia and Rwanda, the peoples who are seeking to come to terms with their suffering must see some connection between their lives and the tribunals' work. They should view the tribunals not as alien institutions designed and manipulated by the major powers, but as responsible partners in a common enterprise. The tribunals can sponsor outreach programs to educate people in the former Yugoslavia and Rwanda about their work.

They can assist governments in the conflict regions in identifying and adjudicating cases of human rights violations. They can provide a public forum in which the personal stories and the historical record are established for future generations. Ultimately, however, the tribunals' power to change the political dynamics in these strife-torn societies is only as great as their ability to provide a justice that is seen and felt by the peoples whose lives they seek to make better.

The United Nations Security Council also established the ICTY and ICTR to advance deterrence by demonstrating the international community's intolerance for gross abuses of human rights. Certainly the tribunals play a critical role in contributing to specific deterrence—preventing those individuals suspected or found guilty of war crimes from committing future violations. This is especially imperative in the case of those who organized and ordered violations of international humanitarian law. General deterrence, the prevention of criminal acts by other potential offenders, is the more long-term, challenging goal. The symbolism inherent in the very creation of the tribunals was intended to advertise to would-be war criminals throughout the globe that there would be no impunity for their actions. The sentences imposed upon the guilty by the ICTY and ICTR are supposed to embody this intolerance in a more tangible manner.

Yet there are limits to what the tribunals can accomplish. Their creation and their judgments may be necessary for deterrence; still, they are not sufficient for its realization. General deterrence requires at a minimum that the penalty be timely and certain so that would-be offenders perceive a linkage between crime and punishment. Some have criticized the ICTY and ICTR for their slowness, especially in trying high-level political and military leaders. Even if justice is swift and certain, however, it may not have the desired impact on high-ranking politicians and generals who see themselves as above the law, or on low-level soldiers and camp guards who look to their leaders, not the international community, to tell them what the law is. Many of the people who are the targets of this message—the political leaders, the paramilitaries, and the rebels who are fighting in remote mountains and jungles the world over—probably have little awareness, let alone appreciation, of the tribunals' actions. Even those who might have been expected to be cognizant of the tribunals' work and apprehend the consequences of their actions nevertheless have committed violations of international humanitarian law. Milosevic's actions in Kosovo and Rwanda's military occupation in the eastern Congo involved the very kinds of atrocities the international community was seeking to deter. As well, ICTY judges have stated in their opinions that while general deterrence of future war criminals is a worthy aspiration, individual sentences must be based on individual crimes, not overarching goals.[6] Limiting the expectation of impunity through the imposition of prison terms on those who violate international law is a necessary, not a sufficient, condition for general deterrence. The justice meted out by the tribunals is a proclamation that must filter into laws and behaviors over time. Deterrence, like peace and reconciliation, depends ultimately on how the ICTY and ICTR fulfill their core mission—to do justice.

Therefore, I hold that to evaluate the work of the tribunals we must begin by focusing on their efforts to achieve justice. The provision of justice is the necessary condition for peace and deterrence that we must first assess, after which and with the passage of time we can evaluate the tribunals' contributions toward these other goals. As justice is a concept and an ideal that has been debated and defined repeatedly over the millennia, it should come as no surprise that its meaning in the context of international criminal tribunals is imprecise and subject to various interpretations. Each individual who works within and each individual who comes to the tribunals, as defendant, victim, witness, or spectator, holds a unique conception of what these trials are designed to achieve. My aim is to analyze two conceptions of justice that inform the work of the tribunals and, in particular, the decisions of the judges. First, there is justice as redress or retribution, which I will argue is sought by both victims and the international community. The outcomes of the tribunals' trials—the verdicts and punishment—are valued the most by these audiences. Second, there is justice as procedural fairness, concerned primarily with the methods by which these outcomes are realized. Procedural fairness is valued most highly by the accused, as well as many human rights and

---

6. "As to general deterrence, in line with the view of the Appeals Chamber, it is not to be accorded undue prominence in the assessment of an overall sentence to be imposed. The reason is that a sentence should in principle be imposed on an offender for *his* culpable conduct—it may be unfair to impose a sentence on an offender greater than is appropriate to that conduct solely in the *belief* that it will deter others" (*Prosecutor v. Dragoljub Kunarac et. al.*, IT-96-23 and IT-96-23/1, p. 840, February 22 2001, www.un.org/icty/foca/trialc2/judgement/index.htm).

lawyers groups. As well, each form of justice is critical to the tribunals themselves.

We should expect that justice as redress and retribution is the most important value guiding the work of the tribunals. Redress is essentially a correction or repair made to individuals and communities that have been victimized. As stated by the ICTY, the goal of redress or retribution is "that punishment shall be proportionate to the crime's gravity and the moral guilt of the perpetrator" (*Prosecutor v. Drazen Erdemovic*, IT-96-22, p. 60, November 29, 1996, http://www.un.org/icty/erdemovic/trialc/judgement/erd-tsj961129e.htm). It represents an acknowledgement and an attempt to rectify wrongs and should be taken more figuratively than literally, for it does not imply that punishment be equivalent in pain and suffering to the crime. Rather, redress, via the tribunals' judgments, represents an acknowledgement of the harm done to the victims and a restoration of the moral equilibrium in their communities through a punishment proportionate, if only symbolically, to the disruption caused. The judges have noted that redress or retribution "is not to be understood as fulfilling a desire for revenge but as duly expressing the outrage of the international community at these crimes" (*Prosecutor v. Zlatko Alexsovski*, IT-95-14/1, March 24, 2000, http://www.un.org/icty/aleksovski/appeal/judgement/index.htm). As well, statements made by members of the Security Council and the language of the tribunals' statutes are replete with references regarding redress and addressing the needs of those who have suffered.[7]

Nonetheless, the tribunals and the international community recognize that the manner in which justice is dispensed is critical to their legitimacy and the verdict of history on their endeavors. If the tribunals' judgments are perceived as biased or rushed, they may ultimately harm the prospects for peace in the Balkans and central Africa, not to mention the cause of international criminal law. The ICTY and ICTR strive to protect the rights of the accused to the greatest extent possible. Yet, when value trade-offs between justice as redress and justice as procedural fairness arise, the ethical and legal imperative to redress tends to be more compelling. Such trade-offs are infrequent and do not occur without significant debate within and without the tribunals. They simply reflect the im-

---

7. See the provisional minutes of the 3217th session (S/Trans. 3217, May 25, 1993), including declarations by Hungary (p. 21), Morocco (p. 17), and New Zealand (p. 22).

possibility of designing an institution that satisfies the demands of all its constituents and can provide perfect justice for all. The rights and suffering of the victims are, ultimately, the impetus for these tribunals.

Providing Justice for the Victims

The need for retribution and the desire to establish the truth are at the forefront of the victims' interests in receiving justice. Justice for the victims of the former Yugoslavia and Rwanda is furthered initially through the opportunity to tell their stories in testimony. Although some who recount their ordeals before the tribunals are reluctant witnesses, many are eager to tell their stories. For some it is a personally cathartic experience; for others it may honor those who were lost; and for still others it is a means of establishing the historical record for future generations. Although the act of testifying can be physically and emotionally harmful to the victims,[8] some research indicates that injured communities can be helped through such public acknowledgement (Hayner, 1994). Telling the truth about the past may prevent the atrocities of tomorrow. This need to allow victims to tell their stories is so strong that the tribunals have even made it possible for witnesses to testify when the accused has not yet been arrested. Rule 61 of the ICTY's "Rules of Procedure and Evidence" (http://www.un.org/icty/basic/rpe/IT32_rev22.htm#61)[9] enables the Prosecutor's Office to present evidence to a Trial Chamber when the accused is not in custody. Rule 61 hearings are designed to facilitate an international arrest warrant, but the judges have also noted that they serve an important purpose because they give victims "the opportunity to be heard in a public hearing and to become part of history" (*Prosecutor v. Dragan Nikolic*, IT-94-2-R61, http://www.un.org/icty/nikolic/trialc/judgement/index.htm). Since the prosecutor may present any exhibits and call any witnesses he or she wishes in these proceedings, some critics have charged that these are trials in absentia, which are not allowed under the tribunals' mandate (Johnson, 1998; Thieroff and Amley, 1998). In this instance, where there appears to be a conflict between the provision of justice to the victims and the rights of the accused, the tribunals have

---

8. In fact, the author saw one witness collapse on the stand at the ICTR in July 2001.

9. I shall rely on the numbering of the "Rules of Procedure and Evidence" of the ICTY. The text is largely the same.

decided in favor of giving the victims their day in court. There seems to be an unstated assumption that these trials will confirm the genuineness of the horrors the world witnessed and the victims lived through.

Punishment, however, is the logical conclusion of redress for the victims. As nearly every defendant brought to the tribunals has pled or been found guilty, punishment, not just verdicts, has been of paramount importance to both victims and observers. It represents a heavily weighted symbolic act by the tribunals, the agents of the international community, to provide a proportionate condemnation, commensurate in some manner to the gravity of the acts of the guilty party. For the victims, it helps restore some semblance of moral order and demonstrates that war criminals cannot act with impunity. Once the judges have established that the accused is guilty beyond a reasonable doubt, they must determine these "just desserts." They are not allowed to fine the guilty, although the judges may order the party to return property to victims that was unlawfully seized, or impose the death penalty. The tribunal statutes and the "Rules of Procedure and Evidence," however, provide only minimal guidance to the judges to assist them in the determination of punishment. Their statutes provide that the judges shall consider "the general practice regarding prison sentences in the courts of the former Yugoslavia" (and Rwanda) and "such factors as the gravity of the offence and the individual circumstances of the convicted person" (http://www.un.org/icty/basic/statut/stat2000.htm#24). Their "Rules of Procedure and Evidence" also allow the judges to consider aggravating factors and mitigating factors, such as cooperation with the prosecutor, in the determination of punishment.

While there are still conflicting opinions within and between the two tribunals over which criteria are appropriate, we have begun to see the emergence of sentencing "norms." The two norms I will examine here are the gravity of the offense and the level of responsibility held by the accused over the commission of these crimes. Both of these norms are intended to provide justice as redress for the victims, but they also reflect the interests of the international community in concentrating energy and attention on the worst of the crimes and those most responsible because these crimes and criminals have received the most attention. However, while a focus by the tribunals on those responsible for the worst and widest violations provides a measure of justice to the victims—it does not always guarantee that the interests of the victims in the pursuit of justice are realized. Below I describe the manner in which the tribunals have attempted to mete out retributive justice to those most responsible for the worst international crimes. I later comment on the degree to which this focus achieves the type of justice sought by the victims of these conflicts.

First, punishment of the guilty in some manner proportionate to the gravity of their offenses is fundamental in providing justice to victims. The ICTY has stated: "By far the most important consideration, which may be regarded as the litmus test for the appropriate sentence, is the gravity of the offence" (*Prosecutor vs. Zejnil Delalic*, IT-96-21, p. 1225, November 16, 1998, http://www.un.org/icty/celebici/trialc2/judgement/index.htm). But in wars where the death tolls reached into the hundreds of thousands and where individuals committed acts of unbelievable savagery, the ordinary sentences available to the tribunals may not provide the morally requisite justice victims demand. The Rwandan government cast the lone "no" vote against the creation of the ICTR in the U.N. Security Council in part because it would not be able to pass death sentences (while Rwandan courts would).[10] How, then, do the tribunals differentiate among the individuals they sentence to make the punishment fit the crime? How is it even possible to classify crimes in this morally and legally dense milieu? Danner (2001) makes the compelling argument that genocide especially, and to a lesser degree persecution, as a crime against humanity, should be treated differently than war crimes and other crimes against humanity because of the bias element in these crimes. Genocide, in particular, is characterized by a special intent to destroy in whole or in part a group of people. Danner argues that because of this bias and because genocidal acts and certain crimes against humanity target groups of people, and thus affect those beyond the immediate victims, they are deserving of more severe sanction than "ordinary" war crimes and other crimes against humanity. She points out, too, that in national courts "bias crimes" against people because of race, religion, and other factors are punished more severely.

Others, especially ICTY judges, have argued that individual punishment must be based upon the specific act(s) committed, and that murder

---

10. The Security Council took note of Rwanda's concerns, but concluded that the global trend toward eliminating capital punishment would not permit its resurrection in this instance.

is still murder regardless of which category of crimes it falls under. The ICTY judges seem to fear that under a scheme such as that proposed by Danner, two individuals who commit the same physical actions would be given different punishments because they are charged under different articles of the tribunal charter. There is a natural concern that this might result in unequal treatment of defendants and perhaps violate their rights to a fair trial. In an Appeals Chamber decision, the majority concluded that the sentence in a given case should be "fixed by reference to the circumstances of the case," and not the broader type of crime committed (e.g., war crimes versus crimes against humanity) (*Prosecutor v. Dusko Tadic*, IT-94-1, p. 32, January 26, 2000, http://www.un.org/icty/tadic/appeal/judgement/index_2.htm). Subsequent Appeals Chamber decisions have followed this precedent in cases from the ICTY, and judges have argued that there should not be a ranking system to distinguish among the four types of general crimes that fall under the ICTY jurisdiction (*Prosecutor v. Anto Furundzija II*, IT-95-17/1, p. 217, July 21, 2000, http://www.un.org/icty/furundzija/appeal/judgement/index.htm). But while ICTY judges have apparently been cognizant of this dilemma in theory, in actual practice their sentences do reflect a relative ranking of general classes of crimes. As well, ICTR judges have often argued that the crime of genocide is a special category of offenses that demands the most severe sanctions and have created their own hierarchy of crimes (*Prosecutor v. Jean Kambanda*, ICTR 97-23-S, September 4, 1998, http://www.ictr.org/).

At the time of writing (December 2005), ICTY Trial Chamber judges have issued verdicts and meted out punishment in fifty-nine cases (only five individuals have been found innocent of all charges), some of which are still on appeal. In some cases the Appeals Chamber has reduced sentences and even rendered not guilty verdicts in other cases. When we consider each individual's sentence in light of the general category of crimes for which he or she was convicted (irrespective of what the Appeals Chamber may have ruled or yet rule), we find that the judges do impose longer sentences on those who are found guilty of committing acts of genocide and crimes against humanity than on those convicted of "ordinary" war crimes. There have been two individuals convicted of committing genocide by the ICTY. General Radislav Krstic, second in command of the Bosnian Serb army that committed the Srebrenica massacre, was sentenced to forty-six years in prison by the Trial Chamber—one of the longest sentences yet handed out by the ICTY (one individual has been sentenced to life in prison, although given Krstic's age his sentence will, in all likelihood, ensure his incarceration for the remainder of his life). The second individual convicted of genocide, Vidoje Blagojevic, was given only eighteen years imprisonment for his lesser role in the Srebrenica genocide. (Both Krstic and Blagojevic were also found guilty of other crimes as well.) If we consider crimes against humanity as the second "worst" category of international criminal offense of which the accused may be found guilty, we find that forty-four individuals have been convicted of this type of crime (they may also have been convicted of war crimes, but not genocide). They have been sentenced on average to approximately fifteen years in prison. The eight individuals who have been convicted of war crimes (and not genocide or crimes against humanity), have received an average sentence of ten years in prison. Thus, if we assume that there is some sort of hierarchy among the general classes of crimes, we do find that those who committed what are arguably the most terrible types of crimes are given progressively longer sentences, despite what the Appeals Chamber may have said in theory about such rankings.

The ICTR judges have been more willing to openly consider the category of the offense in their sentences. The judges often refer to genocide as the "crime of crimes" and have generally punished those guilty of this crime with life imprisonment. If we examine the sentences the ICTR judges have handed down, we see that in most cases to date, where an individual has been convicted on a charge of genocide (including incitement, complicity, and conspiracy to commit genocide) that person is sentenced to life in prison. Individuals who have been found guilty of various counts of crimes against humanity have received more variable sentences, ranging from six years to life imprisonment. It is more difficult, however, to make comparisons within the ICTR, given that the life sentences it imposes make calculating average prison terms problematical. In general, it is evident that those categories of offenses that involve bias or persecution—genocide and crimes against humanity—are treated as more harmful and far-reaching in their consequences than crimes of war. Given that justice for the victims involves communities of people, we would expect that crimes that specifically target these groups would be more severely punished, and this has generally been the case in practice.

The United Nations, and especially the states most responsible for the creation of the tribunals, has been especially interested in the prosecution of the most high-ranking suspects. It is reasonable to assume that when the Security Council created the two tribunals it did not envision that these institutions would be responsible for prosecuting and judging the actions of every suspected war criminal in the former Yugoslavia and Rwanda. Most of the lower-level perpetrators could be tried in those nations. Instead, the time, expense, and energy required to administer institutions of this magnitude and complexity could best be utilized in pursuit of those who gave the orders. Initially, the ICTY did try fairly low-ranking individuals before more high-ranking suspects were brought to its detention unit. Now it is deliberately concentrating on adjudicating cases involving the political and military leaders at the highest echelons of power. In the ICTY's annual report to the United Nations, the president stated: "The Prosecutor's investigative strategy continues to be to prosecute the leaders of the conflict. Lower-level perpetrators will continue to be subject to local/domestic prosecutions and there may, in the future, be a truth and reconciliation process of some kind. However, provided sufficient evidence exists, the Prosecutor continues to believe that a lasting and stable peace in the Balkans will not be achieved unless the Tribunal brings to justice those individuals who were responsible, as leaders on whatever side of the conflict, for the commission of crimes falling within the Tribunal's jurisdiction" (Eighth Annual Report of the International Criminal Tribunal for the Former Yugoslavia, IV, c. 1., p. 189, http://www.un.org/icty/rappannu-e/2001/index.htm).

The ICTR, after its own slow start, now has many of the most notorious figures in the Rwandan genocide in its custody, including the suspected military mastermind of the atrocities, Colonel Theoneste Bagosora, and many of the cabinet officials of the former Hutu power government. Concentrating its resources on the prosecution of these leaders certainly seems to be sound strategy. It helps establish the legitimacy of the tribunals for the peoples of the former Yugoslavia and Rwanda as well as the international community. The trials of those who gave the orders to commit genocidal acts and the like create a more comprehensive and enlightening history of these events that can assist victims in reconstructing their lives and communities. It helps embed the principle that individuals were responsible for those atrocities, not peoples, thereby helping to end the cycle of violence.

Neither the tribunals' statutes nor their "Rules of Procedure and Evidence," however, make explicit mention of the need to more aggressively prosecute or punish those whose decisions led to the violations of international humanitarian law. Yet there is substantial evidence, especially with regard to punishment, that those at the top of the criminal hierarchy receive the longest sentences. In my examination of the cases in both the ICTY and ICTR, I differentiated among low-level war criminals, principally ordinary soldiers and prison camp guards; mid-level officials, such as prison camp commanders, military officers below the rank of colonel, and political figures below cabinet-level status; and high-level officials, including military officials at or above the rank of colonel, and political officials of cabinet-level status or higher. At the ICTY I find that the lowest-ranking individuals found guilty (twenty-one individuals) are sentenced on average to thirteen years in prison, mid-level officials (twenty-six individuals) to fifteen years, and political/military leaders (seven individuals) to twenty-three years in prison on average. At the ICTR, several high-ranking figures have now been sentenced, including former prime minister Jean Kambanda, former minister of finance Emmanuel Ndindabahizi, and former Interahamwe vice president, George Rutuganda. Their sentences have all been life sentences, with one exception. A number of more low-level perpetrators have also been found guilty by a Trial Chamber, such as Georges Ruggiu, a Belgian national, and Hassan Ngeze, both of whom were found guilty of inciting others to commit genocidal acts or other crimes through their positions in the media. The sentences of low-level perpetrators have ranged from seven years for some charges to life in three cases. Those whose level of responsibility lies somewhere in between have received sentences ranging from ten years to life imprisonment. Thus, the ICTY appears to make a sharp distinction between low- and mid-level war criminals and high-ranking officials, while at the ICTR the sentences exhibit much more variation across levels of power. However, those found most responsible for the Rwandan genocide have almost all received life sentences.

The tribunals' sentencing of those found guilty would suggest that, in accordance with their responsibility to provide redress as well as their interest in making the punishment proportionate to the nature of the crime, the severest condemnation is reserved for those who wielded the most influence. Yet, while we might find agreement that prime ministers and generals found guilty of atrocities should receive the lengthiest prison sentences, would we necessarily find that the victims would all agree that this is sufficient justice? The international community may be more interested in punishing those most responsible because their crimes have done the most violence to international law and because of the need to deter other leaders. Victims may, in many respects, be more concerned with the prosecution of those individuals who physically attacked or destroyed their families.[11] Village-level justice may look quite different from international justice, which may seem distant and aloof to the lives of many people in the former Yugoslavia and especially Rwanda. Punishment of the ringleaders may provide victims with a moral victory and further national justice, but if actual perpetrators continue to live in their communities, it will remain an incomplete justice. As well, as long as the tribunals' justice is physically remote (distant from the scene of the crimes and often not accessible to the victims through the media) and politically remote (all those involved in the proceedings are mostly indirectly linked to the actual crimes), the victims will continue to remain emotionally remote from this work and thus find difficult the acts of reconciliation the tribunals are ultimately supposed to foster. In some respects, punishment of the highest-ranking offenders of international law is a first step—critical to the tribunals' legitimacy in the eyes of all—toward the provision of redress to those who have suffered. It fixes guilt on those most responsible and provides a more informative historical record of the crimes committed. The evidence brought to bear in these trials can be used in national courts, where most of the lower-ranking individuals will be tried. Still, justice will not be complete for the victims until those who carried out the orders of the generals and politicians are punished as well. Yet it must be admitted that such comprehensive jus-

---

11. The first president of the ICTY, Antonio Cassese, conceded this in the 1994 Annual Report to the United Nations, in which he stated: "To these victims it may matter less that those in command also be called to account for any responsibility they might bear for instigating or condoning the perpetration of those crimes. 'Command responsibility' is primarily an exigency of the world community, which intends to see to it that 'system criminality'—that is, the obnoxious involvement of policymakers in the widespread and systematic disregard of human rights—be punished too, so that the root causes of international criminality can be eliminated in the country concerned" (http://www.un.org/icty/rappannu-e/1994/index.htm, 51).

tice may well take many years, as the number of alleged low-level perpetrators will often be quite high, thereby rendering other forms of justice, such as truth commissions and community justice (e.g., the Gacaca Courts in Rwanda) more practical as alternatives.

Redress to the victims of war crimes has been perhaps the most fundamental impulse affecting the work of the two tribunals. For better or worse, many of those who follow the tribunals' decisions look upon them as the definitive judgment on the wars in the former Yugoslavia and Rwanda. But can the justice the international community is capable of providing match the expectations and needs of the victims? In a survey conducted in Zagreb and Sarajevo during the second half of the 1990s, researcher Sanja Kutnjak Ivkovic sought respondents' views of the ICTY. Almost all had heard of the ICTY; the vast majority of those surveyed thought the tribunal would conduct its trials justly and make fair decisions, but almost all respondents felt that those found guilty should be sentenced to death or life imprisonment (2001: 310, 323). Some would argue that no judicial solution can ever restore their lives or their communities. The response of one Sarajevo resident to the survey is revealing: "The International Tribunal in the Hague is following the laws and facts, and any punishment to be determined is too lenient for their crime; only we, the people who witnessed the terror, lost our closest and dearest ones, watched and listened to descriptions of the crimes inconceivable to the human spirit, know that there is no adequate punishment for such crimes" (ibid.: 321).

Given the tribunals' inability to impose the death penalty and the perceived "leniency" toward those who are not sentenced to life, the tribunals may not be capable of granting the degree of redress victims seek. This is not surprising, as we might expect that victims' pain can never truly be compensated, but it does point to a fundamental paradox in the mission of the tribunals. If the impetus for justice arises from the harms suffered by the victims, but the standards of justice are imposed by the international community, divisions between the two groups will occur. These divisions make the realization of the tribunals' other objectives—peace and reconciliation—all the more difficult if victims, as well as the accused, fail to understand the reasons behind the tribunals' actions. Not surprisingly, both tribunals expend considerable energy trying to develop a greater appreciation among all affected groups about the need for independent judiciaries, defendants' rights, and international law. In many ways, these efforts at outreach are among the most critical of the tasks facing the tribunals but, as one might expect, quite secondary to the primary mission of dispensing justice.

Providing Justice for the Accused

The international criminal tribunals are expected to administer justice in a manner corresponding to the highest standards in national criminal justice systems. Antonio Cassese, former president of the ICTY, stated that "we believe that we have been able to distill as well as harmoniously amalgamate the most advanced aspects of the various legal systems, within the general framework of the principle of a 'fair trial'" (ICTY Annual Yearbook, 1994: 141). This is an especially important concern given that some view the international tribunals as a form of victor's justice. Since the ICTY and the ICTR were created and are sustained by the major powers through the United Nations, a perception may exist that they are beholden in some manner to these powers and their desire to see blame and punishment allocated. To avoid the perception that they "are merely organized to convict," the tribunals have been at pains to demonstrate their impartiality. According to former chief prosecutor Richard Goldstone, "At all times, in the Office of the Prosecutor, the primary goal was not to achieve convictions, but rather to *ensure that those indicted would enjoy fair processes and procedure*" (2000: 123; emphasis added).

The United Nations Security Council borrowed heavily from the International Covenant on Civil and Political Rights when it drafted the language on the rights of the accused. These are:

1. All persons shall be equal before the International Tribunal.
2. In the determination of charges against him, the accused shall be entitled to a fair and public hearing, subject to article 22 of the Statute.
3. The accused shall be presumed innocent until proved guilty according to the provisions of the present Statute.
4. In the determination of any charge against the accused pursuant to the present Statute, the accused shall be entitled to the following minimum guarantees, in full equality:

a. to be informed promptly and in detail in a language which he understands of the nature and cause of the charge against him;
b. to have adequate time and facilities for the preparation of his defence and to communicate with counsel of his own choosing;
c. to be tried without undue delay;
d. to be tried in his presence, and to defend himself in person or through legal assistance of his own choosing; to be informed, if he does not have legal assistance, of this right; and to have legal assistance assigned to him, in any case where the interests of justice so require, and without payment by him in any such case if he does not have sufficient means to pay for it;
e. to examine, or have examined, the witnesses against him and to obtain the attendance and examination of witnesses on his behalf under the same conditions as witnesses against him;
f. to have the free assistance of an interpreter if he cannot understand or speak the language used in the International Tribunal;
g. not to be compelled to testify against himself or to confess guilt (http://www.un.org/icty/basic/statut/stat2000.htm#21).

The rights of the accused under the tribunals' statutes are designed to ensure that there is at least an "equality of arms" in a procedural sense between the defense and the Office of the Prosecutor. In fact, the Appeals Chamber has ruled that "the principle of equality of arms must be given a more liberal interpretation than that normally upheld with regard to proceedings before domestic courts. This principle means that the Prosecution and the Defence must be equal before the Trial Chamber. It follows that the Chamber shall provide every practicable facility it is capable of granting under the Rules and Statute when faced with a request by a party for assistance in presenting its case" (*Prosecutor v. Dusko Tadic,* IT-94-1, p. 52, January 26, 2000, http://www.un.org/icty/tadic/appeal/judgement/index.htm). In effect, there must be an equality of opportunity for each side to *present* its case. The Trial Chamber cannot guarantee that the defense will take full advantage of this potential. More important, it cannot guarantee that despite using its "every practicable facility," the defense will gain access to whatever witnesses, documents, or evidence it would like. But the Trial Chambers have generally endeavored to assist the defense and have issued numerous rulings favorable to the general interests of defendants.

When the judges must interpret some provision of the tribunal charters or their own "Rules of Procedure and Evidence," they have often chosen the meaning that is the more favorable to the defense. For example, in the *Akayesu* case from the ICTR, when the Trial Chamber judges sought to clarify the meaning of various legal terms, they ruled, "Given the presumption of innocence of the accused, and pursuant to the general principles of criminal law, the Chamber holds that the version more favourable to the accused should be upheld" (*Prosecutor v. Jean Paul Akayesu*, ICTR-96-4-T, p. 501, September 2, 1998, http://www.un.org/icty/basic/rpe/IT32_rev22.htm#89).[12] Similarly, while the prosecutor must prove aggravating circumstances beyond a reasonable doubt to the judges, the defense need only establish mitigating circumstances on balance of probabilities (*Prosecutor v. Zejnil Delalic et al.*, IT-96-21, p. 590, February 20, 2001, http://www.un.org/icty/celebici/appeal/judgement/index.htm). Appeals Chamber judges recuse themselves from cases in which they participated as Trial Chamber judges to avoid any impression of prejudice. Defendants are allowed to enter a plea of "guilty," to which the Prosecutor's Office typically agrees not to oppose a request for "a particular sentence or sentence range" (Rule 62, "Rules of Procedure and Evidence," http://www.un.org/icty/basic/rpe/IT32_rev22con.htm). This has resulted in reduced sentences for several individuals at both tribunals. Defendants can be provisionally released by the Trial Chambers if the judges determine that the accused will appear for trial and does not pose a threat (Rule 65, ibid.). Even those who are suspects enjoy all the rights and privileges of those indicted, such as a right to free legal counsel if needed (see article 18 of the ICTY Statute, http://www.un.org/icty/basic/statut/stat2000.htm#18).

Yet both the tribunals' supporters and their critics have raised concerns about a number of issues that may harm the interests of defendants and prevent an "equality of arms" (Chinkin, 1997; Creta, 1998; DeFrancia, 2001; Ellis, 1997; Fabian, 2000; "Fair Trials," 2001; Johnson, 1998; Leigh, 1996). At the root of many of these problems, real or perceived, are the purposes and composition of the tribunals. If the raison d'être for the tribunals is the attribution of blame and the dispensation of pun-

---

12. At the same time, however, rule 89 of the "Rules of Procedure and Evidence" states that "a Chamber shall apply rules of evidence which will best favour a fair determination of the matter before it and are consonant with the spirit of the Statute and the general principles of law."

ishment, critics charge that the tribunals will be biased against the accused. The formal name of the ICTY, for example, suggests its primary purpose—The International Tribunal for the *Prosecution* of Persons Responsible for Serious Violations of International Humanitarian Law Committed in the Territory of the Former Yugoslavia since 1991 (emphasis added). Some argue that this "bias" is reflected in the organization of the tribunals because while they contain an Office of the Prosecutor, they do not have an Office of Defense Counsel. Such criticisms of the tribunal's independence and impartiality may be inevitable regardless of the standards of procedural fairness by which they seek to operate. Simply because they are ad hoc tribunals, designed to address specific violations of international humanitarian law, and not a permanent criminal court, there may always be concerns that their decisions reflect the political interests that led to their creation.

Many critics point to wide disparities between the quantity and quality of the prosecution lawyers and the defense (Creta, 1998; Ellis, 1997; Johnson, 1998). The Office of the Prosecutor possesses substantial expertise and institutional memory regarding international criminal law that many defense lawyers do not possess (Creta, 1998; Johnson, 1998). And although the ICTY pays attorneys' fees for indigent defendants, the accused are normally allowed to hire only one attorney. They can plead for additional counsel. The Office of the Prosecutor, on the other hand, typically employs multiple lawyers on any one case. Even the *Harvard Law Review* notes ("Fair Trials," 2001: 8): "In the absence of uniformly effective representation, even a robustly pro-defendant statutory and regulatory framework would tend to result in an uneven prosecutorial record, prejudicing defendants whose attorneys do not effectively litigate their claims and simultaneously privileging other defendants of equal culpability who can afford, or are fortunate enough to be provided with more effective attorneys." Certainly the Trial Chambers or the Registry could provide for some sort of official recognition and space (in the case of the ICTY) for the defense counsels within their institutions. This should assist in the creation of a greater reservoir of knowledge from which the defense can draw. Yet it is quite doubtful that the tribunals will pay for the quantity of counsel defendants may seek. Certainly there are a number of highly qualified and diligent attorneys working with the accused, but it will take a much more concerted effort for these lawyers to enjoy the same acceptance and access to resources enjoyed by the Prosecutor's Office.[13]

Several writers have criticized the tribunals for allowing some witnesses to testify in secret and concealing their identities indefinitely in order to protect them and their families from intimidation or retaliatory violence (DeFrancia, 2001; "Fair Trials," 2001; Johnson, 1998; Leigh, 1996; Stapleton, 1999). The same writers and others have also faulted the tribunals for allowing hearsay evidence and written statements in lieu of oral testimony into the record (DeFrancia, 2001; Fabian, 2000). Both sets of concerns raise a number of red flags regarding the rights of the accused to a fair trial. In the *Tadic* case, where anonymous witnesses were used, the testimony of one turned out to be false. At the same time, however, I can find no evidence that such thoroughly anonymous testimony has been allowed since. Rather, witnesses' identities may be kept concealed until they arrive safely at The Hague. While such delays may hamper adequate preparation by the defense counsel, they are not so onerous as complete lack of disclosure. The Trial Chambers have ruled that the use of hearsay evidence and affidavits is permissible because the judges will assess for themselves the probative value of the testimony.[14] In each of these instances, the tribunals' actions that appear to be prejudicial against the rights of the accused were taken in order to satisfy the needs of victims. The tribunals allowed for anonymous testimony and hearsay evidence to protect the interests of those who have suffered the most, especially victims of rape who have been among the most reluctant to testify in public. Victims' rights groups have been especially vocal about the need to maintain these sorts of protections.

More troubling, however, are problems related to the fundamental presumption of the innocence of the accused. This basic protection is readily acknowledged in theory yet occasionally harmed in practice. First, under rule 98, judges can order either party to produce additional evidence dur-

---

13. Some argue this problem also affects the quality and quantity of the investigative team hired by defense counsel. Johnson writes (1998, 190): "Even when at full strength, a defense team cannot compete with teams of investigators and legal advisors in the OTP [Office of the Prosecutor]. An added benefit to continuity is the body of knowledge on the subject of the Yugoslav conflict, rules of engagement, tactics and 'signature' techniques of the warring parties that give OTP investigators a distinct advantage over even the most competent defense investigator working on a single case."

14. Defense counsels are allowed to object to the use of affidavits and may be able to demand the appearance of the witness.

ing a trial ("Rules of Procedure and Evidence," http://www.un.org/icty/basic/rpe/IT32_rev22con.htm). Since the Trial Chambers may request such evidence or testimony of either the prosecutor or the defense, on the face of it this provision is not inherently suspect. Yet the impact of such testimony and evidence on the likelihood of a guilty verdict and length of sentence, assuming guilt, is quite pronounced (Meernik, 2003). When the Trial Chamber itself calls at least one witness, the accused is more likely to be found guilty and is sentenced to a longer prison term on average (ibid.: 318). While we should not ascribe motivations to the judges in the absence of any direct evidence, some have speculated that the judges may call for witnesses and evidence to make more certain a finding of guilt. Johnson (1998: 183) alleges that "'Such action could be an excuse, not to acquit a defendant, but instead, to help fill in the gaps in the prosecutor's case and strengthen the rationale supporting the Trial Chamber's conviction." A more precise but correctable source of this problem lies in the presentation of evidence pertaining to sentencing during trial. Under rule 85, the judges can seek information on mitigating and aggravating circumstances even before a finding of guilt ("Rules of Procedure and Evidence," http://www.un.org/icty/basic/rpe/IT32_rev22con.htm). Not only might this power cause the judges to call for evidence that seems premised on a finding of guilt, it also would seem to violate the defendant's right against self-incrimination. If the accused are forced to produce mitigating evidence prior to the verdict, they may be, in effect, acknowledging guilt. Prior to 1998, the tribunals had bifurcated their decision-making processes regarding guilt and punishment, but they now combine them. This may expedite matters, but it also would appear to violate the rights of the accused with minimal benefit to the cause of justice.

Also of concern are potential violations of the defendants' protections against double jeopardy. First, under article 10 (ICTY Statute) and article 9 (ICTR Statute), the tribunals are allowed to try an individual who has already been tried by a national court under the following circumstances: (1) the act for which he or she was tried was characterized as an ordinary crime; or (2) the national court proceedings were not impartial or independent, were designed to shield the accused from international criminal responsibility, or the case was not diligently prosecuted. While this power has yet to be exercised, there has been considerable debate over the terminology in the provision and whether it protects against trying the same person twice for the same crime if the crime's definition varies between the national court and the international tribunal (Creta, 1998). Second, under article 25 (ICTY) and article 24 (ICTR), the Prosecutor's Office can appeal a verdict if an error of fact "has occasioned a miscarriage of justice." Rule 119 of the "Rules of Procedure and Evidence" also allows the prosecutor to ask for a review of a case when "a new fact has been discovered which was not known to the moving party at the time of the proceedings before a Trial Chamber" ("Rules of Procedure and Evidence," http://www.un.org/icty/basic/rpe/IT32_rev22con. htm). The defense is granted that right indefinitely, while the Office of the Prosecutor has only one year in which to make a motion after final judgment. To date, the Office of the Prosecutor has not had recourse to this provision. Other critics point to the case of Jean-Bosco Barayagwiza at the ICTR as evidence of the tribunals' ability to revisit its errors. The ICTR Appeals Chamber had ordered Barayagwiza to be released immediately from detention because of impermissible delays in his case before he was indicted (*Jean Bosco Barayagwiza v. the Prosecutor*, Appeals Chamber, November 3, 1999). Shortly thereafter the Prosecutor's Office sought a review of the decision and the accused was forced to remain in custody while the Appeals Chamber ultimately reversed itself. Some have charged that political pressures from the Rwandan government resulted in the Appeals Chambers' about-face (International Crisis Group, 2001). Whether it was the Rwandan government or simply the need to fulfill the U.N. mandate to do justice, the failure to release Barayagwiza after the Appeals Chamber ordered his discharge has provided ammunition to tribunal critics who argue the judges put retribution ahead of procedural fairness.

Some observers have been quite disparaging of the tribunals' protections of the rights of the accused (International Crisis Group, 2001; Johnson, 1998). Some have even gone so far as to label the Rwandan Tribunal a "dismal failure" (Crocker, 2001: 293). Many of their points are valid and provide instructive guidance to help improve the performance of the tribunals. Certainly in those instances where justice for the accused seems to conflict only with the tribunals' and international community's desire for expeditious justice (e.g., combining verdicts and sentences), little appears to be gained from infringing upon the rights of the accused. When it has been possible for the tribunals to correct some of these contradictions, we have seen changes in the "Rules of Procedure and Evidence" and Appeals Chambers decisions that have protected the rights of the accused. Nonetheless, many of these criticisms seem to be premised on the notion that procedural fairness should be the most important value guiding the tribunals' work and should be pursued despite its occasional incompatibility with other goals. Yet all institutions that are designed by political leaders and created through political compromise will pursue aims that are often contradictory. Given that the suffering of the victims compelled the creation of the tribunals, it is not surprising that the injustices they suffered often trump the rights of the accused. The trials, after all, are supposed to embody procedural justice in the courtroom and facilitate political justice in the global arena. That broader and rougher justice for the victims, with whom the sympathies of the international community lie, is usually the more morally compelling.

Providing Justice for the International Community

Because so many of its laws were violated, a crucial component of justice for the international community is condemnation of these crimes. After the horrors of the Nazi genocide and concentration camps, the rallying cry among human rights advocates was "Never again." Yet the scourge of genocide and its kindred atrocities, like crimes against humanity and ethnic cleansing, have not been removed from the world. The United Nations Security Council has the power to authorize all manner of methods to address the causes of these atrocities and to take more aggressive action to prevent their outbreak. Whether because of geopolitics, fear of casualties among those who might have to act, or the complexity of the conflicts, the U.N. and the major powers have chosen to provide legal justice after the fact (Bass 2000). By creating a mechanism to determine guilt and mete out punishment, the U.N., and thus the world, has sought to underscore its condemnation of these violations of international humanitarian law. The tribunals exist to further the cause of justice for the international community by establishing truth and consequences and setting norms of expected behavior and precedents for future permanent and ad hoc tribunals. So long as the tribunals remain operative, their judgments at a minimum continually demonstrate international condemnation of these crimes. Justice for the world would seem to require at a minimum

Ad Hoc International Criminal Tribunals 317

the creation and maintenance of institutions to enforce its laws. Whether the "mere" creation of these tribunals evidences true commitment to the "Never again" principle remains to be seen.

Integral to this condemnation and the cause of justice is truth telling. Establishing a historical record of what transpired in the former Yugoslavia and Rwanda protects the world against revisionists and propagandists who would deny or rewrite history. As the U.S. representative to the United Nations, Madeleine Albright, said during the debates on the creation of the ICTY, the world must "establish the historical record before the guilty can reinvent the truth" (quoted in Danner, 2001: 430). This task is particularly important among the peoples of the conflict regions, who lived under extremely repressive regimes that distorted the truth and lied to justify their atrocities. It is just as critical to record these histories for the rest of the international community, for revisionists know no national boundaries. Indeed, they draw their lessons from the willingness of the world to forget the truth, just as Hitler did, and act accordingly. Therefore, the two tribunals have been extremely open institutions that have created extensive databases to document their work, opened their courtrooms to allow the public to watch their trials, and sponsored numerous outreach programs. This transparency and accessibility is a vital element of justice for it can help demonstrate the sincerity and impartiality of these international institutions. This makes it all the more likely that the tribunals' accounts of the horrors of Yugoslavia and Rwanda will be viewed as honest and objective—and, most important, durable.

Although this justification has never been expressly stated as such in any of the resolutions and statements from the United Nations, one aspect of redress for the international community involves righting the scales of justice in a more encompassing sense. "Political" justice may be the most apt literal translation of this concept—providing something of value, whether tangible or intangible, to those who lost something else as a form of compensation. Given that the United Nations and specifically the Security Council powers did not prevent or halt the crimes, despite their power to do so, their failure would seem to demand, morally at least, corrective action. The unwillingness to take action resulted in at least temporary impunity for those who committed violations of international humanitarian law. If the world was unprepared to redress the injustices committed on the battlefield, it could seek to right the imbalance through international law. Interestingly, Bassiouni (1999) argues that the creators of the Nuremberg Tribunal had this same objective in mind when they drafted the London Charter. He writes (119), "the drafters believed that theirs was not a pure exercise in power, but the *redress of a legal imbalance produced by prior abuse of power*" (emphasis added). The ICTY's former president, Antonio Cassese, testified to the tribunal's role in this restoration of justice in the ICTY 1997 Annual Report to the United Nations. He wrote: "The Tribunal's mission is to hear and record for posterity the stories of those who have suffered in the camps and killing fields of the former Yugoslavia *and to dispense justice on that account in the name of the international community*" (September 18, 1997, para. 192, http://www.un.org/icty/rappannu-e/1997/index.htm; emphasis added). When there is a moral vacuum because the international community has failed to abide by its laws, there is an undeniable need to fill it. Justice for the international community requires that the violence done to its norms, laws, and peoples be understood and condemned. Even if it was guilt that compelled the creation of the tribunals, there still exists an implicit recognition of responsibility for righting the judicial imbalance.

Conclusion

There is a unique and fascinating convergence in international criminal law between global interests and individual rights and responsibilities. The creation of the ICTY and the ICTR represents an acknowledgment that the consequences of the crimes committed in the Balkans and central Africa transcend their immediate circumstances to affect broader international concerns. Their precedent-setting decisions will reverberate not just in the field of international law but also in conflict resolution strategies throughout the world. At the same time the "world" has come to appreciate its interests, there is a growing recognition that it is individuals who must be held responsible for violations of international humanitarian law. This trend began with the World War II tribunals and has reached perhaps its final fruition with the establishment of the International Criminal Court. Because *most* states do not trust *some* states to abide by international humanitarian laws, they have established international courts to prosecute the most prominent offenders of these laws. As the international community asserts political and moral interests in upholding humanitarian law, and its right to penetrate state sovereignty to hold individuals accountable, the equilibrium between public order, nationally and internationally, and individual rights becomes its responsibility to arbitrate. International courts have been granted some of the responsibilities of national courts, for they must now define justice and weigh the claims of these individuals and the international community to justice.

If one subscribes to the view that justice requires that paramount consideration be given to those harmed directly (victims) and indirectly (international community), the quality of the rights of the accused may become dependent upon the degree of harm done to victims and the international community. The greater the suffering, the greater the need to punish the accused. If one views the international tribunals as inherently suspect because they are a manifestation of the political interests of their creators, primacy must be given to the rights of the accused because they are in an unequal contest and because all are innocent until proven guilty. One approach sees the victims as symbolic of the perilous existence of many in a world dominated by powers that too readily ignore their suffering. To protect them and the future victims they represent demands that the international community assert its hierarchical authority to redress the wrongs they suffered. The other approach sees the accused, to some extent, as symbolic of the selective exercise of power by the major states whose interests dominate the world. Their protection, and that of others less odious and more innocent who might stand accused tomorrow, demands that individuals be afforded all the same protections enjoyed by defendants in the most advanced legal systems. The tribunals have generally sought to protect the interests of both the victims and the international community, on the one hand, and to provide justice for the accused, on the other. I have argued that when value trade-offs between these groups are unavoidable, infrequent though they may be, on balance the tribunals have favored the interests of victims and the international community in redress and retribution. They have developed enhanced rights for the accused not always enjoyed in the most exemplary criminal justice systems. But in the areas of witness anonymity, the presumption of innocence, and the protection against double jeopardy there are areas of concern. Does this mean that the accused cannot obtain a fair trial? Does this mean that innocent persons may be imprisoned? Given the tremendous amount of work that is invested by the tribunals in the substance and procedures of these trials, it would seem more unlikely than in most national courts. Improvements can and should be made, but the absence of perfection does not mean the tribunals should be dismissed or discarded, as some have argued. As Bass (2000: 310) writes, "Do war crimes tribunals work? The only answer is: compared to what?"

Whatever tensions exist in the tribunals among competing values and goals, they are, by their very nature, endemic to all political institutions. Justice is composed of political values whose supremacy at any one time says more about what most threatens us than any universal vision that unites us. What threatens the security of humanity at the moment are those people and forces who now possess the means to destroy more than at any time in history. As these actors are loosened from the confines of cold war politics and primitive war-making technologies, one of the few binding mechanisms available to the international community to protect its interests is international law. To mitigate those evils that the international community still lacks the will and means to prevent, many states and their leaders now demand that such international criminals be held accountable just as any other wrongdoer. The justice the international community, through the tribunals, is defining is founded on these sentiments.

The ICTY and ICTR, by existing as the exception to the rule of impunity for violations of international law, serve their ultimate purpose by demonstrating that justice must, finally, be done. Thus, by at least one measure of success the tribunals have worked quite well, for it was because of their examples, and based on their statutes and jurisprudence, that a broad majority of states in the world created the International Criminal Court (ICC). These states sought the establishment of a permanent court whose jurisdiction would be more far-reaching both in time and place so that justice would not depend on the accession of the victors or a coalition of the willing on the U.N. Security Council for its realization. Justice for the world's victims, accused, and the states that have ratified the Treaty of Rome is intended to be now a more universal right. But as a criminal justice system becomes part of the international amalgam of institutions knitting the world closer together, it is all the more imperative that the ICC and the justice it delivers be fair and impartial. For unlike most other international institutions that have little independent power of their own, the ICC, and especially its prosecutor, has been accorded substantial discretionary decision-making power that will potentially allow it to weigh in on political and military disputes throughout the world. Maintaining impartiality, both in the adjudication of violations of international laws within such conflicts and across them, may well be the most difficult and important mission of the ICC. Only by demonstrating such impartiality and commanding respect for its adjudicatory processes can the ICC hope to achieve the degree of legitimacy needed to win the ultimate approval of the world's states and citizens that is necessary for the realization of international justice. For if the ICC's justice is perceived as selective or biased, justice for the world will remain a distant goal. Perhaps the best place to begin is by learning from the successes and mistakes of the ICTY and ICTR.

REFERENCES

Akhavan, Payam. 2001. "Beyond Impunity: Can International Criminal Justice Prevent Future Atrocities?" *American Journal of International Law* 95 (January): 7–31.
Bass, Gary Jonathan. 2000. *Stay the Hand of Vengeance*. Princeton: Princeton University Press.
Bassiouni, M. Cherif. 1999. *Crimes against Humanity in International Criminal Law*. The Hague: Kluwer Law International.
Carroll, Christina M. 2000. "An Assessment of the Role and Effectiveness of the International Criminal Tribunals for Rwanda and the Rwandan National Justice System in Dealing with the Mass Atrocities of 1994." *Boston University International Law Journal* 18 (Fall): 163–200.
Chinkin, Christine M. 1997. "Due Process and Witness Anonymity." *American Journal of International Law* 91 (January): 75–79.
Creta, Vincent M. 1998. "Comment: The Search for Justice in the Former Yugoslavia and Beyond." *Houston Journal of International Law* 30:381–418.
Crocker, David A. 2001. "Transitional Justice and International Civil Society." In Alexsandar Jokic, ed., *War Crimes and Collective Wrongdoing*. Maldan, Mass.: Blackwell, 270–300.
Danner, Allison Marston. 2001. "Constructing a Hierarchy of Crimes in International Criminal Law Sentencing." *Virginia Law Review* 87 (May): 415–501.
DeFrancia, Cristian. 2001. "Due Process in International Criminal Courts: Why Procedure Matters." *Virginia Law Review* 87 (November): 1381–1439.
Ellis, Mark. 1997. "Achieving Justice Before the International War Crimes Tribunal: Challenges for the Defense Counsel." *Duke Journal of Comparative and International Law* 7 (Spring): 519–37.
Fabian, Kellye L. 2000. "Note and Comment: Proof and Consequences—An Analysis of the Tadic and Akayesu Trials." *DePaul Law Review* 49:981–1039.
"Fair Trials and the Role of International Criminal Defense." 2001. *Harvard Law Review* 114 (May): 1982–2006.
Goldstone, Richard J. 2000. *For Humanity: Reflections of a War Crimes Investigator*. New Haven: Yale University Press.
Hayner, Priscilla B. 1994. "Fifteen Truth Commissions—1974–1994: A Comparative Study." *Human Rights Quarterly* 16:597–655.

ICTY Annual Yearbook. 1994. The Hague: ICTY.
International Crisis Group. 2001. *International Criminal Tribunal for Rwanda: Justice Delayed.* Nairobi/Arusha/Brussels: International Crisis Group.
Ivkovic, Sanja. 2001. "Justice by the International Criminal Tribunal for the Former Yugoslavia." *Stanford Journal of International Law* 37 (Summer): 255–346.
Johnson, Scott T. 1998. "On the Road to Disaster: The Rights of the Accused and the International Criminal Tribunal for the Former Yugoslavia." *International Legal Perspectives* 10 (Spring): 111–92.
Leigh, Monroe. 1996. "The Yugoslav Tribunal: Use of Unnamed Witnesses against Accused." *American Journal of International Law* 90 (April): 235–38.
Meernik, James D. 2003. "Equality of Arms? The Individual vs. the International Community in War Crimes Tribunals." *Judicature* 86 (6): 312–19.
Paul VI. 1972. "Celebration of the World Day of Peace, January 1, 1972." *http://www.law.duke.edu/journals/lcp/articles/lcp59dFall1996p9.htm#F1*.
Stapleton, Sara. 1999. "Ensuring a Fair Trial in the International Criminal Court: Statutory Interpretation and the Impermissibility of Derogation." *Journal of International Law and Politics* 31 (Winter/Spring): 535–609.
Thieroff, Mark, and Edward A. Amley Jr. 1998. "Proceeding to Justice and Accountability in the Balkans: The International Criminal Tribunal for the Former Yugoslavia and Rule 61." *Yale Journal of International Law* 23 (Winter): 231–74.

14

The Legitimacy of Anticipatory Defense and Forcible Regime Change

DIETER JANSSEN

In the months preceding the recent war against Iraq, the U.S. administration made clear that it sought not only to disarm Saddam Hussein and coerce him to comply with international law but also to force a change of regime.[1] Alongside the legitimacy of preemptive/preventive strikes and the justification of militarily enforcing nonproliferation of weapons of mass destruction (WMD), the problem of forcible regime change was thus brought to the fore of international attention.

Forcible regime change is neither a new phenomenon in international relations nor is it of rare occurrence. Since World War II the United States has forcibly changed regimes in the Dominican Republic (1965–66), Grenada (1983), Panama (1989), Haiti (1994), and Afghanistan (2001). If covert actions like CIA-sponsored or -assisted coups in Iran (1953), Guatemala (1954), and Cambodia (1973) are also regarded as forcible regime changes, the number of violent interventions in the governance of foreign countries rises even higher. Not only the United States but other powerful countries have made ample use of forcible regime change. The So-

---

This chapter is based on a paper published in the *Journal of Military Ethics* 3, no. 2 (2004). I would like to thank the editors of this journal for their kind permission to use this material. I also would like to thank Henrik Syse and Gregory Reichberg for their valuable suggestions.

1. As early as August 2002 the White House made clear that it pursued a policy of forcible regime change to oust Saddam Hussein. See U.S. State Department, 2002; Cirincione, 2003.

viet Union toppled foreign governments in its sphere of influence whenever its rulers feared that a particular country would attempt to leave the Soviet orbit (Butler, 1974; Bennett, 1999). Mark Curtis, who in his book *Web of Deceit* criticizes British interventionism, in a recent article for the *Guardian* called forcible regime change as British as afternoon tea (Curtis, 2003).[2]

From an academic point of view the term *forcible regime change*[3] seems to be central to at least four different but nonetheless interrelated discourses.

In the first discourse "regime change" is considered to be an expression of the alleged neocolonialist aspirations of today's major powers. The proponents of this discourse argue that moral language is used—or rather abused—to gain support for violent interferences into the affairs of foreign nations. Ostensibly regime change serves to ensure democracy and human rights, but in reality, the proponents of this discourse charge, it is a means to ensure hegemony and egoistical national interests of the major powers. Noam Chomsky, Edward Herman, Mark Curtis, William Blum, and others have repeatedly expressed this view in their books and articles.

The second discourse centers on the question of whether there is a right to live in a democracy and whether this right justifies pro-democratic intervention into foreign nondemocratic countries (Byers and Chesterman, 2000; Lecce, 1998; Schachter, 1984; Wippman, 2000).

At the core of the third discourse is the problem of how to deal with regimes that are guilty of grave abuses of the fundamental human rights of their own citizens. "Abuse of fundamental human rights" in this discourse means that large-scale killing, ethnic cleansing, or even genocide have occurred or are still in progress. The main question here is whether forcible regime change should be allowed to remove especially obnoxious regimes that disregard virtually all precepts of humanity. This dis-

---

2. See also Wyllie, 1984. France showed the same inclination as Britain to intervene in its former colonial empire. Paris, e.g., initiated military interventions in Cameroon (1960–61), Mauritania (1961), Gabon (1962), Congo (1960 and 1962), Chad (between 1960 and 1963; 1968), Niger (1963), and the Central African Republic (1967). See Treacher, 2003; Utley, 1998; Verschaeve, 2000.

3. Technically the term *regime* refers to any system of control. In political science it denotes a system of governance or an administration. The word often has a pejorative connotation. It is frequently used to describe governments that are held to be inimical or morally reprehensible. In this chapter the term is used to denote the government of a state.

course often overlaps with the debate on military humanitarian intervention.[4]

In the fourth discourse forcible regime change is discussed under the premise that changing an outwardly aggressive national regime might be necessary to ensure security and stability—either one's own or that of the whole international community. This fourth discourse received broad attention in September 2002 when the Bush administration published its *National Security Strategy*. In chapter 5 of the *NSS* (2002) the authors claim that the United States has a right to preemptively counter the threat of a newly emerged lethal combination of rogue states and terrorists who might use weapons of mass destruction against civilian population centers. This so-called Bush doctrine instantly caused an acrimonious debate on various moral, legal, and political issues associated with a right to preemptive or preventive war.

The debate gained even more immediacy when, in the weeks after the publication of the *NSS*, the confrontation between the allies and Saddam Hussein's Iraq heated up again. On March 20, 2003 the allies eventually attacked Iraq with the clear intent to oust Saddam Hussein and his Baathist regime. This war is widely held to be the first application of the Bush doctrine and thus an important precedent on how the doctrine of preemptive war is meant to be implemented within the international system. In the most recent *National Security Strategy* (March 2006) the Bush administration confirmed its claim to a right to preemptively counter the threat of WMD use—albeit without linking a particular regime to international terrorism:

Our strong preference and common practice is to address proliferation concerns through international diplomacy, in concert with key allies and regional partners. If necessary, however, under long-standing principles of self defense, we do not rule out the use of force before attacks occur, even if uncertainty remains as to the time and place of the enemy's attack. When the consequences of an attack with WMD are potentially so devastating, we cannot afford to stand idly by as grave dangers materialize. This is the principle and logic of preemption. The place of preemption in our national security strategy remains the same. We will always proceed deliberately,

---

4. Neither the concept nor the practice of military humanitarian intervention necessarily need to include regime change, as can be seen by the 1991 intervention in northern Iraq. During Operation Provide Comfort the allies protected the Kurds from Iraqi forces and brought humanitarian relief to them but did not use the occasion to topple the Baath Party regime of Saddam Hussein.

weighing the consequences of our actions. The reasons for our actions will be clear, the force measured, and the cause just. (2006: 23)

Currently, a possible standoff between the United Nations Security Council and Iran, which is deemed to be in violation of the Nuclear Non-Proliferation Treaty, might lead to another invocation of the "right to preemption" in case of a nuclear threat.

This chapter will focus on what I above termed the fourth discourse. In so doing it will address a question that seems essential to the evaluation of the Bush doctrine: Can forcible regime change be justified legally as well as morally as a means to ensure international security and stability? This question obviously has many aspects to it and leads to quite a number of follow-up questions (Boniface, 2003), for example, can such forcible regime change be legally implemented within the present international order without forcing a fundamental change of international law and institutions? Even if security-related forcible regime change is found to be morally and legally justifiable, is it still practicable? How can security-related forcible regime change be implemented in a just way? Who is to decide on regime change? Who is to execute it? How can the right to self-determination be balanced with the right to intervention that would result from the implementation of forcible regime change? What can be done to prevent the cynical abuse of security-related forcible regime change?

This essay will adopt a three-pronged approach to these questions. It opens with an analysis of the preventive military strategy that is outlined in the *NSS* of 2002. The *NSS* became pivotal for the discussion of security-related forcible regime change because of its allegation that a new security situation forces a new concept of "preemptive defense" on those nations that are targeted by terrorists and rogue states. It is important to see what exactly the *NSS* characterizes as the new security threat and what reaction it proposes.

Next, the legality, justice, and feasibility of regime change in the current international order will be discussed. Is regime change contrary to the system of international security that was established with the U.N. Charter? Can and should a right to security-related forcible regime change become part of present international law? Has a right to regime change a positive effect on the security and stability of the international order, or is it detrimental? Can forcible regime change be morally justified? What are the ethical reservations against regime change? Is regime change a viable option, or will it be counterproductive and/or excessively harmful to the peoples living under the control of rogue regimes?

Finally, I will argue that the concept of regime change as part of anticipatory or preemptive defense has an intuitive plausibility that stems from the fact that under very specific circumstances it might seem legitimate to seek to change a foreign regime by force. I will use John Rawls's vision of a "realistic utopia," which he laid out in his *Law of Peoples* (1999) to show that in a strongly idealized context forcible regime change for reasons of anticipatory defense may seem justified. The presentation of this realistic utopia will serve to show that the authors of the NSS must make some idealized assumptions to present their case for a right to preemptive war in the current international order. The realistic utopia of a "Law of Peoples" will also elucidate how far the present international system is removed from these idealized conditions that would be necessary to establish a fair right to regime change.

The *National Security Strategy* and the Legitimacy of Forcible Regime Change

In September 2002, coinciding with the buildup of the crisis over alleged Iraqi programs to construct weapons of mass destruction, the Bush administration published the *National Security Strategy*.[5] Unlike preceding national security strategies, which often amounted to little more than unabashed self-praise of supposed foreign policy achievements of the incumbent administration, the 2002 *NSS* at least on one point proclaimed a fundamental shift in U.S. foreign and security policies.[6]

Chapter 5 of the *NSS* started a heated and controversial debate on the question of the definition and justice of preemptive and preventive military actions. In this chapter the authors of the *NSS* argue that a fundamental change in international relations has taken place since the end of the cold war. The end of mutual nuclear deterrence between the West-

---

5. The obligation of the U.S. president to submit a national security strategy to Congress 150 days after taking office dates back to the Goldwater-Nichols Act of 1986 (see Snider, 1992).
6. A differing view is held by Nichols, 2003: "The fact of the matter is that American leaders have rarely been willing to accept a position of military inferiority; what is different now, however, is that it is apparently no longer considered inappropriate to say so."

ern alliance and the Soviet bloc did not bring about the hoped-for era of general peace and stability. Instead a new threat emerged: a lethal combination of rogue states, international terrorism, and the propensity to acquire WMD for devious purposes.

The *NSS* defines rogue states as regimes that

- brutalize their own people and squander their national resources for the personal gain of the rulers;
- display no regard for international law, threaten their neighbors, and callously violate international treaties to which they are party;
- are determined to acquire weapons of mass destruction, along with other advanced military technology, to be used as threats or offensively to achieve the aggressive designs of these regimes;
- sponsor terrorism around the globe; and
- reject basic human values and hate the United States and everything for which it stands. (2002: 13–14)

Rogue states are perceived to be dangerous to international security mainly for two reasons. (1) If they succeed in the acquisition of weapons of mass destruction they will be in a position to use them for political blackmail. Such states will, for instance, threaten other nations with the use of WMD to shield themselves against reprisals for violations of international law (Weller, 1998). (2) Some rogue states are believed to have contacts with fanatical terrorists. If rogue states share their WMD with such terrorist groups, the latter would possess the means to cause hundreds of thousands of deaths in a single attack. Against terrorists who are motivated by powerful ideologies the usual strategies of deterrence will not work, because such individuals are willing to face death in order to do harm to their enemies, as was demonstrated in the suicide attacks of 9/11. Furthermore, the *NSS* points out that these terrorist organizations often move freely across territorial boundaries, making it hard or even impossible to determine a suitable target for deterrent action.

Since WMD in the hands of terrorists can be "easily concealed, delivered covertly, and used without warning" (2002: 15), it is of the utmost importance to prevent terrorists from acquiring this kind of weapons in the first place. This, the authors of the *NSS* claim, can only be done if rogue regimes are not allowed to obtain WMD. The *NSS* therefore urges a new understanding of the right to preemptive self-defense.

The United States, according to this new understanding, would be justified in attacking any regime that has a record of breaking international law and that is trying to circumvent nonproliferation agreements for WMD. Although the *NSS* does not use the term *regime change*, it seems obvious that the aim of a "preemptive" military strike against a "rogue state" cannot simply be the removal of WMD capabilities. If the rogue regime were to be left in place, it would renew its attempts to acquire WMD as soon as foreign forces are withdrawn. In the long run the invading forces must seek to replace the rogue regime with a friendly or at least neutral government.

Within the Bush administration the idea that forcible regime change might be a necessary instrument in the drive to stabilize and secure the international system seems to have preceded the 9/11 attacks.[7] In a letter from the Project for a New American Century to President William J. Clinton regarding Iraq, dated January 26, 1998, the signers call for regime change in Iraq. Most of the signers of this letter later held important offices in the Bush administration and helped shape its foreign and security policies.[8] The authors of the letter urge the president to aim, "above all, at the removal of Saddam Hussein's regime from power" (Project for the New American Century, 1998). As a reason for this demand the following rationale is given: "It hardly needs to be added that if Saddam does acquire the capability to deliver weapons of mass destruction, as he is almost certain to do if we continue along the present course, the safety of American troops in the region, of our friends and allies like Israel and the moderate Arab states, and a significant portion of the world's

---

7. For a short introduction to the historical nexus between nonproliferation and preemption, see Litwak, 2002–3: 54–58. On the deeper ideological roots of the "Bush doctrine," see Monten, 2005.

8. The Project for the New American Century (PNAC) is a political neoconservative think tank, based in Washington, D.C. Signers (and their subsequent positions) include Elliott Abrams (U.S. assistant secretary of state for Inter-American Affairs), Richard L. Armitage (deputy secretary of state), John Bolton (undersecretary, Arms Control and International Security, then representative to the U.N.), Paula Dobriansky (undersecretary, Global Affairs), Zalmay Khalilzad (special U.S. envoy to Afghanistan and to the Iraqi opposition), William Kristol (editor of the *Weekly Standard*), Richard Perle (chairman of the Defense Policy Board), Peter W. Rodman (assistant secretary of defense), Donald Rumsfeld (secretary of defense), William Schneider Jr. (chairman, Defense Science Board, U.S. Department of Defense), Paul Wolfowitz (deputy secretary of defense), and Robert B. Zoellick (U.S. trade representative). Only six signers did not become members of the Bush administration: William J. Bennett (Heritage Foundation), Jeffrey Bergner (lobbyist), Francis Fukuyama (professor of international political economy at Johns Hopkins University), Robert Kagan (senior associate of Carnegie Endowment for International Peace), Vin Weber (vice chairman of Empower America), and R. James Woolsey (former CIA director).

supply of oil will all be put at hazard" (ibid.). For the authors of the letter, the United States had only one option to ensure its own security and that of allies and friends: "The only acceptable strategy is one that eliminates the possibility that Iraq will be able to use or threaten to use weapons of mass destruction. In the near term, this means a willingness to undertake military action as diplomacy is clearly failing. In the long term, it means removing Saddam Hussein and his regime from power. That now needs to become the aim of American foreign policy" (ibid.).

It was thus made clear that many policy advisers of the Bush administration consider forcible regime change as justified under certain circumstances. These "circumstances" seem to be ingrained in the characteristics given for "rogue regimes." According to this position forcible regime change therefore is legitimate: (1) to stop a regime from violating the basic human rights of its citizens and from plundering the resources of the country, (2) to remove aggressive regimes that continually have violated and still violate international law, (3) to ensure the nonproliferation of WMD, and (4) to fight international terrorism. Regimes that behave in one or more of these ways are endangering peace, stability, and security, and they force their neighbors to arm themselves and to be continuously vigilant. Rogue states, the authors of the *NSS* assume, undermine the international order and impose their style of politics on others. They therefore declare it necessary to change these regimes even if force is the only way to do it.

The Legality, Justice, and Feasibility of Forcible Regime Change

The authors of the *NSS*, as we have seen, argue that a new security situation requires fresh thinking about questions of preemption, prevention, nonproliferation, and aggression. A normative evaluation of the *NSS* must take into account its political as well as its legal context. Therefore the alleged "right to preemption" and the forcible removal of dangerous "rogue regimes" need to be discussed under the angles of legality, justice, and political feasibility.

Legality

With the inception of the U.N. Charter in 1945 the member states of the U.N. sought to outlaw war as a means of international politics. The charter clearly forbids all members to resort to force to settle their international disputes. Article 2(4) obliges all member states to "refrain in their international relations from the threat or use of force against the territorial integrity or political independence of any state, or in any other manner inconsistent with the Purposes of the United Nations." Even the U.N. itself may not interfere "in matters which are essentially within the domestic jurisdiction of any state" (article 2(7)). Only two exceptions from this general prohibition of international violence are made in the charter.

The first exception may be found in articles 39 and 42. The charter concedes to the Security Council the right to mandate member nations to use force in reaction to a "threat to the peace, a breach of the peace, or act of aggression." This somewhat imprecise formulation gives the Security Council considerable leeway on so-called enforcement measures. The creators of the charter, however, thought the veto power of the five permanent members sufficient to protect against the abuse of articles 39 and 42.

The second exception is the right to immediate self-defense outlined in article 51, which holds that member states may resort to armed force unilaterally, if this is the only available means to repel "an armed attack." It seems quite obvious that any legal claim in favor of preemption must appeal to this clause in the U.N. Charter. Whether preemption can be seen as part of a right to self-defense thus hinges on the interpretation of article 51. According to the Vienna Convention on the Law of Treaties, the interpretation of a legal document must be based on three considerations: (1) the ordinary meaning of the disputed term given in a treaty must be ascertained, (2) the meaning of the term must be considered within the specific context of the treaty, and (3) the term in question must be interpreted "in the light of object and purpose" of the treaty.

Self-defense is deemed legal by the charter in the event of an armed attack. Defined as the *action* of striking someone, the ordinary meaning of the word "attack" does not, however, include verbal expressions of the intent to attack, preparations for an attack, or threats to attack. Thus, from the ordinary meaning of the term, one cannot infer that preparations to attack already constitute an attack.

If we take into account the context of this article, it becomes even more obvious that the authors of the charter did not intend violent preventive measures to be included in the right to self-defense. The decisive clause of article 51 reads: "Nothing ... shall impair the inherent right of ... self-defense if an armed attack occurs." It is explicitly stated that the attack must occur. While the Security Council is authorized to take forcible measures preventively to counter a threat to the peace, states may react only to an actual assault (Randelzhofer, 2002; Schmitt, 2003).

The first object and purpose of the U.N. Charter, affirmed in the preamble, is "to save succeeding generations from the scourge of war." The system of international security that the framers of the charter took as a key aim was based on an extensive renouncement of war by all member states. It is therefore consistent with the spirit of the charter to interpret the restrictions to the use of violence in international affairs very strictly.[9]

Some authors, however, maintain that anticipatory or preemptive self-defense is not excluded from the right to self-defense. Common sense, so it is argued, tells us that we should not wait for the first blow to hit us when we unmistakably see it coming and when it would be lethal to us. In this context the criteria for anticipatory defense that were developed by U.S. secretary of state Daniel Webster during the Caroline affair (1837–42) are often quoted. According to Webster's formula, military preemption is allowable when there is "a necessity of self-defence, instant, overwhelming, leaving no choice of means, and no moment for deliberation" (Webster, 1840–41: 1129; see also Stevens, 1989).

The authors of the *NSS* acknowledge that a preemptive strike should respond to an imminent threat. They argue that in the days of conventional warfare the "visible mobilization of armies, navies, and air forces preparing to attack" (2002: 15) provided a rather clear proof of an imminent attack. The fact that terrorists can deliver weapons of mass destruction covertly and without any warning, however, makes it necessary to enhance the present understanding of the term *imminent*.

Conversely, it is hard to see how the *NSS* offers a practicable new understanding of the concept of "imminence." Traditionally, one speaks of an imminent attack when the last stage of preparation for an attack is about to be finished. The authors of the *NSS* seem to consider the mo-

---

9. An even more elaborate interpretation of the charter according to the principles of the Vienna Convention can be found in Bothe, 2003.

ment a rogue state tries to acquire WMD as constituting the last stage of such preparation. This understanding, however, seems to combine two different aspects of an alleged right to anticipatory self-defense: preemption and regime change.

Undoubtedly, terrorists are a grave threat to security; a terrorist attack with WMD would have devastating consequences. According to the classical understanding of preemption, it would be justified to intervene in any state to prevent an impending attack. If the United States, for example, should send a special forces unit into a foreign country to apprehend or stop terrorists boarding a plane to the United States with the intent to highjack it and to crash it into a tightly packed football arena, the act could be interpreted as preemption since it is necessary, the danger it removes is both imminent and overwhelming, and arguably the danger could not be met by other means.

This is not what the authors of the *NSS* have in mind. They claim that it is nearly impossible to get the necessary intelligence to counter terrorist attacks and that therefore possible sources for WMD have to be shut down before terrorists can use them to acquire weapons of such destructive power. For this reason the concept of "preemption" should include the right to attack those states that develop WMD and are suspected of someday supplying terrorists with them. This claim, in fact, boils down to the demand of a right to change rogue regimes because they are conceived to be the possible sources of WMD to terrorists. According to the usual understanding of the terms *preemptive* and *preventive*, this alleged right to change rogue regimes is a right to preventive war.

It is hard to imagine how such a right to security-related regime change could fit into Webster's definition of preemption. Of course, the authors of the *NSS* argue that the traditional concept of preemption is not suitable for the present-day situation. Advocates of the *NSS* thus claim either that Webster's formula has to be rephrased in the light of the new threat of WMD (Slocombe, 2003) or it has to be abandoned as an outdated legal model altogether (Sofaer, 2003). This begs the question why the term *preemption* is used at all.

The recent war in Iraq, if we may consider it as an application of the Bush doctrine, can serve as an example. The British government claimed that Iraq possessed WMD that could be readied for an attack within forty-five minutes of an order from Saddam Hussein (see Prime Minister's Iraq

Statement to Parliament, 2002). The danger was thus alleged to be imminent and overwhelming. Nonetheless, the allies spent several months building up their forces in the region instead of immediately attacking to defuse an imminent threat. Furthermore, the U.N. Security Council already had the situation under deliberation and there was a motion to bring a vote on appropriate countermeasures into the Security Council. The U.N. Charter leaves no doubt that member states may not claim any right to go to war if the Security Council is already addressing the situation in question.

The difference, therefore, between prevention and preemption is that a preemptive strike reacts directly and immediately to an already manifest threat. Prevention is directed against emerging threats that, if left unchecked, would likely become insurmountable in the future. Aside from the question whether the *NSS* is in fact proposing a right to prevention, despite the fact that the argument is framed using the term *preemption,* we need to ask whether the *NSS* could be interpreted to advocate a *lex ferenda*—a new law yet to be constituted.

Two points seem to make such an interpretation difficult. First, the *NSS* does not elucidate whether the new concept of "preemption" is meant to apply to all nations. This would be necessary if preemption were to be regarded as law, since one of the major qualities of law is its universal applicability to all similar cases. India, for example, could point out that Pakistan is supporting terrorists in Kashmir. Pakistan is also a nuclear power and possesses WMD that could be shared with those terrorists. This situation then would constitute a right to preventive action on the part of India. There seems, however, to be a bias in the wording of the *NSS*. Nations are warned not to use "pre-emption as a pretext for aggression" (2002: 15). In the next sentence it is affirmed that the United States cannot remain idle against the "enemies of civilization." This bias becomes even more clear when we consider that one of the criteria to describe rogue nations is their hatred of the United States and all that it stands for (ibid.: 14).

Second, to interpret the concept of preemption as lex ferenda is complicated by the imprecise language that has often been used to describe the criteria for justified preemption. For example, among other criteria, a "rogue regime" has been defined as a regime that squanders a nation's natural resources for the personal gain of the rulers. The "squandering of resources," however, seems to be a hopelessly imprecise criterion to determine the roguish character of a regime. There is thus reason to doubt that these criteria, in their present form, can serve as the basis for the formulation of right in international law.

To sum up the legal discussion, the appeal to an enhanced understanding of preemption, and consequently to a right of regime change for reasons of international security, is a breach of current international law. Furthermore, the authors of the *NSS* fail to make a compelling case for an emerging law or new understanding of present law.

Justice

Some people would argue that the illegality of the Bush doctrine under present international law settles the matter and renders all further discussion unnecessary. Yet present international law is still fraught with inconsistencies and contradictions. The current debate on the problem of military humanitarian intervention is a case in point. It reveals gaps between our moral convictions (help people who are threatened by thugs) and legal provisions (strict prohibition of unilateral intervention). It is therefore necessary to see if our moral convictions correspond to present international law in the question at hand.

Preventive war has been one of the more challenging problems of just war thinking. Most just war theorists criticize the idea of preventive war and security-related regime change. It is argued that according to the criterion of just cause, war may only be the reaction to an injury already received, or at the limit an injury that is imminent. Michael Walzer made this point in a recent speech at the Heinrich Böll Foundation:

Regime change has never been accepted—in just war theory or in international law—as a legitimate cause of war, unless the regime is engaged right now in mass murder. A tyrannical or authoritarian regime isn't a reason for war, first of all, because there would be too many wars. But there is another, deeper reason: just wars are a response to violence; they represent the use of force to stop some far worse use of force: an aggression or massacre that is already happening or that we have good reason to think is about to happen. War is too terrible; the risks it brings, the carnage it brings, make it an instrument that must not be used for any purpose except defending oneself and others against greater risks and greater carnage. Political and religious crusades—to spread Christianity or Islam or socialism or democracy—are not just wars. I suppose that's why, though the US government aimed at regime change in Iraq from the beginning, the official justification for the war had to do with the enforcement of UN resolutions and the disarming of Iraq. Not many Americans would have been prepared to fight for the democratization of Iraq in the absence of any imminent danger posed by Saddam's regime to its neighbors and to the US. (Walzer, 2003)[10]

Walzer's comment shows that there are three major reservations against preventive war.

First, the general license to attack any regime that is considered inimical or a future threat would in fact lead to a *liberum ius ad bellum* (the free right to wage war, whenever one sees fit to do so). This would be the end of the system of collective security that is central to the U.N. Charter.

Second, advocates of preventive war must show that they are able to predict future events—even in the long run—with absolute accuracy. Arthur Schlesinger Jr. (2002) pointed out that this is possible only in science fiction stories like P. K. Dick's *Minority Report*, in which individuals with amazing precognitive abilities predict future crime. The Bush doctrine in fact constitutes a shift of the burden of proof from the accuser to the accused. Foreign governments would have to prove that they are peaceful, law abiding, and well ordered to avoid being "preemptively" attacked.

Third, if preventive war were allowed, probably any fear of attack could itself provoke a war. Along these lines, Richard K. Betts (2003) shows how concern over such a consequence led the United States and Soviet Union to refrain from preventive war against each other. In 1950 the United States did not use its position of greater strength to preventively oust Stalin, and in 1983 the Soviets did not preventively attack NATO countries to decide the ideological confrontation before the United States could implement its Strategic Defense Initiative (Pry, 1999).

Although there is a clear-cut presumption against preventive war, the same cannot be said for preemptive war. Our moral intuitions concerning an imminent attack seem to be different from those concerning projected attacks in the distant future. Most people agree that it would be an outright folly to wait for a blow one sees coming and that probably would

---

10. Walzer exaggerates somewhat when he asserts that regime change has never been accepted in the just war tradition as a just cause of war. As he himself has shown in *Just and Unjust Wars* (Walzer, 1977: 76–78), some representatives of the just war tradition (certainly not all)—Vattel, for instance—have advocated some forms of preventive military action that presumably could aim at regime change. An interesting discussion of the thoughts of classical proponents of the just war tradition on preemptive war can be found in Reichberg, 2004.

be decisive. There is a strong leaning to include preemptive strikes into a wider concept of self-defense.

But how can we decide whether the situation at hand is a case for justified preemption? The criteria outlined by Daniel Webster seem to be a good starting point for determining the answer to this question:

1. Imminence. In all discussions of preemptive vs. preventive war, the criterion of the "imminence" of a threat is at the core of the argument. Preemption is commonly held to be an action aimed at forestalling an imminent attack, while preventive war reacts against an emerging threat. But what exactly is meant by the term *imminent* in regard to preemptive war?

Some analysts suggest that a short time span is essential to the definition of an imminent threat. Neta Crawford (2003: 31), for instance, states: "Immediate threats are those which can be made manifest within days or weeks unless action is taken to thwart them." The vagueness of this attempt to define "imminence" shows one of the many difficulties of this criterion. Since the time needed for mobilization differs according to the kind of weapon systems and the sort of forces needed, it is impossible to determine an exact span of time in which an attack could still be considered preemptive to a threat. "Imminence" must therefore be interpreted in a flexible manner. An attack may be considered a reaction to an imminent threat when the last stage of the mobilization of the critical mass of enemy forces is reached. "Critical mass" here denotes what would be necessary to overwhelm the opposing military, according to a reasonable probability.

In other words: the choice left to us is either to attack first or to suffer extremely dire consequences. This is not the case when a decision on preventive war is made. Here the threat lies well in the future and the resulting attack is merely prospective, not yet certain. Other avenues to diffuse the threat would still be available.

2. Necessity. War necessarily entails killing, destruction, and suffering. If, therefore, there is a less harmful way of achieving one's goals, there is an obligation to sincerely try such means first. War should be the means of last resort when all other proven and promising avenues have failed or according to reasonable foresight are bound to fail.

3. Gravity of threat. The threat that a preemptive attack seeks to repel must be of a specific gravity. Only when the attack of the opponent seriously endangers the capabilities to defend oneself or one's very survival is it justified to thwart a surprise attack beforehand.

4. Due diligence in determining threat. It is important to note that due diligence in determining the true implications of a situation is a prerequisite to any informed decision on war and peace. In the context of the decision to strike preemptively it is essential to make sure that we do not mistake the intentions of our opponent. A mobilization of enemy forces may be considered an imminent threat only when it is clear that the readying of troops or arms is not part of a political bluff or a symbolic act to send a political message. We must therefore have good reasons to believe that our opponent is actually bent on attacking us. Guessing the intentions of an adversary, however, has its very own epistemic problems. Only an intimate knowledge of the political culture, the *Weltanschauung,* and the past behavior of our enemy can help us to judge the situation correctly. Furthermore, to avoid falling into the trap of one's own hysteria, the critical voices of friends and allies should be considered.

Additionally, two criteria of rational action should be taken into account: (1) proportionality of threat and response and (2) reasonable hope of success.

Can the "new" security situation of rogue states that try to acquire WMD and possibly share them with anti-American terrorists be seen as a case for preemptive security-related regime change? Before attempting to answer this question, it is necessary to point out that the *NSS* makes some rather strong suppositions that for the sake of argument shall be accepted for the moment. The first presupposition is that the concept of "rogue regimes" adequately describes certain governments and their behavior. The second presupposition is that rogue regimes actually have connections to terrorist groups that are willing to use WMD against the United States.[11] The third presupposition is that a rogue regime that has developed WMD will share them with those terrorists. The fourth presupposition is that terrorists will use WMD for an attack against the United States and not as bargaining chips or for other purposes.

Even if these presuppositions are accepted there remain three ma-

---

11. A recent study by Mary Caprioli and Peter F. Trumbore suggests that rogue states in fact are not exceptionally aggressive in their interstate relations (2005: 788): "Overall, rogue states as a group are no more likely to become involved in interstate disputes in any given year, are no more likely to initiate militarized disputes, and are no more likely to use force first when disputes turn violent."

Anticipatory Defense and Regime Change 339

jor reservations against the proposed right to security-related regime change, which have not been answered by proponents of the Bush doctrine:

First, the unilateral right or, as some analysts claim, prerogative of the United States to defend itself preemptively/preventively effectively undermines the present system of international security without providing an adequate substitute. If preemptive defense is a universal right, it would destabilize the present world order by considerably broadening the right to go to war. If it applies only to a select group of nations, it would undermine the justice and thus credibility of international law.

Second, how can the right of self-determination of peoples be balanced with *forcible* regime change? Julie Mertus (2003) argues that such a balancing act might be impossible: "Forcible regime change violates the deeply enshrined principle that people should be allowed to choose their own government. The cornerstone human rights document, the Universal Declaration of Human Rights, provides that the only legitimate government is one based on the 'will of the people.' The International Covenant on Civil and Political Rights, a convention ratified by the U.S., recognizes 'self-determination' as a human right and specifies that '[b]y virtue of that right' all peoples have the right to 'freely determine their political status and freely pursue their economic, social and cultural development.'" Without going as far as Mertus, it is interesting to note that the *NSS* does not address this important question at all.

Third, how can the epistemic problem of preemption be solved? If it is nearly impossible to obtain reliable intelligence on the status and existence of WMD programs, it will be all the more difficult to get reliable intelligence about the intentions of foreign regimes and their terrorist affiliates. The Iraq case has shown how difficult it is to acquire objective and dependable information in a situation in which fear of attack (post 9/11) is acute.

The authors of the *NSS* are surely correct in pointing out the dangers of a possible alliance between rogue regimes and terrorists that might result in the use of WMD against civilian populations. To react by declaring a seemingly unilateral "right to preemptive war" and consequently to security-related forcible regime change does not seem to be a suitable reaction to this threat. The Bush doctrine already has strengthened the prejudice that the United States is a heavy-handed hegemon that follows only self-interest and suppresses even legitimate opposition with its military might. Many hold, even among traditional U.S. allies, that the Iraq war turned out to be a blow to the present international order. The *NSS* in its present form could even be interpreted as an attempt to achieve security for the United States by derogating the security of the international community, because one member alone is granted the permission to change regimes without being accountable to any international organization.

Feasibility

The third aspect of security-related forcible regime change is the complex problem of feasibility. Can forcible regime change succeed in substituting a dangerous regime with one that is well ordered, peace loving, and still representative of its own people? In the aftermath of the publication of the *NSS* and the Iraq crisis many contending views on this question were offered. Two main objections against the feasibility of regime change have been made: (1) a forced regime change that results in a stable, democratic, and well-governed nation is next to impossible and (2) the Bush doctrine in the current international order is counterproductive.

The most important empirical criticism of forcible regime change is the charge that outwardly enforced regime change is likely to fail.[12] As early as 1859 John Stuart Mill claimed that democracy cannot take hold if it is imposed on a people. Minxin Pei and Sara Kasper (2003) looked at U.S. attempts at regime change and applied one simple criterion to judge success or failure: Was the supposedly changed regime still democratic after ten years? The results of the study are sobering. All attempts before 1945 failed. After 1945 only two out of six regime changes brought stable and viable democracies to the target countries. In both cases these countries were small (Panama and Grenada) and had good prospects for economic and political development even before the interventions.[13]

The policy exchange study *Regime Change: It's Been Done Before* (Gough,

---

12. This criticism did not remain uncontested. Some researchers come to the conclusion that under certain conditions intervention might set a political system on the right path to democratic reform. See Hermann and Kegley, 1998; Gleditsch, Christiansen, and Hegre, 2004.

13. Von Hippel, 1999 takes a look at interventions and nation-building attempts in Panama, Somalia, Haiti, and Bosnia. While only Somalia in her judgment was a complete failure, the regimes left in charge in the other three cases proved wanting in many respects.

2003) comes to similar mixed results. The study cites regime changes in post–World War II Germany, Italy, and Japan as successes of building democracies by force. But these three cases seem to have happened under very special circumstances. Germany, for example, was utterly defeated in war, physically as well as morally. This gave the democratic elements of that society the chance to take over and to make use of democratic traditions that already existed.[14]

The present-day problems of the allied forces in Iraq illustrate the many difficulties regime change entails (Bacevich, 2005). Even years after the overthrow of Saddam Hussein, the establishment of a stable democratic government seems elusive. It has become clear that far more resources would have been needed to protect the infrastructure against sabotage and to quickly create political institutions that would transfer some political decision making as well as responsibility to the Iraqis. If regime change is to have even a faint chance of success a huge effort like the post–World War II Marshall Plan would likely be needed. A strategy of "regime change light" is always likely to fail (Ignatieff, 2003; Ottaway, 2003).

The second objection states that the concept of preemption is counterproductive in the current international order. Instead of ensuring more security for the United States and other countries, the doctrine of preemption might send the wrong signal (Guoliang, 2003). It is argued that the war against Iraq and the continuing diplomatic initiatives in North Korea have made clear that the United States will attack weak regimes that it considers to be roguish but will not touch rogues that already have some arsenal of WMD. The rational conclusion for the leaders of rogue regimes therefore would be to develop WMD as fast as possible to ward off an attack or the threat of attack. In the end the Bush doctrine would not curb proliferation but be a strong incentive for possible targets of regime change to spend even more resources on acquiring WMD.

The problem of the feasibility of regime change is too complex to be discussed here in full detail. The two objections, however, show that regime change is not a trivial business. It is questionable whether the United States can succeed in diffusing the threat of the axis of rogues-

---

14. See Jowitt, 2003, for an in-depth analysis on the differences of postwar Germany, Japan, and Iraq. An interesting historical overview of attempts to change political systems in foreign countries can be found in Owen, 2002.

terrorists-WMD by changing all regimes that might become dangerous. The experience of regime change in Iraq has shown that the U.S. military faces the danger of "overstretching" its capabilities.

In considering the results of our discussion of the legality, justice, and feasibility of regime change, it becomes clear that the Bush doctrine contained in the 2002 *NSS* is fraught with various problems. The proposed doctrine of preemption is inconsistent with current international law, and indeed seems inconsistent with the affirmation of multilateralism that is at the center of chapters 3 and 4 of the same document. Moreover, the moral basis of the Bush doctrine is highly questionable, (1) because the *NSS* seems to demand a prerogative rather than a universal right and (2) because its underdefined criteria for justified action leave ample possibilities for abuse of the doctrine. The feasibility of forced regime change is, at least, doubtful. It is clear, however, that if regime change is to have even the slightest chance of success, considerable resources have to be spent on the target country. Instead of providing a set of guidelines for meeting newly emerged threats the Bush doctrine rather undermines current international law without establishing a workable alternative.

The "Realistic Utopia" of Regime Change

The Bush doctrine was harshly criticized for the above-mentioned shortcomings. Nonetheless, the argument that it might be necessary to change extremely aggressive regimes in order to prevent the proliferation of WMD and the destabilization of entire regions has some intuitive persuasiveness. One could easily think of regimes that because of their internal instability pose a threat to all their neighbors and thus create an atmosphere of suspicion and tension. An example of this kind of regime would be Idi Amin's Uganda. In October 1978, faced with an army mutiny and riots over the killings of approximately three hundred thousand Ugandans, as well as being diplomatically isolated, Amin ordered his troops to invade Tanzania and annex the province of Kagera. With this maneuver Amin hoped to strengthen his hold on power while keeping a low-intensity conflict simmering that could be used to keep the opposition in check by denouncing their criticism as unpatriotic in times of war. This, however, turned out to be a miscalculation since Tanzanian

Anticipatory Defense and Regime Change   343

president Julius Nyere decided to escalate the conflict and to get rid of Idi Amin once and for all. With the help of Ugandan guerillas his forces invaded the neighboring country and succeeded in ousting Amin from power. It is obvious that if Amin had possessed WMD the crisis would have taken on a completely new dimension.

Should an Idi Amin be stopped before he becomes a danger to an entire region? The late philosopher John Rawls offers in his *Law of Peoples* (1999) a view of a "realistic utopia" that might contain an opening for this kind of admittedly preventive regime change. To avoid any misunderstandings, it must be stated that Rawls does not expressly discuss the problem of forcible regime change and therefore does not delve into the more intriguing questions of why, when, and how to interfere with the governance of foreign countries. I use his idea of a realistically utopian world order as a starting point for a thought experiment that will show why the ideas of preventive defense and forcible regime change cannot a priori be discarded as always contrary to our moral and political convictions. Once we have seen why the concept of security-related regime change might under idealized circumstances seem workable, it will help us clarify to what extent the *NSS* makes use of tacit idealized assumptions that give it a certain measure of superficial plausibility.

Rawls in *The Law of Peoples* explains what developments are necessary to set the present system of states on a course toward a more just, new world order. The most important step is the introduction of the "Law of Peoples" itself. The Law of Peoples, in Rawls's terminology, is the "political conception of right and justice that applies to the principles and norms of international law and practice" (1999: 3). One of the aims of a reasonable Law of Peoples is to guarantee peace, stability, and cooperation among states. International law in Rawls's realistic utopia is thus founded on principles that are in accordance with consensual ideas of justice.

Rawls acknowledges that the international community is a society of peoples living in sovereign states. The different states that comprise this community can be divided into five distinct types: (1) liberal societies, (2) decent societies, (3) benevolent absolutism, (4) burdened societies, and (5) outlaw states. Rawls describes liberal societies in terms of three basic features: "a reasonably just constitutional democratic government that serves [the citizens'] fundamental interests; citizens united by what

Mill called 'common sympathies'; and finally, a moral nature" (1999: 23). The term "common sympathies" denotes a feeling of a common identity and destiny that citizens share with each other. The "moral nature" refers to the fact that liberal peoples in Rawls's view must be both reasonable and rational. "Reasonable" in this sense means that a liberal citizen is willing to cooperate with other citizens in domestic society on fair terms. There can be no doubt that Rawls considers liberal democracy to be the most desirable form of government.

Rawls defines "decent" governments as "nonliberal societies whose basic institutions meet certain specified conditions of political right and justice (including the right of citizens to play a substantial role, say through associations and groups, in making political decisions) and lead their citizens to honor a reasonably just law for the Society of Peoples" (1999: 3).

The term "benevolent absolutism" denotes those governments that do not allow all their citizens to participate in political decision-making processes but have a regard for human rights and respect international law. In today's world some of the Gulf emirates show the characteristics of benevolent absolutist regimes.

"Burdened societies" are those nations that are held back in their development by highly unfavorable internal conditions. These conditions can be historical, economic, social, or a mixture of all three. Because of their difficult situation burdened societies have problems growing into liberal or decent societies, or in more severe cases cannot advance without external help. The term "burdened societies" seems to correspond vaguely to the more common term "failed states." "Failed states," however, usually denotes societies that are in a state of turmoil, civil war, or violent upheaval.[15] Additionally, the term "burdened societies" includes societies that may have reached a certain measure of internal peace. A rigid caste society, for example, may seem relatively free of internal violence. Its fundamentally unjust social system, however, might bar its development into a well-ordered society.

"Outlaw states" are defined as those regimes that refuse to comply

---

15. The *State Failure Task Force Report, Phase III* defines failed states as those political entities that are destroyed by (1) revolutionary wars, (2) ethnic wars, (3) adverse regime changes (shifts away from democracy to authoritarian rule), and (4) genocides/politicides. See Goldstone et al., 2000. See also Zartman, 1995; Rotberg, 2002; Gros, 1996.

with a reasonable Law of Peoples and think that "a sufficient reason to go to war is that war advances, or might advance, the regime's rational (not reasonable) interests" (Rawls 1999: 90). Rawls's idea of "outlaw states" seems to correspond with the term "rogue states."[16] Outlaw states show a selfish drive to aggrandize themselves at the cost of others and have no qualms about using violence as a means of furthering their goals. Because of this strict definition, Rawls also considers Europe's early modern monarchies that continually quarreled among themselves as outlaw states (ibid.: 105–6).

According to Rawls, liberal and decent peoples form the group of the well-ordered societies of the world. He assumes that liberal peoples are unlikely to go to war with other liberal or decent societies. Rawls here agrees with the "democratic peace" hypothesis.[17] Although actual democracies sometimes are marked by "considerable injustice, oligarchic tendencies and monopolistic interests" (1999: 48), Rawls believes that well-ordered societies are most likely to succeed in creating a just and stable international order based on moral principles. The people of these societies, he argues, are aware that in the same way that just and fair internal laws are the prerequisite for peace and stability within a state, a just and fair body of international law is the sine qua non of a stable and peaceful world order.

The well-ordered societies seem to form a core of states in Rawls's conception that establish a just international law and then attempt to move other states to adhere to the law and in time reform themselves along the principles of the Law of Peoples. One of the most pressing problems for the process of enlarging and even maintaining the community of well-ordered peoples is the relation between the well-ordered societies and instable or aggressive regimes.

The instability of burdened societies might lead to the necessity of a

---

16. Rawls seems to avoid the term "rogue state" because critics have accused the governments of the Western world of using this term solely for propaganda purposes. A rogue state would be any state that pursues a policy antithetical to the interests and objectives of the West (Chomsky, 2000). Furthermore, the term "outlaw state" more precisely describes regimes that on purpose remain outside the system established by international law.

17. Rawls (1999: 53) was aware that "the idea of democratic peace sometimes fails. In these cases, my guiding hypothesis leads me to expect to find various failures in a democracy's essential supporting institutions and practices." The United States, for instance, covertly intervened to oust democratic leaders and to install autocratic stooges in Guatemala in 1954 (see Schlesinger and Kinzer, 1982).

military humanitarian intervention. Rawls (1999: 109) gives an example of humanitarian emergencies that might necessitate interfering in the internal affairs of a failing state: "A government's allowing people to starve when it is preventable reflects a lack of concern for human rights, and well-ordered regimes as I have described them will not allow this to happen."[18] Even more dangerous for a just and fair international order are outwardly aggressive regimes: "If the political conception of political liberalism is sound, and if the steps we have taken in developing the Law of Peoples are also sound, then liberal and decent peoples have the right, under the Law of Peoples, not to tolerate outlaw states. Liberal and decent peoples have extremely good reasons for their attitude. Outlaw states are aggressive and dangerous; all peoples are safer and more secure if such states change, or are forced to change, their ways. Otherwise, they deeply affect the international climate of power and violence" (ibid.: 81). Rawls in this passage argues that it is just that well-ordered societies exert pressure on the regimes of outlaw states in order to force them to comply with international law. I will not discuss whether Rawls should be interpreted to advocate forcible regime change or not.[19] It would, however, make sense to assume that in extreme situations the community of well-ordered societies would be justified in using forcible regime change in order to prevent the undermining of a just and fair international law. If, for example, an outlaw state sought to acquire WMD and was clearly intending to use them to threaten its neighbors and to pursue an aggressive policy, this situation could effectively destabilize the international order of the Law of Peoples, because it would force neighboring states to arm themselves, to keep forces in a state of mobilization, and thus it would create an atmosphere of suspicion that would be conducive to conflict. Furthermore, the aggressiveness of outlaw states would cause a relapse of the international community into the kind of anarchy in which only military might would be respected.

It has been argued that exactly this was the case in the Iraq crisis of 2003 and that therefore today's well-ordered societies had to intervene and change the Iraqi regime. But if we look at Rawls's realistic utopia again, we find that some important prerequisites are missing in the present world order.

18. On intended famine, see also Marcus, 2003.
19. For Rawls's position on just war and intervention, see Wicclair, 1980; Giesen, 1999.

First, in Rawls's realistic utopia the well-ordered societies have established a just and fair international law. Rawls does not give details on how he imagines the international law based on the moral and political principles of the Law of Peoples to be implemented. Nonetheless, it can be inferred from his explanations that the institutions to implement international law must conform to the principles of the Law of Peoples, too. This would mean that an organization like the United Nations in the realistic utopia of the Law of Peoples would be founded on principles of justice and fairness and not on the representation of power of the strongest nations.

Second, in Rawls's well-ordered societies we find one important difference with today's democracies. The peoples of the well-ordered societies are of the opinion that a fair and just international order is their most important national interest. Neither economic advantages nor a hegemonic position outweigh the concern for this international order.

Third, Rawls makes clear that the well-ordered societies deliberate and act together when questions of the international order arise.

Rawls's prerequisites suggest solutions to some of the difficult problems that arise apropos of forcible regime change. One of these is how to decide what sort of regimes should be changed and when. It is here that consensus can play an important role. If the quasi-unanimity of well-ordered societies can agree that a particular regime is a danger to international security and stability, the likelihood that this regime is indeed pernicious will be extremely high. For here the intelligence capabilities of different nations will be bundled and for this reason they stand a much better chance of producing sound judgments. Moreover, the point of view of states that need not feel directly threatened may help to distinguish overblown war scares from actually dangerous situations.[20]

Concerning the question of feasibility, it is obvious that an alliance of all well-ordered societies has more resources at hand than any single nation or "coalition of the willing." This does not refer only to monetary resources. When confronted with regime change and nation building, past experience shows that it is even more important to have a vast array of human resources at hand, that is, specialists in all kinds of fields that are

---

20. For further advantages of a cosmopolitan framework for preventive military action, see Buchanan and Keohane, 2004.

necessary to rebuild a country and help transfer political power as fast as possible back to the people of the former outlaw state.

Since well-ordered societies of the Law of Peoples are more interested in a just and fair world order than in more narrowly defined egoistic interests, there is a good chance that the abuse of forcible regime change for cynical purposes is minimized. If we take these idealized conditions into account, preventive defense and forcible regime change might seem justifiable. If we return to the present-day world order, we find that the authors of the *NSS* need to make some tacit idealized assumptions, too, in order to make a convincing case for a right to regime change.

The first tacit assumption concerns the question of decision making. The *NSS* actually leaves the decision on regime change to the discretion of the president of the United States. If this is to be a convincing solution for the decision-making problem, then one must be of the opinion that the U.S. president will not be guided by egoistic national interests, that he will not be swayed by the undue influence of lobbies, that he will balance opposing views impartially and without bias, and that his intelligence sources are as accurate as possible.

The second tacit assumption is that the United States is able to perform a regime change with due regard for the rights of the people of the target country. The moral and legal obligations of the regime-changing nation are to ensure that the target country does not slide into chaos and to help the people on the path to recovery. The authors of the *NSS* in fact ask their compatriots for huge sacrifices, because—if we accept that regime change entails the responsibility to help in the reconstruction—every regime change will involve the expenditure of considerable national resources.

The third tacit assumption is that the United States will not abuse regime change for purposes that are not related to security and human rights. The authors of the *NSS* warn all nations to refrain from using preemption as a pretext for aggression. They do not, however, specify how the United States itself would be prevented from abusing regime change for hegemonic, economic, or other unjust purposes. Here it seems that the authors of the *NSS* are asserting a certain form of American exceptionalism. Only if one accepts that the United States is a virtuous, freedom-loving power, the champion of human rights and liberal democracy in the world, would one be justified in expecting that a U.S. administration will refrain from abusing a prerogative that allows it to initiate regime changes that are forbidden to any other nation.

Yet in the opinion of this writer, these three assumptions lean heavily in favor of an overly positive image of the United States. In this respect the *NSS* cannot be said to offer a consistent argument in favor of the United States' right to effect forcible regime change when necessary.

The more promising way to enhance the security of the United States in the fight against international terrorism may lie in the path that political thinkers such as John Rawls have outlined. This consists in working toward strengthening justice and fairness in the international order by supporting (and when need be creating) democratic international institutions. Most of all this would entail rejecting a narrowly defined national interest as a guide for foreign policy decision making and substituting it with a the kind of multilateralism that the authors of the *NSS* committed themselves to in chapters 3 and 4 of the same document.

REFERENCES

Bacevich, Andrew J. 2005. "Requiem for the Bush Doctrine." *Current History* 104 (December 2005): 411–17.

Bennett, Andrew. 1999. *Condemned to Repetition? The Rise, Fall, and Reprise of Soviet-Russian Military Interventionism, 1973–1996.* Cambridge and London: MIT Press.

Betts, Richard K. 2003. "Striking First: A History of Thankfully Lost Opportunities." *Ethics and International Affairs* 17 (1): 17–29.

Boniface, Pascal. 2003. "What Justifies Regime Change?"*Washington Quarterly* 26 (3): 61–71.

Bothe, Michael. 2003. "Terrorism and the Legality of Pre-emptive Force." *European Journal of International Law* 14 (2): 227–40.

Buchanan, Allen, and Robert O. Keohane. 2004. "The Preventive Use of Force: A Cosmopolitan Institutional Proposal." *Ethics and International Affairs* 18 (1): 1–22.

Butler, William E. 1974. "Soviet Attitudes toward Intervention." In John Norton Moor, ed., *Law and Civil War in the Modern World.* Baltimore: Johns Hopkins University Press, 380–98.

Byers, Michael, and Simon Chesterman. 2000. "You, the People: Pro-Democratic Intervention in International Law." In Gregory H. Fox and Brad R. Roth, eds., *Democratic Governance and International Law.* Cambridge: Cambridge University Press, 259–92.

Caprioli, Mary, and Peter F. Trumbore. 2005. "Rhetoric vs. Reality: Rogue States in Interstate Conflicts." *Journal of Conflict Resolution* 49 (5): 770–91.

Chomsky, Noam. 2000. *Rogue States: The Rule of Force in World Affairs.* Cambridge, Mass.: South End.

Cirincione, John. 2003. "Origins of Regime Change in Iraq." *Proliferation Brief* 6 (5), http://www.ceip.org/files/nonprolif/templates/Publications.asp?p=8&PublicationID=1214.

Crawford, Neta C. 2003. "The Slippery Slope to Preventive War." *Ethics and International Affairs* 17 (1): 30–36.

Curtis, Mark. 2003. "As British as Afternoon Tea." *Guardian*, May 21, 2003, http://www.markcurtis.info/article7.html.

Giesen, K. G. 1999. "Charité paternaliste et guerre juste: La justice internationale selon John Rawls." *Temps modernes* 54 (604): 40–62.

Gleditsch, Nils P., Lene S. Christiansen, and Haarvard Hegre. 2004. "Democratic Jihad: Military Intervention and Democratization." Paper presented at the Forty-fifth Annual Convention of the International Studies Association, Montreal, March 17–20, http://www.isanet.org.

Goldstone, Jack A., et al. 2000. *State Failure Task Force Report: Phase III Findings*. McLean, Va.: Science Applications International Corporation.

Gough, Roger, ed. 2003. *Regime Change: It's Been Done Before*. London: Policy Exchange.

Gros, Jean-Germain. 1996. "Towards a Taxonomy of Failed States in the New World Order: Decaying Somalia, Liberia, Rwanda, and Haiti." *Third World Quarterly* 17 (3): 455–72.

Guoliang, Guo. 2003. "Redefine Cooperative Security, Not Pre-emption." *Washington Quarterly* 26 (2): 135–45.

Hermann, Margaret G., and Charles W. Kegley Jr. 1998. "The U.S. Use of Military Intervention to Promote Democracy: Evaluating the Record." *International Interactions* 24 (2): 91–114.

Ignatieff, Michael. 2003. *Empire Lite: Nation Building in Bosnia, Kosovo, Afghanistan*. London: Vintage.

Jowitt, Ken. 2003. "Rage, Hubris, and Regime Change." *Policy Review* 118:39–40.

Lecce, D. J. 1998. "International Law Regarding Pro-Democratic Intervention: A Study of the Dominican Republic and Haiti." *Naval Law Review* 45:247–62.

Litwak, Robert S. 2002–3. "The New Calculus of Pre-emption." *Survival* 44 (4): 53–80.

Marcus, David. 2003. "Famine Crimes in International Law." *American Journal of International Law* 97 (2): 245–81.

Mertus, Julie. 2003. "The Law (?) of Regime Change." *Jurist*, http://jurist.law.pitt.edu/forum/forumnew98.php.

Monten, Jonathan. 2005. "The Roots of the Bush Doctrine: Power, Nationalism, and Democracy Promotion in the U.S. Strategy." *International Security* 29 (4): 112–56.

Nichols, Thomas M. 2003. "How Really New Is the New Bush National Security Strategy?" *History News Network*, http://hnn.us/articles/1031.html.

NSS. 2002. *The National Security Strategy of the United States, September 2002*. Washington, D.C.: White House, http://www.whitehouse.gov/nsc/nss.html.

———. 2006. *The National Security Strategy of the United States, March 2006*. Washington, D.C.: White House, http://www.whitehouse.gov/nsc/nss.html.

Ottaway, Marina. 2003. "Promoting Democracy after the Conflict: The Difficult Choices." *International Studies Perspectives* 4 (3): 314–22.

Owen, John M. 2002. "The Foreign Imposition of Domestic Institutions." *International Organization* 56: 375–409.

Pei, Minxin, and Sara Kasper. 2003. "The 'Morning After' Regime Change: Should US Force Democracy Again?" *Christian Science Monitor*, January 15.

Prime Minister's Iraq Statement to Parliament. 2002. September 24, http://www.number10.gov.uk/output/Page1727.asp.

Project for the New American Century. 1998. "Letter to President Clinton on Iraq," http://www.newamericancentury.org/iraqclintonletter.htm.

Pry, Peter Vincent. 1999. *War Scare: Russia and America on the Nuclear Brink*. Westport, Conn. and London: Praeger.

Randelzhofer, Albrecht. 2002. "Article 51.'" In Bruno Simma et al., eds., *The Charter of the United Nations: A Commentary*, 2nd ed. Oxford and New York: Oxford University Press, 788–806.

Rawls, John. 1999. *The Law of Peoples*. Cambridge: Harvard University Press.

Reichberg, Gregory. 2004. "Pre-emptive War: What Would Aquinas Say?" *Commonweal* 131 (2), http://www.commonwealmagazine.org/2004/january302004/013004st.htm.

Rotberg, Robert I. 2002. "The New Nature of Nation-State Failure." *Washington Quarterly* 25 (3): 85–96.

Schachter, Oscar. 1984. "The Legality of Pro-Democratic Invasion." *American Journal of International Law* 78 (3): 645–50.

Schlesinger, Arthur Jr. 2002. "Unilateral Preventive War: Illegitimate and Immoral." *Los Angeles Times*, August 21.

Schlesinger, Stephen, and Stephen Kinzer. 1982. *Bitter Fruit: The Untold Story of the American Coup in Guatemala.* London: Sinclair Browne.
Schmitt, Michael N. 2003. "Pre-emptive Strategies and International Law." *Michigan Journal of International Law* 24:513–48.
Slocombe, Walter. 2003. "Force, Pre-emption, and Legitimacy." *Survival* 45 (1): 117–30.
Snider, Don M. 1992. *The National Security Strategy: Documenting Strategic Vision.* Carlisle Barracks, Pa.: Strategic Studies Institute, U.S. Army War College.
Sofaer, Abraham D. 2003. "On the Necessity of Pre-emption." *European Journal of International Law* 14 (2): 209–26.
Stevens, Kenneth R. 1989. *Border Diplomacy: The Caroline and McLeod Affairs in Anglo-American-Canadian Relations, 1837–1842.* Tuscaloosa: University of Alabama Press.
Treacher, Adrian. 2003. *French Interventionism: Europe's Last Global Player?* Aldershot, U.K.: Ashgate.
U.S. State Department. 2002. *White House Reiterates Regime Change in Iraq Is U.S. Policy.* White House Report, August 19, http://usinfo.state.gov/regional/nea/iraq/text/0819wthsrpt.htm.
Utley, Rachel. 1998. "The New French Interventionism." *Civil Wars* 1 (2): 85–103.
Verschaeve, François-Xavier, 2000. *Silence noir: Qui arrêtera la Françafrique?* Paris: Editions des Arènes.
Von Hippel, Karin. 1999. *Democracy by Force: U.S. Military Intervention in the Post–Cold War World.* New York: Cambridge University Press.
Walzer, Michael. 1977. *Just and Unjust War: A Moral Argument, with Historical Illustrations.* New York: Basic.
———. 2003. "Judging War." Speech given at the Heinrich Böll Foundation, Berlin, July 2, http://www.boell.de/downloads/aussen/walzer_judging_war.pdf.
Webster, Daniel. 1840–41. *British and Foreign State Papers.* Vol. 29. London: James Ridgway and Sons.
Weller, Marc. 1998. "The Changing Environment for Forcible Responses to Nontraditional Threats." *American Society of International Law Annual Proceedings* 92 (1-4): 177–78.
Wicclair, Mark. 1980. "Rawls and the Principle of Non-intervention." In H. Gene Blocker and Elizabeth H. Smith, eds., *John Rawls' Theory of Social Justice.* Athens: Ohio University Press, 289–308.
Wippman, David. 2000. "Pro-Democratic Intervention by Invitation." In Gregory H. Fox and Brad R. Roth, eds., *Democratic Governance and International Law.* Cambridge: Cambridge University Press, 293–327.
Wyllie, James H. 1984. *The Influence of British Arms: An Analysis of British Military Intervention since 1956.* London: Allen and Unwin.
Zartman, William, ed.. 1995. *Collapsed States: The Disintegration and Restoration of Legitimate Authority.* London: Lynne Rienner.

15

Genocide

A Case for the Responsibility of the Bystander

ARNE JOHAN VETLESEN

Defining Genocide

After affirming that genocide is a crime under international law whether committed in time of peace or war, the 1948 Convention on the Prevention and Punishment of the Crime of Genocide defines genocide as "any of the following acts committed with intent to destroy, in whole or in part, a national, ethnic, racial or religious group, as such: killing members of the group; causing serious bodily or mental harm to members of the group; deliberately inflicting on the group conditions of life calculated to bring about its physical destruction in whole or in part; imposing measures intended to prevent births within the group; forcibly transferring children of the group to another group" (Gutman and Rieff, 1999: 154). In addition to the crime of genocide itself, the 1948 convention provides that the following acts shall be punishable: conspiracy to commit genocide, direct and public incitement to commit genocide, attempt to commit genocide, and complicity in genocide. The Genocide Convention imposes a general duty on states that are parties to the convention "to prevent and to punish" genocide. In addition to individual criminal responsibility for genocide, the convention also establishes state responsibility—that is, international legal responsibility of the state itself for breaching its obligations under the convention. It is crucial to bear in mind that the main criterion of genocide is that it is directed at individuals "not in their capacities as individuals but as members of the national [or ethnic, racial, or religious] group" (see Helsinki Watch, 1992: 2; Sells, 1996: 24).

The term *genocide* was coined as recently as in the mid-1930s by the Polish scholar Raphael Lemkin, who fashioned it from the Greek word *genos,* meaning race or tribe, and the Latin term for killing, *cide.* Lemkin pointed out that, generally speaking, genocide does not necessarily mean the immediate destruction of a nation. It is intended rather to signify "a coordinated plan of different actions aiming at the destruction of essential foundations of the life of national groups, with the aim of annihilating the groups themselves" (Gutman and Rieff, 1999: 155). Lemkin observed that genocide has two phases: "one, destruction of the national pattern of the oppressed group; the other, the imposition of the national pattern of the oppressor. This imposition, in turn, may be made upon the oppressed population which is allowed to remain, or upon the territory alone, after removal of the population and colonization of the area by the oppressor's own nationals" (ibid.).

Before proceeding, let me briefly note the problems created for nations of a genuinely *multinational and multireligious* kind by the conceptual nationalist bias implicit in the Lemkin-inspired Genocide Convention. In a state such as Bosnia, there is not one—homogeneous—national group that is being threatened. As David Campbell argues, because a "national" group has to be ethnically, racially, or religiously specific to have status according to the convention, a multicultural state, in order to protect itself from partition, would have to "[submit] itself to the very identity politics and territorial division it is seeking to resist" (1998: 108). What the bias in favor of homogeneous, exclusivist identity built into the very premises of the Genocide Convention cannot accommodate, then, are threats to a hybrid, multicultural polity, one where each person is the carrier of multiple identities, thus defying any one-criterion identity mark.

It is important to have this in mind when, in what follows, I invoke empirical material from the so-called civil war in Bosnia (1992–95). My purpose is to raise the issue of responsibility for genocide, in particular with regard to *incitement* to genocide and *complicity* in genocide. My systematic focus will be on the respective roles of two groups: the *bystanders* to concrete acts of genocide and the *intellectuals* who in their professional capacities take part in genocide on the side of the perpetrator group.

A Typology of Bystanders to Genocide

Most often, in cases of genocide, for every person directly victimized and killed there will be hundreds, thousands, perhaps even millions who are neither directly targeted as victims nor directly participating as perpetrators. The moral issues raised by genocide, taken as the illegal act par excellence, are not confined to the nexus of agent and victim. Those directly involved in a given instance of genocide will always form a minority, so to speak. The majority to the event will be formed by the contemporary bystanders. Such bystanders are individuals; in their private and professional lives, they will belong to a vast range of groups and collectives, some informal and closely knit, others formal and detached as far as personal and emotional involvement are concerned. In the loose sense intended here, every contemporary citizen cognizant of a specific ongoing instance of genocide, regardless of where in the world it occurs, counts as a bystander.

Bystanders in this loose sense are aware, through TV, radio, newspapers, and other publicly available sources of information, of ongoing genocide somewhere in the world, but they are not—by profession or formal appointment—involved in it. Theirs is a passive role, that of onlookers. Although what starts out as a passive stance may, when a decision is taken, convert into active engagement in the events at hand, I shall label this category *passive bystanders.*

This group should be distinguished from bystanders by *formal appointment:* those who have been professionally engaged as a "third party" to the interaction between the two parties directly involved in acts of genocide. The stance of the third party to an ongoing conflict, even one with genocidal implications, is in principle one of impartiality and neutrality, typically highlighted by a determined refusal to "take sides." This manner of principled noninvolvement is frequently viewed as highly meritorious (Vetlesen, 1998). A case in point would be U.N. personnel deployed to monitor a cease-fire between warring parties, or (as was their task in Bosnia) to see to it that the civilians within a U.N.-declared "safe area" are effectively guaranteed "peace and security," as set down in the mandate to establish such areas. By virtue of their assigned physical presence on the scene and the specific tasks given to them, such (groups of) bystanders may be referred to as *bystanders by assignment.*

Genocide 355

What does it mean to be a contemporary bystander? To begin with, let us consider this question not from the expected viewpoint, that of the bystander him- or herself, but from the two viewpoints of the parties directly involved in the event.

To put it as simply as possible: From the viewpoint of an agent of genocide, bystanders are persons possessing a potential (one needing to be estimated in every concrete case) to halt his ongoing actions. The perpetrator will fear the bystander to the extent that he has reason to believe that the bystander will intervene to halt the action already under way and thereby frustrate the perpetrator's goal of eliminating the targeted group. That said, we immediately need to differentiate among the different categories of bystanders introduced above. It is obvious that the more knowledgeable and otherwise resourceful the bystander, the more the perpetrator will have reason to fear that the potential for such resistance will translate into action, meaning a more or less direct intervention by military or other means deemed efficient to reach the objective of halting the incipient genocide. Of course, one should distinguish between bystanders who remain inactive and those who become actively engaged. Nonetheless, the point to be stressed is that, in principle, even the initially most passive and remote bystander possesses a potential to cease being a mere onlooker to the events unfolding. Outrage at what comes to pass may prompt the judgment that "this simply must be stopped" and translate into action promoting that aim.

But is not halting genocide first and foremost a task, indeed a duty, for the victims themselves? The answer is simple: The sheer fact that genocide is happening shows that the targeted group has proven itself unable to prevent it. This being so, responsibility for halting what is now unfolding cannot rest with the victims alone; it must also be seen to rest with the party not itself affected but knowledgeable about—which is more or less literally *witnessing*—the genocide that is taking place. So whereas for the agent bystanders represent the potential of resistance, for the victims they may represent the only source of hope left. In ethical terms, this is borne out in Emmanuel Levinas's (1991) notion of responsibility, according to which responsibility grows bigger the weaker its addressee.

Of course, agents of genocide may be caught more or less *in delicto flagrante*. But in the age of television—with CNN being able to film and even interview (!) perpetrators as well as victims on the spot and broadcast live to the entire television-watching world (such as was the case in the concentration camp Omarska in Bosnia in August 1992; see Gutman, 1993)—physically being present at the event at hand is almost rendered superfluous. One need not have been there in order to know what has happened. The same holds for the impact of the day-to-day reporting from the ground by newspaper journalists of indisputable reputation. In order to be knowledgeable about ongoing genocide these days, it suffices to watch TV news or read the front pages of one's daily newspaper.

But, to be more precise, what exactly does it mean to act? What is to count as an action? We need to look briefly at the philosophical literature on the notion of action—as well as the notion of agent responsibility following from it—in order to get a better grasp of the moral issues involved in being a bystander to genocide, whether passive or active.

Acting—and Deciding Not to

"I never forget," says Paul Ricoeur in *Oneself as Another,* "to speak of humans as acting and suffering. The moral problem," he continues, "is grafted onto the recognition of this essential dissymmetry between the one who acts and the one who undergoes, culminating in the violence of the powerful agent." To be the "sufferer" of a given action in Ricoeur's sense need not be negative; either "the sufferer appears as the beneficiary of esteem or as the victim of disesteem, depending on whether the agent proves to be someone who distributes rewards or punishments." Since there is to every action an agent and a sufferer (in the sense given), action is interaction; its structure is interpersonal (Ricoeur, 1992: 145).

But this is not the whole picture. Actions are also omitted, endured, neglected, and the like; and Ricoeur takes these phenomena to remind us that "on the level of interaction, just as on that of subjective understanding, not acting is still acting: neglecting, forgetting to do something, is also letting things be done by someone else, sometimes to the point of criminality" (1992: 157). Ricoeur's systematic objective is to extend the theory of action from acting to suffering beings; again and again he emphasizes that "every action has its agents and its patients" (ibid.).

Ricoeur's proposed extension certainly sounds plausible. Regrettably, his proposal stops halfway. The vital insight articulated, albeit not developed, in the passages quoted is that *not acting is still acting.* Brought to bear on the case of genocide as a reported, ongoing affair, the inaction making a difference is the inaction of the bystander to unfolding genocide. The failure to act when confronted with such action is a failure that carries a message to both the agent and the sufferer: the action may proceed. Knowing, yet still not acting, means granting acceptance to the action. Such inaction entails "letting things be done by someone else"—clearly, in the case of acknowledged genocide, "to the point of criminality," to invoke one of the quotes from Ricoeur. In short, inaction here means complicity; accordingly, it raises the question of responsibility, guilt, and shame on the part of the inactive bystander, by which I mean the bystander who *decides* to remain inactive.

In the view I am advancing, the theory of action is satisfactorily extended only when it is recognized that the structure of action is triadic, not dyadic. It takes two to act, we are tempted to say—no more and no less. But is an action really the exclusive possession—a private affair—between the two parties immediately affected as agent and sufferer? For one thing, the repercussions of a particular action are bound to reach far beyond the immediate dyadic setting. As Hannah Arendt (1958) famously observed, to act is to initiate, to make a new beginning in the world, to set in motion—and open-endedly so. Only the start of a specific action allows precise localization in space and time, allows us to attribute it to a particular agent, as *her* property and no one else's. But as for the repercussions, they evade being traced in any definite manner to any final and definitive endpoint.

To repeat, not all bystanders are equal. In particular, with regard to the question of complicity raised above, some bystanders carry greater responsibility than others. If we continue to confine ourselves to bystanders in the present tense, that is, to bystanders to contemporary, ongoing events, it is clear that some bystanders will be closer to the event than others. "Closer" does not have to denote spatially closer; it may denote closeness by virtue of professional assignment as well, or by virtue of one's knowledge as an intellectual. Indeed, the spatial notion of responsibility and its proper scope is hopelessly out of tune with the moral issues prompted by acts facilitated by context-transcending modern technology (Jonas, 1979). Today, ethics in world politics must take the form of a deterritorialization of responsibility (Campbell and Shapiro, 1999).

Is degree of responsibility directly proportionate to degree of closeness to the event? The answer will hinge on how we conceptualize not only agency but responsibility as well.

To make us see more clearly what is at stake here, some distinctions made by Larry May in his book *Sharing Responsibility* may be helpful. A famous quote from Edmund Burke sets the stage for May's discussion: All that is necessary for evil to triumph in the world is for good people to do nothing. May goes on to observe that "just as a person's inaction makes him or her at least partially responsible for harms that he or she could have prevented, so collective inaction of a group of persons may make the members of that group at least partially responsible for harms that the group could have prevented" (1992: 105). He then defines "collective omission" as the failure of a group that collectively chooses not to act; by contrast, "collective inaction" refers to the failure to act of "a collection of people that did not choose *as a group* to remain inactive but that could have acted as a group" (ibid.: 107). The latter case of collective inaction is particularly salient with respect to what May speaks of as "putative groups," in which "people are sometimes capable of acting in concert but in which no formal organization exists and, as a result, there is no decision-making apparatus" (ibid.: 109). The fundamental premise informing May's discussion is that "once one is aware of the things that one could do, and one then does not do them, then lack of action is something one has chosen" (ibid.: 119).

For my purposes, the central question is whether the harm (read genocide) that took place in Bosnia *could* have been prevented, or at least halted, by the contemporary bystanders to it. Employing the distinction made above between passive bystanders and bystanders by assignment, we shall explore the extent to which both categories can be held responsible for *failing to prevent* ongoing and well-documented instances of genocide.

Collectivizing Human Agency and Moral Responsibility: A Look at Genocidal Logic

So far we have described the nature of genocide only by reference to its juridical definition as coined by Raphael Lemkin and employed by the U.N. and international humanitarian law. In order to answer the question about responsibility among different types of bystanders, we need to take a more phenomenological look at what characterizes the practice of genocide.

Genocide is a collective action. By this I mean that genocide is contemplated, planned, organized, and carried out by a specific organized collective, by a *group*. The defined target of genocide is another group. As a piece of action, then, genocide is the interaction taking place between a perpetrator group and a target group. Typically, the perpetrator group will define itself by reference to the individual members' common identity, be it nation, race, ethnicity, religion, or gender. The target group will be defined by the perpetrator group by the same set of (collectivist, often essentialist) criteria. The antagonism that is produced by this type of identificatory reference takes the form of a one-to-one relationship: if the perpetrator group focuses its identificatory attention upon the *race* identity of the target group, the ideological message conveyed is that the race identity of one's own group is what is first and foremost threatened by the other group. Similarly, if the *ethnic* identity of the target group provides the primary focus, the ethnic identity of the perpetrator group is likely to prevail as what is threatened most directly by the other group.

Political scientist Espen Barth Eide (1997: 10) has noted a principle at work in all the documented instances of genocide in the twentieth century: namely, that "a war of words precedes a war of bodies." Genocide does not occur without preparation, by which is meant not only practical, logistical, strategic preparation and the like, but primarily *ideological* preparation. The chief objective of the last is to mobilize support for the action that will ensue. This includes first and foremost support among members of the in-group, in which some people will be direct participants in the event and others passive and more or less distant bystanders. This preparation often also aims at garnering support from the outside world and thus from among the audience of bystanders, in the common sense of the word as nonparty outsiders to the event. The crucial part played by ideological preparation is captured in article 3 of the Genocide Convention of 1948. Here it is stated that "direct and public incitement to commit genocide" is punishable. We will see below that *intellectuals* form a crucial group in the activities amounting to such incitement. By virtue of the popular impact exerted by prominent academics and writers of various kinds (including TV and radio journalists), they carry a major responsibility for creating what may be deemed a genocidal atmosphere—that is, an atmosphere pervaded by fear, hatred, distrust, contempt, and the like for the group targeted for persecution. The drumming-up of such an atmosphere is a sine qua non for the atrocities to follow, so that the more strongly individuals are implicated in these ideological activities, the greater is their complicity in the consequences that ensue for those targeted.

Not something spontaneous, genocide is reactive—indeed, reactive in the strong sense of *imitation*. If there is one *Gedankenfigur* that is common to the most well-known instances of genocide, it is this: the perpetrator group does exactly what it castigates the target for having done (in some remote or recent past) or being just now about to do toward one's own group. To imitate means to legitimize—when the focus of attention is on past wrongs caused by the target group, legitimation of the action now taken assumes the form of *retaliation;* when the selected focus is on the wrongs (allegedly) planned and just about to be performed by the target group, legitimation assumes the form of *preemption*. In both cases, the ideologically produced upshot is that the action taken by one's own group has the character of *self-defense*. Self-defense provides a moral justification of acts of aggression; it is invoked as a license to kill precisely those *deserving* to be killed.

Doing unto the other what one holds the other to have done, or is contemplating doing, unto oneself: this is often the logic of imitation characteristic of genocide. We noted that genocide is not spontaneous. This entails that genocide never occurs in a social, historical, or cultural vacuum. In particular, the historical past is manipulated so as to become thoroughly mythologized. Thus gestalted, the past is transformed into an arena of *collective*, not individual, agency. In this fashion, the Muslims living in Bosnia today are deemed guilty for what their forefathers are said to have done some six hundred years ago, given that Serb ideologues have picked the battle against the Ottomans (Turks) at Kosovo Polje in 1389 as their "chosen trauma." The categories of agency, including guilt and complicity, are set loose from the original contextuality of events and travel freely as it were through the centuries that have passed since. Once collectivized, human agency in all its (moral as well as spatiotemporal) dimensions is conceived of in such a way that the individual is compelled to answer for everything "his" group does, has done, or is held to be about to do; conversely, the group is made to answer for everything

Genocide 361

a single individual member has done, does, or is said to plan doing. Collectivizing human agency in the manner typical of genocidal ideologues is tantamount to obliterating the morally and legally crucial distinction between individual and group. In a word, it creates a logic that completely undermines the enactment of law. For law to be (re)enacted, disaggregation is required so as to reinstall agency as a property of individuals as distinct from collectivities.

Assessing the Role of Intellectuals

Against this background, we can now turn to the role of Yugoslavian intellectuals. The voluminous literature now existing on the subject agrees that a key document in the ideological preparation for what was to follow in Bosnia is the so-called *Memorandum*. The events in Kosovo in 1999, culminating in NATO's use of force, certainly gives the document a reinforced actuality, since its main theme is the Serbs' relationship to Kosovo.

Although the *Memorandum* was conceived under the aegis of the Serbian Academy of Science and Arts (SANU), its status is that of a nonofficial plea for the safeguarding of Serbian autonomy and integrity in times of crisis, regionalization, and disintegration in Yugoslavia. Under the charismatic leadership of the famous novelist-politician Dobrica Cosic, the document was drawn up by sixteen prominent (mostly Belgrade-based) academics, including economists, scientists, and historians. Work on the text began in June 1985. On September 25, 1986 the Belgrade newspaper *Vecernje novosti* leaked extracts of the unfinished *Memorandum*, causing what has been described by journalists as a "political earthquake" in the whole of Yugoslavia.

When one reads this fifty-page document today, it is difficult to understand why it has come to attain such legendary status. The tenor of the text is that of a conservative, disillusioned, and pessimistic *Zeitdiagnose*. The two first sentences read: 'There has been a growing concern in our country over the stagnation of social development, economic difficulties, the growth of social tensions and open ethnic conflicts. Not only the political and economic system, but the entire public order of the country has come into a deep crisis" (Covic, 1993: 289). The text ends on this note: "The Serbian Academy of Science and Arts, on this occasion too, expresses its readiness to give its whole-hearted best and devote all its strength to these fateful and historic tasks of our generation" (ibid.: 337). What were these tasks?

The major complaint expressed by the intellectuals behind the *Memorandum* concerns the fate of the Serbian people under the 1974 Constitution of Yugoslavia. The Constitution had made Yugoslavia into a federation consisting of eight quasi-autonomous provinces. The complaint is that this "weakening of the unity of the Yugoslav nation" has proved particularly damaging for the Serbian people within the different parts of the country. To quote: "Not all nations are equal: the Serbian nation, for example, did not gain the right to its own state. Parts of the Serbian people, who in considerable numbers live in the other republics, do not have the right, unlike the national minorities, to use their own language and alphabet, to get politically and culturally organized, to develop the unique culture of their nation" (Covic, 1993: 313). The authors repeatedly return to the fate of the Serbs living in Kosovo, using it to strike their grim warning about all Serbs living in diaspora, as a persecuted and vulnerable minority in the various republics: "It is not just that the last of the remnants of the Serbian nation are leaving their homes at an unabated rate, but according to all evidence, faced with a physical, moral and psychological reign of terror, they seem to be preparing for their final exodus" (ibid.: 326). A direct line is drawn from the migrations led by Patriarch Arsenije in 1690 to the present, and the *Memorandum* proceeds to declare: "The physical, political, legal and cultural genocide of the Serbian population in Kosovo and Metohija is the worst defeat in the battles for liberation that Serbia waged from 1804 (Orasac) until the revolution in 1941" (ibid.: 324). In this situation, where (according to the census of 1981) 24 percent of Serbs lived outside Serbia and 40.3 percent outside "inner" (read the Republic of) Serbia, "the Serbian people cannot idly stand by and wait for the future in such a state of uncertainty.... Naturally, Serbia must not be passive and wait and see what the others will say, as it has done so often in the past" (ibid.: 336). Taking an alleged Albanian (Tirana-led) plan to create an "ethnically cleansed" and nationally homogeneous Kosovo as their prime example (i.e., a Kosovo that would be part of a "Great Albania" rid of Serbs), the central message of the *Memorandum* is that Serbs are everywhere threatened by a hostile and powerful anti-Serbian environment. The response advocated by the authors is the achievement of "territorial unity" in the form of a sovereign Serb nation-state, or what has come to be called a "Greater Serbia." This is the only viable solution in the face of the genocide (as we saw, that is precisely the word used) they see as threatening Serb minorities everywhere with virtual extinction.

In order to substantiate my thesis that the genocide (mainly) of Bosnian non-Serbs takes the form of imitation (of the alleged past and future harms caused by the enemy group), a few more statements deserve to be quoted. In the *Memorandum* it is asserted that "there is an obvious tendency to find a political alibi for the violence to which the Serbs are being exposed through the alleged mutual hatred on both sides, through intolerance and retaliation and recently through imaginary activities of 'the outside enemy,' i.e. of Serb nationalism 'from Belgrade'" (Covic, 1993: 325). Making a swift move from 1985, when the *Memorandum* was drafted, to August 1995, a full year after the so-called civil war in former Yugoslavia broke out in Croatia, Darko, a young policeman in the Serb village of Ostra Luka in Bosnia, told English journalist Tim Judah: "We captured documents and lists that prove what the Muslims were going to do to the Serbs here. We found hermetically sealed boxes that they were going to put our kidneys and hearts in which they were going to send to Germany and France in exchange for tanks" (Judah, 1997: 235). Similarly, American journalist Peter Maass, interviewing two Serb women who in the fall of 1992 had just taken over a "vacant" (read formerly Muslim-owned) apartment in Banja Luka in the wake of the city's "liberation" from its Muslim population, was told that, even though there admittedly had been no fighting between Muslims and Serbs in the area, the Muslims had been arrested and taken away (probably eventually detained and possibly killed in a camp). Asking why the Muslims had been arrested, Maass received the following answer: "Because they were planning to take over the village. They had already drawn up lists. The names of the Serb women had been split into harems for the Muslim men. . . . Thank God they were arrested first" (Maass, 1996: 113). Inquiring how they could be so sure that the Muslims now removed were planning to kill the Serb men and create harems for themselves, Maass was told, "It was on the radio. Our military had uncovered their plans." Wanting to know how they could be so sure that the radio was telling the truth, the two Serb women became impatient with the ignorant American and retorted, "Why would the radio lie?" (114).

Claims of the kind cited were legion among Serbs, who had been subject to President Slobodan Milosevic's monopolized TV and radio broadcasting since he took power in 1986. The logic exhibited is that of imitation. Consider the material. It is claimed that Albanians in Kosovo expose Serbs in Kosovo to violence, to exodus, even to genocide, by making references to "imaginary activities" of "the outside enemy," that is, of Serbian nationalism "from Belgrade." What happens? Six years later, with Serbs now at war with non-Serbs everywhere where Serbs are living, be they a regional majority or minority, the Serb propaganda has it that "Croatian nationalism," more frequently referred to as "Ustasha fascism, Tudjman style," emanating "from Zagreb," is threatening the Serbs with extinction in all areas copopulated by ethnic Croats. Or alternatively, the Serb propaganda has it that "Islamic fundamentalists," whose regional stronghold is Izetbegovic-controlled Sarajevo and whose international stronghold is Tehran, are engaging in "secret activities" against Serbs wherever they are coliving with Muslims, activities allegedly including secret plans to take Serb girls and women captive for use in harems. What thus happens is that the exodus said to be forced upon ethnic Serbs in Kosovo comes to be forced instead upon non-Serbs (mainly Croats and Muslims) all over Bosnia and Herzegovina, not to speak of Serbia proper. The harems said to be set up for Serb women materialize instead in the form of concentration camps where Croat and (especially) Muslim women are gang-raped for weeks and months on end in order to force pregnancies on women now compelled to give birth to a new generation of "Serbs," the ethnic identity of the victimized women having been effaced in a final (some would say symbolic) gesture of humiliation. In the end, what prevails as the result of all these (and so many similar) inversions and imitations of the enemy groups' alleged intentions and past or future actions is—in a word—the genocide of non-Serbs (especially Muslims) in Bosnia and Herzegovina, and with that the killing of a once-vital and flourishing multicultural, multireligious, and multiethnic society. The inversion effected by the imitation at work assumes the form of an all-important *role reversal:* yesterday's (alleged) aggressor is turned into tomorrow's victim; yesterday's (alleged) victim is preparing to become tomorrow's aggressor.

I remarked that at first sight the 1986 *Memorandum* makes for rather unremarkable reading. More remarkable, radical, and outspoken documents were soon to follow, in particular the so-called Ram (later Brana) plan authored in Belgrade in 1991 by a team of generals and experts on psychological warfare. I have dealt extensively with this plan elsewhere (Vetlesen, 1997, 1998) and shall not dwell on it here but merely cite one central paragraph: "Our analysis of the behavior of the Muslim communities demonstrates that the morale, will, and bellicose nature of their groups can be undermined only if we aim our action at the point where the religious and social structure is most fragile. We refer to the women, especially adolescents, and to the children." The document then prescribes "decisive intervention on these social figures," to which must be added "a wide propaganda campaign to our well-organized, incisive actions so that panic will increase" (cited in Allen, 1996: 57).

There is a path from the lackluster tone of the 1986 *Memorandum* to the unhidden brutality of the prescriptions advanced by the Ram plan five years later, a path from what started out as ideological war-mongering among Belgrade intellectuals in the mid-1980s to what materialized as mass murder and downright genocide ten years later. To return to my point of departure, intellectuals played an indispensable role in the planning and carrying out of the genocide that was to ensue. Why?

The question needs to be differentiated, of course. Intellectuals in former Yugoslavia, or for that matter in Belgrade, do not form a homogeneous group. Some are longtime dissidents; others careerists and opportunists; still others are dogmatists, fanatically pursuing some version of utopia, be it communist, nationalist, or ethnic. Dobrica Cosic, the principal brain behind the *Memorandum,* was expelled from the Communist Party in 1968 because of independent thinking; as a dissident he used to give philosophical lectures to other independent minds in private flats in Belgrade. One of Cosic's young admirers was Vojislav Seselj. Born in 1950, Seselj had been a brilliant Bosnian Serb student, the youngest Ph.D. in Yugoslavia (his thesis was on Marxism and guerrilla warfare), and in the early 1980s he was a teacher at Sarajevo University (Judah, 1997: 187). In the early 1990s Seselj emerged as head of a Serb paramilitary group called the White Eagles, a group notorious for its studied cruelty in assaults, including gang rape and random killings, against Muslim villages in Bosnia. Despite (or because of) his well-documented record as a war criminal, Seselj is one of the most celebrated war heroes—alongside Arkan (Zeljko Raznatovic, assassinated in 2000), head of the equally notorious Tigers—in Belgrade. In 1998 Seselj became a vice president to Slobodan Milosevic, heading an ultranationalist political party enjoying growing support.

When one looks at the role of Yugoslavian intellectuals in preparing for genocide, the most remarkable story no doubt is that of the so-called Praxis group. The members of this group, mainly philosophers and social theorists well versed in the most sophisticated versions of Western humanist Marxism and in political thinking about a possible "third way" between capitalism and Moscow-oriented communism, were at once the Yugoslav system's (Tito's) most passionate exponents abroad and its fiercest internal critics. Developing close intellectual bonds with prominent Western leftists such as Jürgen Habermas, the Praxis group rose to international recognition during the 1970s and 1980s. Tragically, however, the story of the group came to dovetail with that of Yugoslavian ethnonationalist politics as led by Milosevic. Hence, when Dobrica Cosic, the principal brain behind the *Memorandum*, became president of Yugoslavia in 1992 (only to fall out of favor with Milosevic a year later), he picked the prominent Praxis philosopher Svetozar Stojanovic as top adviser. Mihailo Markovic, the leader of the group, was a coauthor of the *Memorandum;* in 1991, the Partisan hero and onetime humanist Marxist became a vice president to Milosevic and ideologue of Milosevic's Socialist Party. Asked by a Western friend why he had joined the Serb government, Markovic's answer was simple: "I got involved to save the Serbs in eastern Croatia. Otherwise they will be slaughtered" (Sucor, 1999: 37). And in an interview with the *New York Times* in August 1992 (proving, by the way, to be the last straw in his by now estranged relationship with leftists in the West), Markovic told the reporter that the alternative to Milosevic-proposed ethnic partition of Bosnia was the "creation of a Muslim state in the heart of Europe" (ibid.: 38).

It would be senseless to mention by name the many intellectuals who not only went along with the tide of drummed-up anti-Muslim frenzy in Milosevic-led Serbia but who in fact did their fair share of the actual drumming—creating and channeling the tide rather than simply being carried along by it. True, a large number of intellectuals (as well as students) opposed Milosevic's policies and left the country at an early stage; from the Praxis group, suffice it here to record the fate of the philosopher Miladin Zivotic, whose disillusionment with the politics leading to ethnic cleansing was such that he "died of a broken heart" in 1997 (Sucor, 1999: 42). Nevertheless, it is a fact that the ethnonationalist ideology, preparing mentally for what was to follow physically in the form of ethnic cleansing, was not only backed but to a large extent thought out and broadcast by intellectuals. This is not the place to speculate about *why* so many intellectuals, even counting some of the most talented, recognized, and (reputedly) independent ones, could throw themselves behind outright criminal political objectives. For my purposes, it must suffice to maintain that the responsibility they carry for what came to pass is considerable—indeed, it is especially so in cases where, in retrospect, the output of intellectuals can be seen to amount to a remarkably concise blueprint for blatantly illegal and immoral acts.

Conclusion: Three Lessons and One Question

Considering the material I have presented from Bosnia, is there one lesson in particular that needs to be learned here?

In fact, I believe there are three important lessons. The first is that the bystander is the one who decides whether the harm wrought by the aggressor is permitted to stand unrectified or not. The bystander who reacts with nonreaction, with silence in the face of killing, helps legitimize that very killing. When nothing is done in the face of what is unfolding, and when what is unfolding is, beyond doubt, killing of a genocidal nature, the message to the agent as well as to the direct victim is that such killing may continue. Knowing, yet deciding not to act when action would have been possible, entails complicity—that is to say, on general grounds it is to count as moral complicity (Unger, 1996), though we need to inquire further to settle the question of strict *legal*—meaning punishable—complicity (I return to this below).

The second lesson is that there is every reason *not* to downplay but instead take extremely seriously any statement—be it oral or written, broadcast in the mass media or published in journals and books—about specific groups if such statements will contribute to actions that will rob such groups of their humanity and right to live under decent conditions. To allude to Hegel, discourses of *misrecognition* are likely to constitute a phase of ideological preparation for the carrying out of a politics of enforced removal, humiliation, and perhaps eventually downright annihilation of the abused individuals. Deeds follow upon words. Generally speaking, due among other things to their comprehensive reading, traveling, and contacts abroad, intellectuals in different countries, though outsiders to such developments within a given state (region), have a duty to sound the alarm bell upon learning about the spreading of hate speech, *especially* in cases where the hate speech is authorized by the authorities, and even more so if the authorities are undemocratic or downright totalitarian. Although we still await the first indictment of journalists on the charge of incitement to genocide in the former Yugoslavia, Rwanda represents a historic precedent. In 1996, Ferdinand Nahimana, a well-known historian who served as the director of the most popular Rwandan radio station, RTLM, was arrested and delivered to the Arusha tribunal, where he was found guilty of, *inter alia,* "incitement to genocide." It is now an established view that this radio station, in the two months in the spring of 1994 when up to 1 million Rwandans were slaughtered, had one single aim: to incite the Hutu masses to exterminate their Tutsi neighbors (Gutman and Rieff, 1999: 192; Melvern, 2004: 208).

The third lesson is that the failure to act when knowledgeable about ongoing genocide corrupts the bystander—the more so the greater his or her potential for acting. Not only the people falling prey to slaughter are victims here; so, too, is the individual bystander who *decides* to remain inactive and so permits what is happening to go on. Ever since Hugo Grotius's *De jure belli ac pacis* from 1625 (the treatise inspiring the principles behind humanitarian intervention to this day), a central criterion to justify the use of force is that the crime must be so excessively cruel as to shock the society of humankind. Every one of us is an embodiment of the society thus able to be shocked, to be morally outraged at what befalls other human beings—even if it be those unknown to us and far off. The idea is that we inflict evil upon ourselves—and not only upon the victims slaughtered—when we willfully remain passive bystanders. In the spirit of Grotius, Mark Huband writes that, since the U.N. knew that genocide was being planned and once the genocide began nothing was done, this makes what took place in Rwanda in 1994 "more than a crime. It was an event that shamed humanity" (quoted in Gutman and Rieff, 1999: 314). In her thoroughly researched *"A Problem from Hell": America and the Age of Genocide,* Samantha Power (2002: 329–89) presents the case for a devastating critique of U.S.-supported U.N. policies of indifference ("mostly in

Genocide 369

a listening mode") while genocide was carried out in two months' time. I believe the same critique can be made with regard to Bosnia. Indeed, when professional bystanders (which I have earlier called *bystanders by assignment*) to a violent conflict eschew responsibility for the victimized, deciding—precisely—to *stand by* and watch as the slaughter unfolds, giving priority instead to their own security and to that alone, the consequence is that humanity is shamed. Such was the case in Rwanda and in Bosnia alike.[1]

The most well-known case to make the point is the fate of Srebrenica, one of six U.N.-declared "safe areas." After days of U.N. high-level wavering about whether to opt for air attacks in order to defend the thirty thousand civilian Bosnian Muslims gathered within the safe area monitored by Dutch UNPROFOR troops, the Serbs swiftly sent a message to the battalion's commander, Lieutenant Colonel Ton Karremans: in the case of NATO air attacks, Serb forces would kill captured Dutch soldiers and shell the refugees and Dutchbat indiscriminately. The result was that Dutch defense minister Jorge Voorhoeve and U.N. top envoy Yasushi Akashi, independently of each other, immediately ordered an official halt to the air strikes. This is more than a single incident. Rather, it contains a general message, throwing into particularly stark relief a pivotal principle of U.N. policies in Bosnia. "The execution of the mandate [i.e., 'to protect peace and security for the civilians' within the safe areas] is secondary to the security of UN personnel . . . [the] intention being to avoid loss of life defending positions for their own sake and unnecessary vulnerability to hostage-taking." This statement, so effective, so unequivocal, is the key content of UNPROFOR Directive 2/95 of May 29, 1995 (see Honig and Both, 1996: 8; Danner, 1998a). It was given as part of an order—an order to remain inactive—from U.N. military commander General Bernard Janvier to General Rupert Smith, head of the "Rapid Reaction Force" (no irony intended). As a result of a tormented policy of hesitation, vacillation, and inaction, the safe area of Srebrenica fell to the Serbs led by General Ratko Mladic on July 11, 1995. Twenty-three thou-

---

1. We are actually dealing with two different sorts of "bystanders by assignment" here: on the one hand, those who are civilians and whose task it is mainly to verify and be witnesses to unfolding events, or if possible to attempt by strictly *peaceful* means to hinder acts of violence; and on the other hand, those who are militarily equipped peace enforcers or peacekeepers, whose task it is to fulfill their mission, if necessary, by military means. The argument about Srebrenica below deals with the failure of the second kind of bystander to act.

sand women and children suddenly had no one to protect them; seven thousand men of all ages were taken away and massacred.

There is now a rapidly growing literature on the fall of Srebrenica (for some of the early installments, see Honig and Both, 1996; Kadhammar, 1996; Barnett, 1996; Rohde, 1997; Danner, 1998a, 1998b; Vetlesen, 1997, 1998). For good reasons, journalists and scholars hesitate to ask the question head-on, yet it must be raised: What precisely was the responsibility of the U.N. envoys and officers involved—more or less directly—in the tragic fate of the disarmed civilians promised "peace and security" in Srebrenica? (U.N. Security Council Resolution 819 of April 16, 1993 stated that Srebrenica, as one of six safe areas, "should be free from any armed attack or any other hostile act" [Honig and Both, 1996: 5].) The signatory states to the Genocide Convention are under obligation to "punish and prevent" genocide. It is widely agreed that what took place in Srebrenica counts as an instance of genocide as defined in the convention. So what about the individual responsibility of appointed professionals from these states in this particular case? Does failure to prevent genocide— this being their very mandate at the place—amount to complicity? If so, will these professionals ever be indicted? If not, why?

REFERENCES

Allen, Beverly. 1996. *Rape Warfare*. Minneapolis: University of Minnesota Press.
Arendt, Hannah. 1958. *The Human Condition*. Chicago: University of Chicago Press.
Barnett, Michael. 1996. "The Politics of Indifference at the United Nations and Genocide in Rwanda and Bosnia." In Thomas Cushman and Stepjan Mestrovic, eds., *This Time We Knew: Western Responses to Genocide in Bosnia*. New York: New York University Press, 128–62.
Barth Eide, Espen. 1997. *Conflict Entrepreneurship*. Oslo: NUPI.
Campbell, David. 1998. *National Deconstruction: Violence, Identity, and Justice in Bosnia*. Minneapolis: University of Minnesota Press.
Campbell, David, and Michael J. Shapiro, eds. 1999. *Moral Spaces: Rethinking Ethics and World Politics*. Minneapolis: University of Minnesota Press.
Covic, Boze, ed. 1993. *Roots of Serbian Aggression*. Zagreb: AGM.
Danner, Mark. 1998a. "Bosnia: Breaking the Machine." *New York Review of Books*, February 19, 41–45.
———. 1998b. "The Killing Fields of Bosnia." *New York Review of Books*, September 24, 63–77.
Gutman, Roy. 1993. *Witness to Genocide*. Shaftesbury, U.K.: Element.
Gutman, Roy, and David Rieff, eds. 1999. *Crimes of War*. New York: W. W. Norton.
Helsinki Watch. 1992. *War Crimes in Bosnia-Herzegovina*. New York: Human Rights Watch.
Honig, Jan Willem, and Norbert Both. 1996. *Srebrenica: Record of a War Crime*. Harmondsworth, U.K.: Penguin.
Jonas, Hans. 1979. *Das Prinzip Verantwortung*. Frankfurt: Suhrkamp.

Judah, Tim. 1997. *The Serbs.* New Haven: Yale University Press.
Kadhammar, Peter. 1996. *Berättelsen om Srebrenica.* Stockholm: Norstedts
Levinas, Emmanuel. 1991. *Otherwise than Being or Beyond Essence.* Dordrecht: Kluwer.
Maass, Peter. 1996. *Love Thy Neighbor: A Story of War.* New York: Knopf.
May, Larry. 1992. *Sharing Responsibility.* Chicago: University of Chicago Press.
Melvern, Linda. 2004. *Conspiracy to Murder: The Rwandan Genocide.* London: Verso.
Power, Samantha. 2002. *"A Problem from Hell": America and the Age of Genocide.* New York: Basic.
Ricoeur, Paul. 1992. *Oneself as Another.* Trans. Kathleen Blamey. Chicago: University of Chicago Press.
Rohde, David. 1997. *Endgame: The Betrayal and Fall of Srebrenica.* New York: Farrar, Straus and Giroux.
Sells, Michael. 1996. *The Bridge Betrayed: Religion and Genocide in Bosnia.* Berkeley: University of California Press.
Sucor, Laura. 1999. "Testaments Betrayed: Yugoslavian Intellectuals and the Road to War." *Lingua Franca* 9 (6): 26–42.
Unger, Peter. 1996. *Living High and Letting Die.* Oxford: Oxford University Press.
Vetlesen, Arne Johan. 1997. "Ondskap i Bosnia." *Norsk filosofisk tidsskrift* 32 (1–2): 71–106.
———. 1998. "Impartiality and Evil." *Philosophy & Social Criticism* 24 (5): 1–35.

16

The Ethical Core of the Nation-State

A Postscript to Part Two

J. PETER BURGESS

The title of the present volume, *Ethics, Nationalism, and Just War*, announces a daunting project. The countless constellations of war, nation, justice, and peace, past and present, and the wide variety of conceivable ethical approaches to them, resist discrete summary. And yet it should at once be underscored that both the "ethics" in question and the "war" (and peace) to which they aspire to take recourse are of a special brand and breed, belonging to a very specific historical moment. Transformations of the notions both of ethics and of war and peace have accelerated in the course of the twentieth century in unforeseeable ways. Ethics—the systematic mapping of rights and obligations, premises and conditions of conduct—has veered from its classical roots and is no longer understood merely as the systematic search for a singular response to the question What is the Good Life? "War and peace," a constantly evolving pair, has made a leap from the perfunctory character of violence in something like Herodotus's *Histories* to the desperate theses of Baudrillard's *The Gulf War Did Not Take Place* (1995). Today, questions of war and peace are more frequently rediscovered in intrastate relations, in experiments with new weapons technologies, opening new questions of modalities, aims, and means, collateral consequences, circumstances and scope, objects and actors.

Many of the empirical illustrations brought to bear in the arguments of the second part of this book, to which this chapter is meant as a postscript (although I do not comment on all of the articles), deal in one way or another with the issue and the destiny of the European nation-state. All, for better or worse, engage the *European* notion of a three-way synergy (between individual, people, and political institution), the immediate derivative of the political philosophy of the Enlightenment. The contributions to a large extent explore the tension between the particular cultural, spiritual, ethical, and/or religious collective impulse at the heart of any given nation-state and the bare, transparent, institutional structures and universal principles to which they relate. Such principles were already thematized in political and philosophical debates by Locke, Lessing, Bayle, Simon, Schiller, Voltaire, Diderot, Rousseau, Paine, and others at the outset of the European nation-state movements at the close of the eighteenth century in what Reinhart Koselleck called the "pathogenesis" of European bourgeois political culture (1973; Böckenförde, 1999).

The paradox of the nation-state's *ethical* universality was clear from the start, that is, already in the first Enlightenment philosophies of state, people, and rule of law. It was famously dramatized by Kant's thinking on the nature of a cosmopolitan world republic, the natural consequence of the universal principles of the nation-state in his well-known 1784 essay "The Idea of a Universal History from a Cosmopolitan Point of View" and his 1795 essay "On Perpetual Peace" (Kant, 1991a, 1991b). In the currently expanding debate on postnationalism and the limits of nationality, Kant's concept of cosmopolitanism has been repeatedly revisited, in both the debate on the nature of globalization (Bauman, 1998; Höffe, 1999: 64–67; Delanty, 2000), and that on the possible forms of a European superstate (Pogge, 1992; Schultz, 1994; Habermas, 1998; Segers and Viehoff, 1996; Ferry, 2000). Much of the discussion concerns the modifications and clarifications necessary in order to bring Kant's conception of a cosmopolitan world order to a contemporary coherence, in general, or to make it applicable to a possible European federal state, in particular.

The contemporary historical determination of these debates revolves around the geopolitical changes in the wake of the fall of the Berlin wall. Most of these arguments would have been impossible before the *Wende*, the more or less peaceful collapse of the Soviet-steered East Bloc beginning with the dramatic events in October 1989. Before then, the cold war and the ideological borders frozen along the lines of European national borders completely overshadowed the prospects of any sort of philosophical cosmopolitanism. Although globalization was long since a reality, principled questions about the nature of a universal order based on political or ethical doctrine were as good as unthinkable (Fernández-Armesto, 1995).

The less thoroughly scrutinized reality of the Wende is that it marks the birth of a new brand of nationalism. The issues addressed by the chapters in this volume concern phenomena that have become relevant as a consequence of the "liberation" of the East Bloc. The question of the relevance of noncombatants (Johnson), environmental considerations (Reichberg and Syse), humanitarian intervention (Semb), the ethical consequences of nationalism (Smith), European construction (Follesdal), international tribunals (Meernik), regime change (Janssen), and genocide in the Balkans (Vetlesen) all address matters that have redoubled their relevance in the postwall period.

The Ethical Kernel

These wide-ranging essays share a second fundamental characteristic. They all proceed, explicitly or implicitly, from the assumption of a certain kind of national core or kernel. By "kernel" I mean an essence or substance that is essential to the nation but is neither equivalent to it nor reducible to it. The chapters in this collection highlight and explore the ethical nature of the nation-state by looking at its ethical presuppositions and consequences. They examine the relationships between various actors and concrete situations, interpreting them in terms of a network of ethical meaning linked to the nation-state. In his contribution "Maintaining the Protection of Noncombatants," James Turner Johnson in chapter 8 seeks to extend the nation-state-based notion of protection of noncombatants in state-based war to protection in the persecution of armed conflicts. In chapter 9, "Protecting the Natural Environment in Wartime," Reichberg and Syse explore the limits of extending the traditional nation-state protections to the domain of nature. Classical Enlightenment questions of respect and recognition are transferred to the concept of "just stewardship," and the concept of "property" is retraced to its origins in natural law philosophy. Anne Julie Semb in chapter 10 focuses her attention on the possibilities of applying the Enlightenment principle of nonintervention with the borders of a sovereign nation-state to the new perspectives and dangers of U.N.-legitimated "humanitarian intervention." In chapter 12 Andreas Follesdal applies the principle of liberal contractualism to a critique of David Miller's nation-state-based ethics of trust and solidarity itself, extrapolated from the nation-state.

Yet it is perhaps Dan Smith in chapter 11 who comes closest to making explicit the ethical kernel to which I refer when he problematizes the "self" to which the principle of the right to national self-determination refers: "[A] problem lurks at the core of the concept of national self-determination: the problem of what the self is. In the case of a putative right to self-determination, who or what is the right bearer?" Nations are ultimately defined by power and, when necessary, they are created and defended by force. The kernel is a hard one: on the one hand, the nation-state is the original form of the political and ethical principles of self-determination and nonintervention. On the other, the nation-state can still not be dissociated from the violence carried out in its name.

These questions all refer in one way or another to a larger and longstanding debate about the nature of the nation, on the one hand, and on its status as a legitimating agent for violence, on the other. The relatively slow rise of the Anglo-Saxon nationalism literature in the 1980s is in part due to the conflict of faculties, which has traditionally reserved matters of international politics for international politics departments and analysis of intranational conflicts for political sociology and neighboring fields. For the same reason, the scholarly treatment of the question of war and peace—and, finally, its linkage to Scholastic traditions of just war—has come unmistakably late (Özkirimli, 2000: 2–3).

For a theoretician like Michael Mann (1986) it is not simple national zeal that drives the rise in international conflict, in particular in the nation-building period. On the contrary, according to the analysis in Mann's *The Sources of Social Power*, it is the machine that contributes to the rise of the nation-state, fueling it on (Smith, 1998: 89–91). The machinery of war making crosses class, cultural, and ethnic boundaries, uniting peoples and states under national umbrellas. Thus the cultural argument that national militaries first enter a new phase because of the legitimacy provided by an ethnic nationality, or even the notion of justice proposed by the collective moral fabric of a nation, may not be entirely adequate.

Psychoanalysis of the National Self

The Slovenian philosopher and psychoanalyst Slavoj Žižek makes a radical attempt to penetrate this national core by means of a rereading of the post-Wende nationalist crises through the optic of Lacanian psychoanalysis and Hegelian dialectical theory. The result is both innovative and refreshing. Žižek sets aside the traditional discourses of political science and ethics in order to examine the prephilosophical basis of both. The novelty of his approach is that he deploys unorthodox psychoanalytic concepts, such as "need," "desire," and *"jouissance,"* completely foreign to the discourse of political philosophy in an attempt to gain insight into its tacit presuppositions. In this way Žižek brings Hegelian dialectics and Lacanian psychoanalysis to bear on contemporary political situations. With illustrations from postcolonial Europe—the Europe of immigration, globalization, multiculturalism—his project is a kind of psychoanalysis of Western political self-understanding: European nationalism on the couch.

Eastern Europe is, of course, also a part of Europe. It is, in many ways, also a kind of Enlightenment-inspired geopolitical self-image of Western Europe. Western Europe has a long tradition of projecting itself—its values and experiences—on the relatively exotic world of the East (Walters, 1987; Wolff, 1994). Thus the "liberation" of the East Bloc in the wake of the fall of the Berlin wall has had more than a passive importance for West Europeans. To witness the rebirth of the East is to enjoy the projected rebirth of the West. Thus the East is simultaneously intimately known and yet unknown: *unheimlich*, as Freud would put. The West is fascinated by the collapse and rebirth of its eastern Other. According to Žižek, this fascination is based precisely on this paradoxical experience. Western Europe witnesses its own rebirth. The rebirth of the East in the image of the West is in effect the nostalgic rebirth of the West. In Eastern Europe, "the West seeks for its own lost origins, its own lost original experience of 'democratic invention'" (Žižek, 1993: 200).

In psychoanalytic terms, the West sees the East as a happy image of itself: the pure, innocent, idealized, and likeable past, the birth of ourselves, something both identical to us and different. Without a doubt, the reality is otherwise. The situation in the Balkans, as in the other emerging democracies of Eastern Europe, is far from idyllic, far from the Enlightenment model of democracy and well-organized free markets. Just as rapidly as the imagined model of democratic spirit motivated the "soft revolution" of the East, the liberal democratic tendency evaporated in the face of the emergence of corporate national populism and its attendant evils, xenophobia and anti-Semitism, in the new East European democracies (Žižek, 1993: 200).

Yet while geopolitical changes have been taking place in Eastern Europe, the identity crisis that consciousness of these events creates seems to plague the West far more. Late-twentieth-century Western national identification, Žižek claims, is an exemplary case of *external* borders being reflected into *internal* borders. The identity of a nation has two phases, or levels. On the one hand, the nation is defined as against its *external* Other, through differences relative to all that it is not, to other nations, peoples, and groups. But the nation is also, on the other hand, an interior demarcation of the endogenous members of the nation against each other. Even a superficial empirical assessment of any national community shows that no member is completely *proper*. Evoking the example of the English, Žižek underscores that "the final answer is of course that *nobody* is fully English, that every empirical Englishman contains something 'non-English'—Englishness thus becomes an 'internal limit,' an unattainable point which prevents empirical Englishmen from achieving full identity-with-themselves" (1991: 110). The national identity of the exemplary Englishman is shaken by consciousness of the radical changes in the East. That new consciousness has a double effect. The *external* changes observed in the East are empirically new, but they also affect one's way of seeing oneself in one's own immediate situation. In the jargon of psychoanalysis: the sameness of the Other underscores the otherness of the same.

Modernity's Neurosis: Capitalism and Liberal Democracy

According to Žižek, the post-Wende growth of Eastern European nationalism is characterized by two specific dimensions: (1) its eruption from an ideologically saturated socialist system into a late-capitalist system of values and cultural relations and (2) the promises of formal democracy. Capitalism is not just a set of values; it is also a striving for the universalization of those values. A critical feature of capitalism, in particular in the Marxian analysis, is the dissolution of particularities—be they ethnic, racial, cultural, or other—as hindrances to the universality of the capitalist system. The internally configured need for growth and expansion renders it a missionary project. The creation of surplus value is most fruitful, the marginal gain of investment is greatest precisely where the refined mechanisms of investment and exchange are not yet refined. The other side of the global capitalist coin is that the insatiable thirst for expansion and the creation of ever-new surplus value has historically been the very force of technological progress, of the innovation that erases borders, reduces distance, brings on the globalized economic integration. Of course, this process of globalization is a false universalization, since by its very nature it economically ghettoizes the largest part of the globe and increases the marginalization of the poorest parts of the world. These processes of globalization are the same that challenge the viability of the nation-state, of national culture—the same into which the new Eastern democracies are thrust (Žižek, 1992: 162). At the very moment when national identity is challenged by globalization (and more "locally" by European construction and the Eastern expansion), the thirst for a national substance emerges.

According to Žižek, liberal democracy is the other motivation for the crisis of the nation-state. In its ordinary sense, universalization erases particularity. Žižek notes that the universalization of formal democracy can occur only through the abstraction of the individual from all concrete substantial ties. The *ideal* democratic subject has no *particular* ethnic or cultural substance, nothing that can set him or her apart from any other democratic subject. All are equivalent in the eyes of the plebiscite. The persons, groups, or institutions assigned to the place of power by the result of the plebiscite are *external* to the democratic process, or at least external to the phase of equivalence that marks the plebiscite. This is the very sense of formal democracy: social differences are smoothed over in order to assure the coherence of the political voice. It is the aim of liberal democracy to evacuate both power and the ethical good from any *one* subjective place. Any and all individual subjects of liberal democracy must be at any given time closed off from "the Good and the Powerful" in order to participate in its constitution. Moral law can be found only in a pure form (Žižek, 1992: 221). No one person can rule without usurping, without losing purity. That this is the obvious compromise made in any representational democracy does not change its paradoxical structure.

Žižek reminds us that the place of power, law, and justice—the nature of which is decided by a well-functioning democracy—is nonetheless excluded from the democratic moment, from the plebiscite. The place of power and law is occupied by a sovereign who, in precisely the Hobbesian sense, is not an individual political subject but rather a kind of concentration of all the individual subjectivities of the commonwealth. The sovereign—power and law—is not a *part* of democracy, and yet it is inseparable, it is, as Žižek puts it, a "substantial extra," which must be abstracted in order for democracy to function. It is carried along as both superfluous and necessary: "the indivisible remainder" (Žižek, 1992, 1993). Nationalism, in Žižek's sense, is the tendency of the "nation" to usurp this empty space of power left open by democracy, to occupy the necessarily empty or abstract space of justice and power. This "indivisible remainder," this empty space, is the "national remainder."

Both late capitalism and formal liberal democracy contribute to the persistence of this national remainder, this essential part of the national substance, which can be neither institutionalized nor formalized. Žižek associates this paradoxical, irreducible national kernel with what the French philosopher and psychoanalyst Jacques Lacan—following Freud—calls the "Thing" (Lacan, 1992). Here Žižek's approach veers considerably from conventional political science, sociology, or social anthropology. The notion of an irreducible national Thing permits Žižek to formulate two moments in the psychoanalytic model of understanding nationalism: (1) hatred of the Other as hatred of the Other's national enjoyment and (2) hatred of one's own national enjoyment as hatred of the Other in oneself.

The Other's National Enjoyment

Following Lacan, Žižek identifies this irreducible "national Thing" with the pathological and aesthetic notion of *enjoyment (jouissance)*. Žižek is fully aware that the analysis of "enjoyment" rubs the discourse and methodologies of social science and humanities against the grain. Still, one must bear in mind that the intention in his work on nationalism in the Balkans and in Europe at large is to map out the contours of this "Thing." It is an object that more than the social sciences and humanities fail to grasp because it is foreign to them.

The heart of the problem for Žižek, the "place" of the "national Thing," is in the dynamics of national community. The bond linking any community, be it national or ethnic, is, he claims, not some concept of the community—not, as is canonically claimed, the *idea* of shared memories, traditions, and rituals: "The bond linking together its members always implies a shared relationship toward a Thing, toward Enjoyment incarnated. This relationship toward the Thing, structured by means of fantasies, is what is at stake when we speak of the menace to our 'way of life' presented by the Other: it is what is threatened when, for example, a white Englishman is panicked because of the growing presence of 'aliens.' What he wants to defend is *not* reducible to the so-called set of values that offer support to national identity" (1993: 201). If we accept Žižek's category of "enjoyment" and all that it implies in terms of the particularity of national, ethnic, cultural, or religious character, then *nationalism* is to be understood as the moment where enjoyment erupts into "the social field" (ibid.: 202). Yet Žižek goes farther. Nationalism is a *materialization* of national enjoyment. Enjoyment is also an existential element in the very being of the nation. The very existence of the nation (in the cultural or ethnic sense of the term) reposes on the network of tensions in the economy of "national enjoyment." "A nation *exists* only as long as its specific *enjoyment* continues to be materialized in a set of social practices and transmitted through national myths that structure these practices." In this regard, Žižek distances himself from "deconstructive" analyses of nationalism that refuse the biological or transhistorical conception of the nation in favor of an understanding of the nation as "discursive or textual practices" (ibid.).

And yet, like other deconstructive approaches, there is a paradox at its center. For the "national Thing" is both threatened by the Other and utterly inaccessible to him or her. This opposition between self and Other can be witnessed again and again in the formulation of "national identity," "national character," or "national interests." The foreigner menaces "our" national culture by threatening to alter it or render it impure, *and at the same time,* his or her Otherness can never be reduced to something more like "us."

"We always impute to the 'other' an excessive enjoyment: he wants to steal our enjoyment (by ruining our way of life) and/or he has access to some secret, perverse enjoyment. In short, what really bothers us about the 'other' is the peculiar way he organizes his enjoyment, precisely the surplus, the 'excess' that pertains to this way" (Žižek, 1993: 203). The revulsion toward the foreign Other is therefore both pathological and aesthetic. The "danger" of the foreign Other, the threat to my national Thing, is a threat to my emotional and aesthetic experience of my nationality. Once again, the nation is not reducible to the sum of its members, be they citizens or members of an ethnic collectivity. It is clearly not reducible to the political and social institutions that embody the national character. Nor is it reducible to the national principle, to the simple concept of the nation as a set of allegiances, rights, and duties. According to Žižek, whenever we attempt to sum up the nation—conceptually, ontologically, or morally—we are left with a remainder, which both resists totalization and becomes the tenacious anchoring pin of the national self-organization. "Why does the Other remain Other? What is the cause for our hatred of him, for our hatred of him in his very being? It is hatred of the enjoyment in the Other. This would be the most general formula of modern racism we are witnessing today: a hatred of the particular way the Other enjoys. . . . The question of tolerance or intolerance is not at all concerned with the subject of science and its human rights. It is located on the level of tolerance or intolerance toward the enjoyment of the Other, the Other as he who essentially steals my own enjoyment" (ibid.).

Hatred of Oneself as Other

The explosion of ethnic conflict in the Balkans and the diverse conflicts erupting in the new democracies of Eastern Europe are clearly perceived as a threat to the West. This threat perception manifests itself both in the debates on EU enlargement to the east and in the question of the expansion of NATO to include former East Bloc countries or even Russia. The emergence of new capitalist democracies in the East is a glorious opportunity for the West to reenact its own self-perception, to project its own capitalistic and democratic values onto the tabula rasa of the East, to reexperience the validity—and even superiority—of these values reaffirmed like some primal re-creation of the Same.

As already noted, in Žižek's analysis, these movements toward integration into Western Europe are measured along two axes, the democratic and the capitalistic. Both serve to frustrate the processes of national identification. First, formal democracy is based on a notion of subjectivity that erases particular difference. Formal democratic validity places a plenum of subjective equivalence that is at odds with cultural, ethnic, religious, racial equality. Democracy—like justice—must be blind. That is why it is just. Yet the impartiality presupposed by the blindness of democracy is precisely what threatens the particularity of individual cultural and ethical experience in relation to more global interests, be they those of a federation, union, or global society at large. Second, capitalism, according to Žižek's analysis, is equally incapable of creating a properly normative cultural or ethical foundation. The basic feature of capitalism is its inherent structural *imbalance* (Žižek, 1993: 209). Capitalism (not be confused with the simple concept of the free market) is based on a logic of crisis and change, on the need for constant innovation, constant reformulation of values, constant expansion, reinvestment, "the permanent production of excess" (ibid.: 209). As the classical Marxian analysis shows, capitalism produces not only value, innovation, invention, and progress, it also produces the *insatiable need* for these. Capitalism is effective at satisfying human needs by simultaneously manufacturing new ones.

In Žižek's view, part of the crisis of Eastern European expansion is the spontaneous discovery that the "revolution" (democratic and capitalistic) is not toward a solidified identity but rather toward a state of displacement from the former, original sense of self (in formal democracy) and toward a state of cultural-economic displacement. Disappointment is thus inevitable, even structural. Even so, this analysis differs little from classical neoconservative cultural critique: formal democracy and market capitalism allegedly threaten to decouple value systems from their deeper anchoring in tradition. Žižek's conclusion is different. He takes the value-conservative analysis of Eastern capitalistic democracies one step further by insisting on the projection of the Western self-understanding onto the East as its Other. Formulated in another way: the East is the West's Other; at the same time, the West is deeply embedded in it.

In other words, the knife cuts two ways: on the one hand, the East is the good, though empirically imperfect, democratic capitalist Other of the West; on the other, communism is the "evil" empirical Other of the East, which is inseparable from its past but which must be negated in order to integrate the East into what it already "truly" is. For Žižek, this paradox is a symptom of liberal society and, not the least, liberal intellectual self-congratulatory self-sufficiency.

This reveals, moreover, a fundamental flaw in liberal democracy, a flaw that is above all interesting because it falls outside the bounds of the human and social sciences. It is *liberal democracy itself* (or rather the "blind spot" of liberal democracy) that opens the space for nationalist fundamentalism. In the troubled wake of Francis Fukuyama, as much in disrepute as he may be, the only question with which the methodologies of political philosophy are truly confronted is whether liberal democracy is the "ultimate horizon of our political practice" (Žižek, 1993: 221). Once again, the neoconservative response is that fundamentalism is the reaction to the loss of roots brought about by formal democracy and capitalism. Žižek reproaches liberal democratic thinking itself for ignoring this blind spot.

The status of nationalism is ultimately that of the transcendental illusion in the Kantian sense. It is based on the idea that reality is ultimately rational, that there is a kind of transcendental rationality. This transcendental reality of the nation—the national Thing—is ultimately inaccessible, even though its function builds upon an illusion of accessibility. This accessibility to the transcendental essence of the nation, the national Thing, is precisely what formal democracy and capitalism promise. In this sense Žižek's analysis is also a critique of Kantian epistemology. Kant construes Evil, like Good, as a *transcendental* dimension. According to Žižek, Kant is incapable of understanding Evil as "diabolical," as an ethical attitude (1993: 222). From this starting point, the *nation* is only one response to a more deeply human, more pathological and more aesthetic need to fill Being with a center, with a core, to reach toward the transcendental, inaccessible meaning of national belonging. The "nation thing" that Žižek analyzes is one formulation—among many others—of the Thing, this insatiable transcendental place, always apparently possible to fill but never completely satisfied. This is where, according to Žižek, both liberal democracy and capitalism, though indispensable, are symptoms of the nation-state's ethical core—its opening and problematization.

REFERENCES

Baudrillard, Jean. 1995. *The Gulf War Did Not Take Place.* Bloomington: Indiana University Press.
Bauman, Zygmunt. 1998. *Globalization: The Human Consequences.* New York: Columbia University Press.

Böckenförde, Ernst-Wolfgang. 1999. *Staat Nation Europa: Studien zur Staatslehre, Verfassungstheorie und Rechtsphilosophie.* Frankfurt: Suhrkamp.
Delanty, Gerard. 2000. *Modernity and Postmodernity.* London: Sage.
Fernández-Armesto, Felipe. 1995. *Millennium: A History of the Last Thousand Years.* New York: Scribner.
Ferry, Jean-Marc. 2000. *La question de l'état européen.* [Paris]: Gallimard.
Habermas, Jürgen. 1998. *The Inclusion of the Other: Studies in Political Theory.* Cambridge, Mass.: MIT Press.
Höffe, Otfried. 1999. *Demokratie im Zeitalter der Globaliserung.* Munich: C. H. Beck.
Kant, Immanuel. 1991a. *Idee zu einer allgeminen Geschichte in weltbürgerlicher Absicht.* Werkausgabe. Frankfurt: Suhrkamp.
———. 1991b. *Zum ewigen Frieden.* Werkausgabe. Frankfurt: Suhrkamp.
Koselleck, Reinhart. 1973. *Kritik und Krise: Eine Studie zur Pathogenese der bürgerlichen Welt.* Frankfurt: Suhrkamp.
Lacan, Jacques. 1992. *The Ethics of Psychoanalysis, 1959–1960.* New York: Norton.
Mann, Michael. 1986. *The Sources of Social Power.* Cambridge: Cambridge University Press.
Özkirimli, Umut. 2000. *Theories of Nationalism.* Hong Kong: St. Martin's.
Pogge, Thomas. 1992. "Cosmopolitianism and Sovereignty." *Ethics* 103:48–73.
Schultz, Paul F. III. 1994. *Hidden Killers: The Global Landmine Crisis.* Washington, D.C.: U.S. Department of State, Office of International Security and Peacekeeping Operations, Bureau of Political-Military Affairs.
Segers, Rien T., and Reinhold Viehoff. 1996. "Die Konstruktion Europas. Überlegungen zum Problem der Kultur in Europa." In R. T. Segers and R. Viehoff, eds., *Kultur Identität Europa: Über die Schwiergikeiten und Möglichkeiten einer Konstruktion.* Frankfurt: Suhrkamp.
Smith, Anthony D. 1998. *Nationalism and Modernism: A Critical Survey of Recent Theories of Nations and Nationalism.* London and New York: Routledge.
Walters, E. Garrison. 1987. *The Other Europe: Eastern Europe to 1945.* Syracuse: Syracuse University Press.
Wolff, Larry. 1994. *Inventing Eastern Europe: The Map of Civilization on the Mind of the Enlightenment.* Stanford: Stanford University Press.
Žižek, Slavoj. 1991. *For They Know Not What They Do: Enjoyment as a Political Factor.* London and New York: Verso.
———. 1992. *Looking Awry: An Introduction to Jacques Lacan through Popular Culture.* Cambridge: MIT Press.
———. 1993. *Tarrying with the Negative: Kant, Hegel, and the Critique of Ideology.* Durham: Duke University Press.

Contributors

J. PETER BURGESS is research professor at the International Peace Research Institute, Oslo (PRIO), leader of PRIO's Security Programme, and editor of *Security Dialogue*. Burgess has published eleven books and over forty articles in the fields of political science, security studies, philosophy, history, and cultural studies.

ANDREAS FOLLESDAL is professor and director of research at the Norwegian Centre for Human Rights at the University of Oslo. His research largely concerns the political philosophy of human rights and of the European Union, centering on such topics as distributive justice, federalism, minority rights, deliberative democracy, subsidiarity, and European citizenship. He is the founding series editor of *Themes in European Governance* from Cambridge University Press.

KATE LANGDON FORHAN is professor of political science and dean of the College of Arts and Sciences at Northeastern Illinois University in Chicago. She has written extensively on medieval political theory; her works include *The Political Theory of Christine de Pizan* and a translation of Christine's *Book of the Body Politic* for the Cambridge series in the history of political thought.

PHILLIP W. GRAY received his doctorate in political science from Texas A&M University in 2006. Currently he is visiting assistant professor at A&M's Department of Political Science. His research focuses on the just war tradition and ontology, international political theory, and the intersection of religion and politics.

DIETER JANSSEN teaches and researches practical philosophy at the Department of Philosophy at the University of Aachen. He is particularly interested in the ethics of war and peace, just war theory, and humanitarian intervention. He is the author of *Gerechte, heilige und zivilisatorische Kriege* (2004; Just, Holy, and Colonial Wars). With Professor Michael Quante, he coedited *Gerechte Kriege* (2002; Just Wars), and in 2006 he coauthored with Professor Wilfried Hinsch *Menschenrechte militärisch schützen* (To Protect Human Rights with Military Means).

JAMES TURNER JOHNSON is professor of religion at Rutgers University. He has written extensively on the just war tradition, its relation to international law, and the application of both to contemporary armed conflict.

JAMES MEERNIK is professor and chair in the Department of Political Science at the University of North Texas. He specializes in research on U.S. foreign policy, judicial politics, and international law.

GERSON MORENO-RIAÑO currently serves as chair and associate professor, Department of Government, at Regent University. His areas of expertise include the history of political philosophy, with a special emphasis on early modern political ideas and political ethics. Moreno-Riaño's publications include four authored/edited books as well as numerous book chapters and journal articles. His most recent work is *The World of Marsilius of Padua* (2007).

GREGORY M. REICHBERG is senior researcher and program leader at the International Peace Research Institute, Oslo (PRIO). He has been on the philosophy faculties of the Catholic University of America in Washington, D.C. and Fordham University in New York City. Associate editor of the *Journal of Military Ethics,* he has also recently coedited (with Henrik Syse and Endre Begby) *The Ethics of War: Classic and Contemporary Readings* (2006). Reichberg has published numerous articles on the ethics of war and peace, as well as on topics in Thomistic philosophy.

ANNE JULIE SEMB is associate professor in the Department of Political Science, University of Oslo. Her academic interests include interventions, secessions, human rights and minority issues, and indigenous issues.

DAN SMITH is the secretary general of International Alert, the London-based international peacebuilding organization. From 1993 to 2001 he was director of the International Peace Research Institute, Oslo (PRIO). He is the author of several books on peace and conflict issues, including *The State of the Middle East* (2006).

Contributors 387

HENRIK SYSE is senior research fellow at the International Peace Research Institute, Oslo (PRIO) and head of corporate governance at Norges Bank Investment Management (NBIM). He has written and taught on various topics within ethics and political theory, with an emphasis on the ethics of war. Recent publications include *Ethics of War: Classic and Contemporary Readings* (edited with Gregory Reichberg and Endre Begby; 2006) and *Natural Law, Religion, and Rights* (2007).

ARNE JOHAN VETLESEN is professor of philosophy at the University of Oslo. He has written fourteen books, mainly on ethics and social philosophy, focusing on evil. Major publications include *Perception, Empathy, and Judgment* (1994), *Closeness* (1997), and *Evil and Human Agency* (2005).

JOHN VON HEYKING is associate professor of political science at the University of Lethbridge in Alberta. He is the author of *Augustine and Politics as Longing in the World* (2001) and articles on friendship, civil religion, Islamic political thought, deliberative democracy, Nicholas of Cusa, and religious liberties under Canada's Charter of Rights and Freedoms. He coedited volumes 7 and 8 of the *Collected Works of Eric Voegelin* (2003).

Index

Abner (Old Testament), 26
abortion, 233n10, 234
absolutism, benevolent, 343, 344
accused, justice for, 291–92, 298–301, 303, 309–16, 319
actions, x, 6, 28, 42n9, 74n7, 77; collective, 347, 358–61; conflict-causing, 80–82; effects of, 213–16; evaluation of, 42, 86–87, 93, 174–75, 214–15, 218, 241–42, 248; inaction vs., 356–58, 367–70; justifying, 281, 284–85; political, 197–98, 253; rational, 338; right, 4, 13, 27, 45–46, 58, 88, 156–57; serious, 124; types of, 12–24. *See also* double effect; intentions
active life, 16, 18, 31–32
Acts (of the Apostles) 9.1–18, 55
Adeney, Bernard T., 64
Afghanistan, 247, 323
Africa, 255, 260, 299, 318. *See also* Hutu tribe; Tutsi tribe; *and individual African countries*
agents, 354–61, 367, 375
aggression, 221, 331, 334, 346, 348, 360. *See also* force; violence
Agincourt, battle of, 103
Ahrensdorf, Peter J., 16
Akashi, Yasushi, 369
Akayesu, Prosecutor v., 311
Akhavan, Payam, 296
Alaric, 52–53
Albania, 179, 184–85, 362, 364
Albert of Brescia, 106
Albert the Great, 77
Albright, Madeleine, 317
Alexander of Hales, 76, 78n16, 84, 86n32, 206n18
Allen, Beverly, 365
Allison, Graham, 58
al-Qaeda, 11, 53–54, 246
altruism, 197
Ambrose: on Cicero, 24–34, 130; *De Officiis ministrorum*, 24–31, 80n18, 125–30; ethics of, 127–28; just war theory, 25–34, 122, 125–30; pacifism of, 120, 126, 128n22; *On Tobias*, 26–27; on war, 11–15
Amin, Idi, 342–43
amity, civic, 81–82, 84, 198, 205
Amley, Edward A., Jr., 300
anarchy, 33, 279, 346

Anderson, Benedict, 249, 251, 252, 254, 257
anger, 80n20, 140, 206
animals, 127n20, 130, 197, 201
Anscombe, Elizabeth, 41
Antarctic treaty of 1959, 192
antiquity. *See* Classical period
apartheid, 83n27, 227
apocalypse, 22–25, 32–34. *See also* end times
Aquinas, Thomas: *De regimine principum*, 135; ethics of, 76–85, 135–37, 157n1, 192, 213n34; just war theory, 5–7, 40, 42, 45–46, 72–98, 135–39, 143, 160–61, 188, 193–94, 196, 206n19; nature viewed by, 199n8, 200–204; *Secunda secundae*, 74–85; *Summa theologiae*, 5–7, 74–85, 136–38
Arab nations, 33
arbitration, 108, 114
Archibugi, David, 255
Arendt, Hannah, 357
Aristide, Jean-Bertrand, 228
aristocracy, 100–101. *See also* kings; princes
Aristotle, 12, 77n15; active vs. contemplative life, 16, 32, 124n14; influence on Aquinas, 82–83, 92–93, 137–38
armed conflict: authority for, 4–8, 90–91; crimes of, 294n3; decline of, 44; defensive, 135; definitions of, ix–x, 10; environmental effects, 190–217; humanitarian interventions in, 246–48; justifications for, 58, 85, 158, 147, 195–96, 204–13, 331–32; laws of, 164–72, 188, 190–91, 209–10; modern, 152, 171–73; morality of, x, 117–18, 121, 148, 158–59; political, 129, 269; restraints on, 119n5, 212, 374. *See also* force; violence; war
armies, 49, 63. *See also* military; soldiers
Armstrong, Susan J., 199n8
asymmetric warfare, 178
atomic bombs, 42, 47n18. *See also* bombing attacks
atrocities: modern, 1, 49, 290; prevention of, 300, 306, 316–17. *See also* cruelty; ethnic cleansing; genocide; killing; torture
attitude. *See* intentions
Augustine: *City of God*, 20n6, 43, 52–59, 63, 69, 81; *Epistle 185*, 52–54, 57–59, 188; just war theory, 5, 36–71, 73, 84, 89n38, 96, 130–35, 137–38, 143, 159–61; pacifism of, 51–71,

Augustine (cont.)
132n31, 133n33, 188; virtue ethics, 29, 41–46
authority: breakdown of, 104, 219, 236; competent, 209–10, 216; definitions of, 112–13, 141–42; legitimate, 4–8, 39–40, 72, 74n6, 75–76; public, 67, 79; secular, 66–67, 87; sovereign, 5–6, 23, 160–61; for war, 38, 99

Bacevich, Andrew J., 341
Bacon, Francis, 199
Baechler, Jean, 14
Bagosora, Theoneste, 305
Balkans: crimes in, 53, 318; nationalism in, 379; peace in, 299, 305; war in, 376–77, 381. See also ethnic cleansing; and individual states
banditry, 1, 3, 7–8
baptism, 61
Barayagwiza, Prosecutor v., 315
barbarians/barbarism, 15–16, 22, 26–27, 29, 43. See also Goths; Roman Empire
Barnes, Jonathan, 100
Barnett, Michael, 370
Barroso, José Manuel, 267, 287
Barry, Brian, 280–81
Bass, Gary Jonathan, 316, 320
Bassiouni, M. Cherif, 318
Baudrillard, Jean, 372
Bauman, Zygmunt, 373
becoming. See being
Begby, Endre, 58, 75n10, 78n16, 197
behavior: conflict-causing, 77, 80, 82; honorable, 123–24, 132, 284; immoral, 253; military, 152, 172–73, 206; restraints on, 15, 197, 298, 316; in wartime, 151–52, 200
being, 201, 383; and becoming, 135
believers: true, 44, 117n1, 125, 133; unorthodox, 27. See also faith; heretics; schism/schismatics
Bellah, Richard, 276
bellum, 5–6. See also war
benevolence, 80–81, 100, 119, 120, 196
Bennett, Andrew, 324
Berlin, Isaiah, 264
Berlin Wall, fall of, 373–74, 376
Bernard, Count of Armagnac, 102, 110, 112
Betts, Richard K., 248, 336
bias crimes, 302, 304
biological weapons, 167, 210–11, 214
bishops, 7, 53–54, 95. See also National Council of Catholic Bishops
Blagojevic, Vidoje, 304
Blanchette, Oliva, 202, 203
Bloch, Marc, 12
Blum, William, 324
Böckenförde, Ernst-Wolfgang, 373
bombing attacks, 157–59, 165, 167, 179, 181–82. See also atomic bombs

Bonaventure, Saint, 77
Bonet, Honoré, 11, 160, 163
Boniface, 52–54
Boniface, Pascal, 326
Book of Deeds of Arms and of Chivalry, The (Pizan), 101, 111–14, 142–43
Book of the City of Ladies (Pizan), 142n44
borders: external vs. internal, 377–78; national, 374, 375; political, 277–78; problems of, 268; wars to secure, 21. See also nations; states; territories
Born, Bertrand de, 12
Bornstein, Diane, 105
Bosnia: genocide in, 175–76, 295, 303–4, 353–56, 358, 360, 363–69; nationalism in, 25 1n2; nation-building, 340n13; sieges in, 179, 182–83; U.N. intervention in, 231, 248; war in, 172. See also tribunals
Both, Norbert, 184, 369, 370
Botzler, Richard, 199n8
Boutros-Ghali, Boutros, 225–26
Boyle, Joseph, 75n10, 205n17, 214, 215
Breton, Albert, 252
Brown, Chris, 255
Brown, Peter, 51, 53, 54
Buchanan, Allen, 249, 257–60
Burg, Wibren van der, 230, 231
Burgess, J. Peter, 372
Burgundians, 103, 113
Burke, Edmund, 290, 358
Burns, J. Patout, 17, 22, 24, 57
Bush, George W., 246–47; doctrine of, 325–49
Butler, William E., 324
Byers, Michael, 324
bystanders, 352–71; by assignment, 354, 358, 369; contemporary, 355, 358; corruption of, 368; passive, 354, 357–58, 359, 367; responsibilities of, 148–49

Caboche, Simon, 100
Caecilian (bishop), 53
Cahill, Lisa Sowle, 57
Cajetan, 75n9, 76n11
Caleb (Old Testament), 26
Callicles, 119n5
Cambodia: massacre in, 168; U.N. involvement in, 231; U.S.-sponsored coup, 323; Vietnamese intervention in, 223–24
Cameroon, 242n2
Campbell, David, 239, 353, 357
Caney, Simon, 253
canonists: restraints on war, 7–8, 15n3, 33, 86, 159–63; on self-defense, 78n16, 84n28
canon law, 162–63
Canterbury Tales (Chaucer), 105–6
capitalism, 377–79, 381–82, 383
Caprioli, Mary, 338n11
caritas. See charity; love

Carroll, Christina M., 293
Carter, Jimmy, 229
Cassese, Antonio, 307n11, 309, 318
Castel, Etienne de, 109
categorical imperative, 260–61, 263
Catholic Church, 89n58, 127; as agent of Heavenly City, 55–56, 61–62, 66–70; conflicts within, 66–68, 131, 133; history, 7–8, 36; just war theory, 68–71, 76n13, 160, 162; relations with states, 69–70; restraints on war, 7–8, 33, 76; in Rwanda, 175–76; schisms in, 51–71, 87
Central African Republic, 324n2
character, 1, 93, 131, 280. *See also* behavior; identity
charity: restraints on war, 46, 100; sins against, 74, 78, 80–85, 88, 90–91; toward nature, 201. *See also* love
Charles IV (king, France), 101
Charles V (king, France), 102
Charles VI (king, France), 102, 103
Charles VII (king, France), 104
Charles of Orleans, 102, 110, 113
Chaucer, Geoffrey: Cicero's influence on, 142; pacifism of, 115–16, 140–41; "Parson's Tale," 105n1; "Tale of Melibee," 101, 104–9, 114, 139–43; "Theopas," 105n2
chemical weapons, 167, 210–11, 214
Chesterman, Simon, 324
children, killing of, 3, 33, 182, 365
Childress, James F., 72, 75n1
China, 224n3
Chinkin, Christine M., 311
chivalry, code of, 13n3, 52, 53, 59, 99, 100, 160, 162–63. *See also* honor; military
choices, 77, 81, 201, 283
Chomsky, Noam, 324
Chopra, Jarat, 225, 240
Christianity/Christians: attitude toward heretics, 11, 15, 17; Classical period vs., 130, 133n33, 143; ethics, 24–25, 32, 41n7, 100, 125n16; justice and, 132–33; just war theory, 5–8, 12–35, 39, 72–73, 122, 130, 137–39, 143, 159–60, 193; life of, 66, 77, 126–27; medieval, 130n28; military service, 21; nature viewed by, 199; pacifism, 20–23, 42, 129; in Roman Empire, 24, 36, 53; virtues, 31–32, 45–46. *See also* Catholic Church
Christine de Pizan, 115–16, 139, 141–42, 160; *Book of Deeds of Arms and of Chivalry*, 101, 111–14, 142–43; *Book of the City of Ladies*, 142n44; *Lamentation on the Evils of Civil War*, 101, 109–11
Cicero: *De officiis*, 24–34, 123, 125, 129; ethics of, 111, 127–28; influence on Chaucer, 142; on justice, 127–28; just war theory, 12–14, 17–19, 23, 36, 108, 122–24; on war as play, 15–20
cities, 81, 83, 178–85; just, 16. *See also* earthly city; Heavenly City

citizens/citizenship, 154, 344; establishment of, 116, 255, 278–80; moral, 196, 286
City of God (Augustine), 20n6, 43, 52–59, 63, 69, 81. *See also* Heavenly City
civic life, 66, 130
civilians: as bystanders, 369n1; deaths of, 179–80; harm to, x, 1, 44, 49, 147–48, 184–85, 213, 215n35, 247; as human shields, 177–78, 180; in occupied territories, 174–75; soldiers distinguished from, 153–54, 163, 186–87; treatment of, 207, 293, 294n3. *See also* noncombatants
civil wars, 3, 211–12, 268, 344; former Yugoslavia, 291; France, 103, 110–11, 114, 141, 142; Rwanda, 172–73, 187–88, 293; U.S., 164, 174–75
classes, social, 99, 101, 115
Classical period: Christianity vs., 130, 133n33, 143; just war theory, ix, 11–35, 122–24, 138, 142
Clausewitz, Karl von, 119n5, 197
Clement VII (pope), 103
clerics, 77, 100–101, 111, 125; war forbidden to, 89n39, 95–96, 128n22
Cochrane, Charles N., 130
coercion: in matters of faith, 58n4, 51–71; of noncombatants, 178; peace through, 55–58, 63, 67–68, 161. *See also* force
cold war, 218, 246, 320, 327, 373–74
collateral damage, 156, 169, 204–5, 212, 215
collectivity, 253, 281
Collette, C., 114
colonialism, 249n1, 252; anticolonialism, 260; decolonization, 255; postcolonialism, 376. *See also* decolonization
combatants, distinguished from noncombatants, 152–55, 159, 163, 171, 173–75, 177–78, 185–87. *See also* knights; soldiers; warriors
command responsibility, 307n11
common good: defense of, 5–6, 10, 40, 79, 84–85, 137; service to, 160–61, 163; threats to, 87, 198; universal, 47, 81–82, 194, 202–3
communism, 382. *See also* Soviet Union
community: *honestum* in, 127; imagined, 252, 254, 257, 264; individual vs., 250, 253–54; members of, 6, 284, 287; national, 255, 268–69, 276–77; partiality and, 255–56; political, 6, 82–83, 272, 276; rights of, 256–59, 262; unity of, 87, 270, 380; value of, 283, 285. *See also* international community
compassion, 1, 100
concentration camps: Bosnian, 175, 356, 364; Nazi, 316; punishment for guards of, 290, 297, 306
concord, 81–84, 87, 89–90, 132, 205
conflict resolution, 318. *See also* reconciliation
conflict, 89n58; deliberation vs., 130, 142; national, 264; research on, 280; types of, 123–24. *See also* armed conflict; war

Index

Congo, Democratic Republic of, 247, 324n2. *See also* Zaire
Connolly, William, 62
Connor, Walker, 250–51
conquest, 16, 99, 112–13. *See also* domination
conscience, 55, 82n24, 171
consent, 281–83
consequences, 213–15, 316. *See also* double effect; side effects
consequentialism, 37, 41–46, 131, 250, 261
Constantine, 22–23, 32, 137
Constantinianism, 13–14, 20
constitutions, 278–79
contemplative life, 16, 32, 201–2
contention, 80–81, 83, 87, 89n38
contracts, social. *See* liberal contractualism
Contra Faustum (Augustine), 43
convergence, Thomist, 75n1. *See also* Aquinas
conversion, forced, 52, 64. *See also* coercion
1 Corinthians (Epistle to the) 13.12, 28
Cosic, Dobrica, 361, 365, 366
cosmopolitanism, 255, 261, 373–74
Coste, René, 76n13
costs, 241–42, 244
councils of advisers, 101, 106–9, 113–14, 140, 142
counterinsurgency campaigns, 211–12
coups, 228, 237. *See also* revolts
courage, 2, 12, 25, 29, 46, 79, 126
courtesy, 162
courtliness, ethic of, 100. *See also* chivalry
courts, 113–14, 148, 168. *See also* tribunals
Covic, Boze, 361, 362
Crawford, James, 229
Crawford, Neta, 337
Creta, Vincent M., 311, 312, 315
crimes against humanity, 168, 224, 290–94; prevention of, 316–17; punishment fit to, 57, 301–8, 319. *See also* atrocities; bias crimes; war crimes
criminals, 307n11, 356–57; enemies viewed as, 15; punishment of, 7
Crisp, Roger, 41
Croatia: nationalism in, 251n2, 364; war in, 172, 293, 363–64, 366
Crocker, David A., 315
cruelty, 43, 49; nationalism as reason for, 246
Crusades, 37
Cuellar, Javier Perez de, 239
culture: destruction of, 175; European, 373, 378, 382; peace based on, 195; protection of, 167, 257–58; shared, 274–80; value of, 283–84, 286–87; wars over, 187
Curtis, Mark, 324

Daly, Robert J., 17, 22, 24, 57
danger case arguments, 230, 238–39, 243
Danner, Allison Marston, 302, 303, 317, 369, 370

D'Anquentonville, Raoul, 102
Dante Alighieri, 83
David (Old Testament), 26, 29–31, 34
Davis, G. Scott, 169, 175
Deane, Herbert A., 57, 58, 63, 66, 67, 68
decency, 39
decision-making, 6, 348–49, 358; political, 92–94, 285, 344. *See also* interventions; war
decorum, 27–28, 31
deduction, 282
defenders, actions against, 182–83
defensive wars, 30, 46–49, 74–76, 220; anticipatory, 323–51; justice of, 86, 96, 124. *See also* self-defense
defoliation, 200, 208
DeFrancia, Cristian, 311, 313
dehumanization, 11–12, 22
Delalic et al., Prosecutor v., 311
Delanty, Gerard, 373
deliberation: with enemies, 123–24, 140, 142–43; in European Union, 270; moral, 77, 197; process of, 38, 93, 101, 108, 113–14, 347
democracy, 218, 347; as challenge to nonintervention, 227–29, 236–37, 238; Enlightenment model, 376–77; establishment of, 44, 70, 324, 349; European, 270, 381–82; forced, 340–41; liberal, 344, 377–79, 382–83
demons, 15, 22, 58
deontology, 9, 37, 41–46, 119, 131–32
deontotheology, 120n6
Descartes, René, 199
desires, 81, 93, 376
destruction, x, 214–15; environmental, 204–10; extent of, 188, 190–92, 196. *See also* collateral damage; harm; weapons of mass destruction
deterrence: mutual nuclear, 327–30; tribunals as, 291, 295–300, 307
deterritorialization, 357
Deuteronomy 23.19–20, 26
dignity, 77n15, 244, 261
Diocletian, 53
discipline, 64, 68, 172, 199. *See also* coercion; punishment
discord, 80–81, 83, 87, 89n38
discourse, 130, 194
discrimination, 8–9, 181, 204–5, 210–13, 215–16
disintegration, 66
dispositions, inner, 42n9, 206
diversity, of nature, 202–4
divine law, 47, 86, 113, 120, 135n36
Dizdarevic, Zlatko, 182, 184
domination: benevolent, 16; lust for, 43, 48, 57–58; wars for, 172, 205. *See also* conquest
Dominican Republic, 323
Donagan, Alan, 215n36
Donnelly, Jack, 255
Donatists, 38n4, 51–59, 61–64, 69, 151
do no harm, obligation of, 72–75

double effect, rule of, 45–46, 152, 156–59, 180–81, 183–84. *See also* side effects
double intention, 45n14, 156–57
double jeopardy, 314–15, 319
duellum, 5, 7–8. *See also* armed conflicts
due process, 114. *See also* fairness
Dumas, Roland, 224
Duns Scotus, 77
duties: moral, 27, 125–26, 281–83; public, 67, 254; rights and, 42–43, 246; special, 284–86; virtues and, 36–50
Dworkin, Ronald, 281

earth, 191–92, 199. *See also* environment
earthly city: Heavenly City compared to, 40, 55–56, 63–64, 67–68; peace in, 52, 70, 79
ecclesiastical unity, 81
economics, global, 255
economic sanctions, 227–28, 230
education, 1–2, 198–99; coercion as, 64; by tribunals, 296–97, 309, 317
Edward III (king, England), 101, 103, 104
effectiveness, lack of, 235, 237–38, 241
Ehrlich, Ludwik, 78n16
Eide, Espen Barth, 359
Eleanor of Aquitaine, 100
Eleazar (Old Testament), 25
Elisha (Old Testament), 25–26
eliticide, 175
Ellis, Mark, 292, 311, 312
Elshtain, Jean Bethke, 55, 56, 139n39
emotions, 41, 199
empathy, 254, 256
empire, 16–20, 57; wars for, 124n15, 128n21. *See also* Roman Empire; *and individual emperors*
end justifies the means, 3, 14, 45, 117n1, 215–16, 263n3
end times, 23, 36, 68. *See also* apocalypse
enemies: of the Church, 57–58; combatant vs. noncombatant, 152, 172; dehumanizing, 11–12, 22; force used against, 88, 129n25; justice toward, 14, 29–30, 206; love for, 26, 49, 63–64, 120, 126; oaths to, 15, 17–19, 21, 25–26; wholesale attacks on, 8, 154, 159, 172, 173–77
enforcement operations, 240–41
engagement, rules of. *See* war
enjoyment, 80–81, 376, 379–80. *See also* happiness
Enlightenment, 373, 374–77
Ennius, 123
ensoulment, of cosmos, 23, 27–28, 32
environment, the: just war applied to, 202–217; moral view of, 195, 199–204; protection of, 190–217, 374; targeting, 200, 209, 212–13, 215n35, 237; war's effects on, 147–48, 190–217
Environmental Modification Techniques Convention, 191–92, 213n33
equality, 270, 382; of arms, 311–12

eternal life, 27, 31, 125n17, 126–27, 133
ethics, 18, 372–73; of Ambrose, 127–28; Christian, 24–25, 32, 41n7, 100, 125n16; Ciceronian, 32, 127–28; contemporary, 36–37; environmental, 190–217; feminist, 139; kernel of, 374–75, 379; medical, 233n10; medieval, 194; nationalism and, 246–66; pagan, 19–20, 25; political, 357; Thomist, 72–98, 135–37, 213n34; universal, 268, 278–80, 373. *See also* morality; nation-states; virtue ethics; war
ethnic cleansing, 3, 261, 316, 324, 364, 366–67. *See also* genocide
ethnicity, 154, 257, 378, 380, 382; targeting, 159, 167–68, 171–73; wars based on, 152, 186–88, 258, 293n2, 344n15, 352–53, 359. *See also* race
eudaimonea, 130
Eugenius, 24
Europe: creation of nations in, 252, 255, 287; Eastern, 376–77, 381–82; medieval, 99, 287; nationalism, 267–89, 379; nation-states, 373–74; war in, ix, 90; Western, 376–77, 381. *See also individual countries*
European Union, 267–89, 381; decision-making procedures, 269–70; trust and stability, 271–78; welfare regimes, 269–74
Eusebius, 22–23, 25; Constantinianism, 13–14, 20, 32; ensoulment of cosmos, 23, 27–28, 32
evidence, rules of, 311–16. *See also* fairness
evil: avoidance of, 96, 156–57; within Catholic Church, 66–68; determination of, x, 92–93, 383; punishment of, 94, 125, 154; root of, 64; triumph of, 358. *See also* actions; good; intentions; sin/sinners; wrongdoing
expansionism, 16
expediency, 17–19, 26–27

Fabian, Kellye L., 311
failed states, 235, 241, 344, 346
fairness: justice as, 281; principles of, 100, 347–49; procedural, 114, 292, 298–99, 301, 309–16, 320–21
faith, 31, 32, 54, 60; coercion for, 58n4, 54, 58; defense of, 8; justice and, 69, 127–28, 132; reason and, 133n33, 135. *See also* believers
falling dominoes argument, 238–44
Farer, Tom J., 181
Fedayeen Saddam, 177
fellowship, 81
Fernández-Armesto, Felipe, 374
Ferry, Jean-Marc, 373
feudal life, 7, 78
Finnis, John, 74n7, 214, 215
Fixdal, Mona, 247
flushing-out tactics, 208
Follesdal, Andreas, 267, 283, 375
force: authority for, 4–8, 84–85; deliberation vs., 142; justifications for, 75, 153, 196, 229–

force *(cont.)*
31, 255, 258–59, 261, 331–32; presumption against, 72–74, 85–96, 135, 160–61; restraints on, 1, 8, 10, 220, 243; threats of, 219–22; use of, ix–x, 2, 90n43, 123–24, 198, 227, 275, 335, 375. *See also* coercion
foreign policy, 74, 139n59, 197, 247
forests, destruction of, 191, 200, 208
Forhan, Kate L., 99, 139–44
Fortin, Ernest, 38n4, 45, 51–52, 61
Fotion, Nick, 120, 196, 198
Fowler, Robert Booth, 58
fragmentation, 33, 104, 271
France: civil war in, 103, 110–11, 113–14, 141–42, 147; European Union and, 267; interventions by, 324n2; peacekeeping forces, 224; violence in, 7, 100; war with England, 101–4, 105; women in, 116; World War II, 157
Francis Leiber's Code, 164
Franck, Thomas M., 227
Franklin, Benjamin, 99
freedom, 18–19, 69, 77n5, 161; nationalism as, 246, 263–64
French Revolution, 147
Freud, Sigmund, 376, 379
Friedman, Leon, 164
friendship, 82–83
Fukuyama, Francis, 383

Gabon, 324n2
gaming, 16–20, 123. *See also* play
Gandhi, Mohandas K., 193
Gauthier, David, 271, 281
Gellner, Ernest, 249, 252, 258
gender, 114, 359
generosity, 100
Geneva Conventions, 164, 165–69; of 1949, 166, 168–70, 191, 206n20, 207n21, 208n24, 211n30; violations of, 293–94
genocide, 175–77, 183–85, 316, 344n15, 352–71; complicity in, 353, 357, 360, 367, 370; definitions of, 352–53, 370; ideologies of, 367–68; as imitation, 363–64; incitement to, 223, 353, 368; intellectuals and, 353, 357, 359, 361–70; international agreements regarding, 167–69, 172, 185, 291, 293–94, 352–53, 358–59, 370; legitimation of, 44, 360, 367; moral issues of, 354, 356–61; prevention of, 167–69, 187, 324, 355; punishment for, 302–5. *See also* ethnic cleansing
George, Robert, 194, 249, 253
Germany: punishment of, 290–91; regime change in, 341; unification of, 251n2, 373–74, 376; World War II, 49, 158, 316–17
Girard, René, 62
Gleditsch, Nils Petter, 44
globalization, 194, 318–19, 373–74, 376, 382; economic, 255, 271, 378; war and, 148–49

glory, 23–34, 55
God: authority of, 40, 143; as Creator, 202; existence of, 120n6; failure to worship, 64; glory of, 12–13, 20, 23, 55; grace of, 26, 31; judgment of, 14–15; love for, 132; messengers of, 38; plan of, 38n3, 43; war commanded by, 38, 56, 108, 129n26, 134; will of, 5, 27
gods, 14–15, 60
Goldstone, Richard, 309
Goldwater-Nichols Act (1986), 327n5
good, x, 79, 81n22, 82, 262, 383. *See also* actions; common good; evil; intentions
Gorazde (Bosnia), 183–84
Gospels, 23, 25, 126–27
Goths, 24, 52–53
governments, 63, 74n3, 89; de facto, 229, 252; democratic, 218, 258; ineffective, 235, 237–38, 241; legitimacy of, 227–28, 249–50, 262–63, 344; prudence of, 93–94; punishment of, 290; unlawful, 219; world, 47–48. *See also* cities; nations; states
grace, 14, 64, 126–29, 130. *See also* God
Graham, Gordon, 251n2
Gratian, 7, 24, 76n11, 84
Gray, Phillip W., 36, 38n4, 51, 130–32, 135
Great Britain: bombing by, 158; interventions by, 324; involvement in Iraq, 333–34; national identity, 276, 377; peacekeeping forces, 224; revolts in, 100; war with France, 101–4, 105
Great Schism, 103–4
Green, Leslie C., 192
Greenfield, Liah, 249
Grenada, 323, 340
Grimm, Dieter, 270
Grotius, Hugo, 42, 43, 48, 152, 163–64, 368
groups, 358–61. *See also* community
Guatemala, 323, 345n17
Guelff, Richard, 171
guerilla warfare, 185n5, 211–12
guilt: determination of, 295, 301, 307, 314, 316, 360; moral, 299; punishment of, 302–7
Gulf War (1990–1991), 190, 224, 240
Guoliang, Guo, 341
Gutman, Roy, 352, 353, 356, 368

Haas, Ernest, 230
Habermas, Jürgen, 269, 275, 278, 280, 287, 366, 373
Habsburg Empire, 260
Haggenmacher, Peter, 76n11, 80n19, 92n46
Hague Conventions, 165, 167, 169–71, 211n30
Haiti, 228–29, 236–37, 323, 340n13
Halleck, Henry W., 174–75
Hamann, Johann Georg, 264
Hampshire, Stuart, 284
happiness, 20, 31, 124n14. *See also* enjoyment; joy
harm, 38–39, 43, 84, 130, 278, 335; direct vs.

indirect, 152, 155–59, 175, 180–81; environmental, 147–48, 190–217; intentional, 84–85, 129n25, 171, 179–85, 187–88, 204, 209–12, 214; to noncombatants, 147–48, 151–55, 159–60, 163–65, 179–85; redress for, 79, 299, 319
hatred, 79, 80–81, 206–7, 368
Hayner, Priscilla G., 300
Hays, Richard B., 137, 138, 139
heathens, 15, 26. *See also* paganism/pagans
Heavenly City: Catholic Church as agent of, 55–56, 62–63, 66–70; earthly city compared to, 55–56, 63–64, 67–68; peace in, 51–52, 60, 70; pilgrimage to, 40. *See also City of God*
Hegel, Georg W. F., 367–68, 376
Held, David, 255
Helgeland, John, 17, 22, 24, 57
Helsinki Watch, 353
Henry IV (king, England), 103, 109n7
Henry V (king, England), 103
Henry VI (king, England and France), 103
Henry VII (king, England), 103
Herder, Johann Gottfried, 264
heretics: Christian views of, 11, 13; coercion against, 58n4, 51–71; orthodoxy and, 24; prayer for, 59; wars against, 15, 24, 26–27, 33–34, 128n22, 129, 130, 133. *See also* schism/schismatics
Herman, Edward, 324
Herodotus, 372
Heyking, John von, 11, 121–30
Hippel, Karin von, 340n13
Hiroshima, 42, 158
Hitler, Adolf, 317
Hobbes, Thomas, 142, 281, 379
Hobsbawm, Eric, 249, 251n2, 252, 264
Höffe, Otfried, 373
Holmes, Robert L., 38
Holocaust, 168, 316
holy wars, 12, 14, 38, 38n4, 118n2
honestum, 17–18, 26–28, 31, 127. *See also* virtues
Honig, Jan Willem, 184, 369, 370
honor: codes of, 33–34, 49, 162; glory and, 27–29, 33; moral, 2, 45; in war, 15–19, 122–24. *See also* chivalry
Hroch, Miroslav, 252
Huband, Mark, 368
Huizinga, Johannes, 14, 15, 122
human beings: conduct, 151–52; equality for, 253; grace and, 14; life of, 45, 64, 121, 127n19, 196; nature of, x, 58, 127n20, 130, 142–43, 283; as stewards of nature, 194, 200–204, 213, 374; treatment of, 117, 263; will of, 47. *See also* crimes against humanity; mankind
humanitarian intervention, 37, 218–47; justifications for, 47, 49, 97, 231, 239, 240; military, 148, 195, 248, 325, 335, 346; U.N.-authorized, 225–26, 375
humanitarianism, 255–56, 291, 319

humanitas, 142–43
human rights, x, 120–21, 195–96, 381; international agreements on, 274–75, 291, 309–10; laws, 164, 171, 172, 255–56, 319; nonintervention and, 223–26, 250–34, 235, 237–38; violations of, 218–19, 296–97, 324–25, 330, 344, 346. *See also* crimes against humanity
humility, 27, 30–31, 143
Hundred Years' War, 101–4, 105
hunting, 106n4
Hurka, Thomas, 253
Hussein, Saddam, 323, 325, 329–30, 341
Hutu tribe, 175–77, 180, 296, 305, 368

identity: common, 273, 344, 359; differences of, 172; national, 148, 268–80, 286–87, 377–78, 381; political, 279, 353
ideologies, x, 186–87, 359–61, 366–67
Ignatieff, Michael, 33, 34, 255, 541
immorality. *See* morality
immunity, 163, 169. *See also* noncombatants
impartiality, 354, 382
imperialism/*imperium*, 16–20, 25, 128, 130
inaction. *See* actions
independence: constitutional, 221–22, 223, 225–27; movements for, 148; national, 249–50, 260; political, 277
India, 334
individuals: communities vs., 250, 253–54, 373; interests of, 281, 283, 285; responsibilities of, 370; rights of, 253–59, 261–62, 318–19
infidels, 11, 26, 33
Ingierd, Helene, 209
injuries, 38–39, 84, 335
injustice, 15, 17–18, 128–29, 198; domestic, 231, 235, 241, 257; presumption against, 37, 73–74, 96–97, 135–39; punishment of, 48, 74n6, 76, 88, 96–97, 161, 206, 261, 290, 316–18. *See also* justice
innocence, presumption of, 313–14, 319
Innocent IV (pope), 84n28
instant case arguments, 230, 238–39
institutions, 64; compliance with, 276, 280, 284–86; democratic, 349; establishment of, x, 7; just, 281–83, 286; law-enforcing, 316–17; political, 373, 381; preventing war, 45, 48; shared, 278
insurrections. *See* coups; revolts
intentions, 131; conscience and, 82n24; double, 45n14, 156–57; right, 39–40, 63, 72, 84, 100, 112, 134, 160–61, 196, 204–7, 215–16; wrong, 6, 73, 88, 135, 205–7. *See also* actions
international community, 48, 343; justice for, 291–93, 298–99, 301, 307–8, 316–21
International Criminal Court (ICC), 292, 308, 318, 320–21
International Criminal Tribunal for Rwanda (ICTR), 291, 293–321

International Criminal Tribunal for the former Yugoslavia (ICTY), 291, 293–321
International Crisis Group, 315
internationalism, 100, 148
international law, 4, 309, 334–35, 339, 346; environmental protections, 191–92, 195, 201, 208n24, 209–11, 216; foundations of, 15–16, 43–44, 343–44; humanitarian, 164–71, 358; intervention issues, 221, 227–29, 342; just war and, 42, 171; Law of Peoples, 345, 347; modern, 37, 46, 48; noncombatant protection, 169–71, 173, 185; positive, 159, 164–71, 174; self-determination under, 229, 261; violations of, 168, 221, 290–95, 297–98, 306–7, 312, 316–21, 328–30, 335, 352; of war, 8–9, 76, 119n5, 152, 158–59, 167, 179, 187–89, 207
international order, 47–48, 85, 326–27, 330, 340–41, 345, 348
international relations, 74, 139n39, 197, 247
interventions, 241; decisions regarding, 234n11, 240–43; ethics of, 247–48; justifications for, 218–19, 227, 252–54, 243–44; presumption against, 222, 258–59, 335; U.N.-authorized, 218–45; unauthorized, 220, 242–43; unilateral, 335–36; U.S.-sponsored, 323. *See also* humanitarian interventions; nonintervention; occupations; regime changes; slippery slope argument
intolerance, 246, 264, 381
Iran, 323, 326
Iraq: oil field attacks, 190; regime change in, 329–30, 335–36, 339–42; U.N. intervention (1991), 223, 224–25, 239, 240, 325n4, 326; U.S. invasion (2003), 148, 173, 177–78, 247, 323, 325, 333–34, 346
Ireland, 251n2, 286. *See also* Northern Ireland
Isaiah, 127
Islam, 8, 195. *See also* Muslims
Israelites, 25–26. *See also* Jerusalem
Italy, 251n2, 341
ius ad bellum, 6, 72, 114–15, 117, 148, 206–7, 218, 336; criteria for, 91–92, 94, 99–100, 205n16; defensive, 74, 96; morality of, 121. *See also* force; war
ius cogen, 236
ius in bello, 8, 39, 115, 117, 121, 212, 218. *See also* war
Ivkovic, Sanja Kutnjak, 308

Jackson, Robert H., 225, 292
James, Alan, 221
Janssen, Dieter, 323
Janvier, Bernard, 369
Japan, 290–91, 341
Jerusalem, 179–80
Jesus Christ, 28, 69, 80n20, 127, 130
Joan of Arc, 103–4
John (king, France), 102

John, Duke of Berry, 102, 110, 111
John of Gaunt, 106
John Paul II (pope), encyclicals of, 69
Johnson, James Turner, 3, 12n2, 13n5, 33, 37, 39, 73, 76, 90–92, 94, 105, 135, 151, 152, 162, 374
Johnson, Scott T., 300, 311, 312, 313, 314, 315
John the Fearless, Duke of Burgundy, 102, 110
Jonas, Hans, 357
Jonathan (Old Testament), 25
Jones, Peter, 253
Josephus, 179–80, 181
Joshua (Old Testament), 25–26, 38
jouissance. *See* enjoyment
journalism/journalists, genocide role of, 367–70
joy, 80–81, 379–80, 376. *See also* happiness
Judah, Tim, 363, 365
Judaism, 195, 199
Judas Maccabeus, 25
Julius Caesar, 18, 19
just cause: Classical theory of, 18, 25; criteria for, 48, 112–13, 204–8, 335, 336n10, 337–38; medieval theory of, 69, 90–91, 134, 196; modern theory of, 216. *See also ius ad bellum*; just war
justice, 100, 121–43, 161–64, 206, 290–322, 379; for accused, 291–92, 298–301, 303, 309–16, 320; Ambrose on, 125–30; Augustine on, 130–35; authority and, 4–5; blind, 382; Christian, 132–33; Ciceronian, 127–28; community, 84, 307–8; commutative, 79; comparative, 91–94, 96; divine, 38, 126–27; toward enemies, 29–30; faith and, 69, 127–28, 132; natural, 119n5, 138; toward nature, 200–201; peace and, 56, 82–83, 162, 295–300; perception of, 92; Pizan on, 142; political, 195, 316–17, 320, 343–44; principles of, 4, 282–86, 347–49; pursuit of, 37, 47; as redress, 112–13, 292, 298–99, 306, 320; restoration of, 85, 318; as retribution, 79n17, 161, 291–92, 298–300, 302, 320; true, 57, 93, 133, 143; universal, 119, 269, 278–81, 307; for victims, 291–92, 296–309, 313, 316, 320; violation of, 57, 74, 91; virtue of, 48–49, 80, 90n4, 94; war and, 39–40, 45. *See also* injustice
just war, ix, 99–101, 121–43; Ambrose's theory, 128; Augustinian theory, 56–71, 137–38, 143, 159–62; Catholic Church's theory, 68–71, 76n13, 160, 162; Chaucer's theory, 101, 104–9; Christian theory, 72–73, 130, 143, 159–60; Classical theory, 11–35, 76, 122–24, 138, 142; criteria for, 1–10, 37–42, 192–95; environmental considerations, 199–217; ethical considerations, 190–217; international law on, 42, 171; Kant's theory, 44–45; medieval theory, ix, 1–10, 12–13, 42, 99–101, 109, 117–45, 159–64, 200, 205, 216; modern theory, 37, 48, 96, 131, 159, 163–64; morality of, 37–41, 88, 119n5,

281, 335; motives for, 12–14, 25, 32, 87–88; noncombatant protection, 159–64; nonintervention and, 222, 335–36; Pizan's theory, 101, 109–14, 141–42; punishment as, 92n47; Scholastic theory, 375; secular theory, 70; Thomist theory, 72–98, 135–39, 143, 160–61, 193–94, 196, 206n19; tradition of, 152–53, 159–64, 196, 218

Kabila, Laurent, 176
Kadhammar, Peter, 370
Kambanda, Jean, 306
Kant, Immanuel: categorical imperative, 260–61, 263; cosmopolitanism, 373; just war theory, 44–45, 134; moral philosophy, 195, 250; nationalism, 383
Kasper, Sara, 340
Kellogg-Briand Pact, 220
Kelsay, John, 185
Khmer Rouge, 168
killing: of children, 3, 33, 182, 365; intentional, 75, 84–85, 185, 191, 209–12, 293n1; justifications for, 30, 129n25, 134, 367; mass, 44, 173, 175, 187, 252, 318, 524; restraints on, 174; of unorthodox believers, 27; in war, 21, 33, 121, 136, 159, 214. See also ethnic cleansing; genocide; murder
kingdoms/kings, 26, 29–31, 34, 38n3, 81, 83, 115, 135n36
Klosko, George, 281
knights, ix, 1, 78, 105n2; armed conflict among, 3, 5, 7–8, 163; behavior of, 49, 141n43, 162; culpability of, 111, 112
Köhler, Martin, 255
Koselleck, Reinhart, 373
Kosovo: battle at Polje, 360; ethnic cleansing in, 184–85, 294, 298, 361–64; war in, 179, 242n16, 243, 259
Kosovo Liberation Army (KLA), 185n5, 259
Krstic, Radislav, 303–4
Kuper, Leo, 223
Kurds, 224–25, 325n4. See also Iraq

Lacan, Jacques, 376, 379
Lactantius, 80
laity, 45, 100–101, 115
Lamentation on the Evils of Civil War (Pizan), 101, 109–11
language: identity and, 173, 251n2, 256; of necessity, 67; serious, 105
Last Judgment, 68. See also apocalypse; end times
last resort, 39, 215
Lavere, George J., 46
law: defense of, 112; establishment of, 298; human, 171, 172, 192; interpretation of, 331; moral, 378, 379; national, 81, 257; obedience to, 15, 281–82; rule of, 198, 373; violations of, 166, 361. See also armed conflicts; canon law; divine law; international law; natural law; war
Law of Peoples, 327, 343–49
lawyers. See canonists
leadership: authority for war, 38, 40; civic, 73; courageous, 24, 141n43; military, 2, 32, 92–93, 297, 305–7; political, 78, 92–93; suffering by, 50. See also authority
League of Nations, 220
Lecce, D. J., 324
legitimacy, 227, 280, 281–83. See also authority; nations; nation-states; states
Leigh, Monroe, 311, 313
Lemkin, Raphael, 353, 358
Leppig, Linda, 110
Levinas, Emmanuel, 355
lex ferenda, 334–35
liberal contractualism, 269, 280–86, 375
liberalism, 29, 74n3, 276, 279, 346
liberation theologies, 139
Libero arbitrio, De (Augustine), 47
libertarianism, 274
liberty, 18–19, 69, 77n15, 161; nationalism as, 246, 263
Lichtenberg, Judith, 249
Licinius, 22
licitum, 86
life. See active life; Christianity/Christians; civil life; contemplative life; eternal life; human beings; religious life
Lillich, Richard B., 232
limited-war theory, 74n3
line-drawing argument, 231–38
literature, didactic, 105–6, 111–12
Louis, Duke of Anjou, 102
Louis, Duke of Orleans, 102
Louis of Guyenne, 110
love, 5, 48, 79–81, 196, 206; Christian, 30, 32, 54; ontology of, 131–32, 135; punishment as, 63–64, 66–67; violence in name of, 57–58. See also charity; enemies
loyalty, 162
lust, 43, 48; war-inspired, 39

Maass, Peter, 363
Macedo, Stephen, 281
MacIntyre, Alasdair, 41, 283
Maimonides, 179
Malthusians, 193n3
Manichean heresy, 62
mankind: enemies of, 17–18, 33; salvation through war, 22–23. See also human beings
Mann, Michael, 375
marginalization, 378
Marie de Champagne, 100
Marie de France, 116
Maritain, Jacques, 274

Markovic, Mihailo, 366
Markus, R. A., 61, 63, 64–68
marriage, 89n39, 114; intermarriage, 173, 175
Marxism, 377–78, 382
massacres. *See* ethnic cleansing; genocide; killing
mass media, 367. *See also specific types of media*
Matthew (Gospel of) 5.16, 28
Mauritania, 324n2
May, Larry, 358
Mayall, James, 224
McCoubrey, Hilaire, 227
McKim, Robert, 253
McMahan, Jeff, 120, 253, 258
mediation, 114. *See also* reconciliation
Meernik, James, 290, 314
mercenaries, 112
mercy, 25, 28, 29, 80–81
Mertus, Julie, 359
Middle Ages: Christianity in, 130n28; environmental philosophy, 199–204; ethics in, 194; Europe during, 99, 287; just war theory, ix, 1–10, 12–15, 42, 109, 117–45, 159–64, 200, 205, 216; political theory, 11–35; war in, ix, 12, 49, 99, 121–30
Midgley, Mary, 255
military, the: behavior of, 152, 172–73, 206; civilian integration with, 153–54; codes of, 152, 164–65; service in, 21, 52, 77–79, 95–97; strategies, 242n16. *See also* humanitarian interventions; leadership; occupations; officers; soldiers
military-industrial complex, 196
military necessity, 191, 208, 214, 337
Mill, John Stuart, 259, 340
Miller, David, 268–87, 375
Miller, Richard B., 72, 73, 74n2, 85–85, 88, 89n38, 91, 135, 249, 253, 254, 255
Milosevic, Slobodan, 70, 298, 364, 366
minorities, 262–63, 279, 286. *See also* ethnicity; race
Mladic, Ratko, 369
moderation, 28, 197
Molina, Luis de, 76n11
monism, 122
morale, 158, 207
morality, 86n34, 344; ambiguous, 136–37, 262–64; categorical imperative, 260–61; national, 118n3, 375; of nature, 201; personal, 198; political, 47, 239, 253; of self-determination, 248–49, 255–63; universal, 120n6. *See also* genocide; just war; war
moral reflection: lack of, 140; medieval, 5–10, 12, 72–73, 93; modern, 160, 164, 185–89; on war and environment, 192–95, 204. *See also* right; wrongdoing
Moreno-Riaño, Gerson, 36, 117
Moses, 30, 58

multiculturalism, 267, 376
murder, 21, 85, 134, 201, 302–3. *See also* killing
Murphy, Mark C., 282
Murray, John Courtney, 196, 198
Muslims: ethnic cleansing against, 175, 183–84, 360, 365–66, 369; European, 267, 287. *See also* Islam

Nagasaki, 42
Nagel, Thomas, 253–55
Nahimana, Ferdinand, 368
Nairn, Tom, 252, 263–64
National Council of Catholic Bishops, 11, 72–73, 91n45, 135
nationalism, 139, 148, 246–66, 379–80; definitions of, 248–54; European, 267–89, 373–74, 376–77; fundamentalist, 383; moderate, 276; nation distinguished from, 250–53, 257; post-nationalism, 373; theories of, 254–55; trust and stability within, 271–78
nationality, 268–80, 286, 373; crimes against, 352–53, 359; wars based on, 171–72, 184–85, 293n2. *See also* identity
National Security Strategy (NSS, Bush administration), 325–49
nation-building, 340n13, 347, 375
nations, 17n5, 254–55, 353, 383; creation of, 251–52, 255–57, 260–62, 380–81; culture of, 276–79; defense of, 139; definitions of, 250–53, 259, 261; interests of, 4, 6, 90–93, 197–98, 243–44, 270–71; legitimacy of, 171, 279; nationalism vs., 250–53, 257; rights of, 258, 261–62; security of, 139, 268, 324; self-determination by, 248–50, 252, 255–63, 277, 286, 359, 375
nation-states, 92, 148, 198, 260; borders of, 375; ethical core of, 372–83; European, 373–74; lack of cohesion in, 35; legitimacy of, 268, 271; sovereignty of, 277, 279
NATO. *See* North Atlantic Treaty Organization
natural law, 6, 82n24, 86, 138, 160, 211, 374
nature, 190–95, 199–204, 261–62, 344, 374. *See also* environment
Nazis. *See* Germany
Ndindabahizi, Emmanuel, 306
Nederman, Cary, 15
need, 376
neglect, 356–57
neighbors, 78n16, 82, 132
neocolonialism, 324
Netherlands, the, 267
neutrality, 354
newspapers, 356
Ngeze, Hassan, 306
Niebuhr, Reinhold, 47
Niger, 324n2
nihilism, x
noncombatants: combatants distinguished from, 13, 152–55, 159, 163, 171, 173–75, 177–78,

185–87; definition of, 165–66, 170, 177–78, 186–87; harm to, 111, 147–48, 151–55, 159–60, 163–65, 171, 176–78, 185, 214; immunity of, 7–9, 33, 70, 163, 169, 181; in just war tradition, 159–64; laws regarding, 164–71; protection of, 74, 100, 119, 151–89, 374; targeting of, 151–52, 167–69, 171–85, 191, 209–12, 247. *See also* civilians
nonintervention: challenges to, 222–29; doctrine of, 218–22, 259, 375; justification for, 232–34; presumption of, 236n12; softening of, 219–20, 230–44. *See also* intervention; slippery slope argument
noninvolvement, 354
North Africa, 51, 53–54, 60
North Atlantic Treaty Organization (NATO), 243, 259, 361
Northern Ireland, 44, 276
North Korea, 341
Norway, 208n24, 215n35, 233n10
Nuclear Non-Proliferation Treaty, 326
nuclear weapons, 154, 167, 209, 211, 215n35, 326
Numidia, church of, 53–54
Nuremberg tribunal, 290–91, 318
Nyere, Julius, 343

occupations, military, 165, 166, 174–75. *See also* interventions
Octavian (emperor), 22
offensive war, 37, 48, 74–76, 86, 90n43, 97, 220
Officiis, De (Cicero), 24–34, 123, 125, 129
Officiis ministorum, De (Ambrose), 24–31, 125–30
On Idolatry (Tertullian), 20–21
On the Crown (Tertullian), 20–21
On Tobias (Ambrose), 26–27
Operation Provide Comfort, 224, 242, 325n2
Operation Restore Hope, 226, 240
oppression, 161, 239, 263, 353
optimists, 193n3
Orasac, 362
order: Augustinian theory, 55–56, 131–32; moral, 120n6; natural, 6, 38, 56, 138; political, 160–62; public, 7; restoration of, 301, 319; social, 161–64, 281
Origen, 11, 13, 20, 21–22, 23
Orleans, battle of, 103–4
Østerud, Øyvind, 249, 252
Ostrom, Elinor, 273
Other: defense of, 46–49, 128n21; East European concept of, 376–83; as enemy, 173–77; good of, 82
Ottaway, Marina, 341
Ottoman Empire, 260, 360
outlaw states, 343, 344–48. *See also* rogue states
Özkirimli, Umut, 375

pacifism, 11–14, 84, 96, 120–21, 209; of Ambrose, 126, 128n22; of Augustine, 135n33; of Chaucer, 139–41, 143; Christian, 20–23, 42, 129; justice and, 125n17; of Origen, 11, 13, 20, 21–22, 23; of Pizan, 141–42; political realism and, 117, 193, 195–99; secular, 120; of Tertullian, 11, 13, 20–21, 23, 80; Thomist, 73, 91, 137
paganism/pagans: ethics of, 19–20, 25, 46; schismatics and, 59–64; wars and, 12–13, 23, 24, 25–26. *See also* heathens; heretics
Pakistan, 334
Panaetius, 125n17
Panama, 323, 340
Pangle, Thomas L., 16
paramilitary fighters, 173, 177–78, 297
Paris Peace Agreement (1991), 223–24
Parousia, 21
partiality, 250, 253–56
particularism, 254, 258
passions, 93, 198
passive resistance, 30
patriotism, European, 267–89
Paul (New Testament) 28, 55, 127
Paul VI (pope), 291
peace: Augustine's views on, 51–71, 132n31; Cathaginian, 181; coercion and, 55–58, 67–68; democratic, 345; de Pizan's views on, 109–14, 139; earthly, 52, 56–57, 59–60, 61, 63, 68–70; ethics of, 372, 375; as goal of war, ix, 13, 17, 21, 38–40, 44, 47, 56, 59, 67, 84, 137, 188–89, 205–6, 215–16, 290–91, 358; heavenly, 56–57, 59, 63, 68, 70, 81n23; honorable, 124n15; internal, 544; interstate, 195, 286; justice and, 56, 82, 162, 280, 295–300; lasting, 43, 45, 48, 63; maintaining, 85, 161–64, 343, 354, 369–70; medieval, 99; national, 261, 264; political, 195; presumption for, 72; reconciliation as, 308; Thomist views on, 79–82, 89n40, 135, 138; threats to, 6, 80–81, 219–21, 224, 226–28, 230, 232, 235–38, 246–47, 293, 330–32
peacekeeping forces, 70, 224–25, 228–29, 240–41, 369n1
Peace of God movement, 7–8, 161–26
Peace of Westphalia (1648), 43, 218
peasant revolts, 100, 102
Pei, Minxin, 340
people, the: rights of, 229, 236, 258; states and, x, 372; will of, 339
perfection, 30–31, 40
per molestias eruditio. See teaching by inconveniences
perpetrator groups, 359–61. *See also* agents; criminals
persecution, 66–67, 302, 304
Peter Lombard, 77
Philip VI (king, France), 101
Philip the Bold, Duke of Burgundy, 102
philosophers/philosophy, 32, 125n17; Christian,

philosophers/philosophy *(cont.)* 22–23; just war tradition and, 4, 193; moral, 41, 166; of nationalism, 250; political, 383; of war, ix. *See also* Scholastics
pillage, 95, 165–67
pirates, 18, 33–34
Pius XII (pope), 76n13
Plamenatz, John, 252
Plato, 16, 32, 119n5, 133
play, war as, 12, 13, 14–20, 26–27, 32–33, 122–24
pluralism, 69, 275
poets, 99–116, 139–44
Pogge, Thomas, 373
police actions, 70
polis, 16–20
political realism, 4, 118–19; Augustinian, 58–59; pacifism and, 117, 193, 195–99; Thomist, 91, 96
political theory, 11–55; contemporary, 36–37, 254, 270; medieval, 121–30, 161
politicians/politics, 1–2, 131–32; genocide and, 366–67; identity, 353; international, 47, 58, 246, 255, 331; laicization of, 45, 100–101; modern, 283, 376; national, 252, 262; poets and, 99–116; punishment of, 290–91, 297, 305; violence as instrument of, 119. *See also* actions; order; power
Pol Pot, 223
popes, 87, 103–4. *See also individuals by name*
postmodernism, 33–34
power: balance of, 290, 318; desire for, 99, 127n18; despotic, 16; international, 346; laicization of, 115; national, 261, 375, 379; political, 23, 52, 66; right to, 260–62; struggle for, 59, 119
Power, Samantha, 368–69
practices, 278, 281–86, 343
Praxis group, 366
prayer, 59, 126; battle via, 21–22, 23
precautionary principle, 213
preemptive actions, 323, 348; justifications for, 148, 247, 325; legality of, 334–35, 341–42, 360; for self-defense, 39n5, 327–33, 336–39
prejudice, 264, 381
preventive actions, 323, 332–35; defensive, 327, 337, 343; justifications for, 117n1, 148, 325, 339
pride, 17n5, 31
princes, 5–7; culpability of, 92, 110–11; duties of, 1, 5–7, 141–42; just war and, 74n6, 76n11, 112; mirrors for, 101, 106–9, 114, 115
prisoners of war, 1, 33, 43, 123, 165, 175
Project for the New American Century (PNAC), 329n8
Promised Land, 25–26
propaganda, 178, 364–67
property: destruction of, 207, 293n1; protection of, 165–67; recovery of, 39, 74, 112, 125, 161; rights, 211, 374; stealing, 87n36, 113
proportionality, priniciple of, 8–9, 39, 42, 191, 204–5, 212–13, 215–16, 338
protection tactics, 208
prudence, 78–79, 93–94, 109, 114; pacifism based on, 120, 139–40, 143
Pry, Peter Vincent, 336
Psalms (Book of) 81.4, 161
punishment: as act of love, 63–64, 66–67; fit to crime, 299, 301–9; God's, 126, 134; just, 83–84, 88, 128, 296, 316; just war as, 57–58, 61, 92n47. *See also* tribunals; wrongdoing
putative groups, 358
Pyrrhus, 15, 122n9, 123

quasi-states, 225, 235

race, 378, 381–82; wars based on, 3, 167–68, 171–72, 293n2, 302, 352–53, 359. *See also* genocide
radical particularists, 258
radio, 359, 363–64, 368
Rahner, Hugo, 14
raison d'etát, doctrine of, 90, 197, 284
Ram (Brana) plan, 365
Ramsey, Paul, 74, 90, 152, 154, 157n1, 158, 186
Randelzhofer, Albrecht, 332
Ranger, Terence, 252, 264
rape, 1, 33, 313, 364, 365
Rawls, John, 195, 269, 275, 278, 280, 283, 284, 285–86, 327, 342–49
Raymond of Peñaforte, 78n16, 84n28
Raznatovic, Zeljko, 365–66
realism, 118n3, 120–21, 137. *See also* political realism
realistic utopia, 327, 342–49
realpolitik. *See* political realism
reason, 127–28, 383; faith and, 133n33, 135; lack of, 140, 201
rebels, punishment for, 297. *See also* coups; revolts
recognition, 374
reconciliation, 96, 291, 295–300; truth and, 83n27, 305, 307–8
Red Cross Conventions, 33, 164, 166
redemption, 22, 23, 31, 64, 70–71
redistribution, in European Union, 270–75, 278, 287
Reformation, 8, 57, 69, 164
refugees, 176–77, 180–81, 183–84, 224
regime change: forcible, 323–51; interventions and, 229, 231, 236, 237–38, 241; justification for, 324–42, 348–49; preemption and, 148
Regimine principum, De (Aquinas), 155
Regulus, 15, 19, 31, 34, 123n12
Reichberg, Gregory M., 37, 38, 48, 72, 75n10, 78n16, 135–39, 190, 197, 374

relief operations, 225, 240
religion: crimes against, 302, 352–53, 359; equality of, 382; freedom of, 277; identity from, 173, 256; just war tradition and, 4–8, 166, 195; wars based on, 3, 8, 38–39, 42, 57–58, 117n1, 152, 157–59 164, 167–68, 171–72, 184–88, 293n2. *See also* faith; *and specific religions*
religious life, 32, 77
Renaissance, 90, 116; just war theory, 109
Renan, Ernest, 281
Renaud de Louens, 106
repression, 246, 264
resources, natural: destruction of, 207, 209–10; ownership of, 212–13; squandering of, 334–35; wars for, 14, 19, 192, 199–200. *See also* environment
respect, 120, 203, 374
responsibility, 318–19, 355
restraints, 88, 186, 212, 242–43. *See also* armed conflicts; violence; war
retribution, 79–80, 291–92, 298–300, 302, 315, 319
revenge, 43, 114, 360; alternatives to, 296, 299; as just war, 38–39, 75n10, 124; prohibitions against, 100, 108, 112–13, 126, 140, 205, 206
Reventlow, Henning Graf, 56
revolts, 43, 87–88, 100, 102, 344n15
Rhodesia, 227
Richard II (king, England), 103, 106
Ricoeur, Paul, 356–57
Rieff, David, 248, 352, 353, 368
right, determination of, x, 17–19, 27, 92–93, 248, 253
rights, 15–16, 119, 253–59, 261–62; duties and, 42–43, 246; political, 343–44; responsibilities and, 318–19; of victims, 300
Roberts, 171, 192, 207n21, 211, 226
rogue states, 148, 246, 325–26, 328–35, 338–42, 345
Rohde, David, 370
Roman Empire: army, 21, 24; emperors, 21, 22–23; as instrument of Gospel, 64–65; just war theory, 24–25, 39, 142; law of, 160; sacking of, 36, 52–53, 60, 65, 133–34; war customs, 18–19, 52, 90, 123n13. *See also individual emperors*
Romans (Epistle to the) 13, 138; 13.4, 5, 74n6, 161
Rousseau, Jean-Jacques, 141
Ruggui, Georges, 306
rule/rulers: advising, 101, 115–16; art of, 17n5, 114; Christian, 57, 65, 67–68, 70–71; defense of society by, 135; good, 5–6, 107, 114; punishment of, 57; rights and duties, 5–6, 42, 44, 87, 111, 162; wars over, 16, 172; wisdom for, 109. *See also* kings; princes; tyrants
rules, 281–82, 284–85; consequences and, 37, 42–44. *See also* evidence; law; war
Russell, Frederick H., 12, 23–24, 77n15, 128

Rutuganda, George, 306
Rwanda: Catholic Church in, 175–76; Congo occupation, 298; genocide in, 175–77, 185, 291, 293, 300, 305, 307, 317, 368–69; U.N. failure to intervene, 241–42; war-crime trials, 166, 168, 296, 302, 315; war in, 147, 172–73, 187–88, 293, 295–96, 308. *See also* tribunals

saeculum theology, 38, 64–69
safe haven designations, 183, 224, 369
safety, as motive for war, 17–18, 26, 137
salvation, 22–23, 31, 52, 54, 64, 70–71
2 Samuel (Book of) 16.5–14, 30
sanctions, 272–73, 278; economic, 227–28, 230
Sarajevo, wars in, 178–84
Scanlon, T. M., 280–81
Schachter, Oscar, 324
Scharpf, Fritz, 270–71, 287
Schauer, Frederic, 230
schism/schismatics: Augustinian views of, 51–71; coercion against, 51–71; pagans and, 59–64; Thomist views of, 80–81, 87–88. *See also* Great Schism; heretics
Schlesinger, Arthur, Jr., 336
Schmitt, Michael N., 213, 352
Scholastics, ix, 75n8, 76n11, 100, 117n1, 194, 213, 375
Schultz, Paul F., 373
scorched-earth tactics, 206, 208
Scotland, 251n2, 276
scriptures, 21, 54–55, 86n32, 126–27, 143. *See also specific books*
secession, 172, 249n1, 250, 257–58, 260
Second Vatican Council, 69
secular unity, 81, 87
security: maintaining, 48, 268, 325–26, 330, 332, 335–36, 354, 369–70; restoring, 290–91; threats to, 224, 226, 228, 246–47, 293, 319, 330, 333, 339
sedition, 8on21, 81, 83, 87, 88
Segers, Rien T., 373
self: hatred of, 381–83; love of, 5; national, 257–58, 262, 375, 376–77; preservation of, 120–21
self-defense: just war as, 14, 25, 37, 46–49, 75–75, 84–85, 87–88; national, 97, 118n4; preemptive, 39n5, 328–33, 337–39; regarding genocide, 360; right to, 220, 331–32; wars of, 78n16. *See also* defensive wars
self-determination, 248–50, 252, 255–63, 277, 286, 359, 375
self-interest, 29, 47, 114, 118–19, 140–42. *See also* nations
self-sacrifice, 15, 24, 29
self-sufficiency, 30–32
Sells, Michael, 175, 353
Semb, Anne Julie, 218, 374–75
Sen, Amartya K., 272
Sentences (Lombard), 77

September 11 (2001), 147, 149, 219, 246, 328–29
Serbia: control of Kosovo by, 259; ethnic cleansing by, 175, 182–85, 303–4, 360–67; nationalism in, 251n2
Serbian Academy of Science and Arts (SANU), 361–66
Sermon on the Mount, 42n9
service, war as, 29–30, 32
Seselj, Vojislav, 365–66
Seton-Watson, Hugh, 251, 252, 257, 259–60
Shapiro, Michael J., 357
Shell, Susan, 45
shelling, 182, 183, 184
shields, human, 177–78, 180
Shimei, son of (Old Testament), 30
side effects, 42, 75n10, 204, 210, 213–16. *See also* double effect
sieges, 163, 178–85
sin/sinners, 1, 27, 38n3; battle with, 30–32, 34, 64; original, 57–58; punishment of, 40, 68; war as, 5, 46, 48, 74, 80–81, 85–90, 95, 137. *See also* evil; vices; wrongdoing
slippery slope arguments, 219–20, 230–44; conceptual or logical, 251–58; empirical, 238–44. *See also* intervention; nonintervention
Slocombe, Walter, 333
Slote, Michael, 41
sloth, 81
Smith, Dan, 246, 247, 248, 249, 251n2, 252, 375
socialism, 252
societies/society, 226, 253, 283; Augustine on, 64; burdened, 344; defense of, 135; effacement of, 364–65; liberal, 343–44, 345, 346; well-ordered, 270, 345–47
Socrates, 16
Sofaer, Abraham D., 333
Solages, Bruno de, 82n24
soldiers, 1–2; Christian, 30; civilians distinguished from, 163, 177–78, 186–87; punishment of, 290, 297, 306; rights and duties of, 21, 38, 44, 77, 84, 162, 209n28, 307n11; risks to, 94, 157, 242; statesmen as, 26; treatment of, 151, 207, 293. *See also* knights; terrorism/terrorists; warriors
solidarity, 271, 274, 375
Somalia: nation-building, 340n13; U.N. intervention, 225–27, 231, 235, 240–42
Song of Roland, 12
souls: of the cosmos, 23, 27–28, 32; duties of, 126; great, 18–19, 27, 31; salvation of, 52, 54, 70–71; war's effects on, 42–43, 45–46
South Africa, 227
Southeast Asia, 260
sovereignty, 47–49, 249n1, 276–77, 319, 379; national, 148, 268. *See also* authority; self-determination; states
Soviet Union (USSR): dissolution of, 235, 260, 373–74, 376, 381; forcible regime change by, 324; relations with U.S., 336
speech, 27–28, 277, 368
spoudaios. *See* actions
Srebrenica, 183–84, 303–4, 369–70
St. Petersburg Declaration, 207n21
stability, 271–80; maintaining, 286, 325, 343, 345; threats to, 330
Stapleton, Sara, 313
statecraft, 160, 188, 198
states: authority for war rests with, x, 4–6; Catholic Church relations with, 69–70; de facto, 218, 225–29, 234–36, 238; de jure, 234–36; empirical, 226–27; European, 282; formation of, 6, 264; ideal, 124–25; interests of, 91–93, 119, 227–28, 243–44, 248; legitimacy of, 249–50, 262–63, 279; modern, 68, 235; peoples and, x, 373; policies of, 118n4; profits of, 118–19; punishment of, 57, 90; relations between, 16–17, 219, 221, 286; rights and duties, 42, 118n3, 352–53; safety of, 17n5, 197–98; secular, 70; sovereignty of, 16, 75n10, 220–50, 254–56, 259–40, 244, 277–78, 319, 343; violence by, 60, 90, 195–86; wars within, 147, 172–73. *See also* failed states; outlaw states; quasi-states; rogue states
statesmen: activities of, 15–17, 23, 26; just, 29, 32, 96, 111, 196–97
Stevens, Kenneth R., 332
Stevenson, William, 38, 40, 47
Stojanovic, Svetozar, 366
strength, 30–31
strife, 80–81, 82, 87, 88
style clergiale, 105–6
Suarez, Francisco, 5–7, 42, 75, 76n11
success, probability for, 240–41, 244, 338
Sucor, Laura, 366, 367
Sudan, 148, 247
suffering: Augustine on, 43, 45; of David, 30–31; goal of, 34; mitigation of, 241, 243, 248; noncombatant, 148, 152, 247; redress for, 292, 296, 300, 316, 319
Summa theologiae (Aquinas), 5–7, 74–85, 136–38
Swift, Louis J., 13, 20, 22, 23, 24, 58
Synan, Edward, 77–78
Syse, Henrik, 36, 38, 48, 75n10, 78n16, 150–52, 154n33, 135, 190, 197, 209, 374
system criminality, 307n11

Tadic case, 313
taking sides, 354
Talmud, 179–80
Tamir, Yael, 249, 255, 258, 276, 284
Tanzania, 342–43
target groups, 359–61
targeting: environmental, 200, 209; genocidal, 359–61; intentional, 157–59, 167–70, 179–85;

military, 210–12; soft, 187. *See also* noncombatants
taxation, 100, 102, 103, 151
Taylor, Charles, 283
teaching by inconveniences, 51, 54–55, 63, 69, 131
technology, 120n7, 320. *See also* weapons
television, 355–56, 359, 364
territories: congruence in, 260; divisions in, 355, 357; just war to secure, 25, 77n15; shared, 277–78, 286–87. *See also* borders; nations; states
terrorism/terrorists, x, 3, 33, 44, 173, 207, 248; fight against, 325–26, 328–30, 352–53; rogue states and, 338–42. *See also* al-Qaeda; Donatists; war on terror
Tertullian, 130, 133n33; pacifism of, 11, 13, 20–21, 23, 80
TeSelle, Eugene, 56, 57, 62
testifying, 300–301, 313
theft, 87n36, 201, 202
Theodosius, 24
theologians/theology, 13n3, 38, 64–69, 76, 86, 138, 159–61
Thieroff, Mark, 300
Thing, national, 379–81, 383. *See also* Other
third-party principle, 30
Thirty Years' War, 164
Thrasymachus, 119n5
threats, imminent, 332–38. *See also* peace; security
Tilley, Maureen A., 54
Tobias, Sarah, 159n39
Tokyo tribunal, 290–91, 318
tolerance, 381
torture, 191, 293n1
totalitarianism, 44, 49
trading, 86n33, 95–96
traditions, 256, 264, 283
traditores, 53–54
Treaty of Rome, 320
Treaty of Troyes, 103
tribunals, 148, 165–68, 290–322; mandates for, 295–300; mission of, 308–9, 316–17; procedural fairness, 298–99, 301, 309–16, 320–21; Rules of Procedure and Evidence, 300–301, 306, 311–12, 314–16; sentencing norms, 301–9, 314; verdicts, 298, 305–7, 314
triumphalism, Christian, 27, 128
Truman, Harry S, 42
Trumbore, Peter F., 338n11
trust, 268–69, 271–80, 284, 286, 375
truth, 201–2; establishment of, 292, 300–301, 308, 316–18; reconciliation and, 83n27, 305, 307–8
Tutsi tribe, 175–76, 368
twentieth century, 1, 21n8, 290, 359, 372, 377
twenty-first century, 1, 44, 247, 287

Tyler, Wat, 100
tyrants, 47n17, 70; removal of, 87–88, 95, 241, 291. *See also* regime change

Uganda, 342–43
underdetermination, 282
Unger, Peter, 367
union of affections, 82–83
United Nations (U.N.), 347; Charter, 220–21, 223, 228, 230, 243, 351–52, 354, 356; Commission on Human Rights, 293; Convention on Certain Conventional Weapons, 191; failures to intervene, 368–70; General Assembly, 221, 294; genocide conventions, 167–69, 172, 185, 352–53, 358–59, 370; International Covenant on Civil and Political Rights, 309–10, 359; International Covenants on Human Rights (1966), 223; interventions by, 48, 148, 218–45, 354, 375; mandate for justice, 315; Resolution 688, 224; Resolution 794, 226–27, 235, 240; Resolution 819, 370; Resolution 841, 228–29; Resolution 940, 228–29, 236; safe haven designation, 183, 224, 369; Security Council, 219–21, 224, 230–31, 233, 235, 237–44, 291–95, 297, 299, 305, 309, 316–17, 320, 326, 331–34; Universal Declaration of Human Rights (1948), 223, 249n1, 359
United States (U.S.): Army, 191; Civil War, 164, 174–75; hatred of, 334; Iraqi invasion of 2003, 148, 173, 177–78, 346; peacekeeping forces, 224; regime changes by, 229, 247, 325–27, 329–30, 333–34, 345n17, 348–49; relations with Soviet Union, 356; threats to, 338–39. *See also National Security Strategy*; war on terror
universal nationalism, 258, 269, 278–80, 285–86
Urban VI (pope), 103
USSR. *See* Soviet Union
usury, 26–27, 129n25
utile. *See* expediency

Valens, 24
values, 3–4, 160, 274–75, 277–80
Vattel, Emmerich de, 17n5, 174, 336n10
vengeance. *See* revenge
Vermork Raid (World War II), 215n35
Vetlesen, Arne Johan, 352, 354, 365, 370
vices, 29, 77, 80–82, 96–97, 133n33, 197; in war, 42, 46, 131. *See also* sin/sinners
victims: of genocide, 354–61, 367; justice for, 291–92, 296–309, 313, 316, 319
victors, 188, 205, 290, 292, 309, 320. *See also* war
Viehoff, Reinhold, 373
Vienna Convention on the Law of Treaties, 351
Vietnam, intervention in Cambodia, 223–24
Vietnam War, 190
Vincent, R. J., 222
Vincent of Beauvais, 77n15
vindicatio, 76n11, 80n19

violence: Augustine's teachings on, 41–46; end to, 124, 296, 306, 316–18; force distinguished from, 198; international, 346; justified, x, 137–39; medieval, 7; nationalism as reason for, 246, 375; peace as goal of, 42n9; political, 119, 345; presumption against, 73–74, 83–84, 120; punishment of, 318; religious, 57–58; restraints on, 1, 76, 174, 195–96, 332, 335; sexual, 191; unjust, 21, 82n24, 207. *See also* barbarians/barbarism; genocide; killing; rape; torture; war

virtue ethics, 37, 41–46, 131–35

virtues: acquisition of, 33, 49, 124; Ambrose's theory of, 125n17, 126, 129; Augustinian theory of, 135; Christian, 31, 46; civic, 16–17, 19; Classical theory of, 12–13, 24; duty and, 36–50, 125–26; glory and, 18–20, 26–34; justice as basis of, 1; moral, 96–97; Thomist theory of, 77–80

Visegrad Drina Bridge (Bosnia), 175

Vitoria, Francisco de, 48, 75n8, 75n10, 76n11, 86n32, 92, 152, 163

Voorhoeve, Jorge, 369

Wales, 276

Walters, E. Garrison, 376

Walzer, Michael, 1, 152, 156–58, 179, 181, 209n28, 222, 232, 241, 253, 258–60, 282, 335–36

war, 81–82, 87; Augustine's views on, 52, 59–60, 63–64; Christian, 132–33; codes of, 39, 164–65; conduct of, 100, 119n5, 122–24, 160–64, 172, 180, 186, 188–89, 205n16, 206–8; consequences of, 115, 175, 261, 345; context of, 49, 104; customs of, 33, 166, 168, 184, 293–94; decisions regarding, x, 1–2, 72, 82n24, 113, 140, 158, 160–61, 209–10, 339; declaration of, 18, 48, 75n8, 101; definitions of, 83, 137, 201; destructiveness of, 120n7, 148–49, 154–55; elimination of, 1, 11–12, 22, 45, 72, 115, 143, 155, 186, 331–32; environmental effects, 147–48, 190–217; ethics of, ix–x, 2, 78, 118–50, 139, 147–48, 190–95, 198–99, 206, 372, 375; evils of, 43–44, 46, 88, 91, 131, 135, 143, 155, 187; glory of, 12–14, 16–20, 23–27, 32, 122–24, 130; goals of, 40; humanizing, 92n46, 124; internal, 147, 172–73; as last resort, 337; laws of, 152, 164–71, 175, 181, 184, 188, 192, 207, 294; means of, ix, 1, 15, 18, 88, 122, 175, 191, 218; medieval, 3–35, 194; modern, 1, 3–11, 13–14, 32–33, 68, 90n43, 131, 147–48, 151, 153–54, 159, 186, 196; morality of, ix–x, 3–10, 39, 45, 46, 96n51, 120–21, 136–37, 155, 157–59, 173–75, 177–78, 181, 188, 192–99, 204, 212; motives for, ix, 1, 12–14, 17–18, 23, 72–76, 80n19, 85, 99, 108, 112–13, 122, 149, 172, 218, 234n11; peace as goal of, ix, 13, 17, 21, 38–40, 44, 47, 56, 59, 67, 84, 137, 188–89, 205–6, 215–16, 290–91, 338; practice of, 112, 141–42, 164; presumption against, 37, 72–98, 120, 135–37, 142–43; punitive, 79n17; restraints on, 1, 15, 91, 99, 166, 169, 172, 188–89, 222; right to, 129n25, 334, 336, 339; rules of, 1–2, 15, 18, 32, 33–34, 43–44, 131–32, 164–66, 171, 174; as service, 29–30; as sin, 74, 85–90, 95; spiritualizing, 21, 23; Thomist theory, 72–98, 137; total, 154–55, 174, 188; unjust, 290; waging, 13, 88, 136, 139, 141–42, 173, 192, 200–201, 375; winning, 188, 205. *See also* civil wars; defensive wars; ethnicity; holy wars; Hundred Years' War; just war; offensive wars; play; race; religion

war crimes, 155, 158, 178, 186, 208n24. *See also* tribunals

warlordism, 7–8

war on terror, 147, 149, 246–47, 349

warriors, 8, 11–35, 100, 160. *See also* chivalry; knights; soldiers

water, 182–83. *See also* sieges

weapons: environment as, 192; modern, 154–55, 172, 186–87, 196–97; regulation of, 9, 43, 155–56, 167, 169, 209n25; spiritual, 21–22, 23, 59, 95, 126

weapons of mass destruction (WMD), 167, 169–70, 209–11, 214, 215n35, 326–27; forcible nonproliferation of, 323, 325, 329–30; prohibitions against, 154–55, 187; rogue states and, 246, 338–42; threat of, 3, 148, 237, 328, 343, 346

Weber, Thomas, 193

Webster, Daniel, 332–33, 337

Weiss, Thomas G., 225, 239, 240, 248

welfare regimes, European, 269–72

well-being, x, 38, 141, 203, 262

Weller, Marc, 328

Wende, 373–74, 376–77

West, the: internal wars, 44; just war theory, 8, 152, 159; moral tradition, 185, 194; noncombatancy theory, 163–64; politics of, 376–77; threats to, 33, 381. *See also* Europe; United States

Westing, Arthur, 190

Wheeler, Nicholas, 239

White, Nigel D., 227

will: direct vs. indirect, 213n34; of God, 5, 27; human, 47, 81; popular, 236, 339

Williams, Bernard, 233

Winwright, Tobias L., 57

Wippman, David, 324

witnesses, protection of, 313, 319

Wolff, Christian, 208n22

Wolff, Larry, 376

women, 29, 100, 111, 114, 115–16. *See also* rape

Wood, Neal, 61

world order, 47–48, 548

World War II, 44, 49, 208n24, 215n35, 341;

bombing, 147, 157, 158; postwar tribunals, 166, 290–94, 518
wrongdoing, x, 88–89, 248; punishment of, 25, 38–40, 47–49, 73–79, 85, 91, 112–13, 138, 161, 207. *See also* punishment; schismatics/schisms; tribunals

Yugoslavia, former: constitution (1974), 235; dissolution of, 235, 260; genocide in, 168, 300, 305, 307, 313, 317–18, 361–68; nationalism in, 251n2; NATO action against, 243; war-crime trials, 166, 168; wars in, 173, 178–84, 187–88, 259, 291, 294–96, 308, 313n13, 363. *See also* tribunals

Zabelka, George, 158
Zaire, Rwandan occupation of, 173, 176, 187–88, 298. *See also* Congo, Democratic Republic of
Zelikow, Philip, 58
Zepa (Bosnia) 183–84
Zhou Enlai, 147
Zivotic, Miladin, 366–67
Žižek, Slavoj, 376–81

www.ingramcontent.com/pod-product-compliance
Lightning Source LLC
Chambersburg PA
CBHW031229290426
44109CB00012B/212